Long-Range
Economic Projection

NATIONAL BUREAU OF ECONOMIC RESEARCH

CONFERENCE ON RESEARCH IN INCOME AND WEALTH

Studies in Income and Wealth, Volumes One-Three, Six, Eight, Ten-Fifteen
Outlay and Income in the United States, 1921-1938
Income Size Distributions in the United States, Part I
Changes in Income Distribution during the Great Depression
Analysis of Wisconsin Income
Long-Range Economic Projection

Long-Range
Economic Projection

Studies in Income and Wealth

Volume Sixteen

BY THE

CONFERENCE ON RESEARCH

IN INCOME AND WEALTH

A REPORT OF THE

NATIONAL BUREAU OF ECONOMIC RESEARCH, NEW YORK

PUBLISHED BY

PRINCETON UNIVERSITY PRESS, PRINCETON

1954

Printed in the United States of America by
Princeton University Press, Princeton, New Jersey

Relation of National Bureau Directors to Publications Reporting Conference Proceedings

Since the present volume is a record of conference proceedings, it has been exempted from the rules governing submission of manuscripts to, and critical review by, the Board of Directors of the National Bureau. It has, however, been reviewed and accepted for publication by the Director of Research.

*(Resolution adopted July 6, 1948
and revised November 21, 1949)*

PREFATORY NOTE

This volume of *Studies in Income and Wealth* is devoted to the discussion of long-term projections. It contains the papers delivered at the May 1951 meetings of the Conference on Research in Income and Wealth together with the comments of participants.

Grateful acknowledgment is made of the services of Simon Kuznets, Chairman, Gerhard Colm, and E. M. Hoover, who organized the meetings, and of Richard Ruggles, who edited the volume. We are also indebted to H. Irving Forman, who prepared the charts.

CONTENTS

Introduction, by Richard Ruggles   3

PART I

Concepts and Assumptions in Long-Term Projections of National Product, by Simon Kuznets   9

COMMENT

Gerhard Colm   38
Solomon Fabricant   40

Long-Term Projections of the Labor Force, by Harold Wool   43

National Productivity and Its Long-Term Projection, by John W. Kendrick   67

PART II

Projections in Agriculture, by James P. Cavin   107

Some Considerations in Appraising the Long-Run Prospects for Agriculture, by Rex F. Daly   131

Specific Industry Output Projections, by Harold J. Barnett   191

COMMENT

A. W. Marshall   227
Stanley Lebergott   230

Productive Capacity, Industrial Production, and Steel Requirements, by Paul Boschan   233

PART III

Long-Term Tendencies in Private Capital Formation: The Rate of Growth and Capital Coefficients, by William Fellner   275

Problems of Estimating Spending and Saving in Long-Range Projections, by Mary W. Smelker   333

Long-Run Projections and Government Revenue and Expenditure Policies, by Arthur Smithies   365

COMMENT

Mary W. Smelker   371
Morris A. Copeland   373

Conceptual Problems Involved in Projections of the International Sector of Gross National Product, by Jacques J. Polak   377

COMMENT

Solomon Fabricant   419

PART IV

Regional and National Product Projections and Their Interrelations, by Walter Isard and Guy Freutel   427

Index   473

Long-Range
Economic Projection

INTRODUCTION

RICHARD RUGGLES
YALE UNIVERSITY

IN RECENT YEARS it has become popular to say that since the essence of science is prediction, the ultimate objective of economic science should be to predict with accuracy and certainty the course of future economic events. In this vein, it might seem that progress to date in making projections is a measure of the real achievement of economics and that this volume on long-term projections should record the progress of economists in making such predictions. A careful reading of these papers, however, should convince even the most enthusiastic proponent of long-term projections that we are a long way from general long-term projections which can be regarded as unconditional forecasts of the future.

Indeed, we may never be able to make such forecasts of future economic events in any significant degree. For the determinants of future economic events may not be in the province of economics alone but also in the province of the physical sciences and the other social sciences, and prediction, therefore, may be fully as much the problem of these other sciences.

Furthermore, unconditional forecasts of future events can never have a completely scientific basis. There will always be factors exogenous to any observable system. It follows, therefore, that accurate unconditional forecasts of the future may be impossible. The inaccuracies may be small, or they may be large. Thus, for example, should the concept of free individual action, independent of all other stimuli, be correct, prediction in the sense of forecasting future events might well be impossible so long as human actions are not entirely random and some few individuals exercise an important influence on events.

For these reasons, the success or failure of long-term projections as accurate unconditional forecasts should not be construed as a test of whether economics is succeeding as a science. It would be entirely possible for economics to reach a high point of development as a science, even though long-term projections of economic magnitudes remained highly unreliable as unconditional forecasts.

Although the making of forecasts may never be wholly a scientific exercise, valid scientific observation about the nature of the relationships among the important variables in the system will be useful in improving the quality of forecasts. The absence of important exogenous factors alone is not sufficient for accurate forecasts; the theory of the economic relationships used in the forecast must be valid. Furthermore, economics as a science is not solely on the contributing end of this process of developing accurate forecasts. A great many problems in economics will be better understood if looked at within the framework of forecasting.

Such is the role of economics in the forecasting problem, but a major question still to be answered concerns, as Fellner points out, "the usefulness of specific kinds of theory for a definite problem of qualified prediction."[1] Reliance upon observed past relationships, assuming their continued existence in the future, may not be warranted on the basis of economic theory, but instead may be based on such factors as the availability of statistics relating to the different variables, and the need for obtaining a concrete method of projecting the future. Such *ad hoc* methods of projection, of course, may well be considerably less reliable than methods well grounded in both theory and statistical findings. Fortunately, it is not necessary that theory always find the complete set of determinants for each given situation. In many cases, a relatively small number of variables may suffice; although in fact there may be many other variables related to the situation, they may either be of minor importance quantitatively or tend to balance each other out. It may be possible in the area of projections to add variables as they are needed, much as additional cases are added to a sample following the principle of sequential analysis.

The contributors to this volume have concerned themselves mainly with the conceptual problems of long-term projections, and the manner in which economic problems are involved. Even those papers that present statistical information are generally more concerned with the problem of translating theory into statistical technique than with the problem of obtaining specific statistical projections. Therefore, no attempt has been made to separate the papers according to their theoretical or statistical nature. Instead, they are arranged according to the areas of the economy with which they are concerned. Kuznets' paper deals

---

[1] "Long-Term Tendencies in Private Capital Formation," Section B, below.

with the problem of long-term projection as a whole. Wool's and Kendrick's papers deal with elements which are perhaps most basic to all long-term projection—the problems of population, manpower, and productivity. Cavin, Daly, Barnett, and Boschan are all concerned with the problem of projecting the growth of the various industrial parts of the economy. Fellner, Smelker, Smithies, and Polak are concerned with projections of different sectors of the economy. Finally, Isard and Freutel are concerned with a breakdown different from those in any of the previous papers; their contribution lies in the area of regional projections.

PART I

PART I

CONCEPTS AND ASSUMPTIONS IN LONG-TERM PROJECTIONS OF NATIONAL PRODUCT

SIMON KUZNETS

UNIVERSITY OF PENNSYLVANIA

A. NATURE OF PROJECTIONS

ALL statements about the future must necessarily employ data on past events: even the wildest fantasies are not without reference to what has been observed. The very purpose of a statement is to communicate something intelligible; and one can be intelligible only in terms of past experiences of others. In that sense, all pronouncements about the future are translations from the past.

However, in the present discussion we distinguish between statements about the future derived from tested or testable propositions concerning the past,[1] and those based on theories or hypotheses that are beyond empirical description and testing. The latter, which include religious and other mystical prophecies, utopias, social and esthetic myths of various description, and plain personal hunches, are not discussed here—but not because they are unimportant. Indeed, many of them, e.g., the messianic myths of many social groups, have played strategic roles in history. We confine the discussion to statements about the future that claim to be derived from empirically tested propositions concerning the past; and we use the term *projections* to describe them.

Even if we have in mind only those projections concerning social or economic events, there is a wide variety of types. The broad distinction most useful for present purposes is between statements of *expectations* and of *intentions*. In the former, the observer is, as it were, outside the object to be projected; and, on the basis of past behavior, infers likely patterns for the future. In the latter, the observer is inside looking out—viewing the past as a succession of realized or unrealized intentions related to desirable goals, and considering the future in terms of goals and programs rather than in passive expectation. That statements of expectations must be based upon empirical observation of the

---

[1] For simplicity we omit references to the present. At any given moment there are only the past and the future.

past is obvious. But even in statements of intentions or goals, empirical data play a crucial part. For these statements of goals, programs, plans, desirabilities—whether individual or social—are usually assumed to be *feasible*: otherwise they would have little sense. And feasibility can be inferred and judged only from past performance. The past, therefore, not only colors and determines the choice of what seems desirable;[2] but, more important here, empirical observation of the past is essential to sound judgment of feasibility.

We are interested in both expectation and intention projections that are based upon the empirically observable past and are therefore assumed to be valid. What is the precise basis upon which the translation from the past to the future is made, and how much validity can be assigned to it?

B. BASIC PREMISE

There is a chasm between the past and the future. Empirical observation can relate to the past alone; the future is defined as the time ordinate of events not yet experienced. This does not mean that these future events are somehow there, predetermined and inexorable, awaiting only the lifting of the curtain of time to reveal themselves to helpless mankind. We do have choices within some limits set by the past. But it does mean that any projection from the past into the future cannot possess empirical validity in the way that a proposition having an identifiable referent in the past can. We cannot ask about a statement con-

---

[2] Statements concerning desirable social ends, particularly those designated "needs" or "requirements," are governed by present, socially conditioned sets of values, thus reflecting the historical past. For example, in the goals specified in J. F. Dewhurst's *America's Needs and Resources* (Twentieth Century Fund, 1947), the purely biological or natural requirements of man play only a minor part. The "needs" are a rough approximation to what people want; and what they want and consider desirable is determined by how society lives, and, in a given class structure at a given level of cultural performance, by the values set by certain classes (often not at the peak of the social pyramid, not at the bottom, but somewhere near the middle). This observation is advanced not to deprecate the value of such statements: the goals are no less important because they are conditioned by the history and institutions of a given society. Indeed, it would be next to impossible to formulate "needs" in relation to physiological and biological requirements alone, and disregard the patterns of a society in supplying goods to its ultimate consumers. But such statements should not be confused with dictates of natural science—with the goals which the latter might formulate were it to define them in a *tabula rasa* condition—uncomplicated by a historical heritage of set social patterns.

10

cerning the future, "Is it true?" as we can about one relating to some past event. All we can ask is, "Is it likely to be true?" meaning, "Are there weighty grounds for accepting it?" The answer to this question, no matter how strongly supported by elaborate empirical study of the past, is merely a judgment that cannot be fully tested; and is, in that sense, an act of faith.

The nature of this act of faith must be explicitly stated, for it involves the basic premise underlying all projections into the future. One indispensable element of the premise is the assumption of some identifiable relation between the past and the future. What is denied is *indeterminacy* of the relation between the past and the future. If such indeterminacy is admitted, within *wide* limits, if it is admitted that past events have no recognizable bearing upon the future, the very possibility of projections is denied.

But this is not sufficient, if the projection is to serve any useful purpose. Were we to view the past as a chaotic mixture of events without semblance of order, assuming that the future will be like the past could not yield useful projections since they would not limit the path of events. Nor would it help us to assume that the future, unlike the past, will show some order, since the nature of the order could not, by definition, be derived from the past. Thus projections are warranted only if the basic premise includes two elements—an identifiable relation between the future and the past, and a minimum of order in the past that can be translated into some specific pattern for the future.

The existence of order in the past is a proposition testable in the light of empirical observation and related analysis. It is the empirical foundation of this model of the past that distinguishes the projections we speak of from prophecies, utopias, myths, and hunches. It follows, therefore, that the whole possibility of projections depends on the extent to which study of the past has yielded an empirically testable picture of order in the universe. In that sense, projections were impossible before empirical science brought knowledge and understanding of the universe. The current interest in long-term projections of national product is a result of the recent development of measures covering a sufficient period and of their analysis, by which some elements of order and continuity in past changes in national product were observed. Furthermore, as our picture of an orderly universe becomes more accurate, greater control of at least some of the natural and social processes becomes possible; and this may in turn introduce an element of order where chaos or wide mutability existed before. Our greater knowledge of causes of death and the higher level of technical arts in general has resulted in a much more "orderly" pattern of population growth than that which characterized, say, the Western countries during the Middle Ages. The finding of order in growth of population during the last century and a half was facilitated, not only by greater knowledge, but also by better *control* of disturbing factors. The dependence of the orderly view of the past upon accretion of past study is thus a double one: it is affected directly by a greater knowledge of the past, and indirectly by the imposition of order by human controls based in turn upon such knowledge.

The act of faith in the basic premise is concentrated in its first element—the assumption of an identifiable relation between the past and the future. This assumption is most acceptably expressed by saying that there is no evidence that the possible future changes will exceed the limits of changing conditions under which order, i.e., some invariant or stable relations, was found in the past. Since changes in the future are hidden in that all their antecedents cannot be fully known today, the transition from the statement that there is no evidence to the contrary to the statement that there *is* an identifiable relation between the past and the future is a jump—which we refer to as an act of faith. But if any statement about the future is to be based upon knowledge of the past, i.e., have any empirical foundation, this assumption based upon absence of evidence to the contrary is the only one that can be used. The alternative is either not to make any statements about the future, which is a natural consequence when impending or current changes are so upsetting or so divergent from the past as to negate any bearing that it may have upon the future; or to indulge in prophecies or hunches, also a rather common practice when no apparent order can be found in the past or when conditions bear a strongly apocalyptic tinge.

C. MAJOR PROBLEMS IN ECONOMIC PROJECTIONS

The finding of some orderly pattern in the past and the assumption of a determinable relation between the past and the future encounter major difficulties in economic projections, particularly those expressible in quantities. These difficulties, in connection with long-term projections of national product, are discussed in general terms in Sections C and D of this paper and the more specific questions relating to the structure of the totals, character of the levels, and time extension are treated in later sections.

As already indicated, establishing some order for the past depends upon the extent to which accumulation and analysis of data have revealed some persistent pattern. The major difficulty in finding such patterns for national product arises partly from the scarcity of data, and partly from the limitations of past analysis. The limitations will be clearly perceived if we assume what actually is not so: that we have a tested theory of the economic growth of nations which demonstrates that long-term changes in national product invariably follow a specific pattern expressible by a given curve; that this pattern is securely founded upon a causal explanation that traces it to underlying factors that in turn display persistent patterns of change—say, trends as clear-cut and as invariant as in the growth processes of a biological species. With such a theory, the estimation of specific constants for any given nation for any given period would still raise questions ordinarily involved in fitting a theoretical model to a body of empirical observations. But these questions would be minor compared with the difficulties, and the pitfalls, that loom in the absence of such a theory, or when the study of the past has yielded hypotheses so vague that an uncomfortably wide choice of systematic patterns of long-term change to describe the past is possible.

So far as I know, we have no adequate theory of economic growth of nations, and none that would securely establish a specific model of long-term change in national product. Without it, attempts to find such patterns are based upon direct observation of specific series relating to national product (or its immediately determining components, such as population and per capita product), and result in models chosen on the basis of such observation alone, without explicit reference to the varieties of experience that would be subsumed in a tested general theory.

Under such conditions, the pitfalls are numerous indeed, and, despite our cognizance of them, cannot easily be avoided. To illustrate: When we state that the per capita product in the past increased, on the average, x percent per decade and use this observation as a basis for projection, we imply that this particular pattern of change, this increase of x percent per decade is a reflection of some force, some element of invariancy that persisted in the past despite changing historical conditions. But if this

x percent is a simple average for n decades, there is no assurance that it represents a persistent pattern. Were we to divide the decades into two groups, the earlier one might show an average increase of $x + a$ percent per decade, and the later of $x - a$ percent. And if we try to handle this complication by simple curves that allow for a systematic acceleration or deceleration of the rate of increase, we find that a great variety of curves can provide a fairly adequate description—each, however, yielding different projection levels for the future.

Since these problems are familiar to anyone who has experimented with fitting lines of secular movements to economic time series, guided by purely empirical criteria of goodness of fit, there is no need for elaborate discussion. The crux of the difficulty in establishing an orderly pattern of long-term change lies in the fact that, in the absence of effective theory or even of working hypotheses, a great variety and wealth of data are needed to discriminate among the many models that can be used to describe the major characteristics of change. Yet no such variety of data is available, within the limits of societies reasonably similar to ours. With the available data, it is extremely difficult to choose even among the simple models used to describe the underlying, primary secular trends. Yet our projections into the future will differ significantly as we use one model rather than another. This can be demonstrated by fitting three curves—the logarithmic parabola, the simple logistic, and the simple Gompertz—to, say, estimates of real national product in this country, either total or per capita, for the period 1870-1940, and then extrapolating to 1980. If, in addition, we cover under long-term changes secondary secular movements, trend cycles, or long cycles, whichever term one wishes to use, the possibility of deriving a given pattern becomes even more remote. The power of discrimination which our limited data permit us to exercise in choosing among the possible patterns for purposes of projection is still weaker.

But let us assume that this major difficulty of selecting the proper pattern of systematic change to describe the past has been solved. We still face the next problem: Can this pattern be projected into the future?

This problem must be treated in the light of the following considerations. First, the future will necessarily contain some elements that did not exist in the past, if merely because it comes later on the scale of history. Indeed, at any given time, there are indications or portents of impending changes, and taking an inventory of them for purposes of appraisal is one way of dealing with this translation from the past to the future. But our knowledge of such portents, no matter how rich, is never adequate; and particularly it must be evaluated to ascertain whether these "new" changes are similar to those that accompanied or entered into the pattern of past change which we are ready to project, or are so entirely new as to belong outside the range of past changes.

This introduces the second consideration, that of the range of changing circumstances under which the persistent pattern of long-term movement was found for the past. If we establish empirically a long-term trend for a period during which great changes in *possibly relevant* conditions occurred, this pattern has more significance than one established for a period during which the potentially relevant conditions changed but little. For unless it can be assumed that the future will be relatively free of changes in relevant conditions, projecting into it a pattern whose persistence has not been tested by a diversity of historical conditions is a risky step.

Whether the past can be projected into the future thus hinges upon whether possible future changes, insofar as they can be foreshadowed at present, can be compared with the range of relevant changes in the past within which the systematic pattern persisted. Such a comparison requires: (1) knowledge of the factors and conditions that are *relevant* to the object of the projection, i.e., that can exercise significant effect upon it; (2) ability to appraise the magnitude of impending changes in relevant factors; and (3) ability to appraise the magnitude of past changes in relevant factors.

Little can be said about the first aspect, except to stress that at this point also the absence of a well-founded theory is crucial. Such a theory not only establishes the connection between the dependent variable and some independent variables and yields some general model of the pattern of change in the former over time; but also provides a relatively *complete* system, which permits us to treat everything outside it as irrelevant. For example, if the theory held that the basic and only factors in long-term changes of national product were growth in technology and in the number of workers (with these in turn reducible to, say, hereditary genius phenomena governed by biological law and

15

by invariant tendencies to human reproduction), then we could ignore political changes and revolutions, institutional habits, international disagreements, exhaustion of natural resources, and the thousand and one items included under these broad heads. But we have no such theory, and hence the field of our vision is distressingly wide and the possibly relevant factors numerous. When we attempt to find the past variations in relevant factors that accompanied the persistent pattern established in growth of national product, we flounder in a motley variety of historical events. Likewise, when we ask whether the changes in the future, whose antecedent signs we see, or think we see, today, are within the range of changes that characterized the past and yet yielded a persistent pattern, the answer can only be a rough judgment.[3]

Thus two major problems in economic projections are establishing a systematic pattern of past change and gauging the variety of relevant conditions under which this pattern was found

[3] It is perhaps dangerous to look at the greener pastures of the experimental scientists and ask how they do it—dangerous because in our ignorance we may misinterpret and overaccentuate the difference. But when a change can be deliberately imposed for the purpose of studying its effects, the situation is different from that for economic projections. The value of the controlled experiment lies in the power of the observer to isolate the object of study from the variety of circumstances that might affect it, and in such isolation to distinguish the major determining factors and exclude the irrelevant ones. It is immediately possible to discriminate finely among alternative theoretical models, and to specify the conditions under which the model selected remains invariant. If these specified conditions can be reproduced, as they ordinarily can at least *en gros*, and if the object of study has an empirical referent, the controlled experiment results in an admissible projection into the future to the extent that if certain conditions are fulfilled (and they can be at will), recognizable results will follow either invariably or with a tolerable margin of variance. For example, if certain recognizable material elements are heated under specific reproducible conditions, and the pressure on the walls of the vessel is measured, this pressure will follow an invariant pattern. These invariant conditions can be reproduced and this model has a recognizable counterpart in reality. In the social sciences, where controlled experiment is impossible, one can *simulate* controlled conditions by the use of the imagination. But then the object of study loses its empirically identifiable character and becomes a construct for which there is no direct counterpart in reality. The conclusions established in this manner could be "projected," but they would not be useful because they would bear no determinate relation to the real world— essentially because the conditions cannot be reproduced as they can in a genuine controlled experiment. For example, we can deduce the behavior of "economic man" in a given market situation, under static conditions; and we can project it into the future by assuming the persistence in time of both "economic rationality" and static conditions. But this would hardly be useful because the imaginary conditions thus set cannot actually be reproduced.

16

to persist. The former difficulty is fairly familiar, and the various technical means for dealing with it, as well as the pitfalls to be avoided, are reasonably well known. The latter is less amenable to technical solution, and is in practice resolved by a whole variety of assumptions. These assumptions are crucial and deserve separate discussion.

D. TYPES OF ASSUMPTION

Any economic projection, particularly an inclusive one like national product, carries with it a host of assumptions—so great and varied that any attempt to group and describe them will probably be incomplete. The summary below bears this unavoidable qualification.

1. The first group of assumptions concerns continuity of physical nature: that the laws that govern the physical universe, as observed by empirical science in the past, will continue—whether they relate to inanimate nature, biological species, or the psyche of man. Since all human activity rests upon a physical foundation, such an assumption is indispensable in any social projection. It is never stated explicitly in presenting, say, a projection of national product because it is taken for granted. But this assumption, which is borrowed from sciences relating to factors exogenous to human society as such, is still an assumption—no matter how deeply ingrained our belief in it is. Furthermore, economic and other social projections would be impossible without the antecedent development of our understanding of the processes of physical nature; e.g., in the intellectual climate that existed prior to the development of empirical science and when there either was no assumption of order and continuity in the physical universe; or when such order was attributed to some mystical force that could change in unknown ways and whose ungovernable changes could radically modify the physical basis of social life.

2. Another type of borrowed assumption relates to factors or forces that may be outside and not affected by the social system but which may affect it much more specifically than the borrowed assumptions under (1). The expectation that physical nature will operate as it did in the past *permits* us to state that society will continue to function on the same broad physical foundation, but it does not limit or specify any particular magnitudes for the

17

performance of human society. With all the laws of physics operating, national product can go up and down by very wide margins. But there may be data about the physical universe, truly exogenous to social phenomena, that can determine future social magnitudes in a rather specific way. We might call these the "specific borrowed projections," which trail a whole host of assumptions behind them. For example, an assumption derived from technological study might be that rise in efficiency of power use represented by BTU output per unit of input of a given mineral follows a given specific curve. A still better example would be the as yet nonexistent science of technological change that might supply economists with specific assumptions about the pattern of future technological change, which could then be used directly as independent variables to derive specific national product projections.

These borrowed assumptions, or borrowed specific projections of determining factors outside the economy *may* relate to factors that are not truly exogenous, but are in fact partly determined by social processes. Consider the population projections borrowed by economists from demographers. These projections are accepted on the ground that demographers use all available information on past patterns of births, deaths, and migration, and are better judges than economists of the specific assumptions that can most reasonably be made. That much is true; yet it is also true that population growth is not truly exogenous but is dependent upon economic and social conditions. Hence, these specific projections mean borrowing also some specific assumptions concerning social and economic factors, and these borrowed assumptions may well conflict with those the economist explicitly makes when he develops his own premises. For example, it is not clear to what extent recent and current estimates of population growth are based on the assumption of full employment and of all that it portends for the birth rate, family formation, etc. Nor is it clear what the population forecasts assume about peace or war. And what is true of projections for population may well be true of borrowed specific projections for technological change, state of irreproducible natural resources, and the like. Indeed, the exogenous character of *any* specific projection should be suspect when it is borrowed by an economist, because it may bear directly upon the specific magnitudes of his projection of national product—unless it can be proven otherwise.

3. The third group might be designated "general assumptions concerning social continuity." Because such continuity is somewhat more doubtful than that of the physical universe, these assumptions are usually explicitly stated, e.g., a projection is made on the assumption that the United States economy will remain one of private enterprise, business competition, democratic government, etc. Such statements, however, do not bar all changes: they presumably permit some modifications compatible with the continuity of broad bases of social and economic organization. The difficulty is to know which changes do and which do not violate this assumption of continuity. In national product projections accompanied by statements using the language just employed, would a continued extension of large-scale enterprise to the point of reducing effective competition in most industries be considered a break in continuity? Would nationalization of a few basic industries, say, coal mines and the iron and steel group, constitute such a break? Or formation of overpoweringly strong trade unions? Or, for that matter, further development of the recent practice of using resources for foreign aid without an economic *quid pro quo*?

It is easy to be overimpressed by current or impending changes, and to view the past as sharply severed from the future. Yet even a glance at the succession of past changes that seemed revolutionary to many contemporaries, and are not unimportant even in retrospect, shows that many systematic patterns established for the past persisted amid quite a turbulent stream of historical events. When the land frontier was closed, when the trust movement began, when the income tax was introduced, when free immigration was suspended—there were always contemporaries who viewed the change as the end of an era. Yet certain basic patterns of change in the country's national product and its major components persisted through and after these changes. There is, therefore, a sound instinct, if only an instinct, for assuming a general continuity of social behavior—except when the evidence of catastrophic or extraordinary change is overpowering.

Since the assumption of continuity is essentially a judgment to the effect that possible changes in the future, foreshadowed at present, are within the range observed in the past, the observer usually resolves his doubts by attaching limiting conditions. For example, a statement may be attached indicating that the projection is based upon the assumption that the relatively peaceful

19

conditions of the past will persist, and that the occurrence of a war will invalidate the projection. By doing this the author of the projection appears to transfer the responsibility to the user— having warned him in advance of the possible contingency that clashes with the basic assumption used. But is such a shift of intellectual responsibility genuinely possible? The very *raison d'être* for the projection, and its publication, is to indicate acceptable possibilities. Otherwise, one could always convert the projection into an irrefutable tautology by attaching a statement that it is valid "if the future changes are like those in the past." But such tautology is completely useless, since strictly speaking the future can never change in exactly the same way as the past. If anything more than a tautology is involved, we must express a judgment as to reasonable probabilities and bear the responsibility for it. Any specific condition that is attached, e.g., that of "no war," is usually made explicit precisely because it is a possibility; otherwise there would be no reason to formulate that specific limiting condition rather than another. A projection with such a limiting condition is justified only if, in the author's judgment, the probability of the limiting condition is significantly lower than that of the assumption of continuity.[4]

4. The last category of assumptions may be designated "specifying conditions." They specify in advance either the magnitude of some components of future national product, or some goals which the projection must satisfy. The reasons for making such assumptions vary. In some cases they are made because intentions of certain economic agents, e.g., of specific government programs, are known, and these intentions are expected to be carried out. In other cases, we may have a program aiming at a general goal, viewed as a socially overriding objective, e.g., full employment; and satisfaction of this goal becomes a specifying assumption to which the projection is geared. In still other cases, certain future contingencies, not necessarily revealed in the past, may be considered highly probable, regardless of their desirability; and they are therefore specified to assure that sufficient attention will be given to them in arriving at the projections.

When these specifying conditions or assumptions are within the range limits of past changes, no particular difficulty is met in using them. For example, if future government programs are

4 See Harold F. Dorn's "Pitfalls in Population Forecasts and Projections," *Journal of the American Statistical Association*, September 1950, pp. 311-34.

known, and are close in magnitude and type to those observed in the past, their inclusion in a specifying assumption can only help in making a projection—since concrete values are provided for some components, without disturbing the persistent relations within the system of components that prevailed in the past and that can be extrapolated into the future. But in other cases, the specifying condition is explicitly formulated precisely because it represents a change from the past—something new that either has not been observed before, or has been observed under circumstances that do not permit an easy translation into the future. Such specifying assumptions may well be in conflict with the basic assumption of social continuity under (3); and their acceptance and proper application involve grave intellectual risks.

Consider two specific illustrations to which we have already alluded. The first is the assumption of full employment. Even if we succeed in defining this condition precisely, say, in terms of maximum frictional unemployment allowable for given secular levels of national product, how can we use the data for the observable past when full employment was absent—except in highly transient phases of business cycles which by that very fact did not provide a reliable picture of secular levels and relations? In trying to fit this new element into the picture, we must revise the version of the past, and somehow find analogues to secular conditions under full employment. Similarly, in the second illustration, that of the unfortunately necessary current assumption of *continued* cold war or hot peace, the specifying condition cannot be observed in our past. It is certainly not found in years of peace, and the experience of our all-out wars is not a proper parallel, since it is for short-term efforts rather than long-term ones. Any attempt to incorporate such a specifying assumption must, therefore, adjust the picture of the observable past in some imaginative way to provide a reasonably acceptable analogue.

This subcategory of specifying assumptions referring to something really "new" is in a different class from the three other types of assumption described above, or from the specifying assumptions that clearly stay within the limits of the past. All the other assumptions stress continuity; the present subcategory specifies discontinuity. Assumptions in this group introduce large elements of judgment and uncertainty into the projection.

No general account of the solution to this problem can be given: it constitutes a substantial part of the several papers that

21

deal with the various components or aspects of national product projections. But we point out that the problem exists because it is assumed that large sections of the economy will continue to operate as free agents; and it is their reactions that are difficult to gauge under conditions so different from the observable past. If, however, we extend the specifying conditions or assumptions to cover by fiat the whole economy, the problem disappears, or is at least modified. It ceases to be a matter of the probability or cogency of a projection, and becomes essentially one of technical feasibility of an over-all plan.

To state the character of this shift more explicitly: the specification of an over-all plan as a condition implies the full exercise of coercive power by a necessarily authoritarian state—even if the decisions of the latter may follow some discussion of desirabilities. We assume here an established authoritarian state, past the turmoil and stress of the period of its coming into being—without relevance to any current or possible experience in this country. Once the over-all plan has been decided upon, the question is one of technical feasibility—of availability of physical resources, including man. The decision upon an over-all plan implies disregard of the economic and social values of individuals as free agents. Economic attainment may cease to be a question if the paramount objective is to be reached regardless of sacrifice and costs. It is in this sense that the problem becomes one of technical feasibility, rather than of economic probability.[5] This perhaps overdrawn picture is useful here because it points up the observation that the problem of feasibility involved in national product projections lies in the reconciliation of certain specifying assumptions that represent overriding intentions or programs of a type unknown in the past with such free behavior in the major sectors of the economy as represents continuity with our observable past. Obviously the problem can be resolved only tentatively and with a wide margin of error. Also, its effective handling requires a clear line of demarcation between the overriding intention and the free sectors of the economy; a limit at which this intention

[5] This has been the experience with over-all economic plans whenever introduced. That short-term economic objectives are assured under such conditions of pressure by an authoritarian state does not preclude a distinct possibility that the system may prove far less efficient in the long run than a social organization in which less centralized planning and a much greater scope for individual decisions by free economic agents prevail.

stops by design or must be curbed by the area assumed for the free economic activity.

E. STRUCTURE OF THE TOTALS

In projecting national product, we must obviously go beyond over-all totals and differentiate major components. National product measures a cross-section of a continuous stream of economic activity, of a flow of resources into production, and of the outflow of finished products which in turn yields new resources and further production. A proper structuring of the totals—differentiation of components that are direct antecedents, contents, and effects of national product—is indispensable, no matter what uses the projection may serve. Even if the over-all totals can be derived without breakdown into components, the latter are needed for a more careful check on the reliability of the projection in the light of past experience—a check in terms not only of global indexes for the whole economy, but of the projected performance of various sectors which stand for institutionally distinct groups in society whose habit patterns may be sufficiently known to permit judgment as to the acceptability of the projected levels. If, for example, the over-all projection implies magnitudes of food output for domestic consumption that yield an unreasonably high per capita figure, the total itself may be questioned. If specifying conditions or assumptions are introduced that set the magnitudes of some components in advance, then, even though an over-all total may be derived directly, the other components must be approximated to see whether their relation to the assumed components violates expectations based on past behavior. In other words, the very technique by which national product projections are derived and tested requires that as many components be distinguished as there are sectors in the economy characterized by different behavior patterns. Over and above this need, such breakdowns are indispensable in any use of projections for analysis or for policy action, since the latter should be geared to separate sectors of the economy—not necessarily to the nation's economy as a whole.

In practice, many current projections of national product are first calculated as over-all totals, usually by multiplying labor force (derived in turn from specific projections concerning population growth) by per worker productivity. Then, on various

23

bases, the several components of national product at different stages of circulation are projected (at the level of production, distribution of income shares, consumption, and investment). Next, these components are tested for consistency with each other (whenever determinate relations exist), consistency with the past, and finally consistency with the over-all total first derived. At the next round, modifications are made in components and/or in the over-all totals to attain a consistent set of estimates of both the totals and the various components. This oversimplified description omits several rounds of revision and reconciliation, some of which may involve substantial adjustments of steps that yielded inconsistent or otherwise unacceptable results. But it indicates, at least, the reciprocal checking of the over-all totals against the parts, and of the parts against each other.

We are interested here only in how this breakdown of the totals affects the reliability of the projection—not its uses for analytical or policy purposes. And if we ask how such a subdivision yields a more acceptable projection than one limited to a single over-all total derived in the customary way (or any other manner, except that proceeding by parts), the answer must be sought in the light of the following considerations.

First, it may be stated, on purely empirical evidence, that the over-all totals show a greater inertia, a much simpler discernible pattern of movement over time, than most of the components usually distinguished. This observation is clearly illustrated in a comparison of the secular movements of total population in the United States and in a much narrower area within it, say, a single state. Clearly, the trend lines in the former display a simpler and steadier pattern, and their changes over time seem much more limited. The same conclusion would be reached if we compared long-term changes in total national product with those in product originating in any industrial sector, any geographical region, the shares represented by any income type, and the like. This does not mean that it would be difficult to find *some* components whose secular trends move as slowly and apparently as evenly as those of the over-all totals (the discussion throughout is in "real" terms, free from the disturbing mobility of price level). But it does seem true that the over-all totals display more stable patterns of change over time than most components.

The theoretical explanation of this empirical finding is beyond my power to provide. The direct reason can be clearly seen. Total national population is blocked off by legislation and other barriers from violent changes by immigration and is moved largely by rather inexorable factors underlying birth and death rates; whereas in the case of population for a single state, internal migration, a more volatile process, may be of paramount importance. Likewise, given the basic trends in total population, and deeply set institutions determining labor force participation, consumer habits, and the like, we have a basis for expecting stable trends in total output, unless major disturbing conditions are assumed; whereas in any single industry, the possible impact of technical change and of change in taste may produce violent fluctuations over short periods. But these are superficial observations; the underlying mechanism that explains this relative stability of over-all totals combined with the competing and offsetting and more rapid changes in the components is far from clear.[6]

Second, and in contrast, it is easier to understand both the trends and the limits of the narrower areas of observation—the components—than those of the over-all totals, whose composition is so variegated and complex. If the present domestic consumption of prunes per capita is 2 pounds a year, and has varied within a range of, say, 1.5 to 2.5 pounds over the last fifty years, a

[6] Cancellation of random changes, which makes for greater stability (narrower sampling errors) in measures treated in statistical theory, is hardly relevant here. In the changes in components, fluctuations that can be attributed to random factors are among the least important. It is rather that when we deal with a social aggregate, certain patterns, traceable perhaps to some basic characteristics of human nature or to deeply ingrained institutional habits, emerge and are impressed on the resulting totals. Thus it is generally true that for society as a whole, an increase in per capita income is accompanied by a decline in the proportion of income spent on food; the same two variables are differently associated when the several subgroups of food or of society are considered. It is generally true that in societies permitting consumers some freedom (and even in some authoritarian societies), the secular level of the savings-income ratio has a fairly low upper limit; this is not true for some subgroups in the society. Both results may be traced to the nature of human wants and to the general habits of the human race in apportioning its resources and attention between the present and the longer future. And yet it may be dangerous to generalize about these patterns of behavior of social aggregates, except within some limits set upon characteristics of social organization. One might ask, thinking of the Lucullan feasts, whether in Roman society an increase in per capita income over time was accompanied by a decline in the proportion of expenditures on food; and whether in a well-established authoritarian society like Egypt in its ancient heyday, the upper limit of the secular savings-income ratio was confined to the 15-20 percent range that seems to have been typical of Western societies of the nineteenth and twentieth centuries.

25

projection of per capita consumption to a date fifty years from now that yields a value of 10 pounds per capita can be treated as suspect—because we know what prunes are and can limit the possibilities involved. But if we substitute for prunes total consumer expenditures per capita or total product per worker, we can no longer be intuitively knowledgeable because these entities include so much. It is, therefore, difficult to see why the possible changes in them should be limited.[7]

In the light of these considerations, how can the distinction of components serve as a check upon the projected national product totals? It cannot provide a check directly: an over-all total derived by summation of projections for parts is not necessarily more acceptable than one derived on a global basis. The check can be provided on only one of two assumptions. The first is that some of the specific components are of strategic significance as determinants of total national product levels; and that a check on their magnitudes in the light of what we can tell about their reasonable limits is possible. This is the essence of all national product projections guided by the Keynesian stress on the strategic role of capital investment as an offset to savings. Acceptance of the theory, in its full implications of the possibility of secular disparity between *ex ante* savings and possible outlets for capital investment, would compel an author of a projection, after deriving an over-all total, to check whether the implicit volumes of business capital formation needed to offset the implicit savings are at all likely, in the light of what we know from the past about business capital formation and savings habits. The difficulty with this and similar theories, in their use along the lines suggested, is that we know relatively little about past behavior of such processes as flow of savings or business capital formation. It is, therefore, difficult to assign relatively accurate values to their

[7] The easier understanding of trends in narrower components should not be taken to be, in and of itself, a safe basis for setting limits to their possible changes in the future. If it is suddenly discovered that prunes contain the elixir of youth, a rise in consumption to 100 pounds per capita is not out of the question. However, for these narrower areas, more specific information may be at hand to provide a basis for intelligent judgment concerning the limits of future changes. This does not deny that for the larger aggregates the empirically observed basis for assuming relative stability in secular movement is much wider; and that study of these wholes, rather than the parts, may reveal some effects of social processes that cannot otherwise be clearly discerned. That the whole is greater than the sum of its parts is clearly reflected in the common reference to the economic or social "system"; by definition, "system" is much more than a sum of parts.

projections, at any rate as compared with the greater relative accuracy of the over-all totals themselves, and particularly to pass judgment on their acceptability. I would, therefore, be inclined to argue that this way of using the strategic components to check on the plausibility of over-all totals is a weak reed.

There is another way provided by a different assumption. The past growth of national product was accompanied by a fair amount of internal shifting of components. As already noted, the relatively stable trends in the over-all totals are due to the combination of more rapidly moving, diverse trends of components. The projection of any over-all total into the future, yielding a certain secular rate of change, implies some further shifting in relative weights of various components. The breakdown of the total may reveal how much shifting is implied in the projected change of the over-all total; and comparison of the extent and character of the shifts so implied with those observed in the past can shed some light on the acceptability of the projection. Assume for the sake of illustration that a projected total implies a shift out of agriculture involving a reduction of the farm population to one-half its current size in 20 years, or a shift of labor force from the East to the West of proportions not hitherto observed, or that are extremely unlikely with the much smaller mobility of population than existed in the nineteenth century. The question is whether we can use the breakdown to compare the rapidity of the implied shifts of resources or of changes in economic behavior patterns with those observed in the past and considered likely from present observations.[8]

Our knowledge of the past may not be sufficient to permit this type of testing of over-all projections. But as our knowledge of relations among components increases, as our understanding of the factors that determine the mobility of resources in their shift from one sector of the economy to another grows, and as our information concerning behavior patterns is more thoroughly analyzed, the value of subdivision of totals into significant components for checking the whole projection, even the over-all totals, will become greater. But even at present, it may be well

[8] Under conditions of authoritarian compulsion, this problem of mobility of resources and changes in behavior patterns is greatly reduced, although not completely removed. In such states, mobility and change in behavior patterns are subject to forceful manipulation. This is much less true in non-authoritarian states, although the latter may use stimuli that are not much less efficient in the longer run.

to pay more attention to the past movements of the components as indicators of the rapidity with which shifts of resources, or changes in patterns, can occur. They may be useful not only in testing the over-all totals, but also in assigning some margins of error to the component parts of the projections themselves.

In this connection, a comment might be made concerning one assumption ordinarily attached to national product projections that is ambiguous in meaning. Projections usually refer to national product totals and components in a given year's fixed prices. The ambiguity is revealed when one considers that the projection must involve changes in relative weights of components over time. Does the assumption mean that not only the general price level, but also the relative prices of goods in various sectors of the economy, are fixed? Does it mean that the price ratios of various groups of goods remain as they were in the year that marks the date of the assumed price level? If it does, then one major element that permits shifts in the relative importance of various sectors and that presumably helped to bring about such shifts in the past is forcibly removed by the assumption; and this removal jeopardizes the economy's ability to adjust to the shifts implicit in the projected secular changes in the national total. If the assumption of a constant *general* price level still permits shifts in *relative* price ratios, should not such shifts be explicitly introduced in the formulation and calculation of the components of the projections? In this case, the projections for the components must be shown in both the prices of the given year (current) and those of the year that dates the projection.

In this whole area of structure of projected national product totals, past shifts must be studied from the standpoint of capacity of the economy for making the adjustments involved in any over-all rate of growth, and the ambiguity involved at present in the assumption of constant prices must be cleared up. One concluding observation may be made. When a national product projection is fully presented with both over-all totals and a variety of significant components, the errors attaching to at least some, if not most, of these components are relatively greater than those attaching to the broader totals. We recognize that it is not easy to specify the margins of these errors. But at least some indication of the difference between the margins of error for the totals and for the components should be given, and the range of pos-

28

sible variation in the distribution of the projected over-all totals among various possible combinations of components indicated.

F. CHARACTER OF LEVELS

When national product (or any other) projections are described as "long-term," the levels are assumed to be descriptive of the longer run, rather than of any short period. Even if the projection is labeled for some single year in the future, it is still implied that the secular level is being approximated, not the level for a single year that would reflect the phase of the business cycle or other transient phenomena. The same implication is often expressed in the term "sustainable" applied to a projection: sustainable means presumably a level which, with allowance for limited short-term fluctuations about it, will describe a long period —not just a level barely attained in a short-term shift, to be succeeded by persistently lower ones.

Furthermore, this long-term character of the levels is assumed to apply not only to the over-all totals, but also to the significant components: it is not only the national product level, but the levels of the various components and the relations among them that are assumed to be sustainable. Any ambiguity or difficulty attaching to this characterization of levels will, therefore, apply both to the over-all totals and to the significant components.

This ambiguity resides in the relative, rather than absolute, character of the concept of long-term, secular, or sustainable levels. Secular levels, usually defined as movements in one direction as contrasted with cycles or other shorter-term changes which involve a frequent reversal in the direction of movement, are a relative concept. On a scale of centuries, many of what we now call secular movements in time series would be cycles. Contrariwise, we may, on the kind of time scale with which we operate, distinguish primary and secondary secular movements, underlying trends and trend-cycles. What level are we considering in long-term projections of national product? For how long a period are we concerned with sustainability?

The problem may seem to be easily resolved by defining sustainable levels as those that are maintained without any long-term *absolute* decline, specifying the "long term" as a period of over three years. For example, a projection of national product of X billion dollars for 1980 is meant to be a long-term level for

29

that year, not one caused by a cyclical boom condition, and we seem to remove ambiguity by saying that no negative departure from that level lasting more than three years (or two or one) is expected after 1980. This answer may appear to free us from the need of worrying whether by a secular level for 1980 we mean a level on the primary trend line sustainable over periods associated with recognition of long cycles, or a level on the line that includes both the underlying trend and the long trend-cycle (or secondary secular movements).

But there are two difficulties with this easy solution. The first is suggested by the following illustration: Assume that the condition set, no absolute decline after 1980, is fulfilled, but that the percentage rates of increases in 1981, 1982, and so on are barely perceptible, whereas before 1980 the projection showed substantial rates of increase. Would the level for 1980 still be considered sustainable? Does not sustainability refer to the level as an item in a systematic long-term change, i.e., to the rate of change over time, and not merely to the absolute level? If so, the possibility of variations in the rate of secular growth itself introduces some ambiguity. Should we allow for such short-term variations in the rate of secular growth, in the rate of change in the long-term levels predicted by our projections? And if so, within what limits?[9]

The second difficulty with the easy answer concerning non-reversibility of absolute changes as definition of sustainability lies in the components. If we accept variations in the rate of secular change in over-all totals as compatible with the criterion of sustainability, if we say that the projection represents a sustainable

[9] An illustration of this difficulty is provided by calculations recently made at the National Bureau in the study of capital formation and financing in the American economy. In this calculation, nine-year moving averages of national product and its components were computed from annual estimates based largely on data for overlapping decades originally published in *National Product since 1869* by Simon Kuznets (National Bureau of Economic Research, 1946). These moving averages remove almost all the short-term fluctuations associated with business cycles. They reveal rather marked longer-term swings in the rate of growth. Thus from 1873 to 1883 (dates of midyears of the moving averages) the rate of increase per decade in gross national product (1929 prices) is 91.0 percent; from 1883 to 1892 it is 37.3 percent; from 1892 to 1905 it is 53.4 percent; from 1905 to 1911, 30.6 percent; from 1911 to 1926, 39.0 percent. In no case does the absolute level of the moving averages decline; the swings are in the percentage rate of growth. Should projections of sustainable secular levels correspond to these variable rates of growth or to the primary trend lines underlying them? If the latter, how much variation in the rate of growth around that line should we permit?

level, even if the subsequent rise in total national product is limited to one-thousandth of a percent per decade (as compared with 30 percent prior to it), we must also allow for the nonsustainability of some components, since they, unlike the total, would show absolute declines. This follows from the observation, for which there is substantial empirical evidence, that the shorter-term variations in the rate of secular change are much more prominent in some components of the national product (e.g., in construction, particularly residential, and in investment in transportation) than in others. Will it violate our criterion of sustainability if the projection permits, shortly after establishment of the levels assumed in it, substantial absolute declines in some important components of real national product?

I am raising these questions not because I have an answer to them, but because we should be aware of them, and because the meaning of sustainable long-term projections needs clarification. The ambiguity resides partly in possible differences in the meaning of cycles whose removal is identified with the long-term levels, i.e., with sustainability; and partly in the question whether such sustainability, however defined, is to be applied to the over-all total alone or to its major components also.[10]

However these questions are answered, accumulated experience and analysis from the past are required to distinguish between secular levels and shorter-term fluctuations associated with business cycles, and between various types of long-term movements within secular levels. It is in this connection that the scarcity of data for the past is particularly limiting, since these problems require information and analysis for a fairly long stretch of experience. If we have a theory, or at least a set of working assumptions, that permits us to consider social processes in the United States in, say, 1870 and 1950 as comparable, then we should have and use data for the full period to discern various types of secular movements and distinguish them from business cycles. It was the lack of such data that led in some recent projections to an attempt to use the short stretch from 1929 onward as a basis for long-term extrapolations. Yet the attempt to derive from what are essentially short-term adjustments some bases for

10 The same question applies to the definition of full employment, which is a closely related concept. Does full employment allow for frictional unemployment for the *longer* range, unemployment that may be associated not with the shorter cycles in general economic conditions, but with the 18-year cycles in residential construction?

estimating the longer-term movements of the economy is particularly likely to lead to fallacious results.

One other point is relevant here. Projections into the future are ordinarily built up from the current year. But one cannot start with the data for the most recent year and assume that they are at a secular, sustainable level. The current year may well be above or below the trend line, however one defines the latter. At any given time we are at some phase of the cycle, not necessarily where it crosses the trend line (even if we disregard other transient disturbances not included in the concept of business or economic cycles). True, in some procedures, attention has been paid to this point and some magnitudes and relations for the current year have been disregarded or adjusted on the assumption that they have been affected by transient circumstances. But such an adjustment is not an easy matter. We are never sure in what phase of the cycle we are, until the cycle has been completed; and we are never sure that a given cycle is completed until the next cycle has definitely begun. In other words, how a given year relates to the secular level, to the sustainable trend line, can be determined only when the year is safely past, and when enough time has intervened to define the pattern of shorter-term changes. Yet in projecting forward, one is always tempted to start with the very latest date for which information is available, since thereby one extends the period under study and secures data for the most recent performance of the economy upon which to build the picture for the future. Consequently a conflict exists between the need for an assuredly secular, sustainable level as a springboard for a projection of secular, sustainable levels in the future and the desire to start with the most recent levels which the economy has attained. How this conflict is resolved can best be discussed in specific terms. But some cognizance of it helps us to make a proper choice and, particularly, reminds us that long-term projections should not be automatically based on the latest year for which figures are available.

G. TIME EXTENSION

The comments just made concerning sustainability of levels in long-term projections have a direct bearing upon their time extension, i.e., the period of time ahead which they have in view. When a projection is calculated for 1980, it would seem at first that the reference is to a point 30 years from today, and not beyond. But when we say that the levels are sustainable, it means that they lie on some line of secular movement—which implies that they are part of a series of changes that will not reverse its direction shortly thereafter. A projection of sustainable or secular levels for 1980 is by definition a projection beyond this date—how far beyond depends upon the character of the secular trend implied. One must therefore envisage a long-term projection into the future as having a time extension significantly beyond its specified date, only gradually fading away into the more distant horizons of time.

While this observation may at first seem a formalistic fancy, it has an important kernel that should be made explicit. This can be done by an extreme example, similar to that cited in the preceding section. Assume that in the projection for 1980, which we characterized as one at sustainable levels, we accepted specific conditions or assumptions (say, some investment-inducing legislation) that would favor the attainment of these levels by 1980 but would cause an extraordinary pressure on reserves and resources of the economy which would not necessarily be reflected in any customary depreciation measures. If analysis were to show that the specifying assumptions of the projection were as described, and if it were also to show that there is little ground for doubting the attainability, under these specific assumptions, of the national product levels posited for 1980, would we still be willing to describe the projection for 1980 as sustainable? And if we hesitate to do so, is it not because we foresee that after 1980 the past rate of secular increase would be jeopardized by the means taken to achieve the 1980 levels? If so, it is clear that when a given national product projection is said to describe sustainable levels for 1980, the implicit time extension of that statement reaches well beyond 1980.

This basic consideration gives rise to other, related questions. The first concerns the limit beyond which the time extension of any projection cannot go. There is obviously no infinite series by which a projection of sustainable levels for 1980 implies some vaguer projection for the year 2010, and by which the latter implies another projection concerning the year 2040, and so on. Social phenomena do not lend themselves to such mathematical play. This kind of time series is quite sharply terminated by the realization of our ignorance. Our knowledge of the past, insofar as it refers to concrete manifestations of the behavior of the social aggregates we call nations, states, etc., tells us clearly that the cumulative events have a pattern that can, at best, be dimly discerned only a short time ahead; and that as the period is extended, the possible errors pile up so fast that the result is useless. In dealing with a relatively short period into the future, we can actually observe some of the factors that will determine it—because they already exist today. For example, if we wish to look 20 to 30 years ahead in population growth, we are helped by our knowledge of the population living today—since the latter will directly produce the population 20 years hence. But if we wish to know the population 2,000 years from now, there are many unborn generations whose character and composition we would have to estimate today and which we could certainly not observe during the current year. And what is true of population of human beings is true also of population of capital, whether of material or of ideas, and of any other human institutions that have a survival power some distance into the future.

This limit to our knowledge is at the bottom of our refusal to deal with projections of a long-time extension into the future. This recognition of ignorance may assume different forms. For example, one is the refusal to *act* upon the longer future—a refusal which unconsciously expresses a sound instinct. Since no policy is feasible, the stimulus for many a long-term projection far into the future is also absent. Another form is purely mathematical. The divergence in extrapolation of various curves, all fitted as equally good models to an observable past, compels us to limit the extrapolation to a relatively short segment beyond the current end of the observable series. Clearly, if we knew more about the future, we could discriminate among the several extrapolations. But whatever form this recognition assumes, it eliminates any infinite series of sustainable projections into the future.

Indeed, in some cases, the time extension may be reduced too much: sustainable levels may be projected too short a distance into the future for the projection to be of much value. Assume an extreme case: that on the basis of secular levels established for the current year, the projection unfolds *secular* levels for the next year. Obviously any addition to our knowledge, any interpretation of significance, made with such a projection lies in setting secular levels for the current year, not in their projection for the next year. For once the secular levels are established and some approximation to past secular trends found, little variation is possible in the quantitative magnitudes of the projection. Only extraordinarily large and variable secular movements would render such a short-span projection of longer-term changes interesting.

It follows that establishing the proper time distance of a long-term projection is a compromise between the desire not to exceed the limit of our knowledge, and the attempt to learn as much about the future as can be drawn from the past. This compromise should be made in the light of the character of the levels implied in the sustainability assumption, discussed in the preceding section; and in the light of the observation just made concerning the implicit extension of any sustainable movement beyond the date at which the levels are specified.

One further comment is relevant. If some assurance of sustainability beyond a specified date is sought, the projection must define the path leading from the present to the date in the future attached to the levels. If today we project national product to 1980, it is not enough to calculate and present the levels in 1980. We must also show in the projection how the totals and the various components change from the secular levels of today to those of 1980. There may be different paths from a given level to a projected level, and these paths may have different meanings in terms of how much they contribute to or detract from the possibility of sustained movement *after* 1980. For this reason alone, even disregarding the value of such path projections for continuous checking and possible revision with the passage of time, it is desirable to trace the path from the present to whatever year the author wishes to label as the formal end of his anticipation of the future.

H. USES OF PROJECTIONS

Our discussion is necessarily in general terms. In this paper we cannot deal with the more specific problems that arise in handling the various components, or with the relations among them that are often the substance of, and the *raison d'être* for, many projections. These more interesting questions are treated in the specific papers that follow. Our comments, largely introductory, deal with the central questions in all long-term national product projections—which are necessarily questions of almost formal logic, inference, definition, etc.

The general tenor of the discussion might justifiably lead some readers to conclude that the formal grounds for long-term projections of national product are tenuous indeed, and that many ambiguities remain in current formulations of such projections. Indeed, a rigorous scrutiny of the bases was bound to yield somewhat disturbing results. The rapidity and complexity of economic changes and the difficulty of objective study of human society are formidable obstacles to the formulation of tenable theories, and consequently to the establishment of elements of order in the past and the testing of generalizations against changes in relevant conditions—the two indispensable bases for valid projections. Nor, since the past is so imperfectly understood, is it surprising that there are difficulties in determining the proper limits of aggregation and disaggregation in structuring the projections, questions as to the meaning of the usually assumed stability of price levels, and ambiguities in the definition of levels projected as sustainable and of the time span to which they are supposed to apply.

The attempt to bring these problems to the surface was not made to read projections out of court. It was made rather in the hope that recognition of the problems might stimulate a more specific treatment of assumptions and contents. Such treatment is important because projections are a form of peering into the future and the latter is an indispensable part of active life.

Extrapolations into the future, whether empirically founded projections or hunches that are revealed only by their consequences in action, are being made and will continue to be made. We live in the present and cannot avoid the future; the decisions we make today will affect tomorrow. Indeed, many of them must look toward a longer-range future. Such decisions, whether made against the background of articulated forecasts or out of a subconscious but often quite strong feeling about the climate of life to be expected, imply projection in the sense of some view of the future. The choice is not between making and not making an extrapolation into the future; it is between making the projections in overt and sometimes quantitative terms, and proceeding by feel and by faith. Even inaction implies some picture of the future.

Thus the fact that it may be difficult, in the kind of examination that was carried on above, to establish the validity of the projections or to follow through fully on their implications does not deny their usefulness. The major use of these intellectually hazardous undertakings is naturally for policy-making. Action is directed toward the future, and the choice of action can be assisted by some specification of the future. The need for action may be motivated by some desirable goals, actively pursued—in which case the projections are often made to demonstrate that the desirable goals can be attained. Or the need for action may arise from some overriding necessity, not always pleasant or desirable—in which case the projection is made to see how the unpleasant necessity can be met without more cost or unpleasantness than need be. Or sometimes the need for action is on the part of an agent who must accommodate himself to whatever national product levels can be reasonably expected, e.g., a business enterprise wishes to have a glimpse of the national economy in the future so as to guide its actions more intelligently.

There are other types of uses, however, to which national product projections are *not* put, and it is of interest to list these. I know of no long-term projection that has been prepared in order to test a *theory* of long-term growth of the economy—the way a prediction would be used to test a theory in some of the more developed experimental sciences. National product projections have not been used in this way because there is no existing theory sufficiently articulated and empirically founded to warrant such a test. Nor are national product projections used for drawing alternative pictures of the future for choice by society—the kind of forward-looking statements that might focus public opinion upon important issues as an aid to their solution. National product projections are too detailed and technical to serve well (like utopias, and many a highly superficial but general theory) as the focus of widespread public discussion. With this country's passion for statistics, however, there has been some attempt to broadcast national product projections far and wide as expressions of economic ideals and goals. These attempts suffer from the fact that such projections, intended as elaborate *quantitative* pictures of feasibility, are limited to too narrow a set of assumptions. Many socially desirable ends that should be considered in any useful discussion of alternative actions for economic society cannot be translated into projections because the empirical bases for a quantitative statement are lacking.

This limitation of national product projections to uses closely geared to *action* may seem so obvious as not to require emphasis.

Nor does one need to emphasize that if action is considered, it is desirable to have even a rough and approximate picture of prospects that has some empirical foundation, granted that (for reasons brought out earlier) it involves some basic assumptions that cannot be fully validated and some ambiguities and margins of errors due to an incomplete picture of the past. All this is obvious enough. But if national product projections find their justification primarily in their use for policy problems, if they are calculated *despite* their roughness and despite their possibly inadequate basis because they are better than proceeding by hunch and by guess, their authors and users ought to recognize this. Indeed, one might argue that presentation of any national product projections should begin with a clear statement of the types of action, of the lines of policy choice involved, that justify the effort to project despite the limitations, difficulties, and unavoidable margins of error in the result. Such a statement of uses might provide a guiding line for many decisions that must be made in formulating the projection and its various parts. It might also serve to prevent unwarranted uses of the projections, and make it clear that projections are not predictions thoroughly grounded on empirical observation or on an established theory of change of the national economy.

COMMENT

GERHARD COLM, *National Planning Association*

At the very end of his paper, Mr. Kuznets states that in considering policy actions, a rough and approximate picture of the prospects can be of value, as long as the limits and possible errors are recognized. This, he believes, is too obvious to require emphasis. I believe that his last paragraph, far from being obvious, could stand considerable elaboration. Most of Kuznets' paper consists of a very discouraging enumeration of all the difficulties in long-term economic projection. If, in his final paragraph, Kuznets reaches the conclusion that these projections can be of some service in considering policy action, why, then, must he be so discouraged? I believe he is discouraged because subconsciously he measures the validity of economic projections by a yardstick borrowed from "the greener pastures of the experimental scientists" (see Section C, footnote 3), and from "some of the more developed experimental sciences" (Section H). Economic projections obviously do not stand up if measured with a yard-stick that is not applicable. If Kuznets is skeptical about our ability to make unqualified long-range economic forecasts, I share his skepticism. I am satisfied, however, if projections are suitable for the role they were devised to play, namely, to serve as an aid in economic policy deliberations.

Kuznets is longing for a theory of economic growth which "demonstrates that long-term changes in national product invariably follow a specific pattern expressible by a given curve" (Section C). Any such theory would miss the essence of social or political economics. It is incompatible with the peculiarities of economic development, which is largely influenced by individual and collective responses to economic facts and aspirations. It is futile to search for a formula or curve by which past data can simply be extrapolated into the future. On the other hand, Kuznets is right in saying that no meaningful statement about the future is possible unless we assume that some future economic relationships and responses can be estimated on the basis of past experience. That, however, is not the same as thinking that the curve of the future gross national product in the aggregate and component parts can be found by the extrapolation of past data.

Kuznets believes that if the future is not determined by the past, "the very possibility of projections is denied." The principle of *indeterminacy*—that observation influences the behavior of the subject matter under observation—plays a role in some fields of physics without preventing the possibility of statements about probabilities in those fields. The same principle is of paramount importance in economics, where the behavior of individuals, groups, and governments is influenced by conscious action, which in turn is influenced by observation.

Kuznets recognizes "intentions" as one of the specifying conditions in preparing projections. The necessary introduction of this sort of assumption destroys the possibility of the mathematical projection for which he is longing. But it does not destroy the use of projections in studying the economic implications of the possible behavior of individuals, groups, and governments. For example, we may want to assess the probable economic implications and effects of an armament program, a change in tax rates, an increase in wage rates, or a change in business sentiment. The answer to such questions cannot be found by extrapolating the national product according to any curve or formula. But the study of policy problems of this kind can gain greatly by the use of long-range projections.

The fact that projections can be directly related to the exploration of policy measures has been mentioned in the discussion in a manner that may lead to misinterpretation. The policy objective enters the projection in the formulation of the question and in the interpretation of the answer. The preparation of the projection itself should not be influenced by any policy considerations. If the question is, for instance, what inflationary pressure is likely to result from a $50 billion defense program, assumptions must be made as to the attitude of business and consumers. It would be wise to prepare projections under two alternatives: (1) that consumers and business believe the international situation is serious and may deteriorate even further; (2) that consumers and business believe that a relaxation of international tension is in sight. The first assumption leads of course to greater, the second to smaller, inflationary pressure. If both attitudes have a certain degree of probability, it would be wrong for the economist to overlook either of them.

In deriving recommendations for a long-range anti-inflation program, however, it may be wise and appropriate to consider only the case in which the effect of the additional defense spending is aggravated by the expectation that defense spending may have to be continued over a considerable period of time or even may have to be stepped up. Whether this is or is not the most *probable* assumption, it is the *safest* assumption for formulating a policy program. It is easier to relax anti-inflationary policy measures if and when the community anticipates an early curtailment in the defense program, than to tighten up measures in case of expectation of increased international tension. This is what I believe Arthur Smithies has called the strategic assumption of projections. It might also be called the "umbrella" principle. We take an umbrella with us not only when the weather forecast is that rain is most probable, but also when some possibility of showers is forecast. But in this case, as in economic projections, we do not want the forecast colored by a "strategic" bias. We want to decide for ourselves when we prefer the risk of getting wet to the discomfort of carrying an umbrella.

SOLOMON FABRICANT, *New York University*

Among his many acute observations, Mr. Kuznets rightly points to the ambiguity involved in the assumption of fixed relative prices. With our attention thus drawn to the question of prices, we may go on to wonder about the significance of the assumption of constancy in the general price level.

There are two reasons for presuming that this question may be of some interest. First, there has been a good deal of speculation about, and some belief in, the influence of rising and falling general price levels on national product and on its composition and distribution. The gold and silver discoveries of the New World are said to have aided in the establishment of capitalism—that is, in helping to tilt upward the trend of national product—and to have done so by expropriation of the landed interests, lags in wages, etc. Similarly, some believe business expansions to be longer and contractions shorter—that is, growth more rapid— when price trends are up, with and perhaps because of related effects on income distribution.

Second, when so many economists think continuing inflation is in the cards, its possibility and its consequences must be given explicit recognition in projections of the aggregate and composition of national product. Some pessimists emphasize the possibility of an ultimate "big bust," while others talk of gradual expropriation of the capitalists—but both seem to believe that the force which may have helped bring capitalism into the world will now help bury it.

Whatever one may think of the merits of these speculations about the effects of general price trends—and I confess to considerable skepticism—should they not be referred to? Anything like a full-scale analysis would, of course, become extremely involved. What effect, for example, would continuous inflation have on profits and thus on income and excess profits taxes, and thus on investment, and so on, first, in the absence of a major revision of current accounting practices, and, second, in the event that revision occurred and were widely accepted? But to admit that the question is exceedingly complex is in itself an interesting comment on the nature of long-term projections.

Mr. Kuznets has elsewhere emphasized a point that must also be remembered here: Projections for a country are projections for one member of an evolving society of nations. The impact of the world economy will, of course, be recognized in a general assumption as to war or peace and in particular assumptions about the factors determining the international investment balance, but it needs recognition in connection with other matters also, such as change in industrial structure. For example, the decline in agriculture and increase in manufacturing in Britain and the United States were associated with important developments in other countries. Therefore projections of change in these industries assume that certain changes are taking place elsewhere.

LONG-TERM PROJECTIONS OF
THE LABOR FORCE

HAROLD WOOL

OFFICE OF MANPOWER UTILIZATION

DEPARTMENT OF DEFENSE

PROJECTIONS of the labor force and labor input have provided logical steppingstones for the construction of forecasts of the nation's future productive potential. Thus the various post-World War II "full-employment" models and, more recently, the five-year projections of the Council of Economic Advisers used forecasts of the population and labor force as a point of departure and then allowed for frictional unemployment and hours of work to arrive at projections of man-hours of labor input. These were translated into projected or "goal" levels of the gross national product, by allowance for over-all productivity trends in the economy, i.e., gross national product per man-hour.

Despite the pivotal importance of the population and labor force trends in the appraisal of future levels of economic activity, economists have dealt only lightly with the assumptions and techniques underlying these projections. For example, until very recent years, they have tended to accept at face value projections of the population conveniently prepared for them by the demographers—in effect, treating population trends as exogenous to the economic climate being projected. Moreover, the labor force, as a percentage of the population, has been regarded as either independent of, or only mildly sensitive to, peacetime changes in the level or pattern of economic activity.

From the standpoint of fairly short-term projections, of five or ten years ahead, the assumption of relative stability in the labor input factors does not appear unreasonable, on a priori grounds:

1. From any given base year, the population of working age can normally be projected with a fair degree of accuracy, up to 15 years in the future, simply by a survival of existing population

Note: When this paper was prepared the author was with the Branch of Manpower Studies, Bureau of Labor Statistics. In developing the statistical materials he was assisted by Sophia Cooper and Stuart Garfinkle, of the Branch of Manpower Studies. The report was also reviewed in preliminary form by members of the staff of the Population Division, U.S. Bureau of the Census, and by Dr. Clarence D. Long, The Johns Hopkins University, who made many helpful suggestions.

cohorts and a realistic allowance for immigration. This is possible because of the general stability of mortality rates and the limited amount of immigration possible under current legislation.

2. Available data suggest that apart from wars or major cyclical movements, labor force propensities of particular population groups are fairly stable and slow-changing, since they are based in large part on deeply rooted social institutions and customs as well as on the prevailing geographic and occupational structure of employment. Once a proper base level is determined, consistent with the economic climate being forecast, extrapolation of past trends for specific population groups provides a reasonable point of departure. Moreover, an assumption of linearity—clearly unfeasible in the long run—may prove adequate for shorter-term periods.

3. Similarly, institutional and structural factors affecting "frictional" unemployment and hours of work can also be assumed to be fairly stable over the short run, in a given socio-economic environment.

However, a shift in time reference from "short-term" or "intermediate" to "long-term" introduces major qualitative changes in the problem of projecting levels of labor force and labor input. Trends in population, labor force, and hours of work can no longer be conveniently considered as autonomous forces, but are themselves influenced—in varying degree and at different time intervals—by basic structural changes in the economy and by many related socio-economic factors. For example, even within the broad framework of a peacetime "full-employment" economy, it is possible to construct sharply contrasting models, with different implications for labor force levels and trends. A consumption-orientated economy, with relatively low savings and investment rates, and stable or declining prices, would probably be accompanied by a lower labor force and lower average hours of work than an economy with high investment or defense expenditures, and predominantly inflationary tendencies.

The task of the analyst is rendered even more difficult by the fact that, although he may be able to judge the general effect of economic movements upon the separate labor input factors, he cannot—with available data and techniques—attempt to quantify these effects with any "scientific" precision. At best, he can present some rough approximations or a broad range within which the "true" level may be expected to fall.

44

The specific problems of long-term population and labor force projection are discussed separately in the following sections.

A. POPULATION

Labor force projections, until the past few years, have been based, with few exceptions, upon the series of detailed population forecasts initiated in 1928 by P. K. Whelpton of the Scripps Foundation for Population Research and revised at periodic intervals until 1947. The Scripps projections published by the National Resources Planning Board in 1943 (and revised in 1947 in joint sponsorship with the Bureau of the Census) have been most frequently followed in projections of 1950 full-employment models during the past decade.[1]

The Whelpton method involved separate projections of three factors affecting future national population trends—mortality, fertility, and migration—by empirical analysis of past trends, by analysis of comparative, geographical statistics, and by evaluation of the influence of relevant social and economic trends. By applying the projected age-specific mortality rates to the last actual population, and "filling in" for births and for an assumed rate of migration, it is thus possible to project not only the size, but the composition, of the future population. The results of these projections have been presented in terms of a range, allowing for "high," "medium," and "low" assumptions as to fertility, mortality, and net immigration, and for various combinations of these assumptions.

1. *Fertility trends*

Of the three factors affecting long-term population trends, fertility is the most difficult to project and the most significant in terms of its impact upon future population growth in the United States. Prior to World War II, the existence of a long-term downtrend in the birth rate, both in the United States and in other industrialized nations, was accepted as a basic postulate in any analysis of future population and economic trends. The growing pattern of family limitation, reinforced by such factors as the movement from farm to city, was identified by demographers as the determining influence in this declining trend. Changing eco-

[1] For bibliographical references, see Harold F. Dorn, "Pitfalls in Population Forecasts and Projections," *Journal of the American Statistical Association*, September 1950.

nomic conditions, with their observed relation to cyclical fluctuations of marriages and births, were recognized as of primary importance in movements around the long-term trend. But these economic changes were interpreted as affecting only the timing of births in individual families—not the ultimate number of children per family. From the standpoint of long-run economic trends, prewar studies indicating a general inverse relation between fertility, on the one hand, and income levels and socio-economic status, on the other, appeared to strengthen the conclusion that a rising standard of living would be accompanied by a decline in the birth rate. The "medium" fertility projections in the various Scripps forecasts, therefore, allowed for a long-term downtrend in fertility from the rates prevailing at or near the base period.

The sharp divergence between the population forecasts and actual fertility experience during 1945-50 has already been subjected to intensive analysis and requires no detailed documentation here.[2] In the earlier, 1943 projection, the "medium" estimate of births for 1945-50 had been set at 13.1 million. On the basis of information available by October 1945, this had been increased to 13.5 million. By the end of 1946, and prior to the publication date of the 1947 forecast, the latter estimates were already obviously too low, and a revised "medium" estimate of 15 million births for the 1945-50 period was indicated. These forecasts contrast with actual births of 18 million during that five-year period. After attaining an all-time high of 3.8 million in 1947 (following the marriage "boom" in 1946) births continued at a near-record level of approximately 3.6 million in 1948-50, still 50 percent above the 1935-39 average of 2.4 million.

From the standpoint of long-term fertility trends, the maintenance of near-record births after 1947 is particularly significant since it occurred in the face of a sharp decline in marriages, from 2.3 million in 1946 to 1.6 million in 1949. To the extent that the initial postwar baby boom was due to a "catching-up" process following a period of depression and of wartime separations, the postwar baby boom could be regarded as a temporary phenomenon whose effects would wear off in the long run. However, after 1947, the over-all birth rate was sustained —not by initial births to newly wed couples, but by progres-

[2] Dorn, *op.cit.*, and Joseph S. Davis, *The Postwar Population Upsurge in the United States* (Stanford University, 1949).

sive increases in second-, third-, and even fourth-birth rates. Most demographers still tend to regard this phase as temporary— a "borrowing" of extra births from the future as well as the past. However, there is reason to believe that we have experienced no merely temporary postwar spurt, and that some portion of this recent rise in fertility rates will persist in future years, if a goal of sustained full employment and rising living standards is to be approached in this country.

Two pieces of collateral evidence may be cited for this hypothesis. First, surveys conducted by the American Institute of Public Opinion in 1941 and 1945 showed a marked upward shift in the attitudes of young women as to the "ideal" number of children per family. This was attributed by Whelpton to "the psychology and economic conditions of the war."[3] Secondly, the Indianapolis survey of factors affecting fertility, based on intensive case-history studies, has revealed that for those families which do practice effective family limitation, fertility rates tend to increase rather than decrease with rising income and socio-economic status.[4] These facts—still inconclusive and partial—do, however, suggest that from the standpoint of over-all fertility trends, the downward pressure of a continued trend away from very large families could be offset, at least in part, by the positive influence of a higher rate of marriage and by a reverse movement away from very small families, under conditions of sustained prosperity and general economic security.

2. Mortality and immigration

Although at present of lesser quantitative importance, the relation between economic trends and the other two major determinants of population growth—mortality and immigration—should also be taken into account. In both cases there is reason to believe that, other factors being equal, high levels of employment and progressive increases in living standards are positively associated with population growth.[5]

[3] P. K. Whelpton, Forecasts of the Population of the United States, 1945-75 (Bureau of the Census, 1947).

[4] Clyde V. Kiser and P. K. Whelpton, Social and Psychological Factors Affecting Fertility (Milbank Memorial Fund, 1949), p. 413.

[5] From the standpoint of shorter-term projections, mortality and immigration are the only factors affecting trends in the population of working age, i.e., 14 years and over. That variability in these factors is not negligible

In recent years, the tremendous strides of medical science through the succession of "wonder drugs" have been cited as the major cause for the relatively sharp reduction in mortality rates. Perhaps of equal importance is the fact that with our relatively high living standards and improved medical care facilities, it has been possible to diffuse the benefits of these discoveries at a very rapid rate through the entire population.

As in the case of mortality, the association between the rate of immigration and domestic economic conditions is fairly evident. Prior to World War I, when immigration was uncontrolled, wide cyclical movements of immigration coincided closely with the general business cycle. Within the much narrower limits set by current immigration legislation, there is still room for sizable variation. For example, during the 1930's, immigration came to a virtual standstill, while in the period 1946-50, the net legal inflows into the United States averaged about 300,000 annually. The postwar immigration was due in part to strictly temporary circumstances (e.g., in the case of war brides and displaced persons). However, it also represented in part a response to favorable employment and other economic conditions here.

3. Census "illustrative projections," 1950-60

The mere recognition of some degree of correlation between the economic climate and the rate of population growth is not of direct value to the economic forecaster, unless he has some technique for identifying the relative importance of the economic factor. No such convenient tool exists at the present time. As a practical matter, the economist can select one from a range of available population projections, expressed in terms of projected trends of demographic factors, if he believes that it is reasonably consistent with the broad framework of his economic or other assumptions.

A current set of population projections which is suitable for this purpose was issued by the Bureau of the Census in August 1950.[6] These projections, cautiously identified as "illustrative,"

---

is indicated by the fact that the "medium" 1943 Scripps projection of the population 14 years and over for 1950 was nearly 2 million below the actual, while the corresponding 1947 Scripps-Census projection proved to be 1 million too low.

[6] Jacob S. Siegel and Helen L. White, *Illustrative Projections of the Population of the United States, 1950 to 1960* (Bureau of the Census, Series P-25, 43).

use the postcensal population estimate of July 1, 1949 and the recent postwar experience in fertility, mortality, and immigration as a point of departure, and then allow for a relatively wide possible variation in trend from this level. Thus, the "medium" and "low" series assume a resumption (at different rates) in the long-term downtrend in fertility, but the "high" assumes a continuation of the high age-specific birth rates prevailing in 1948. A wide range is also allowed for in mortality trends and immigration—in the latter case, ranging from a low of "no net immigration" to a high of 350,000-400,000 annually. As a result of these factors, the projected total population of the United States in 1960 ranges from a "low" of 161.7 million to a "medium" of 169.4 and a "high" of 180.3 million. About 13 million or over two-thirds of the difference between the low and the high projections is due to the difference in fertility assumptions, while slightly over 5.5 million is due to the range in the mortality and immigration assumptions.

In order to illustrate the implication of these alternative projections of *total* population for longer-range trends in the population of working age, the census projections of the population 14 years and over have been extended in this report to 1975. These estimates were constructed by a cohort-survival method, i.e.: (1) using as a base the census "low," "medium," and "high" projections of total population for 1960, by age and sex; (2) estimating births in 1961 at about the same absolute level as projected, under each assumption, for 1960 (in order to derive the cohort aged 14 in 1975); (3) "surviving" the projected 1960 populations by an extension of the trends in the census "high," "medium," and "low" mortality rates to 1975; and (4) assuming continued net immigration in 1960-75 at the same level as projected by the Census Bureau between 1955 and 1960 under each of the assumptions.

As shown in Table 1, differences between the projected populations 14 years and over remain relatively small—although widening gradually—until 1965. By the latter year, the "high" projection is 9.8 million, or 7 percent above the "low" projection. This difference is almost entirely accounted for by the different assumptions as to immigration and mortality trends. However, in the following ten-year period, the cohorts born in the decade 1950-60 will be entering working age and as a result, the projections show a much wider divergence by 1975, to 29.4 million, or 21 percent.

TABLE 1

PROJECTIONS OF POPULATION 14 YEARS AND OVER, 1950-75
UNDER "HIGH," "MEDIUM," AND "LOW" ASSUMPTIONS[a]
(IN MILLIONS)

Year	High	Medium	Low	Difference between "High" and "Low"
1950	112.3	112.1	111.8	0.5
1955	119.4	117.9	116.4	3.0
1960	128.8	125.9	123.1	5.7
1965	142.1	137.0	132.3	9.8
1970	155.2	145.3	136.9	18.3
1975	168.3	151.6	138.9	29.4

[a] Projections for 1965-75 prepared by the Bureau of Labor Statistics by extension of projections for 1950-60 given in *Illustrative Projections of the Population of the United States, 1950-1960* (Bureau of the Census, Series P-25, 43).

The sources of the differences in the projected populations are more clearly identifiable in Table 2, which compares the three projections for 1975, by age and sex groups. Of the total difference between high and low projections of 29.4 million, 15 million is in the age group 14-24 years and is due very largely to the wide spread between the "high" and "low" birth-rate assumptions.

In view of the critical importance of the birth-rate trend in the next 10 years, as a determinant of the size of the population of working age a generation hence, it is necessary to evaluate the effect of relatively short-run social and economic forces upon fertility during the coming decade. It is noteworthy that after the preparation of the census projections in early 1950, the actual trend of births continued at a near-record annual rate of about 3.6 million during calendar year 1950 and then rose to a new high of 3.8 million in 1951. This rise can be traced to the direct and indirect effects of the Korean outbreak: the reactivation of Selective Service inductions, the increased tempo of economic activity, and the general heightening of international tension and uncertainties. These same factors are likely to exert continued upward pressure upon the birth rate during the next few years and perhaps for a decade or more. In view of these factors, the "low" projection, which assumes a rapid decline in births, to about 2.3 million in the second half of the decade, must be rejected as unrealistic—except under the explicit assumption of a sharp and sustained decline in economic activity. If a high level

TABLE 2

Projected 1975 Population 14 Years and Over, by Age,
under "High," "Medium," and "Low" Assumptions[a]
(in millions)

Age	High	Medium	Low	Difference between "High" and "Low"
14 years and over	168.3	151.6	138.9	29.4
14-19	22.9	16.7	13.1	9.8
20-24	19.0	15.9	13.5	5.5
25-29	18.1	17.7	17.1	1.0
30-34	14.6	14.2	13.7	0.9
35-39	12.1	11.6	11.0	1.1
40-44	11.4	10.9	10.2	1.2
45-49	12.3	11.7	11.0	1.3
50-54	12.4	11.8	11.1	1.3
55-59	11.2	10.5	9.9	1.3
60-64	10.0	9.3	8.7	1.3
65-69	8.2	7.6	7.1	1.1
70-74	6.4	5.8	5.4	1.0
75 years and over	9.4	8.0	7.2	2.2

Detail does not necessarily add to totals because of rounding.

[a] Estimated by the Bureau of Labor Statistics from data in *Illustrative Projections of the Population of the United States, 1950-1960* (Bureau of the Census, Series P-25, 43).

of defense spending and "full" or "near-full" employment continues during the greater part of the decade (without the actual outbreak of major hostilities), the "high" series, providing for an average of about 3.8 million births annually, may prove to have been the most probable. Somewhat more conservatively, we can assume that the population of working age in 1975 is likely to lie somewhere between the "medium" and "high" series, i.e., between 152 and 168 million.

B. LABOR FORCE

The level of the labor force and variations in its size are to a significant extent functions of the concepts and enumeration techniques used in labor force measurement. Prior to 1940, data on the size and composition of the United States working population were available only from the decennial censuses of population. In these censuses, statistics on the "gainfully occupied" population (or "gainful workers") were derived as a by-product of data on occupational attachment of persons of working age.

With increasing concern and interest in employment problems during the 1930's, this approach proved to be inadequate and a "labor force" concept was adopted in the 1940 census. At about the same time, a monthly sample survey of the labor force was initiated which is currently conducted by the Census Bureau and published as the "Monthly Report on the Labor Force" (MRLF).

The current labor force concept differs from other approaches to labor force measurement in two major respects: (1) A person's relation to the labor market is determined primarily by his activity in a given week (i.e., working or looking for work), with supplemental provision for inclusion as employed of persons who have a job attachment, but who are not actually working for certain temporary causes, and for inclusion as unemployed of some "inactive" workers, if their failure to look for work is due to certain specified causes, such as indefinite layoff or short-term illness. (2) Labor force attachment, as thus defined, takes priority over other types of activity or status, such as student, housewife, or retirement. Thus a student, enrolled full-time in school, would be included as in the labor force if employed one hour or more during a given week for pay or profit, or for 15 hours or more as an unpaid family worker.

The above definitions have proved generally effective as a sensitive barometer of month-to-month and year-to-year changes in employment and unemployment and of the changing composition of the working population. The MRLF was an indispensable tool for measuring and evaluating the great wartime expansion of the labor force and the transition to a postwar high-employment economy. However, the use of the activity concept and the systematic inclusion within the labor force of "fringe" groups, such as students and housewives, when actually employed or seeking work, has resulted in a high degree of seasonality in the labor force totals (with a typical range of nearly 4 million from "high" to "low") and has tended to make the series relatively sensitive to cyclical changes in the level of labor demand. This volatility means that special care must be taken in selection of base levels, and in evaluation of past data for purposes of long-term projection.

In addition to the influence of seasonal and cyclical factors, experience with the labor force survey during the past decade has revealed that the labor force estimates are highly sensitive to even minor changes in enumeration procedures. Thus, the addition of a "probing" question on employment status in the MRLF survey in July 1945 and subsequent months resulted in an upward revision of 1.5 to 2 million in the labor force estimates, due largely to more complete enumeration of marginal workers, such as women and youths. The contrast between the preliminary sample results of the 1950 decennial census recently published and the comparable MRLF estimate for April 1950 is even more striking. The employment status questions in the 1950 census were almost identical to those in the monthly sample survey; yet the estimated total labor force in the decennial census of about 59.9 million (including armed forces overseas) was 3.5 million lower than the comparable MRLF estimate. This difference was attributed by the Census Bureau mainly to a difference in the levels of experience of the field staff.[7]

Comparison of the preliminary census results with the MRLF in Table 3 indicates that the greatest differences for 1950 occur among "marginal" groups, including women and teen-age boys, while much smaller differences are shown for adult men aged 25 years and over. In terms of trends, it will be noted that the general direction of the changes between 1940 and 1950 is similar for most of the age-sex groups, expressed as percentages of the corresponding populations, but that the over-all labor force increase shown by the census data is much smaller than that shown by the MRLF data. Thus, the net increase in the labor force was about 6.6 million between 1940 and 1950 on the basis of the decennial census data, or about 2.2 million below the MRLF increase of 8.8 million over the decade.[8]

Unpublished census checks of the labor force enumeration in the 1950 decennial census compared with the MRLF indicate that, despite the greater sampling variability of the latter survey, the higher labor force total in the MRLF is probably the more accurate. However, from the standpoint of analysis of trends

[7] "Employment and Income in the United States, by Regions: 1950," *1950 Census of Population*, Preliminary Reports, Series PC-7, No. 2, p. 1.

[8] This comparison slightly understates the "true" increase, based upon decennial census data, since the preliminary census report for 1950 excludes from the labor force about 1.2 million persons 14 years and over whose employment status had not been reported. The corresponding census estimates for 1920-40 as shown in Table 3 have been adjusted by Durand to include a portion of the "not reported" group in the labor force. In 1940 about one-fourth of this group was estimated to be in the labor force. A corresponding adjustment for 1950 would have increased the decennial census labor force estimate by about 300,000.

TABLE 3

COMPARISON OF CENSUS AND MRLF ESTIMATES OF TOTAL LABOR FORCE, BY AGE AND SEX, APRIL 1940 AND APRIL 1950

AGE AND SEX	TOTAL LABOR FORCE (IN THOUSANDS)						PERCENT OF POPULATION IN LABOR FORCE					
	Decennial Census		MRLF		Net Change 1940-50		Decennial Census		MRLF		Net Change 1940-50	
	1940	1950a	1940	1950	Census	MRLF	1940	1950a	1940	1950	Census	MRLF
Total, 14 years and over	53,299	59,857	54,739	63,513	6,558	8,774	52.7	53.4	54.1	56.8	0.7	2.7
Male, 14 years and over	40,284	43,533	40,898	45,429	3,249	4,531	79.7	78.9	80.9	82.4	−0.8	1.5
14-19	2,619	2,594	2,833	3,096	−25	263	35.4	39.9	38.3	47.5	4.5	9.2
20-24	5,035	4,563	5,077	5,129	−472	52	88.5	82.5	89.2	86.9	−6.0	−2.3
25-34	10,076	10,741	10,133	10,920	665	787	95.8	91.5	96.3	94.4	−4.3	−1.9
35-44	8,741	9,903	8,851	9,933	1,162	1,082	95.4	94.2	96.6	96.5	−1.2	−0.1
45-54	7,381	7,851	7,457	8,147	470	690	92.7	91.7	93.7	94.6	−1.0	0.9
55-64	4,573	5,502	4,636	5,746	929	1,110	84.5	82.9	85.7	85.1	−1.6	−0.6
65 years and over	1,859	2,379	1,911	2,459	520	548	42.2	41.6	43.4	45.0	−0.6	1.6
Female, 14 years and over	13,015	16,323	13,841	18,084	3,308	4,243	25.7	28.6	27.4	31.9	2.9	4.5
14-19	1,395	1,458	1,460	1,679	63	219	19.0	22.5	19.9	26.4	3.5	6.5
20-24	2,688	2,492	2,820	2,603	−196	−217	45.6	42.5	47.8	44.4	−3.1	−3.4
25-34	3,607	3,792	3,821	4,053	185	232	33.3	31.5	35.3	33.5	−1.8	−1.8
35-44	2,500	3,718	2,680	4,061	1,218	1,381	27.3	34.6	29.2	38.0	7.3	8.8
45-54	1,691	2,870	1,830	3,246	1,179	1,416	22.4	33.0	24.2	36.9	10.6	12.7
55-64	859	1,491	920	1,868	632	948	16.6	22.8	17.8	27.3	6.2	9.5
65 years and over	275	503	310	576	228	266	6.0	7.6	6.7	9.5	1.6	2.8

a Preliminary census data adjusted by the Bureau of Labor Statistics to include estimates of armed forces overseas and to exclude persons whose employment status was not reported. (See footnote 8 to text.)

Sources: 1940 decennial census from John D. Durand, Labor Force in the United States, 1890-1960 (Social Science Research Council, 1948). All other data from Bureau of the Census.

between 1940 and 1950, no definite conclusions can be drawn from the currently available data. It is likely that, to some extent, the greater labor force increases shown by the MRLF over the decade may reflect progressive improvements in enumeration techniques by the census sample survey staff. If this hypothesis is valid, it is possible that, for purposes of comparison with the decennial census data prior to 1940 (when similar limitations in training of enumerators existed), the 1940-50 decennial census changes may be the more consistent.

For purposes of the present paper, the preliminary 1950 decennial census results are used for comparison with earlier census data in analysis of past trends, while the level of the current MRLF series as of April 1950 is used as a base for projecting future trends.

1. *Factors affecting long-term trends*

The brief review of some of the problems of labor force measurement illustrates one of the basic limitations of any long-term labor force projection. Clearly, a projected labor force can be no more realistic than the past or current data upon which it is built. It is doubtful that censuses prior to 1940 were any more accurate than the more recent ones; they may well have been less so. In addition, the necessity of adjusting "gainful worker" data to levels comparable to the current labor force concept adds another element of uncertainty to the analysis of long-term trends. Detailed cross-classifications of labor force status by such pertinent characteristics as family status or school enrollment are also generally lacking in censuses prior to 1940. These factors, alone, are sufficient to proscribe any elaborate statistical manipulation of past census data, as a basis for extrapolation of future long-term trends.

Despite these limitations, the general direction of labor force trends for broad population groups, as reflected in the available data, has been fairly consistent over a period of decades, with some notable exceptions. Table 4 summarizes the labor force participation rates (or "worker rates") by sex and age groups since 1920.[9] The over-all ratio of labor force to population 14

[9] Data prior to that date are not shown because of major difficulties of comparability (particularly in the case of the 1910 data) and because the relevance of movements prior to World War I for coming decades is somewhat questionable.

years and over has shown little net change since 1920, with the exception of the war period, but this has been a net effect of a complex of social and economic forces which have had contrasting effects on the work propensities of different population groups. Thus, the continued decline in the importance of agriculture in the economy and the accompanying movement from farm to city have tended to reduce the gainful activity of teen-age youth and of older men, but have expanded employment opportunities for women. Other major occupational shifts, such as the rising importance of the white-collar occupations and of semiskilled industrial jobs, have also operated in this direction.

TABLE 4

PERCENTAGE OF POPULATION IN THE LABOR FORCE, BY AGE AND SEX, 1920-50

AGE AND SEX	COMPARABLE WITH DECENNIAL CENSUS DATA				COMPARABLE WITH MRLF DATA		
	1920	1930	1940	1950[a]	1940	1945	1950
Total, 14 years and over	54.3	53.7	52.7	53.4	54.1	62.3	56.8
Male, 14 years and over	84.5	83.1	79.7	78.9	80.9	87.9	82.4
14-19	51.5	40.1	35.4	39.9	38.3	67.2	47.5
20-24	89.9	88.8	88.5	82.5	89.2	96.3	86.9
25-34	95.7	96.0	95.8	91.5	96.3	96.6	94.4
35-44	95.4	95.7	95.4	94.2	96.6	98.2	96.5
45-54	93.5	93.8	92.7	91.7	93.7	97.4	94.6
55-64	86.3	86.5	84.5	82.9	85.7	88.4	85.1
65 years and over	55.6	54.0	42.2	41.6	43.4	49.9	45.0
Female, 14 years and over	22.7	23.6	25.7	28.6	27.4	37.0	31.9
14-19	28.3	22.8	19.0	22.5	19.9	39.6	26.4
20-24	37.5	41.8	45.6	42.5	47.8	55.6	44.4
25-34	23.7	27.0	33.3	31.5	35.3	39.7	33.5
35-44	19.2	21.7	27.3	34.6	29.2	41.6	38.0
45-54	17.9	19.7	22.4	33.0	24.2	36.4	36.9
55-64	14.3	15.3	16.6	22.8	17.8	27.4	27.3
65 years and over	7.3	7.3	6.0	7.6	6.7	9.4	9.5

Data refer to April, except the 1920 decennial census, which refers to January.

[a] Preliminary census data adjusted by the Bureau of Labor Statistics to include estimates of armed forces overseas and to exclude persons whose employment status was not reported. (See footnote 8 to text.)

Sources: Decennial census data: for 1920-40, John D. Durand, *Labor Force in the United States, 1890-1960* (Social Science Research Council, 1948); for 1950, Bureau of the Census, Series PC-7, No. 2.

In addition, there have been specific forces affecting the changing work propensities of the major population groups. In the case of youth, the extension of compulsory education and child labor laws intensified the effect of other basic socio-economic factors, such as urbanization and rising levels of family income. Similarly, in the case of older men, a long-term decline in relative employment opportunities has been accompanied by increased provision for social security and pension benefits.

For women, the rapid expansion of the white-collar fields and of lighter industrial jobs has been a major factor creating an increased demand for their services. At the same time, the pre-war decline in the birth rate, the introduction of many labor-saving household appliances, and the shift of many functions from the household to the market economy have released an increasing proportion of women for work outside the home. The extent to which a change in any one of these factors can influence the over-all trends in labor force participation for the group is highlighted by the decline in worker rates among women aged 20-34 between 1940 and 1950, in contrast to the pronounced uptrend in earlier decades. This reversal is directly associated with the postwar upsurge in marriages and births: a much larger proportion of young women in the central child-bearing ages are currently fully occupied with the care of young children and are therefore not available for gainful employment. On the other hand, among older women past the child-bearing age, the uptrend in labor force activity has been particularly sharp, reflecting in part, perhaps, the relative shortage of younger women in the current labor market.

The relative influences of the various demographic, social, and economic factors upon historical trends in labor force participation have been the subject of intensive analyses by Wolfbein and Jaffe, Durand, Long, and others. Wolfbein and Jaffe, by standardizing changes in the over-all rates of labor force participation between 1890 and 1930 for the effects of specific demographic factors (i.e., age, sex, color, nativity, and marital status, for females), concluded that "social and economic forces are much more important than measurable demographic factors in accounting for changes in the proportion of the population in the labor force."[10] Durand performed a detailed "factorial" analysis for

[10] S. L. Wolfbein and A. J. Jaffe, "Demographic Factors in Labor Force Growth," *American Sociological Review*, August 1946, p. 396.

the period 1920-40, with additional allowance for the effects of changes in fertility among women and for urban-rural changes in residence. Partly because of his identification of urban-rural migration as a "demographic" factor, Durand has tended to give somewhat greater weight to the role of demographic changes, although recognizing the importance of socio-economic influence.[11] Long, in his study of the labor force under changing conditions of employment and income, found an inverse relation between income and labor force participation among areas and individuals, but found no such correlation over time, and concluded that the over-all relationship of labor force to population was independent of the income level and remarkably constant.

Despite these intensive studies of factors affecting past labor force trends, the application of the findings to projections of the future labor force has been carried through to only a limited extent. For example, Durand has published a detailed projection of the labor force to 1960, based on projections of the population by age, sex, color, and marital and family status of women, but without correspondingly specific projections of the socio-economic factors affecting each of the separate population groups. It was necessary for Durand to assume that, for each population group, the net effects of these factors would tend to operate in about the same way in the future as in the past.

One possible danger in this assumption may be cited here. The contrast has been noted between the inverse correlation of income of family head with labor force participation of married women *at a given time*, on the one hand, and a positive correlation of rising income with rising labor force activity of married women *over time*, on the other. These observations are not, of course, necessarily contradictory. They merely serve to highlight the fact that, in a free economy, where a significant area of choice exists between working and other types of activity for certain population groups, visible changes in patterns of labor force participation are the *net* results of a whole complex of dynamic influences. It is quite conceivable that at some future date, the balance of these forces may be altered. In the case of married women, available data strongly indicate that the pull of expanding job opportunities, combined with a set of social values which has placed great emphasis on an expanding material standard of

[11] John D. Durand, *The Labor Force in the United States, 1890-1960* (Social Science Research Council, 1948), p. 67.

living, has been a dominant factor in their steady flow into the labor force. There may be some theoretical rate of employment or level of real consumer income at which—under dynamic conditions—the benefits of further increments to family income will be offset by the disadvantages of less adequate household or child care, the loss of leisure, and the other real sacrifices resulting from the dual responsibilities of working women to their family and their job.

However, we need to know much more than we do about the basic relationships among these factors, under both static and dynamic conditions, in order to test a hypothesis of this type and incorporate it into a quantitative projection. Meanwhile, the analyst who is called upon for labor force projections today must still rely upon oversimplified extrapolations, reflecting the net effects of these various forces upon specific population groups, rather than attempt the much more complex task of forecasting their separate influences.

2. *Major assumptions*

In an extrapolation of this type, the major socio-economic assumptions are, in a sense, identified by the choice of base levels and of the method of estimating past trends. For purposes of projecting a peacetime "full-employment" labor force in 1975, the MRLF pattern of labor force participation by age and sex prevailing in April 1950 provided a convenient point of departure. The level of unemployment of 3.5 million, or 5.7 percent of the civilian labor force in April 1950, was somewhat greater than "frictional," but not sufficiently so to materially affect the over-all level of labor force participation as compared with the earlier postwar period of "full employment," in 1947-48.

One minor abnormality in the 1950 data from the standpoint of long-term projection was the temporary absence from the labor force of about 750,000 World War II veterans, mainly in the age group 20-34 years, who were attending schools under the G.I. Bill of Rights. Since nearly all of these veterans are expected to complete their training in the next few years, an allowance was made for this group in the 1950 worker rates for men aged 20-34 years, based upon a comparison of veteran and non-veteran worker rates in these age groups and upon related data on veterans' school enrollment trends.

Apart from this temporary factor, analysis of past labor force trends reveals no significant change in the worker rates for men in the age groups 25-54 years, apart from minor statistical aberrations. In these ages, nearly all men typically work or seek work except for a small percentage who, at any time, may be disabled, confined in institutions, or otherwise unavailable for work. The projected worker rates for these age groups were held constant at the adjusted April 1950 levels.

For all other age-sex groups, projections of worker rates were based on net rates of change between 1920 and 1950, with a special adjustment (for adult women) based on postwar trends between 1947 and 1950. (See Table 5.) The selection of the 1920-50 period was based on the following considerations:

1. Labor force data prior to 1920 were subject to larger relative errors of measurement and were too far removed from the operation of recent socio-economic forces.

2. Both 1920 and 1950 were years of relative prosperity, and followed—with somewhat varying time lags—a period of large-scale mobilization. In these respects, they are more comparable than the intervening decennial years, 1930 and 1940.

3. The time span of 30 years is sufficiently wide to reflect the operation of a number of major socio-economic trends: the continued relative decline of agriculture in the economy, the rapid growth of mass-production and other large-scale enterprise, the rising importance of the white-collar occupations, the establishment of social security and pension programs, etc. It was a period of rising productivity and of a general increase in the standard of living. It seems reasonable to assume that these broad trends will continue into the future, although probably at different rates.

4. Finally, the proportion of women with young children in 1920 more closely resembled that of the postwar period than did the proportion in either of the two intervening decennial years.[12] The effects upon worker rates for women due to intervening movements of the marriage and birth rates have thus been minimized.

In projecting worker rates to 1975, average annual rates of change between 1920 and 1950 were extrapolated to 1975 for those age-sex groups with declining trends in labor force participation, i.e., the 14- to 19-year olds, males aged 20-24 years, and

[12] This is indicated by comparisons of the proportion of mothers of children under 10 years among native, white, married women in 1920, 1930, 1940, and 1946, appearing in Durand, *op.cit.*, p. 231.

males 55 years and over. A relative, rather than an arithmetical, change in worker rates was applied, as the latter would have ultimately resulted in negative values. In the case of women in age groups 20 years and over, either an arithmetic or an exponential trend fitted to the rising pattern of worker rates would ultimately yield values over 100 percent. For these groups, the

TABLE 5

PERCENTAGE OF POPULATION IN THE LABOR FORCE, BY AGE AND SEX, ACTUAL (1950) AND PROJECTED (1975)[a]

| | | PROJECTED, 1975[b] | |
| | ACTUAL | Based on | Adjusted for |
AGE AND SEX	1950	1920-50 Trend	Postwar Changes
Total, 14 years and over	56.8	56.2	57.2
Male, 14 years and over	82.4	78.8	78.8
14-19	47.5	38.4	38.4
20-24	86.9	83.7	83.7
25-34	94.4	96.0	96.0
35-44	96.5	96.5	96.5
45-54	94.6	94.6	94.6
55-64	85.1	82.3	82.3
65 years and over	45.0	35.3	35.3
Female, 14 years and over	31.9	35.1	37.1
14-19	26.4	21.8	21.8
20-24	44.4	48.1	48.6
25-34	33.5	39.2	40.7
35-44	38.0	48.0	49.0
45-54	36.9	46.7	52.2
55-64	27.3	33.4	35.4
65 years and over	9.5	9.8	11.8

[a] Comparable to current MRLF at April seasonal level.
[b] Percentages for group totals computed on basis of "medium" population projections.

average annual rate of decline between 1920 and 1950 in the proportion of women *not* in the labor force was projected to 1975. The worker rates were then derived as the complements of the projected "nonworker" rates in 1975.

For adult women aged 20 years and over, average annual rates of increase in labor force participation were significantly higher in the postwar period 1947-50 than in the longer period 1920-50. It is doubtful whether the recent rates of increase in labor force participation can be sustained for any long period. However, allowance was made for the continuation of the higher recent rate of increase for the equivalent of five years in the future,

61

partly in recognition of possible lasting effects of the current defense program.

As in any other simple extrapolation of complex social variables, the extension of constant rates of change in worker rates for the coming 25 years is clearly subject to question. Over a sufficiently long period of time, this procedure would result in worker rates approaching zero for youth and older men, and in worker rates approaching unity for women—both of which extremes seem highly unreasonable at the present time. As more detailed information becomes available on factors affecting labor force participation, through analysis of the 1950 decennial census results and other sources, it may be possible to substitute more explicit assumptions and more refined methods for those described above. A range in projected labor force participation rates from "high" to "low" would also be desirable as a basis for constructing alternative economic models.

One approach toward projection of worker rates which may prove fruitful is through analysis of geographic differences for specific population groups. Preliminary analyses of this type, based on the 1940 decennial census and on sample census surveys of 34 metropolitan areas in April 1947, indicated that the relatively high projected worker rates for women in 1975 already prevailed in certain urban areas in the United States. Similarly, sharp geographic differentials in school enrollments support the possibility of a continued long-term decline in work activity among youth, simply as a result of a "catching-up" process in the more backward areas. The projected decline in labor force participation among older men, although consistent both with prewar and with recent postwar trends, is subject to a particularly wide margin of error. In an expanding economy and with a more highly trained and flexible labor force, it may be possible for a greater proportion of men than shown in the projection to remain in gainful employment until advanced ages.

3. The 1975 labor force

On the basis of the projected pattern of worker rates and of the "medium" and "high" projections of the population for 1975, projections of the labor force are shown in Table 6, by age and sex. These indicate that, in the next 25 years, the United States labor force will increase by between 23 and 31 million above the level prevailing in April 1950, or at an average annual rate of

TABLE 6

Projected Total Labor Force, by Age and Sex, 1955-75 (in millions)

AGE AND SEX	ACTUAL 1950	BASED ON "MEDIUM" POPULATION PROJECTION[a]					BASED ON "HIGH" POPULATION PROJECTION[a]				
		1955	1960	1965	1970	1975	1955	1960	1965	1970	1975
Total, 14 years and over	63.5	67.3	71.6	77.1	82.6	86.8	68.1	73.2	79.6	86.9	94.4
Male, 14 years and over	45.4	47.2	49.0	52.1	55.3	57.7	47.7	50.1	53.7	58.1	62.6
14-19	3.1	3.2	3.7	4.4	3.8	3.3	3.2	3.8	4.6	4.6	4.5
20-24	5.1	4.7	5.0	6.1	7.6	6.7	4.8	5.0	6.2	7.7	8.1
25-34	10.9	11.4	10.8	10.8	12.5	15.5	11.6	11.1	11.0	12.8	15.9
35-44	9.9	10.5	11.1	11.4	10.9	10.8	10.6	11.4	11.8	11.3	11.3
45-54	8.1	8.7	9.3	9.8	10.4	10.8	8.8	9.5	10.2	11.0	11.4
55-64	5.7	6.0	6.2	6.6	7.1	7.5	6.0	6.4	6.9	7.5	8.0
65 years and over	2.5	2.7	2.8	2.9	3.0	3.1	2.7	2.9	3.1	3.2	3.4
Female, 14 years and over	18.1	20.1	22.6	25.0	27.3	29.1	20.4	23.1	25.9	28.9	31.8
14-19	1.7	1.7	2.0	2.4	2.1	1.8	1.7	2.0	2.5	2.5	2.4
20-24	2.6	2.4	2.6	3.3	4.1	3.8	2.5	2.7	3.3	4.2	4.6
25-34	4.1	4.3	4.2	4.3	5.0	6.4	4.4	4.3	4.4	5.2	6.6
35-44	4.1	4.7	5.2	5.5	5.4	5.5	4.7	5.3	5.7	5.6	5.8
45-54	3.2	4.0	4.9	5.5	6.0	6.3	4.1	5.0	5.6	6.3	6.6
55-64	1.9	2.2	2.6	3.0	3.4	3.8	2.3	2.7	3.1	3.6	4.1
65 years and over	0.6	0.8	1.0	1.1	1.3	1.5	0.8	1.0	1.2	1.5	1.7

Detail does not necessarily add to totals because of rounding.

[a] Comparable to current MRLF at April seasonal level. The corresponding annual average level for total labor force is about 1 percent higher, on the basis of recent seasonal movements.

Sources: Actual 1950 from Bureau of the Census; projected 1955-75 from Bureau of Labor Statistics.

about 1 million per year. The projection is based on the fundamental assumptions of a continuation of past trends in labor force participation (as reflected in changes between 1920 and 1950 and in the recent postwar period) and of maintenance of an expanding economy with high levels of employment opportunity. It also presupposes that there will be no major war, or other disaster, which might substantially alter the previous work patterns of the population.

The rate of labor force growth may be expected to vary considerably over the next 25 years. On the basis of population trends and projected trends in worker rates, a smaller than average annual increase would be expected during the coming five years, when the relatively small population group born during the 1930's will be entering working age. A sharp rise in labor force growth is then indicated for the late 1950's and the decade of the 1960's, resulting from the wartime and postwar baby booms. Thereafter, the rate of labor force growth will be dependent in large measure upon the trends of the birth rate during the current decade. For example, if births during the current decade are at the "medium" level, a pronounced decline in the rate of labor force growth will occur in the period 1970-75; however, if fertility is maintained at the projected "high" level, annual increments to the labor force in the early 1970's may continue to rise.

Apart from population movements, annual changes in the size of the labor force will be significantly affected by cyclical movements in business activity, by changes in the international situation and in the level of munitions production (short of all-out war), and by a complex of other short-term factors. For example, the Bureau of Labor Statistics has projected a labor force increase of 3.2 million, or about 1.4 million greater than "normal," between late 1950 and late 1952, in response to the demands generated by the national defense program.[13] If the rate of defense production levels off or declines after 1952, this may be offset by smaller than normal increases in subsequent years.

It is noteworthy that the over-all ratios of labor force to the population 14 years and over, as projected for 1975, show very little net change from 1950. This would not necessarily hold true

[13] *Projected Manpower Requirements and Supply for the Defense Program, 1950-52*, Manpower Report 7 (mimeographed, Bureau of Labor Statistics).

for the relationship of labor force to total population; the latter, however, has not been projected in view of the uncertainty as to future birth-rate trends. The empirical observation of a fairly stable peacetime relation of the labor force to population 14 years and over in recent decades and in our projection for 1975 does not by itself warrant any broad, theoretical generalization. It is the net result of a number of contrasting trends which have largely offset each other; i.e., declining rates for youth and older men, increasing rates for women, and changes in the age-sex structure of the population. There is no a priori reason to believe that these forces will have the same effect for an indefinite period in the future.

4. Implications of labor force projections

The projected labor force trends for the separate population groups have many implications for the working life pattern of the American population and for major issues of social and economic policy. Some of these are noted briefly below.

Women. Women will account for nearly half of the projected labor force growth between 1950 and 1975. The greatest relative increases for any age group will occur among women aged 35-54 years, of whom about half are expected to be in the labor force in 1975, as contrasted to a worker rate of less than two-fifths in 1950 and less than one-fifth in 1920. On the other hand, relatively small increases in work activity are projected for younger adult women in the age group 20-34 years, since under assumed prosperity conditions, marriage and birth rates are likely to remain high. This trend accentuates the U-shaped pattern of labor force participation of women over the life cycle, with an initial high rate in the late teens and early 20's, before most women marry and start families; a decline during the central child-bearing period of the late 20's and early 30's; and a return flow into gainful activity as children grow older and leave home, with a consequent reduction in household responsibilities. Planning for a "second working life" and for a longer average period of gainful activity will therefore become increasingly important in the education and counselling of women.

Youth. A declining trend in labor force activity is shown for teen-age youth of both sexes and for young men aged 20-24 years, reflecting a continued extension in the period of schooling. The projected reductions in worker rates are relatively moderate

65

and do not fully reflect the assumed increase in school enrollment at the high school, college, and postgraduate levels. In recent years, about one-fourth of all students in the age group 14-19 years have also been in the labor force, mainly on a part-time basis. Under full-employment conditions, a continuation of a pattern of work outside of school hours (and particularly during vacation periods) may be expected and will limit the net decline in labor force participation for these age groups.

Older men. A slight decline of labor force participation among men 55 to 64 years of age and a larger decline (from 45 percent in 1950 to 35 percent in 1975) for men 65 years and over have been projected. If past trends are to be arrested, positive social and economic measures will have to be adopted by industry, labor, and government agencies, in order to avoid the economic wastage and individual frustrations resulting from premature separations of many older persons from gainful activity.

NATIONAL PRODUCTIVITY
AND ITS LONG-TERM PROJECTION

JOHN W. KENDRICK

NATIONAL BUREAU OF ECONOMIC RESEARCH

THE PHYSICAL volume of production in the economy is a function of the quantities of the factors of production utilized, and their joint efficiency or productivity. Long-term projections of gross national product basically involve projections of factor input and productivity. Because of the current limitations of our statistical information, it is more practicable to project in terms of labor, or man-hour input, and the partial productivity measure, real gross national product per man-hour, than in terms of a complete production function. This paper is concerned with the productivity sphere of the projection problem.

Successful projection of productivity involves first of all a clear concept of the variable under consideration, and the chief factors which determine its movement. Since real gross national product per unit of factor input, in aggregate and by industry, differs in important respects from most other productivity measures, considerable space will be devoted to clarifying the concept. The main factors which affect the movements of this type of productivity measure will be discussed theoretically.

As Dr. Kuznets pointed out in his introductory paper, projection involves a knowledge of persistent patterns of behavior in past periods. Accordingly, another section of this paper describes calculations of secular trends in national productivity over several past decades. Productivity trends in the farm and nonfarm sectors of the private economy are measured separately in order to illustrate the industry approach to productivity analysis.

The discussion of projections of productivity is largely related to technique. The types of adjustment which would have to be made in extrapolations of past productivity trends in order to obtain a projection articulated with the relevant details of the economic projection as a whole are developed. Finally, the areas are indicated in which further data, analysis, and theory are

Note: At the time this paper was prepared, the author was acting chief of the National Economics Division of the Department of Commerce. He bears full responsibility, however, for the views expressed herein, as well as for the supporting estimates.

needed to advance our knowledge of productivity and thus our ability to project.

A. PRODUCTIVITY CONCEPT IN A GROSS NATIONAL PRODUCT FRAMEWORK, IN THE AGGREGATE AND BY INDUSTRY

There are many distinct concepts and measures of productivity. Real product per man-hour, in the aggregate or by industrial origin, used in connection with over-all economic projections, differs in a number of important respects from other types of productivity measures. Understanding of the distinctive features of productivity measurement in a real product framework is essential to its use for analysis or projection.

1. *Real product dividend—a net output concept*

Gross national product measures the market value of the nation's economic output of final goods and services. The concept upon which the discussion in this paper is based is that of the Department of Commerce. It is clear that different concepts and measures of national product could affect the derived movement of productivity. Differing definitions of final product as opposed to intermediate product, for example, could have a significant influence on the derived productivity measures.[1] On the other hand, the line drawn between economic and noneconomic activities, while affecting the movements of total national product, should not be very important in productivity measurement, since the delimitations chosen would affect both output and input.

The influences of price changes are eliminated from gross national product by dividing the current dollar expenditure estimates, in the finest possible product detail, by appropriate indexes of market prices. This procedure ideally yields the same result as weighting the physical volume of output of the various types of final goods and services by base period market prices. The problems of price deflation, and possible biases in movements of constant dollar ("real") product, are discussed else-

---

[1] Some critics maintain that part of government purchases of goods and services as measured by the Department of Commerce represents intermediate products furnished business, and should be excluded from gross national product. See "Discussion of the New Department of Commerce Income Series," *The Review of Economics and Statistics*, Vol. xxx, No. 3, August 1948.

where.[2] Although any such measure has certain imperfections, it is currently the most practicable way of estimating the total physical volume of final output in the economy. For one thing, physical volume measures are not available for all industries. Most of the available industry measures are on a gross output basis, which differs from the gross national product concept.

Gross national product, in current and in constant dollars, is "gross" in that no deduction is made for business and institutional consumption of capital goods. It is "net," however, in the important sense that all other intermediate products, such as raw materials, semifinished goods, or components—other than those entering the net change in inventories—are excluded.

This factor may quite significantly affect the movement of real product relative to the volume of gross output, and the productivity measures derived therefrom. For example, economies in the use of intermediate products, given the same gross output in two periods, are reflected in an increase in real product. Input factors remaining constant in relation to outputs, an increase in productivity would result, because of both the increase in real product and the decrease in man-hour inputs, as man-hours engaged in intermediate production are reduced. Composite physical production series based on gross output would not only show no increase under these circumstances, but, if they covered the entire economy, would decline because of the smaller volume of output of intermediate products. A composite productivity series, based on gross output dividends, would show no change, abstracting from the effect of interindustry shifts.

The gross national product by individual industries of origin, while gross with respect to capital consumption, is likewise net with respect to intermediate products consumed. Estimated from the product side, gross industrial product is, broadly speaking, measured by the value of gross output (and inventory changes) less the value of intermediate products consumed in the production process. If intra-industry sales are included in the value of gross output, then an equivalent amount, representing intra-industry purchases, would be included in the deduction for value of intermediate products consumed. If, however, value of gross output is defined and measured net of intra-industry sales, then

[2] George Jaszi and John W. Kendrick, "Estimates of Gross National Product in Current and Constant Dollars, 1929-49," *Survey of Current Business* (Department of Commerce), January 1951.

69

the value of intermediate products represents purchases from other industries. In either case, the industrial product estimate is the same, and is additive to the gross national product estimates for other industries.

Gross industrial product, as a value-added type of concept, is equivalent to the sum of income accruing to the factors of production, plus indirect business taxes and capital consumption allowances. For deflation purposes, however, the product data are essential. Real industrial product is obtained as the difference between the value of gross output, adjusted for price changes by detailed product groupings, and the value of intermediate products consumed, deflated likewise.

Thus, the real product of an industry will move differently from the physical volume of gross output if the ratio of real purchases of intermediate products to the real value of gross output varies. Most productivity measures are based on gross output, and therefore do not allow for changing proportions of intermediate products consumed. Yet this factor is definitely relevant to productivity measurement.

These points are illustrated in the hypothetical model shown in Table 1 for individual industries and the economy as a whole. For the sake of simplicity, the model relates to an economy composed of two industries, A and B.

In industry A, because of the increasing proportion of intermediate products consumed, the national product rises less than the value of gross output. In industry B, the reverse is true. Because of the greater importance of industry B in the economy as a whole, the over-all proportion of intermediate products consumed declines and the total national product rises more than the value of the total gross output.

These examples are hypothetical, but not necessarily unrealistic. The real gross farm product in the United States has behaved like the national product of industry A. (See Section B-2-a.) This behavior may be typical of extractive industries generally, when there is a strong tendency toward diminishing returns. The extractive industries, however, currently account for a minor proportion of gross national product.

The hypothetical data for industry B may generally typify manufacturing industries, although good data over time concerning intermediate products consumed would be required for verification. Certainly scientific industrial controls, which have

TABLE 1

THE NATIONAL PRODUCT OF A HYPOTHETICAL ECONOMY
(IN MONETARY UNITS OF CONSTANT VALUE)

	TIME PERIODS		PERCENT
	I	II	CHANGE
Industry A			
Value of gross output			
Final products	100	100	
Intermediate products	50	100	
Total	150	200	+33
Value of intermediate products consumed	50	80	+60
National product of Industry A	100	120	+20
Industry B			
Value of gross output			
Final products	200	620	
Intermediate products	50	80	
Total	250	700	+180
Value of intermediate products consumed	50	100	+100
National product of Industry B	200	600	+200
Total economy			
Value of gross output	400	900	+125
Value of intermediate products consumed	100	180	+80
Total national product	300	720	+140

helped to economize the utilization of raw materials, and the increasing degree of processing have tended to reduce the proportion of intermediate products consumed.[3] This tendency may prevail in the economy as a whole. The net-versus-gross comparison for any individual minor industry would depend on the industrial classification scheme followed. The scheme would have to be consistent for the period studied if the tendency toward increasing specialization were not to be reflected as an increase in the intermediate product ratio for any one industry.

In any case, it is apparent that gross output data may be misleading in an economic sense. Consumption of intermediate

[3] Mr. V. R. Berlinguette, of the Dominion Bureau of Statistics of Canada, in a paper presented to the September 1950 meeting of the Econometric Society, "Limitations on Measurement of Physical Production," reviewed the few scattered attempts to measure the volume of net industrial output, and presented statistics relating to Canadian industry. On the basis of a study of 21 industries representing close to 25 percent of the total net value of manufacturing production for the period 1935-47, he concluded: "On balance, the index based on net output was significantly higher than that based on gross production, indicating that the degree of processing per unit of output had increased over the period covered." See summary of paper in *Econometrica*, Vol. 19, No. 1, January 1951, pp. 71-72.

products represents an important real cost of production, and for most purposes of economic analysis allowance should be made for changes in this variable relative to changes in gross output. This is especially true as regards productivity measurement, since efficiency in the use of materials is usually a relevant aspect of the problem. It is this writer's opinion that allowance for changing ratios of intermediate products consumed is better made in the dividend of the productivity equation, reserving the divisor for use as a measure of factor input.

Capital consumption allowances have also varied as a percentage of gross national product. If it were possible to make meaningful estimates of real capital consumption allowances, it would undoubtedly be desirable to measure productivity in terms of "net national product" in constant dollars.

2. The factor input divisor—the real cost of productive services

The physical volume of production is a function of the quantity and quality (or "efficiency") of the factors of production employed. The basic factors are customarily defined as: land, in the broad sense of natural resources; capital—plant and equipment, and working stocks; and the human labor force. These factors form stocks, or social and economic capital, while the employment or input in production of the factors represents flows of productive services, or "real costs."

The physical volume of input of the factors must be defined and measured carefully to avoid counting changes in efficiency as changes in physical volume. If changes in efficiency of each of the factors could be measured separately, and were counted as changes in the volume of input, then there would be no change in productivity, since the changes in output relative to input would have been imputed to the various input factors.

For each factor, the physical unit input or real cost can be measured as the physical volume of the stock in productive employment times the base period rate of remuneration or cost of the flow of factor services. The total of this constant-dollar flow of services from all factors would provide a measure of the composite physical volume of factor input.

It would seem logical to measure real factor costs for each industry separately. If relative prices or costs of factors, as well as of final products, in the base period, are accepted as a yardstick of relative physical volumes, then shifts of factors to industries with higher than average unit cost should be reflected as increases in the volume of input.

Most productivity measurements have related output to labor input only in terms of man-hours. This has been partly due to expediency, and partly due to the greater interest attaching to production in terms of persons or man-hours employed, possibly because of the close relationship of this concept to the ideas of real income and standards of living. However, it is clear that the real volume of input of the other factors relative to labor input influences the movement of the productivity quotient, as well as the efficiency of all the factors.

To make more explicit the assumptions involved in using a man-hour productivity measure, Table 2 has been set up, carrying the data of Table 1 a step further to show the relation of the input measures to each other, and to the real gross products in the component industries and in the hypothetical economy as a whole. The figures in parentheses are the series by which the

TABLE 2

REAL FACTOR INPUT, BY TYPE, RELATIVE TO REAL PRODUCT
IN A HYPOTHETICAL ECONOMY
(IN MONETARY UNITS OF CONSTANT VALUE, AND MAN-HOURS)

| | TIME PERIODS | | PERCENT |
	I	II	CHANGE
Industry A			
National product	100	120	+20
Factor cost	100	106	+6
Labor cost	70	70	0
(Man-hours worked)	(100)	(100)	
Property cost	30	36	+20
(Real value utilized)	(500)	(600)	
Industry B			
National product	200	600	+200
Factor cost	200	480	+140
Labor cost	120	240	+100
(Man-hours worked)	(100)	(200)	
Property cost	80	240	+200
(Real value utilized)	(1,000)	(3,000)	
Total economy			
National product	300	720	+140
Factor cost	300	586	+95
Labor cost	190	310	+63
(Man-hours worked)	(200)	(300)	+50
Property cost	110	276	+151
(Real value utilized)	(1,500)	(3,600)	+140

base period factor costs were moved—except for the total, in which case they are the unweighted sum of the data by industries. For the sake of simplicity, the returns to land and capital have been lumped as "property cost."

Before discussing the relationship of the various measures of factor input, a few words should be said concerning the conceptual and statistical problems involved in measuring actual total real factor input in the United States economy.

In the first place, to obtain an equivalence between factor cost and national product in the base period, real product would have to be revalued in terms of factor prices, which would mean deducting indirect business taxes and capital consumption allowances from the Commerce data, and adjusting the data for subsidies and statistical discrepancy.[4]

Labor cost in the base period should be inclusive. That is, the labor compensation element in entrepreneurial income should be segregated and included with the wages, salaries, and supplements of all types of employees.

Base period labor cost (by industry) would be moved by man-hour data. Although some productivity measures relate to average employment only, average hours worked measures the rate of utilization of employed workers, and is a closer approximation to labor input.

All types of labor should be included in the man-hour data— and are, in the data presented later: entrepreneurs (business and professional) and family workers; management and other administrative workers; and production workers, direct and indirect. Productivity measures related only to certain types of labor are influenced by the movement of the ratio of uncovered labor to the type of labor included in the divisor.

The property cost shown in the table includes the rents and royalties of land, and the return on capital. There would be difficult problems involved in obtaining a segregation in the base period. Some capital is leased, so that data on "rents" include part of the return on capital as well as the rents of land. On the other hand, the data on corporate profits and entrepreneurial income include rent (imputed) on land owned by the business. The income accruing to capital would include net interest and the

---

[4] This procedure raises difficult, statistical problems, especially when carried through on an industry basis. The general discussion in this paper of real product at factor prices, and of total real factor cost, is purely theoretical.

profit element of entrepreneurial income and corporate profits after inventory and depreciation valuation adjustments.

The real input of land would be computed as the base period ratios of net rent to the total value of land employed in the various industries moved by the quantities of land, the latter possibly adjusted by a use-intensity ratio.

The real cost of capital could be computed as the base period return on the net value of capital (buildings, equipment, and inventories) moved by the constant-dollar net value of capital employed, times a factor representing the degree of capacity utilization. Needless to say, estimating the constant-dollar value of capital assets and depreciation valuation adjustments would present difficult statistical problems.[5]

In the example, total man-hours show a smaller increase than real labor cost. This would always be true when there is a relative shift of labor toward higher-pay industries. Man-hours are interchangeable with real labor cost only on the assumption that there has been no shift in the industrial composition of man-hours employed.

Total real factor cost shows a greater increase than labor cost. This would be so whenever the ratio of the total real value of property per man-hour is increasing, which has probably been true generally of progressive economies. Thus, aggregate productivity would show a smaller secular rate of increase than labor productivity alone.

In my opinion, it will be salutary when productivity measurement and projection can be done in terms of total factor input, so that explicit account may be taken of property input. When only labor productivity is used, projections should be made at least with awareness of the property factor. Projections of past rates of increase imply not only that technical advance will keep up with past trends, but also that the relationship of real property input to labor input will continue according to past patterns. If this assumption is not consistent with other aspects of the economic projection, the productivity projection should be modified accordingly.

3. Productivity quotient—joint efficiency of the factors of production

"Productivity" is not an independently observable variable, but

[5] See Raymond W. Goldsmith, "A Perpetual Inventory of National Wealth," *Studies in Income and Wealth, Volume Fourteen* (NBER, 1951).

is a meaningful abstraction. Mathematically, it is the quotient of output and factor input, however defined. The precision with which it can be measured depends on the quality of the underlying data. Economically, the content or meaning of productivity change depends on the definition of the concept.

Defined as real product per unit of factor input (whether total real factor cost, real labor cost, or man-hours), composite productivity changes reflect changes in the joint efficiency of the factors, because of both technical and economic forces—as well as the influence of the real volume of input of uncovered factors if only part of factor input is used.

Changes in output of specific types of goods and services relative to factor input reflect technical forces. Productivity advances in this sense stem from increases in knowledge concerning production, and their application to productive procedures and instruments through technology. This type of "pure" productivity measure for broad segments of the economy is usually approximated by combining productivity series by a system of constant weights.

Aggregate real product per unit of factor input is also influenced by the effect of variable input weights applied (implicitly) to productivity movements of individual industries. This influence may be termed economic, since it stems from shifts in relative demand. By taking separate account of this influence, productivity analysis and projection can be more precise.

a. ECONOMIC EFFICIENCY

Real product per unit of factor input changes not only as productivity in the component industries change, but also as the weights used to combine the real products per unit of factor input in the various industries change.

These weights are, implicitly, the relative real factor costs in the various industries in any given year. This factor is economic, since it depends on the relative demand for the productive factors by industry, which, in turn, is a result of the relative demand for final goods and services. Final demand shifts as tastes change, and in response to changes in relative prices which reflect changes in relative costs. In a sense, relative changes in productivity itself are a partial cause of the industrial composition of factor input, since they influence the relative costs of the factors in the various industries.

In the case of real product per unit of aggregate factor input, a shifting composition of aggregate factor input by industry affects the movement of productivity only insofar as productivity movements by industry differ. If, on net balance, factor input shifts toward industries whose productivity rises more rapidly than the average, the rise in aggregate productivity will be greater than that indicated by application of base period weights to the component industrial productivity series.

In the case of real product per unit of labor input (real cost or man-hours), aggregate productivity is affected not only by differential productivity movement by industry, but also by the different *levels* of real product per unit of labor input in the various industries. If, on net balance, labor input shifts toward industries with higher levels of real product per unit of labor input than the average, total real product per unit of labor input will rise, apart from any changes in labor productivity in the various industries. This effect will be reinforced, of course, if the industries with higher than average real product per unit of labor input are also those in which productivity is rising more rapidly than the average.

From an aggregate economic viewpoint, the influence of the shift of resources among industries should be reflected as productivity changes. A shift of resources toward industries in which the real product per unit of factor cost is higher than average represents a real gain to the community, since the utility in terms of base period relative values, created by the factors in their new employment, is greater than in the old. Thus the factors are more "efficient" in an economic sense.

The effects of variable factor cost weights may be seen in Table 3, which spells out the productivity implications of Table 2.

It was seen in Table 2 that industry B has a higher value added per unit of labor input than industry A and also shows a greater increase in productivity. The higher real product results from a higher ratio of real property to labor and higher rates of return to both property and labor.

However, in the case of real product per unit of total factor input, since productivity in both industries is unity in the base period, aggregate productivity is influenced only by the shift of input toward the more rapidly rising productivity series.

77

In the case of labor productivity, the shift of labor toward the industry with the higher level of productivity also influences the aggregate productivity. Since the differential in levels of productivity is greater in the case of man-hour productivity than for productivity based on real labor cost, the shift of relative man-hours between industries causes a greater increase in aggregate

TABLE 3

PRODUCTIVITY MEASURES IN A HYPOTHETICAL ECONOMY
USING DIFFERENT INPUT MEASURES AND DIFFERENT WEIGHTING SYSTEMS
(IN MONETARY UNITS OF CONSTANT VALUE)

| | TIME PERIODS | | PERCENT |
	I	II	CHANGE
Industry A			
National product per unit of:			
Total factor cost	1.00	1.13	+13
Labor cost	1.43	1.71	+20
Man-hours	1.00	1.20	+20
Industry B			
National product per unit of:			
Total factor cost	1.00	1.25	+25
Labor cost	1.67	2.50	+50
Man-hours	2.00	3.00	+50
Total economy (variable input weights)			
National product per unit of:			
Total factor cost	1.00	1.23	+23
Labor cost	1.58	2.32	+47
Man-hours	1.50	2.40	+60
Total economy (constant input weights)			
National product per unit of:			
Total factor cost	1.00	1.21	+21
Labor cost	1.58	2.21	+40
Man-hours	1.50	2.10	+40
Effect on aggregate productivity of variable input weights			
National product per unit of:			
Total factor cost			+2
Labor cost			+5
Man-hours			+14

productivity on a man-hour basis than the shift in real labor cost causes on that basis.

It should not be thought that the increases in productivity on a man-hour basis are any less real because they show a larger influence of the shifting distribution of man-hours among industries. The meaning and movement of any productivity measure is relative to its definition. Man-hour productivity is certainly a

78

legitimate concept, and can be used as a projection tool. It is merely based on an incomplete measure of factor input, and one that probably rises less rapidly than total real factor cost. These characteristics should be consciously considered in using the measure.

b. TECHNICAL EFFICIENCY

Most conventional composite productivity measures attempt to isolate changes in technical efficiency by using constant weights to combine individual industrial productivity index numbers. Insofar as the relative weights are of the value-added type, corresponding to the relative gross products originating in the various industries, these composite index numbers correspond to the productivity measures using constant weights based on relative factor input shown in Table 3.

The economic factor is not entirely eliminated from such constant weighted indexes, however, since intra-industry shifts of the factors among products with differing productivity levels and/or changes affect the movement of productivity in the individual industry. "Pure" productivity change based on technical factors alone could be measured only in terms of individual products. But it is true that a composite productivity index for the economy as a whole, using constant weights for the component industrial productivity series, comes closer to the concept of pure technical productivity than one using variable weights.

The causes of the changes in productivity from the technical angle lie in the fundamental activities which result in changes in efficiency, or output capacity of a given quantity of the factors in combination.

It is impossible to segregate the changes in efficiency attributable to any one factor, although, obviously, changes in joint productivity can be related to, or measured in terms of, any one factor. This is because changes in efficiency of one factor usually require and are accompanied by a progressive adaptation of the other factors to the changed shape of the services rendered by the factor initiating the change in production technology. For example, new machinery requires retraining of workers and possibly a reorganization of plant layout, work flows, and the like.

The fundamental activities producing improved efficiency of the factors relate to improvements in technology and to the rate of incorporation of technical innovations into the body of factors

79

employed. Technological innovations rest on advances in human knowledge, which in systematized form may be called scientific progress. Advances in knowledge result from research, whether formalized as a distinct function or not. These advances are frequently directed toward, or may be adapted to, improvements in concrete procedures or instruments of production, resulting in technical innovations, or "inventions."

Research and development work is directed not only toward improving productive plant and equipment. It is also devoted to raising the level of physical and mental health, and the efficiency of human beings in their productive activity and in the rest of their lives, which also bear importantly on work efficiency. Much of the investment in personal efficiency is made by individuals themselves, as, for example, with education.

Research and development activity is also devoted to the problems of land and resource use to increase the productivity of land with a given input of the other factors. It is also devoted to problems of the use, improvement, and substitution of materials, which, as we have seen, affect real product per unit of factor input through the dividend of the equation.

A measure of real research and development outlays, with a distributed time lag, should show a high degree of correlation with changes in technical productivity. No attempt is made here to tackle the difficult problem of precise definition and measurement of the volume of research and development activity. However, as such activity increasingly becomes a distinct, organized function in business firms, the possibility of such measurement becomes greater.

Indeed, this type of intangible work, which represents current expenditures devoted (directly or indirectly) to the object of increasing productive efficiency in the future, might well be classified as "investment" in the national accounts, instead of being charged to current expense, as is done in the case of the business economy.

If such a procedure were eventually adopted, the gross business product would be higher by the amount of expenditures for research and development. On the income side, profits would be higher by a like amount. Government and personal purchases falling in the "intangible investment" category could also be segregated, but since these expenditures are already counted as final product, no adjustment of the totals would be required.

The rate of adoption of new developments and adaptation of productive organization to technical change also affects productivity. This is hard to measure in respect to personnel procedures, plant layout, organization of work flows, and the like. It is a more tangible factor in the case of plant and equipment, where the average age of the capital furnishes an index of the rate of incorporation of new devices into the body of productive capital. Likewise, changes in the average education, training, and health per worker are susceptible to rough measurement. The spread of improved methods of land management and resource use is likewise relevant, but probably difficult to measure.

Even this brief review of some of the dynamic factors which cause changes in productivity shows the difficulty of devising a quantitative measure of these forces. What can be done is to relate productivity measures to time, and (after abstracting from the effect of changing weights) to consider the average annual rate of increase in productivity as the net effect and measure of the combined influence of the various dynamic forces behind factor efficiency.

Projection of a past rate of growth in productivity is based on the implicit assumption that intangible investment per unit of factor input and the rate of incorporation of new technique into productive capacity will proceed at past rates.

B. PAST TRENDS IN NATIONAL PRODUCTIVITY

Long-term projection is basically a matter of extrapolating past trends modified by introducing the effects of anticipated or assumed abnormal changes in relevant factors. This section describes the calculation of past productivity movements and trends in the private economy. A brief description of the underlying estimates follows in Table 4.

The estimates of gross private product in constant (1939) dollars from 1929 forward are those published by the Department of Commerce.[6] The gross government product, which is equivalent to compensation of general government employees according to the Commerce concept, was excluded from the total. This was done because in the constant dollar series this item, by major categories, was moved by employment or man-

[6] See 1951 "National Income Supplement" to the *Survey of Current Business* (Department of Commerce), Part IV.

TABLE 4

Gross National Product in Constant (1939) Dollars, Man-Hours Employed, and Real Product per Man-Hour by Major Sectors of the United States Economy, 1909-50

YEAR	GROSS NATIONAL PRODUCT (IN BILLIONS OF 1939 DOLLARS)			MAN-HOURS EMPLOYED (IN BILLIONS)			REAL PRODUCT PER MAN-HOUR (IN 1939 DOLLARS)		
	Private (1)	Farm (2)	Private Nonfarm (1)−(2) (3)	Private (5)+(6) (4)	Farm (5)	Private Nonfarm (6)	Private (1)÷(4) (7)	Farm (2)÷(5) (8)	Private Nonfarm (3)÷(6) (9)
1909	46.2	5.1	41.1	89.7	25.2	64.5	0.515	0.202	0.637
1910	47.3	5.3	42.0	91.5	25.1	66.4	0.517	0.213	0.632
1911	48.1	5.6	42.5	90.0	24.9	65.2	0.534	0.224	0.652
1912	51.4	5.6	45.8	92.3	24.8	67.4	0.557	0.224	0.680
1913	51.6	5.6	45.9	92.4	24.8	67.6	0.558	0.227	0.679
1914	50.3	5.9	44.4	89.9	24.8	65.2	0.560	0.237	0.682
1915	49.7	6.0	43.7	90.2	24.7	65.5	0.551	0.243	0.668
1916	54.6	5.7	48.8	96.1	24.8	71.3	0.568	0.230	0.685
1917	56.4	5.6	50.8	101.8	24.3	77.4	0.554	0.232	0.655
1918	58.6	5.5	53.1	103.1	23.8	79.3	0.569	0.233	0.669
1919	59.0	5.5	53.4	94.9	23.4	71.6	0.621	0.237	0.747
1920	56.6	5.2	51.4	93.8	23.8	70.0	0.603	0.219	0.733
1921	51.5	5.1	46.4	82.7	21.9	60.8	0.622	0.232	0.763
1922	58.0	5.6	52.4	89.8	22.7	67.1	0.646	0.245	0.781
1923	65.6	5.8	59.7	97.0	22.9	74.2	0.676	0.256	0.805
1924	65.3	5.7	59.5	94.5	23.1	71.4	0.691	0.247	0.834
1925	70.8	5.7	65.1	98.8	23.6	75.2	0.716	0.242	0.866
1926	74.6	5.9	68.6	102.6	23.7	78.9	0.727	0.250	0.870
1927	75.3	6.0	69.3	102.4	22.8	79.7	0.735	0.263	0.870
1928	76.1	5.9	70.2	103.7	23.2	80.5	0.733	0.255	0.871

TABLE 4 (concluded)

YEAR	GROSS NATIONAL PRODUCT (IN BILLIONS OF 1939 DOLLARS)			MAN-HOURS EMPLOYED (IN BILLIONS)			REAL PRODUCT PER MAN-HOUR (IN 1939 DOLLARS)		
	Private (1)	Farm (2)	Private Nonfarm (1)−(2) (3)	Private (5)+(6) (4)	Farm (5)	Private Nonfarm (6)	Private (1)÷(4) (7)	Farm (2)÷(5) (8)	Private Nonfarm (3)÷(6) (9)
1929	81.5	5.9	75.6	107.5	23.0	84.5	0.758	0.258	0.895
1930	73.5	5.5	68.0	100.1	22.8	77.3	0.734	0.242	0.879
1931	67.7	6.3	61.3	91.2	23.4	67.9	0.742	0.271	0.904
1932	57.4	5.9	51.4	81.2	22.5	58.6	0.707	0.264	0.877
1933	56.5	6.1	50.4	80.5	22.5	58.0	0.702	0.271	0.868
1934	62.0	5.0	57.0	81.9	20.0	61.9	0.757	0.249	0.922
1935	67.6	5.9	61.8	86.4	20.9	65.5	0.783	0.281	0.943
1936	76.4	5.3	71.1	92.7	20.2	72.4	0.824	0.260	0.982
1937	80.9	6.3	74.6	98.7	21.9	76.8	0.820	0.289	0.972
1938	76.4	6.5	69.9	90.4	20.5	69.9	0.845	0.318	1.000
1939	83.7	6.6	77.1	95.2	20.6	74.6	0.879	0.320	1.034
1940	92.1	6.6	85.5	99.4	20.5	78.9	0.927	0.322	1.084
1941	106.2	7.0	99.1	108.2	20.2	88.0	0.981	0.348	1.126
1942	116.5	7.5	109.0	116.9	21.1	95.8	0.997	0.358	1.138
1943	125.3	7.1	118.3	121.1	20.9	100.2	1.035	0.339	1.180
1944	133.0	7.1	125.9	119.9	20.8	99.2	1.109	0.340	1.270
1945	129.7	6.7	123.0	113.9	20.0	93.9	1.139	0.334	1.310
1946	125.6	6.8	118.7	116.3	19.8	96.6	1.080	0.346	1.230
1947	128.8	6.5	122.3	120.6	19.5	101.2	1.068	0.334	1.209
1948	133.7	7.0	126.7	122.0	19.5	102.5	1.096	0.361	1.236
1949	133.2	6.7	126.5	117.4	19.4	98.0	1.135	0.346	1.291
1950	143.8	6.9	136.9	120.8	18.8	102.0	1.190	0.368	1.341

hours, because of the lack of objective means for measuring output and productivity in large areas of government activity. Thus, the productivity estimates are based on the real product originating in the private economy, including purchases by government from the private sector, but excluding product originating in government.

The Commerce Department gross national product estimates and price deflators were extrapolated by detailed components from 1929 back to 1909 by the author, using sources described in the Appendix. Although the estimates for the earlier period were made as carefully as a few months' time permitted, they are subject to a considerable margin of error and should be superseded by more authoritative series on the Commerce concept which may appear. The estimates of real gross farm product are those published by the Department of Commerce.[7]

The private nonfarm employment estimates from 1929 to 1950 are based on Department of Commerce estimates and include proprietors as well as full- and part-time employees. Numbers of unpaid nonfarm family workers were added. This series, by industries, was extrapolated back from 1929 to 1919 by Bureau of Labor Statistics estimates and from 1919 to 1909 by National Industrial Conference Board data.[8] The employment estimates, by major industries, were multiplied by estimates of average hours worked per week (derived from various sources, mainly the Bureau of Labor Statistics), and raised to an annual level. Average hours worked by industries and by types of labor for which data are unavailable (especially in the earlier periods) were assumed to move as the average for the covered industries and types. Man-hours worked on farms are Bureau of Agricultural Economics estimates for 1917-50 extrapolated back by an employment series from the same source. It should be noted that the BAE estimates are based on a somewhat different concept and methodology from those used in the nonfarm estimates.[9]

More intensive reworking of past data is needed, especially

---

[7] See "Gross National Farm Product in Constant Dollars, 1910-50," by John W. Kendrick and Carl E. Jones, in *Survey of Current Business* (Department of Commerce), September 1951.

[8] *Monthly Labor Review* (Bureau of Labor Statistics), October 1949; and *The Economic Almanac* (National Industrial Conference Board) for 1946-47.

[9] See Department of Agriculture *Technical Bulletin No. 1020*, December 1950, "Gains in Productivity of Farm Labor," by Reuben W. Hecht and Glen T. Barton.

for the period prior to 1929. The productivity trend calculations presented below, while probably of the right general order of magnitude, are subject to revision when better underlying estimates become available.

1. *Productivity trends in the private economy as a whole*

Chart 1 shows the net regression on time of productivity in the private economy, fitted to data for the years 1909-41. A second independent variable, the ratio of civilian employment to civilian labor force, was employed in the equation and held constant at 96.5 percent in the calculation of the "net trend." Because of the

CHART 1

Real Gross Private Product per Man-Hour, 1909-50

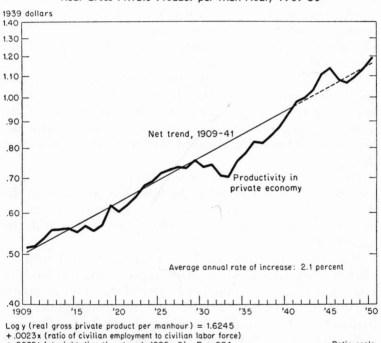

Log y (real gross private product per manhour) = 1.6245
+ .0023x (ratio of civilian employment to civilian labor force)
+ .0089t (straight-line time trend, 1925 = 0); R = .984   Ratio scale

various violent disturbances associated with depression, war, and postwar readjustment, which have affected the American economy from 1929 to date, it did not appear wise to fit a simple trend line to the entire period.

The war and postwar periods involved forces which affected

estimated productivity to such an extent that the period since 1941 was omitted altogether. The lack of comparability of munitions with nonmunitions, rationing, quality deterioration, and other disturbances render the meaning of real product during World War II dubious. Even if a conservative relative valuation for munitions is used, real private product per man-hour in the later war years swings well above the computed net trend line.

In the early postwar years, on the other hand, productivity falls well below the trend. Apart from continuation of some of the wartime disturbances, this is to be expected in the light of restrictions on new gross private domestic investment in peacetime industries during the war. Such investment restrictions resulted in a postwar capacity which was older than the prewar average, and the industrial distribution of which was imbalanced in relation to postwar demand. It was to be expected that heavy postwar expenditures for new plant and equipment would gradually raise productivity to the prewar trend line, and by 1950 this appears to have taken place.

As the 1940's fade into history, the 1942-49 period could probably be included in productivity trend calculations without distorting the results appreciably. But coming at the end of the historical period now under consideration, it was felt that the long-term trend would be distorted to some extent by inclusion of these years.

The problem of the 1930's is a different one. By 1933, productivity had fallen well below the trend line, and whereas the discrepancy was subsequently made up gradually, it was not until 1941 that productivity was almost back in line with the historical trend.

The depression period must have been associated with inefficiently low rates of utilization of capacity and low levels of new investment, with consequent aging of the stock of capital per worker, to mention the most important characteristics. The introduction of a variable describing the cyclical factor was indicated if use was to be made of the 1929-41 data in calculating the trend. For this variable, the ratio of civilian employment to the civilian labor force was used, based on Census Bureau and BLS estimates. The employment ratio not only takes account of fluctuations in the rate of capacity utilization, but approximates the cyclical factor generally as it affects the movement of various causative factors bearing on productivity.

When the employment ratio is held constant, the average annual rate of growth of real private gross product per man-hour implied by the regression equation is 2.1 percent. The net trend line shown in Chart 1 is computed on the basis of holding the employment ratio constant at 96.5 percent, taken to approximate a full-employment level.

Other types of curves would, of course, yield somewhat different results. It does appear that a constant rate of growth is implied by the data for the period covered. Possibly data for earlier decades would give a different impression. Real product comparisons become increasingly tenuous, however, the longer the period included, especially when there are radical shifts in product composition.

It is interesting to note that the trend line has almost exactly the same slope as is obtained by using the period 1909-29 only, and without a third variable. The average annual growth implied is also almost the same as is computed from the real private product data for 1929, 1941, and 1950, all years of relatively high employment, and relatively free from unusual economic disturbances.

If, however, the coefficients for the same variables employed in the formula are computed for the period 1929-41 only, the implied average annual rate of productivity growth is somewhat higher—almost 2.2 percent. The longer-term picture is probably a better guide to the future, however, despite the poorer quality of the data in the early years.

2. Productivity trends in sectors of the private economy

It was pointed out in Part A that real gross private product per man-hour in the private economy is a composite of real gross product per man-hour in the various private industries, combined by variable man-hour weights. For projection purposes, insofar as productivity trends by industry differ and the percentage distribution by industry of man-hours worked changes, it is desirable to handle various industries separately.

Practically no work has been done to develop historical productivity estimates by industry on a real gross product basis. This is partly because of insufficiency of data. Data being developed for interindustry relationship tabulations hold promise for the future, however.

Relatively complete data for the period since 1909 already

exist for the farm economy. This makes possible computations of real product and productivity in the private nonfarm sector. Presentation of these two sectors of the private economy separately will serve to illustrate the methodology involved in analyzing real product per man-hour by industry, and the effects on aggregate productivity of interindustry shifts of labor input.

a. PRODUCTIVITY TRENDS IN THE FARM ECONOMY

Farm productivity has been computed by a number of agencies. Generally, these computations are based on one variant or another of the physical volume of gross farm output. Such productivity computations, based on gross output, show a larger average annual rate of increase than the real gross farm product per man-hour series, shown in Table 4. This is because in real gross farm product estimates, the real value of intermediate products consumed is subtracted from the real value of gross farm output. Gross farm product is "gross" only in the sense that it includes depreciation charges; otherwise, it is "net" in that it excludes purchases of intermediate products consumed in the production process.

The ratio of the real value of intermediate products consumed to the real value of gross farm output has increased significantly during the period 1909 to 1941, so real gross farm product has increased substantially less over the period than the various measures of the physical volume of gross farm output.

It should be noted that the real value of gross farm output used here differs somewhat in concept, and in movement, from the several physical volume series used in other farm productivity series. The series used in the real gross farm product estimates follows the Commerce concept, which includes in the value of gross output the following items: cash receipts from farm marketings and Commodity Credit Corporation loans, the value of farm products consumed on farms where they were produced, the value of the net change in all farm inventories, and the gross rental value of farm homes.

But the most important factor distinguishing these estimates from the conventional ones remains the increasing ratio of the real value of intermediate products consumed to the real value of gross farm output. The relevant figures are shown for selected years in the following table:

88

	Billions of 1939 dollars		Percent change
	1910	1941	
Value of gross farm output	7.08	10.69	+51
Value of intermediate products consumed	1.75	3.73	+113
Gross farm product	5.33	6.96	+31

Thus, the real gross farm product increased 31 percent from 1910 to 1941, as contrasted with a 51 percent increase in the real value of gross farm output. This was because of the much greater relative increase in the real value of intermediate products consumed than in the real value of gross farm output, reflected in an increase in the ratio of the former to the latter from 25 to 35 percent over the period covered. By 1950, the ratio approached 45 percent, as real expenditures for operation of vehicles and machinery, for fertilizers, and so forth continued to climb more rapidly than the volume of production.

These comparisons would be more clearly in line with the concepts outlined in Part A if the value of gross farm output were net of sales to other farmers, and the intermediate products represented exclusively purchases from other industries. The inclusion of intra-industry sales (or purchases) in both places does not affect the gross product figure, and the movement of the "intermediate product" ratio should closely approximate the movement of a "purchases from other industries" ratio.

Most calculations of farm productivity have been on a "per worker" basis, because of the paucity of reliable average-hours-worked data for agriculture. However, in order to tie in with man-hour productivity data in the private nonfarm sector, and obtain man-hour productivity data for the private economy as a whole, a Bureau of Agricultural Economics series on man-hours worked in agriculture was used with a small adjustment for the early years. This series was derived from intensive man-hour requirement studies for various time periods. When divided by farm employment data, the man-hour series implied only a small secular decline in average hours worked over the period, much less than is apparent in the private nonfarm sector. Thus, man-hour productivity computed using this series would not differ much from a per worker productivity calculation.

The man-hour productivity series obtained by dividing the real gross farm product by the man-hours data is shown on Chart 2. The employment ratio is not relevant to this computation, but it was used in order to make possible an exact reconciliation of the farm and nonfarm productivity trends with the trend in the private economy as a whole.

The net regression on time indicates an average annual increase of 1.2 percent in farm productivity. The coefficient of multiple correlation is not as high as for the regression equation

CHART 2

Real Gross Farm Product per Man-Hour, 1909-50

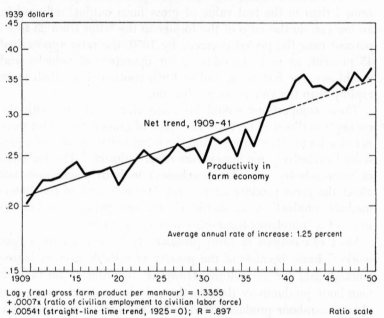

Log y (real gross farm product per manhour) = 1.3355
+ .0007x (ratio of civilian employment to civilian labor force)
+ .00541 (straight-line time trend, 1925 = 0); R = .897   Ratio scale

fitted to private nonfarm productivity, because of the greater importance of external influences in farming.

It will be noticed that most of the years in the 1940's are somewhat above the trend line. This may be partly because of unusually favorable weather conditions, but to some extent may represent real gains in productivity over and above the trend. The deviations above the trend in the 1940's are not as great, however, as in the productivity series based on gross output, since gross production gains were partly attributable to higher relative purchases from other industries, which are not reflected in this productivity computation.

b. PRODUCTIVITY TRENDS IN THE PRIVATE NONFARM ECONOMY

The real gross private nonfarm product shown in Table 4 is obtained by subtracting the real gross farm product from the total real gross private product. When divided by man-hours worked in the private nonfarm economy, the productivity series shown in Chart 3 emerges.

CHART 3

Real Gross Private Nonfarm Product per Man-Hour, 1909-50

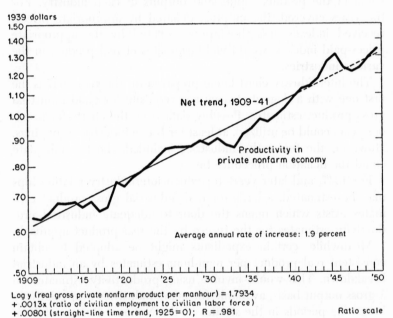

1939 dollars

Log y (real gross private nonfarm product per manhour) = 1.7934
+ .0013x (ratio of civilian employment to civilian labor force)
+ .0080t (straight-line time trend, 1925=0); R = .981

Ratio scale

As would be expected, the movements of real private nonfarm product per man-hour are similar to those of the productivity series for the private economy as a whole—since real farm product comprised less than 10 percent of the total real private product in the period as a whole.

The same variables employed in the private productivity equation were used to describe private nonfarm productivity over the same time period, 1909-41. Holding the employment ratio constant at 96.5 percent, the average annual rate of increase of the net regression on time is 1.9 percent. The difference between this growth factor and that for the private economy as a whole is due to the influence of farm productivity—its rate of growth, a downward influence, and its level, an upward influence, because of the shift of labor from the farm to the nonfarm economies, which will be discussed in the next section.

It would be desirable if real product per man-hour could be computed for individual nonfarm industries. But the real product estimates necessary for such computations do not exist. The data being developed in studies of interindustry relationships give promise for the future. This approach rests on estimates of the value of the product inputs and outputs of each industry. For the years covered, the outputs, deflated by appropriate prices-received indexes, less the inputs, deflated by the appropriate prices-paid indexes, would yield estimates of real product in the various industries.

The interindustry chart being prepared for the year 1947 is the first one with a degree of accuracy requisite for good industrial gross product estimates. Possibly data from the charts for previous years could be utilized, at least for broad industrial groupings. However, the fewer the industries included, the less adequate could the deflation procedure be.

For 1947, and later years for which interindustry relationships may be estimated, a basis for real industrial gross product estimates exists which opens the door to adequate industrial productivity estimates for the future by the real product approach.

Meanwhile, certain expedients might be adopted to obtain consistent real product per man-hour estimates by an industrial breakdown. This would involve using productivity estimates on a gross output basis, available for many industries over relatively long time periods in the studies of the National Bureau of Economic Research, the Bureau of Labor Statistics, and others.

If it is assumed that the ratios of the real value of intermediate products consumed to the real value of gross output in the industries concerned have not changed significantly over the period covered, then the available productivity series could be used to move a base period gross product per man-hour in the various industries. The industrial gross product estimates for the base period could be approximated by appropriately adjusting the estimates of national income by industrial origin, or could be estimated from interindustry data.

Either procedure would, however, be an expedient. The assumption of a constant intermediate product ratio is dubious.

92

Also, productivity data for large areas of the economy are not available—notably, for trade, service, and finance. Thus, no check could be made by summating industrial real products and comparing them with the over-all estimates.

It would be possible, however, to multiply real product per man-hour for the covered industries (derived by the procedure described above) by the corresponding man-hour data and obtain a total real product for the covered areas. By subtracting this total from total real private nonfarm product, the implied real product of the uncovered industries as a whole would be obtained. By dividing this residual real product by the residual man-hours, an approximation to productivity in the uncovered areas would emerge and could be assessed for reasonableness.

If reasonable, the area not covered could be projected as a whole, in conjunction with the productivity data by industry in the covered area. It is probable that, because of the generally higher rate of growth of productivity in the covered areas than that indicated for the private nonfarm economy as a whole, the average rate of productivity growth in the area not covered, chiefly trade, service, and finance, was below the average rate. Much more work needs to be done in defining the concepts and measuring productivity in these areas before intelligent projections can be made.

3. Effect on productivity of interindustry shifts

It was pointed out in Part A that composite real product per man-hour reflects changing proportions of labor input among industries, quite apart from changes in technical efficiency within the component industries. The economic, or weighting, factor in productivity change is usually minor compared with technological factors, but it is significant enough to warrant special treatment in analysis of past trends, and in trend projections.

a. THE FARM-TO-NONFARM SHIFT

Over the 1909-41 period covered by our trend analysis, the ratio of man-hours worked on farms to the total worked in the private economy declined from almost 30 percent in the early part of the period to about 20 percent in the latter part. Since real farm product per man-hour averages out at less than one-third of real private nonfarm product during the period, it is clear that the relative labor shift would have an upward influence on real private product per man-hour.

The influence of this shift can be measured by comparing real private product per man-hour with variable man-hour weights as computed in Part B-1, on the one hand, with real private product per man-hour computed by weighting real farm product per man-hour and real private nonfarm product per man-hour by constant (1939) man-hour weights, on the other. An index of the influence on productivity in the private economy of the farm-to-nonfarm shift is obtained by dividing the variable weighted series by the constant weighted series. This index is plotted in Chart 4.

The general upward trend during periods of relatively full employment is marked. During periods of depression the index moves down, since a reverse shift takes place in depressions, when

CHART 4

Effect on Productivity in Private Economy of
Farm-to-Nonfarm Shift of Man-Hours, 1909-50

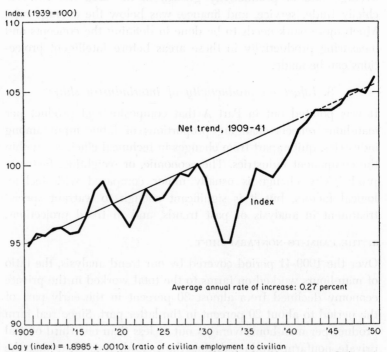

Index (1939 = 100)

Log y (index) = 1.8985 + .0010x (ratio of civilian employment to civilian
labor force) + .0011t (straight-line time trend, 1925=0); R = .904   Ratio scale

94

the volume of farm output holds up well relative to nonfarm output as a whole.

The net regression on time, computed from the index of the influence of the farm-to-nonfarm shift on productivity in the private economy, holding the civilian employment ratio constant, yields an average annual rate of increase of 0.27 percent.

Without the influence of the farm-to-nonfarm shifts, productivity in the private economy as a whole (using constant, 1939 man-hour weights to combine farm and private nonfarm real products per man-hour) shows an average annual rate of increase of 1.84 percent. This is smaller than the 1.91 rate of growth of productivity in the private nonfarm economy, because growth of productivity in the farm sector is less. But by adding the average rate of increase occasioned by the farm-to-nonfarm shift of 0.27 percent, we obtain a reconciliation with the over-all average annual rate of increase in the private economy as a whole of 2.11 percent.

b. SHIFTS AMONG NONFARM INDUSTRIES

Since estimates of real product per man-hour for the nonfarm industries are not at hand, it is not possible to compute precisely the effect on private nonfarm productivity of relative shifts of labor among the nonfarm industries.

A crude approximation of the effect of such shifts can be made on the basis of the Department of Commerce employment and national income data for 60 private nonfarm industries for the period 1929-49. This approximation involves the broad assumption that relative levels of national income by industry approximate relative levels of real gross product by industry, and that shifts in the proportions of persons engaged among industries approximate shifts in man-hours worked among industries.

The total number of persons engaged in the private nonfarm industries was distributed for all years by the base period (1939) proportions, and the products of given-year national income per person by industry times persons engaged distributed by industry were summated. By dividing the calculated total into the actual total private nonfarm national income for the various years, an index was obtained which reflects the effects of a shifting distribution of labor input.

This index (1939 = 100) was 96.1 for 1929 and 100.9 for 1949. Contrary to what might be expected, excluding the war period, there appears to be an inverse correlation between the index and the employment ratio. During the war period, the index reached 104, reflecting the shifts to higher value-added industries. The average annual rate of increase between 1929 and 1949 is approximately one-quarter of one percent. Inspection indicates that this result is close to what would be obtained by fitting a trend line mathematically to all the observations.

More refined analysis over a longer time period is clearly needed. A highly tentative conclusion is that relative shifts of labor input among private nonfarm industries have been in the direction of increasing the trend of productivity in the private economy. Such shifts in aggregate have apparently been not more important than the farm-to-nonfarm shift alone. If this is true, then interindustry shifts of labor input in the private economy as a whole have accounted for not more than about one-fourth of the secular increase in real private gross product per man-hour.

C. TECHNIQUE OF PRODUCTIVITY PROJECTION

The chief factors involved in productivity projections have already been implied in the discussion of productivity concepts and measurement. It remains to tie together the factors involved and relate them to the economic projection as a whole.

1. Over-all projection—first approximation

Before the forecasters of consumption, investment, and government expenditure patterns go to work, they need a general idea of the total dividend. A first approximation to real gross national product can be obtained by multiplying the projection for the target year of total private man-hours by a projection of real gross private national product per man-hour, and adding a projection of real government product based on a projection of government employment (if government product is treated according to the present Commerce concept).

If the first projection of private real product per man-hour is based on the past growth trend, several major assumptions are implicit:

a. Continuation of past rates of change in the real volume of capital and land per worker, or man-hour, as in the past.

In the case of plant and equipment, the past average rate of replacement and addition would involve rising levels of real

96

expenditures for new capital goods, although the future ratios to total gross product could not well be established without actually working out estimates of the total real volume of capital in the past.

The past secular trend of real plant and equipment expenditures represents an average over the business cycle. If the projection for the target year assumes a pathway between now and then under conditions of close to full employment, either the past average rate of new investment would be used, in which case a policy of stimulating other offsets to saving would be implied; or, if a rate of new investment consistent with past periods of high-level employment were assumed, some policy of assuring this high rate would be implied. A program of investment incentives, such as accelerated depreciation allowances, might be the assumption. Under these conditions, in which a higher rate of new investment was assumed than prevailed on the average in the past, an upward adjustment would be called for in the projected rate of growth in productivity.

b. A continuation of the same net effect on over-all private productivity of the shifting distribution of man-hours employed among industries would be assumed.

This assumption becomes increasingly untenable the longer the projection period. It should be checked against the distribution of final demand in the target year by industries. This check, however, would have to be done in a second approximation, since a first approximation to real product is needed before a product and industry break can be made.

c. The same rate of increase in real intangible investment (research and development expenditures) per unit of real factor input as in the past would be assumed.

A fairly steady secular rate of growth in technical productivity seems to be among the more persistent features of a highly industrial economy. In the absence of specific assumptions or forecasts which would alter the tendency to devote increasing amounts of resources to research and development, extrapolation of past rates of aggregate growth seems reasonable.

Insofar as the assumptions for the target year, and the pathway to it, implied special policies accelerating (or retarding) intangible investment, the past rate of pure productivity increase would be modified accordingly. Since the correlation between intangible investment and pure productivity measures has not

97

been quantified for past periods, any adjustments in the productivity projection would, of necessity, be subjectively based.

d. Finally, it is clear that projection of past rates of productivity growth assumes no major changes in the socio-economic structure. Social changes might not only alter the conditions covered in the first three points, but could change the general atmosphere within which the economy operates, with particular respect to economic incentives. For example, further substantial alteration in the relative roles of government and the private sectors of the economy could accelerate or retard productivity change via government expenditures, the tax structure, and the general legal framework of the economy.[10]

The remarkable stability of the production function, or the trend in productivity, over a period during which much cumulative change has taken place leads me to believe that only radical social change would be likely to alter past trends substantially. And long-run projections have little meaning unless a relatively high degree of social continuity is assumed.

2. Productivity projections by industry— successive approximations

Projection of productivity by as fine an industry break as possible would aid in refining the economic projections for the target year. First of all, they would be of use in arriving at approximations of relative prices, which, in conjunction with total real income and other relevant factors, would be needed to make a final product distribution of total real gross product in the target year.

This breakdown of real product could be translated into a chart of interindustry relationships, which, as we have seen, can be used to obtain real product estimates by industry.

Real product estimates by industry for the target year, in conjunction with industrial productivity projections to the target year, would yield estimates of man-hour requirements. The total man-hour requirements for the target year could then be compared with the projected man-hours-available figure, and any surplus, or deficiency, used to adjust the total real product projection.

If the industry productivity projections were, in aggregate, con-

---

[10] Mr. Fabricant commented in this connection that the new role of government "may tend to prevent productivity from rising as rapidly in the future as it has in the past."

sistent with the original over-all productivity projection translated into a constant weighted aggregate, the difference between the final approximation to real product and productivity in the target year, on the one hand, and the first approximation, on the other, would be due to a different set of relative factor input weights than those implied by the first approximation, which assumed a continuation of past trends in relative factor input.

The projection of productivity by industry would also have to take account of the factors spelled out above in connection with the over-all projection. Additional complications would be present in industry productivity projection, however. For one thing, it is likely that the productivity function for many minor industry groups would be more complex than for broader aggregates, with differential rates of productivity change in various phases of industry development.

At this stage of our knowledge, it is unlikely that the aggregate of productivity projections for individual industries would be more accurate than an aggregate projection alone. For this reason the former should probably be tied into the latter on a constant-weight basis. The specific adjustments for shifts in weights based on the product distribution in the target year should, however, result in a desirable refinement of the projection of aggregate national productivity. It would be dangerous to assume that the shifts of input factors among industries for a long future period would follow those in the past.

If the spelling out of real product by industry in the target year were accompanied by estimates of capital requirements by industry, a modification of the over-all investment assumption might be required. This would be indicated only insofar as shifts of labor input from industries with lower to those with higher capital per unit of labor input deviated from past patterns.

If product prices in the target year were spelled out in some detail, it would be interesting to revalue the total gross national product in the take-off year by the prices of the target year. This would probably serve to reduce the indicated rate of increase in total real product and productivity, since the products for which demand increases relatively more rapidly are usually those in which productivity increases relatively more rapidly, and relative prices decline. By using target year relative prices as the base for price deflation, less weight would be given to the more rapidly

99

expanding outputs, and thus to the related industrial product and productivity measures.

This phenomenon is apparent in measurement of historical aggregate real product and productivity movements in general—the more recent the price base, the smaller the increase. This does not mean that productivity measurement is an illusion. It merely means that the essence of economics is the relativity of values—at one point in time and over time. The particular set of values chosen as weights in assessing the real product dividend of productivity measures depends on one's point of view relative to the specific problem.

3. Areas for further productivity research

This brief analysis of the projection problem points up the need for much more information regarding productivity.

Although the concept of productivity has been clarified to some extent in this paper, more extensive theoretical thought is needed. This theory would be particularly fruitful if related to the practical problems of productivity measurement. The concept of industrial productivity on a real product basis, in particular, needs to be sharpened, especially in the noncommodity areas, where the definition of output lacks precision.

On an over-all basis, more work needs to be devoted to refining annual estimates of gross national product in constant dollars, especially prior to 1929. Available data on labor force, employment, and average hours worked per week need to be reworked for earlier periods, and the best possible estimates made.

Annual estimates of the total real wealth of the country in terms of productive capital and land will be necessary to obtain productivity measures related to total factor input. Although such estimates are rough at best, they would aid in interpreting past trends, and make possible productivity projections consistent with real investment projections.

Finally, work on productivity by industries needs to be refined and extended. The field of estimates by industry of real product per unit of total factor input is virgin territory. Not only estimates of real product for most industries are needed, but also estimates of man-hours and real property employed in various industries. Even measures of gross output per man-hour have not yet been made for many industries. Annual estimates of total productive capacity, and percentages of capacity utilized, in terms of physical units, would also have considerable bearing on the productivity problem, especially in its cyclical aspects.

In many of these areas, it may be impossible to construct adequate historical productivity series. It is never too late, however, to commence gathering and processing data, which, as time passes, will add to our knowledge of this important area of economics. Future generations of economic analysts, forecasters, and policy makers will find their task made more comprehensible by our initiative.

APPENDIX

Sources of the Real Product Estimates Underlying the National Productivity Estimates, 1909-29

The 1929 Department of Commerce estimates of gross national product, by product groupings, and the corresponding price indexes necessary for deflation were extrapolated back to 1909 by data from the sources listed below.

1. Personal consumption expenditures for commodities: Current-dollar estimates by product groups were extrapolated back by value of output data from William H. Shaw, *Value of Commodity Output since 1869* (NBER, 1947). These data, already adjusted for exports and imports, were further adjusted, in the aggregate, for changes in inventories. No adjustment was made for changing distributive markups, so the 1929 average markup is implicitly extrapolated for the entire earlier period.

The price deflators are Shaw's, linked to the implicit Commerce deflators for corresponding minor product groupings as of the year 1929, and thus converted to a 1939 base. Deflation was then carried out by the minor product groupings.

2. Personal consumption expenditures for services: The Commerce current-dollar data by minor groupings were extrapolated back by corresponding groupings from J. Frederick Dewhurst and associates, *America's Needs and Resources* (Twentieth Century Fund, 1947) for 1909, 1914, 1919, and subsequent odd years through 1929.

Expenditures for housing services (rent) were deflated and interpolated separately. The deflator back to 1914 was the rent component of the Bureau of Labor Statistics consumer price index. Interpolations to the constant-dollar data were made on a straight-line basis. The 1914 constant-dollar rent figure was extrapolated back to 1909 on the basis of the number of dwelling units in the United States, given in *Historical Statistics of the United States, 1789-1945* (Bureau of the Census).

Current-dollar expenditures for other services for the available years were deflated by a weighted average of the "miscellaneous" component of the consumer price index and the "fuel, electricity and ice" component (Bureau of Labor Statistics). Ratios of the constant-dollar other-service expenditures to the constant-dollar nondurable goods expenditures were computed, interpolated on a straight-line basis, and the estimates for the missing years obtained by applying the interpolated ratios to the constant-dollar nondurable goods estimates for those years.

3. New private construction: The 1929 estimate for new private construction (other than oil and gas well drilling) in 1939 dollars was extrapolated back to 1915 on the basis of the 1939-dollar estimates contained in *Construction and Construction Materials Report—Statistical Supplement* (Construction Division, National Production Authority, Department of Commerce, May 1951). This series was linked in 1915 to series H-47 for residential construction in *Historical Statistics of the United States,* and lagged permit data for nonresidential construction in Clarence D. Long, Jr., *Building Cycles and the Theory of Investment* (Princeton University Press, 1940), both deflated by the cost index implicit in series H-78 and H-79 of the former source.

Oil and gas well drilling expenditures, in constant dollars, were extrapolated back of 1929 on the basis of "footage drilled" and "number of wells drilled" data from *The Oil Weekly.*

4. Producers' durable equipment: The current-dollar data, by product groupings, were extrapolated back by data from Shaw, *op.cit.,* with rough adjustments for inventory change. The value of output of new passenger cars, included by Shaw in consumer durables, was used to extrapolate back the Commerce estimate of passenger cars for business use. The Shaw deflators were linked to the Commerce deflators as of 1929, and used to deflate the current-dollar estimates by minor groups. Estimated government purchases were explicitly excluded for the World War I years.

5. Change in business inventories: The annual data for the change in nonfarm business inventories, 1919-28, from Simon Kuznets, *National Product since 1869* (NBER, 1946), were converted to 1939 dollars. Rough estimates for prior years were based on a relationship between total nonfarm inventories and gross

102

national product excluding services, both in constant dollars, for the period 1918-50. The change in farm inventories was derived from the Bureau of Agricultural Economics estimates for the entire period.

6. Net foreign investment: The current-dollar series, by receipts and payments components, 1919-28, computed by the International Economics Division, Office of Business Economics, Department of Commerce, appears in *Historical Statistics of the United States.* The commodity part of the balance was carried back to 1909 on the basis of export and import data. The "invisible" items were extrapolated back on the basis of the ratios of the receipts and payments for these items to commodity exports and imports, respectively, for the periods 1896-1914, and 1914-18, based on data from the same source, applied to the commodity exports and imports for the individual years 1909-18. The Department of Commerce unit value indexes for exports and imports for 1913, 1919, and subsequent years were used to deflate receipts and payments separately, with interpolation and extrapolation based on the BLS wholesale price index.

7. Government purchases of goods and services: Federal government expenditures were extrapolated by averages of data for fiscal years, adjusted to exclude interest payments, pensions, and other transfer payments from the *Annual Report of the Secretary of the Treasury.* Unpublished data of Raymond Goldsmith[1] were used for the World War I period to improve the phasing. The deduction for compensation of federal general government employees was extrapolated back to 1929 on the basis of data in Simon Kuznets, "National Income, 1919-1938," *Occasional Paper 2* (NBER, 1941), and from 1919 back on the basis of numbers of federal general government employees times an extrapolation of the average annual earnings implicit in the Kuznets series. The employment series was based on Civil Service Commission data, and the average earnings series on data presented in Paul H. Douglas, *Real Wages in the United States, 1890-1926* (Houghton Mifflin, 1930).

The federal government purchases from the private economy were broken down between "new construction" and "other" by subtracting estimates of the former, based on the Construction Division data cited above, from the total. The 1929 price de-

[1] Soon to be available in Dr. Goldsmith's *A Study of Saving in the United States* (Princeton University Press).

flator for new federal construction was extrapolated back to 1915 by the implicit deflator for new public construction from the Construction Division data. The "other" purchases deflator was extrapolated back to 1915 by the BLS wholesale price index, and the implicit deflator for all federal purchases in 1915 extrapolated back by the same index.

State and local government purchases were extrapolated back of 1929 by census expenditure data for selected years shown in the *Historical Review of State and Local Government Finances* (No. 25, Bureau of the Census, June 1948). Provision for debt retirement, aid paid to other governments, interest payments, and contributions to trust funds and enterprises were subtracted from total general expenditures, and interpolations made between the adjusted totals for census years. Compensation of state and local general government employees was extrapolated by methods analogous to those used in the federal segments. Deflation of the purchases from private business was based on the series used for federal purchases.

PART II

PART II.

PROJECTIONS IN AGRICULTURE

JAMES P. CAVIN

OFFICE OF STATISTICAL STANDARDS, BUREAU OF THE BUDGET

A. INTRODUCTION

THIS paper reviews a number of economic projections which have
been made by the Bureau of Agricultural Economics of the
United States Department of Agriculture during the postwar
period. I shall describe briefly the nature and purpose of these
projections, summarize the methods used, and discuss a few of
the problems involved.

Agriculture is only a segment of the national economy, but an
important one. Net income from agriculture usually represents
about 10 percent of total national income; about 18 percent of
the population of the United States lives on farms; agricultural
exports usually account for 25 to 30 percent of total exports; and
American consumers spend over 35 percent of their total disposable income on such agricultural products as food, clothing,
and tobacco.

The field of agricultural economics has traditionally been separated from the main body of economic analysis. The artificial
character of this separation shows up sharply when long-term
projections of the national product are under consideration. On
the one hand, the agricultural economist becomes involved in
many of the problems of population, labor force, productivity, the
cost-wage-price structure, money supply, and the consumption
function that confront the more general analyst. On the other
hand, the general analyst must employ reasonable assumptions
about the agricultural labor force, agricultural production, farm
income, the prices of farm commodities, and the consumption of
food, or some of his more general projections may become distorted.

This is not to imply that there is no room for specialization.
The agricultural analyst, for example, needs a more detailed set

Note: The assignment to prepare this paper was undertaken while the
author was head of the Division of Statistical and Historical Research,
Bureau of Agricultural Economics, Department of Agriculture, and completed while he was, as he is now, a member of the staff of the Office of
Statistical Standards, Bureau of the Budget. It does not necessarily represent
the views of either agency.

107

of projections for the agricultural segment than for the non-agricultural segment; while the reverse is true for the analyst specializing in problems of commerce, industry, or labor. Nevertheless, projective analyses, even with specialized objectives, must reckon with many factors whose influences permeate the entire economy.

B. LONG-RUN PROJECTIONS

The Bureau of Agricultural Economics has published two sets of relatively long-run projections for agriculture. The first appeared in a series of bulletins published in 1945 entitled *What Peace Can Mean to American Farmers*. The actual analysis was done largely in 1944, and the projections were for the year 1950. The second, published in 1948, was *A Study of Selected Trends and Factors Relating to the Long-Run Prospect for American Agriculture*, prepared for the Committee on Agriculture of the House of Representatives. The analysis was done in 1947 and the projections were for a postwar period described as being about 1955-65, with some selected trends projected to 1975. This study is usually called the "Hope Report." This was not due to any wishful character, but to the fact that the request for its preparation came from the Hon. Clifford Hope, chairman of the House Agriculture Committee. We are now working on projective analyses in connection with river valley developments, flood control, soil conservation, and the activities of various agricultural lending agencies, all of which require consideration of whether future economic returns will justify current investment costs.

Before analyzing our longer-term projections, I shall dwell briefly on our outlook work. Each fall we make systematic appraisals of the economic prospects for agriculture during the coming calendar year. This work has been described elsewhere in some detail.[1] Our work on longer-term projections grew out of these efforts at short-term forecasting, and to some extent a common methodology is employed.

C. SHORT-TERM APPRAISALS

In making our short-term appraisals, we first estimate the levels of domestic and foreign demand for farm products during the

[1] J. P. Cavin, "Forecasting the Demand for Agricultural Products," *Agricultural Economics Research* (Bureau of Agricultural Economics), Vol. IV, No. 3, July 1952, pp. 65-76.

coming year. This requires an estimate of disposable income and of the value of agricultural exports. From a number of sources we develop forecasts of gross private investment, net foreign investment, and government purchases of goods and services. These forecasts provide an estimate of nonconsumption expenditures from which we can estimate gross national product, personal income, and disposable income.

From the GNP forecast, plus information about foreign aid programs, we can estimate the anticipated value of agricultural exports. Cash receipts from livestock, livestock products, and crops marketed domestically can be estimated as a function of disposable income; while cash receipts from export crops can be estimated as a function of disposable income and the value of agricultural exports.

From our knowledge of the quantity of livestock, feed supplies, and crop conditions, we can estimate the probable level of farm output and farm marketings. Given the latter, together with the estimate of cash receipts, we can derive an estimate of the level of prices received by farmers. Furthermore, because of the close relationship between cash receipts and the realized net income of farm operators, an estimate of the former will usually yield a pretty fair estimate of the latter. I shall not try to give any of the details involved in these estimates, except to say that linear relationships, fitted by least squares, are employed throughout.

In making our general forecasts of farm prices and income, we do not rely exclusively on these over-all relationships. Our analysts specializing in the various commodity fields, who are responsible for outlook reports appraising the factors affecting the prices of their respective commodities, provide us with independent estimates of the prices and quantities involved, which we can use to substantiate or modify the forecasts for the larger aggregates.

Neither our short-term forecasts nor our longer-term projections hinge on any single method. We try to use and consolidate all relevant knowledge. We examine long-time trends in production, consumption, and technology; we employ various types of statistical relationships; and we utilize the specialized knowledge of commodity analysts, farm management experts, marketing specialists, and the like. We continually try new hypotheses and new statistical techniques, and attempt to bring within our grasp problems which we had to leave unsolved in earlier projective efforts.

The ways in which our longer-range projections differ from those employed in short-term forecasts are largely matters of degree. As we move further into the future, we must rely increasingly on long-time trends; relationships which are satisfactory for measuring year-to-year changes must be modified in the light of assumptions about the structure of the projected economy; and problems which are of relatively small concern in the short run assume greater importance when longer periods are considered. For example, the problem of the general price level assumes much greater significance in longer-run projections than it has in the short-term outlook.

D. "WHAT PEACE CAN MEAN TO AMERICAN FARMERS"

Between May and December 1945 the Bureau of Agricultural Economics published four reports under this title.[2] The first described economic conditions likely to be associated with full employment or various levels of unemployment during the post-war years, and indicated probable effects of these different levels on prices and incomes received by farmers. The second report discussed the means of maintaining full employment, while the third was concerned with means of expanding foreign trade. The fourth report dealt with agricultural programs and policies appropriate to alternative conditions of domestic economic activity and foreign trade.

The first of these reports contains the first set of projections with which this paper is concerned. The key projections in the report are reproduced in Table 1. Their purpose was in large measure an educational one. As stated in the introductions:

"If farm people are to help develop constructive programs in the post-war period, they must understand their direct interest in national and international economic decisions which of necessity will be made at the close of this war—and understand the more basic relations of agricultural affairs to over-all national and international policies. The purpose of this analysis is to provide an aid to such understanding by describing the economic

[2] Department of Agriculture, Misc. Pub. 562, May 1945; 570, July 1945; 582, October 1945; 589, December 1945.

BLE 1

MPLOYMENT, INCOME, AND PRICES IN THE UNITED STATES, 1935-39 AVERAGE,
43, AND ESTIMATES FOR 1950 UNDER ASSUMED CONDITIONS

Item	Unit or Base	1935-39 Average	1943	1950 Full Employment	1950 Intermediate Employment	1950 Serious Depression
tal labor force[a]	Million	53.8	62.6	60.0	60.0	60.0
med forces	do.	0.3	9.1	2.0	2.0	2.0
tal unemployment[a]	do.	10.2	1.1	2.0	7.0	17.0
tal civilian employment[a]	do.	43.3	52.4	56.0	51.0	41.0
tal agricultural employment	do.	9.3	8.3	8.0	8.5	9.0
tal nonagricultural employment	do.	34.0	44.1	48.0	42.5	32.0
ross national product[b]	Billion $	81.9	187.8	188.0	130.0	76.5
ational income[b]	do.	65.4	149.4	150.0	105.0	57.5
ash income from farm marketings	do.	8.0	19.2	17.0	12.5	6.5
et income of farm operators	do.	4.2	11.4	9.3	6.5	3.0
ices received by farmers, index	Aug. 1909– July 1914	107.0	193.0	165.0	125.0	75.0
ices paid, interest, and taxes, index	do.	128.0	162.0	165.0	140.0	120.0
arity ratio (prices received vs. prices paid)	do.	64.0	119.0	100.0	89.0	62.0
holesale prices, all commodities, index	1926	81.0	103.0	103.0	87.0	66.0
ood consumption per capita, index	1935–39	100.0	106.0	118.0	110.0	100.0
gricultural production, index	do.	100.0	129.0	135.0	125.0	115.0

[a] Revisions in data resulted in some differences for these items from comparable items in able 3.
[b] Department of Commerce series as published prior to 1947. For differences between old nd new series see "National Income and Product Statistics of the United States 1929-46," *upplement to Survey of Current Business,* July 1947.

conditions likely to be associated with various degrees of employment and unemployment in the post-war period, and to indicate
the most probable effect of these conditions on the price-and-
income position of agriculture. *The estimates presented are not
forecasts of what will happen after the war, but are intended to
illustrate what is most probable under stated alternative assumptions with respect to employment, price levels, productivity of
labor, and related factors."*

111

1. *Estimating procedures*

To estimate the total labor force in 1950, we settled on an increase of approximately 1 percent a year from the total labor force reported by the Census for 1940. An allowance of 2 million persons was made for the armed forces and an additional 2 million for frictional unemployment. These deductions gave a total civilian employment of 56 million persons, of which we assigned 8 million to agriculture. This last was lower than the number employed in any prewar year, and was designed to allow for the usual movement away from the farm during prosperity and for continuing technological advance in agriculture.

The next step was the estimation of gross national product and national income. These estimates were expressed in terms of the general price level in 1943, as indicated by the average level of the retail consumer price index.[3] However, the agricultural components were adjusted downward because prices received by farmers in that year appeared to be about 15 percent above their normal relationship with the general price level. A compensating upward adjustment was made in the nonagricultural component.

Nonagricultural productivity levels in 1950 were estimated for two principal groups: group A—consisting of mining, manufacturing, transportation, electric power and gas utilities, and construction industries; and group B—consisting of wholesale and retail trade, finance, government, personal and professional services, and miscellaneous industries. Productivity per man-hour was estimated by fitting straight-line trends to the productivity data for each of the two groups. To obtain net income produced by each group, it was necessary to estimate the proportions of the 48 million nonagricultural workers that would be employed in the respective groups. For this purpose, we used the same proportions that prevailed in the high-employment year of 1929. This resulted in placing 20.6 million workers in group A and 27.6 million in group B.

An estimate of net real income produced by each of these groups in 1950 was obtained by multiplying the respective productivity indexes by the corresponding percentage increases in employment. These estimates of real net income were combined and converted to a total in terms of 1943 prices. This total amounted to approximately $134 billion. To this was added $2

[3] Consumers' price index of the Bureau of Labor Statistics.

billion for income produced by persons in the armed forces. On the basis of its past relationship to nonagricultural net income, agricultural net income was estimated at $14 billion. The sum of these three estimates gave a national income of $150 billion and a corresponding gross national product of $188 billion.

Given these over-all assumptions with respect to national income and the general level of prices, price specialists in the Bureau developed an integrated pattern of production, disappearance, exports, imports, and prices for each of the principal agricultural commodities. In making these projections, it was further assumed that there would be no support-price or production control programs (except the sugar quota system); that exports would revert to approximately the prewar pattern; and that high levels of employment would prevail in the principal industrial countries of the world. Most of these individual commodity projections, including prices received by farmers, production, and exports, were published in this first report.

Estimates of domestic disappearance and exports were converted into equivalent farm marketings. Cash receipts from these marketings were derived by multiplying quantities marketed by corresponding estimates of prices received. The sum of the cash receipts from all items totaled $16.7 billion, which was consistent with the net-income-produced figure of $14 billion.

2. Checking estimates

Results of this general estimating process were subjected to certain cross-checks. The index of prices received by farmers, estimated on the basis of past relationships between that index and the consumer price index, approximately equaled the index resulting from the summation of the individual farm price projections. The cash receipts estimate of $16.7 billion arrived at by the summation process proved lower than the results given by an over-all regression analysis, in which cash receipts were expressed as a function of national income and the value of agricultural exports. This equation indicated a level of $18 billion. However, since the multiplier effect on farm income which this equation assigned to agricultural exports seemed suspiciously large, we relied on the results obtained in the individual commodity analyses, and used a final cash receipts figure of $17 billion in the over-all model.

Estimates of domestic disappearance for food use at the farm

113

level were checked, and in some instances modified, on the basis of estimates of per capita consumption at the retail level. These per capita estimates were obtained by a combination of two approaches. First, a size distribution of the projected national income was constructed. The projected population was broken down by income groups, and estimates of consumption by these groups were obtained from income-group consumption data contained in the consumer purchases studies of 1935-36 and 1942.[4] These were finally converted to estimated average consumption per capita. Secondly, estimates of per capita consumption of individual commodities were projected by time series analysis. Consumption of meats, dairy products, fats and oils, and sugar was estimated principally on the basis of correlation analyses in which consumption was regarded as a function of retail prices and per capita income. Consumption of other products, principally fruits, vegetables, and grains, was derived largely from long-time trends. When estimates from the two approaches were combined, they gave an index of per capita food consumption 18 percent above the 1935-39 level. This was consistent with a correlation analysis in which the index of per capita consumption of all foods was regarded as a function of disposable income per capita and the ratio of food prices to nonfood prices at retail. Furthermore, when the index of per capita food consumption was converted to an index of total consumption, it was found to be consistent with the index of total food production implicit in the individual commodity production estimates.

Estimates of domestic disappearance for nonfood use at the farm level were also checked by separate analyses, but it was not possible to do this as thoroughly as for the food items. However, the farm level projections for cotton and tobacco were fairly well substantiated by estimates of cotton consumption at the mill level and of cigarette consumption at the retail level. It was not possible to develop any definitive analysis of wool consumption. Projections of livestock product consumption were checked against projected feed supplies, prices, and trends in feeding efficiency in order to achieve internal consistency for this important input-output relationship.

In this first report, similar estimates were made within the

---

[4] *Consumer Expenditures in the United States* (National Resources Committee, 1939); and *Spending and Saving of the Nation's Families in Wartime* (Bureau of Labor Statistics, Bul. 723, 1943).

agricultural segment under conditions of intermediate employment and of serious depression. The intermediate situation was
visualized as being analogous to the year 1941, and the serious
depression as analogous to something between the very low level
of 1932 and the average prewar level of 1935-39. The basic estimating procedures within these lower level assumptions were
essentially the same as for the full-employment model.

In developing our projections for this report, we undertook to
discuss the several models with agricultural economists in various
sections of the country. A considerable number took rather strong
exception to our full-employment model, which they regarded as
improbable, if not fantastic. According to them, everyone knew
that full employment was an unattainable ideal and that something like the agricultural depression of the 1930's would certainly
reappear as soon as the war was over! Although we were not
attempting actually to forecast conditions in the year 1950, we
naturally hoped that it would turn out to be a year of approximately full employment. This would not only enable us to con-
found our critics, but, more important, would give us an opportunity of finding out whether or not we had been able to visualize
the nature of a full-employment postwar economy with any degree of accuracy.

Unfortunately, the year 1950 was not ideally suited to this purpose. Conditions in this year ranged from continued decline in
the economy during the first quarter, particularly with respect
to agricultural prices and income, to an inflationary boom in the
latter part of the year, arising out of the Korean situation. However, examination of quarterly data indicated that average conditions prevailed in the second and third quarters, approximating a
full-employment situation not yet too seriously distorted by government expenditures for war purposes or by price inflation. Accordingly, I attempted to compare our 1950 projections made in
1944 with conditions as they existed in those two quarters converted to an annual basis. I reconstructed the 1944 projections
using all original assumptions and relationships with the exception of the price level, where the actual indexes of consumer prices
and wholesale prices were used. I did not attempt to work out the
projection in all its commodity detail, but simply confined myself
to over-all relationships between national income, on the one
hand, and some of the principal items in the agricultural segment,
on the other. Results are given in Table 2.

TABLE 2

COMPARISON OF 1950 FULL-EMPLOYMENT PROJECTIONS ADJUSTED TO 1950 PRICE LEVELS
WITH ACTUAL CONDITIONS IN SECOND AND THIRD QUARTERS OF 1950

ITEM	UNIT OR BASE	1950 FULL-EMPLOYMENT PROJECTIONS Original Projections[a]	1950 FULL-EMPLOYMENT PROJECTIONS Adjusted for 1950 Price Level[b]	ACTUAL 195((BASED ON 2ND ANI 3RD QUARTER
Total labor force	Million	60.0	60.0	65.1
Armed forces	do.	2.0	2.0	1.3
Total unemployment	do.	2.0	2.0	3.0
Total civilian employment	do.	56.0	56.0	60.8
Total agricultural employment	do.	8.0	8.0	8.1
Total nonagricultural employment	do.	48.0	48.0	52.7
Gross national product	Billion $	188.0	265.0[c]	277.7
National income	do.	150.0	225.0[c]	236.5
Cash income from farm marketings	do.	17.0	23.6	27.5[d]
Net income of farm operators	do.	9.3	12.7	13.0[d]
Prices received by farmers, index	Aug. 1909– July 1914	165.0	238.0	256.0
Prices paid, interest, and taxes, index	do.	165.0	239.0	256.0
Parity ratio (prices received vs. prices paid)	do.	100.0	100.0	100.0
Wholesale prices, all commodities, index	1926	103.0	160.0	160.0
Food consumption, per capita, index	1935–39	118.0	118.0	112.0[e]
Agricultural production, index	do.	135.0	135.0	137.0[e]

[a] From *What Peace Can Mean to American Farmers*, Department of Agriculture, Misc. Pu
562, 570, 582, 589 (1945).

[b] 1950 projections calculated on same basis as in 1943, except for differences between actu
and assumed general price levels.

[c] Including adjustment to bring these aggregates in line with Department of Commer
income concepts.

[d] Not available on an annual rate basis. Approximated from estimates of volume of far
marketings and prices received by farmers.

[e] Actual estimate for calendar year 1950. Not available on part-year basis.

3. Comparison of estimates with actual

Our projections of farm employment, farm income, prices received by farmers relative to prices paid, and the level of total
agricultural production were fairly good. The projected level of
food consumption was too high and our index of farm marketings,

116

which is not shown on this table, was too low relative to agricultural production. Disparity between the projected and actual situations was enhanced by the fact that agricultural exports in 1950 continued unusually high because of government aid programs, while the very considerable error in the population and labor force projections had pervasive influences on the estimates of the 1950 economy level which are very difficult to untangle. For example, there was no way of knowing offhand just how much of the miscalculation of the level of per capita consumption was due to population increase, how much to retarding factors in the production of meat, and how much to fundamental errors in the statistical relationships used in forecasting the consumption of food. I do not believe there is any point in pressing the comparison between actual and projected conditions much further. I shall leave the grading of this exercise to disinterested observers.

E. AGRICULTURE LOOKS AHEAD

There are both important differences and important similarities between the Hope Report and *What Peace Can Mean to American Farmers*. Although both studies contain projections of the economic condition of agriculture under various levels of economic activity, the Hope Report took the position that "in general it appears reasonable to expect a relatively high level of employment over the 25 years ahead" and that "the prospect for American agriculture over the next quarter century is relatively good" (p. 3). In analyzing the long-time prospects in this second report, we distinguished between certain long-run trends, which appeared to be of a rather stable nature, and certain variable factors, whose future behavior is more conjectural. Further comments on differences between the two reports will be made at the end of this section.

1. *Long-run trends*

With respect to long-run trends, we visualized a steady growth in the national economy as a whole. This growth is the result of upward trends in total population, labor force, and productivity per worker. The trend analysis of population is shown in Chart 1. On the basis of trends in gross national product per worker from 1880 to 1930, we concluded that the long-time trend in productivity per worker probably lay within the range of 1.5 to 2 per-

117

cent a year. Assuming a population in 1975 midway between the high and medium projections in Chart 1 (that is, 174 million persons), a labor force of about 71 million, and—to avoid exaggerating the long-time trend—an average increase in productivity

CHART 1

Population in the United States, 1910-49;
Projected, 1950-75

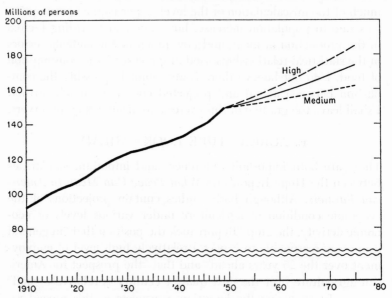

Basic total population estimates are from the Bureau of the Census.
High projection based on high birth rates, low death rates, 200,000 annual net immigration.
Medium projection based on medium birth rates and death rates, no net immigration.

per worker of 1.5 percent a year, we derived a long-time trend for the gross national product. The comparable trend for disposable income in 1935-39 dollars is shown by the upper trend line in Chart 2.

We also visualized a long-time upward trend in farm output, despite a continued downward trend in farm population. The trend in farm population is shown in Chart 3, while the trend in farm output, associated with a projected high level of economic activity, is shown in Chart 4. Even with a declining farm population, it appears that agricultural production will continue to rise. Long-time upward trends in farm mechanization, production per unit of breeding livestock, and crop yields per acre were

118

CHART 2

Consumer Income in the United States, 1921-48;
Projected, 1950-75

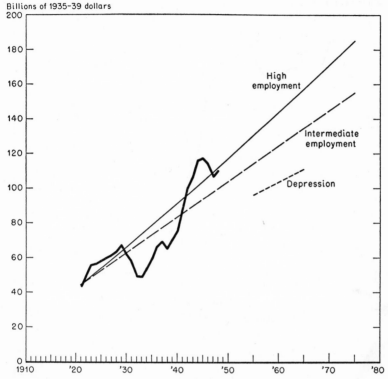

Billions of 1935-39 dollars

Disposable personal income in current dollars deflated by Bureau of Labor Statistics index
of consumer prices.

assumed to be continuing agricultural characteristics. The increased crop yields were predicated on trends in fertilizer input,
soil-conserving and soil-building practices, and the substitution
of new land—created by drainage, irrigation, and clearing—for
old land retired from cultivation. It should be noted here that the
long-time projection of total farm output was based not only on
analysis of trends in time series but also on a cooperative study
carried out by the land-grant colleges and the United States Department of Agriculture. Assuming average weather and relatively favorable prices for farm products, committees in each
state estimated what improved farm practices it would pay
farmers to adopt and what the effects would be on crop yields.

119

CHART 3

Farm Population in the United States, 1910-49; Projected, 1950-75

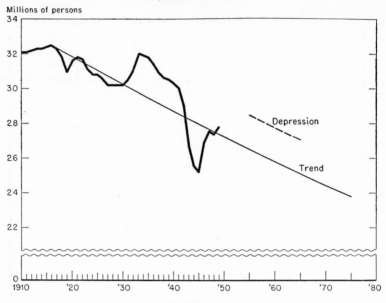

Millions of persons

CHART 4

Farm Output in the United States, 1910-50; Projected, 1951-75

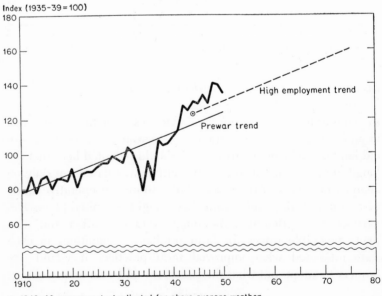

Index (1935-39=100)

⊙ 1942-46 average output adjusted for above average weather.

In addition, analysis was made of trends in farm costs, marketing costs, and food consumption. This report also discussed the continuing trends toward fewer and larger commercial farms, toward more part-time farms and rural residences, and toward the urbanization of rural life.

Following this presentation of selected long-run trends, we discussed what appeared to be the more variable factors—employment, the general price level, and the foreign demand for agricultural products—and presented a set of projections based on a number of alternative assumptions as to the general level of economic activity. These projections are given in Table 3, and apply to the decade centering on 1960.

The high-employment level in this model was based primarily on the trends selected as likely to be predominating influences over the next 25 years. It represents what was in our judgment the most probable economic environment in which agriculture would find itself in the long-run period. This is in contrast to the projections in *What Peace Can Mean to American Farmers*, where we did not attempt to determine which of the alternative situations calculated for the year 1950 was likely to prevail.

2. *Other problems*

Beside incorporating these long-time trends into the high-employment model, we dealt also with problems of the general level of prices, and the relation of farm prices and incomes to nonfarm prices and incomes.

It appeared to us that 1947 was characterized by a degree of price inflation that would not persist. Nonfood prices were markedly above their past relation to unit labor costs. We felt it advisable to bring this relationship back in line. After allowing for some further increase in wage rates during 1947, we assumed that the general price level would gradually adjust itself downward during the 1950's, with prospective increases in productivity per worker being about equally divided between increases in money wage rates and decreases in prices. We felt, therefore, that prices in the long-run postwar period under conditions of high employment would be something like 40 to 50 percent above 1935-39, but perhaps as much as 10 percent below those which prevailed in 1947. This was obviously a tentative approach to the long-run price level problem, but it did seem desirable to get away from the price abnormalities of the year 1947. Since then, the Bureau

TABLE 3

EMPLOYMENT, INCOME, AND PRICES IN THE UNITED STATES, 1935-39 AVERAGE, 1947, AND ESTIMATES FOR 1955-65 UNDER DIFFERENT ASSUMPTIONS

ITEM	UNIT OR BASE	1935-39 AVERAGE	1947 PRE- LIMINARY	High Employ- ment	Average Level	Depres
Total population	Million	129.0	144.0	158	154	154
Total labor force	do.	54.3	61.6	66	66	66
Employment	do.	44.9	59.5	62	58	53
Unemployment	do.	9.4	2.1	4	8	13
Gross national product	Billion $	84.0	231.8	265	205	165
Disposable income	do.	66.2	175.6	200	155	130
Cash receipts from farm marketings	do.	8.0	30.0	23	17	11
Realized net income of farm operators	do.	4.8a	18.0a	14	9	6
Net farm income to all farm peopleb	do.	5.4a	20.0a	16	11	7
Consumer prices, index	1935–39	100	159	145	125	115
Wholesale prices, index	1926	81	152	125	105	85
Prices received by farmers, index	1910–14	107	278	200	150	100
Prices paid by farmers,c index	do.	128	231	200	175	150
Ratio of prices received to prices paidc	do.	84	120	100	85	67
Farm output, index	1935–39	100	129	143	138d	135
Food consumption per capita, index	do.	100	116	121	115	110

ALTERNATIVE SITUATIONS, 195
Intermediate
Employment

a Includes government payments.

b Net income accruing from agriculture to all farm people, including farm laborers living farms. Includes value of farm products consumed in the farm household and the rental v of the farm dwelling.

c Index of prices and rates paid by farmers, including allowance for interest and taxes.

d Probably exceeds, by small amounts, quantities marketable through normal channel relative price levels specified.

of Agricultural Economics has given further attention to the price level problem involved in long-term projections.

We also faced the problem of agricultural prices and incomes in relation to nonagricultural prices and incomes. Although historical relationships between farm prices and income, on the one hand, and other economic variables, on the other hand, have given quite satisfactory results for short periods, there was doubt as to their reliability for making long-run projections at levels of population and national income far beyond anything previously experienced. Unqualified use of these relationships gave forecasts of farm prices and incomes that appeared high. After taking into consideration the long-time downward trend in agricultural income as a percentage of national income, and introducing the assumption that under full employment the per capita income of persons on commercial farms would be roughly equivalent to incomes of persons not on farms, we found ourselves obliged to make decisions within a range. For a number of important agricultural series, these ranges were as follows: cash receipts from farm marketings, $23 to 26 billion; prices received by farmers, 200 to 220 (1910-14 = 100); and a parity ratio of 100 to 106. A conservative choice was made in this matter, with weight being given to the uncertainty in export prospects, the possibility that the long-time trend in farm output may have been understated, and the further possibility that estimated per capita demand for food (as indicated by the index of average per capita food consumption) may have been too high. Events before Korea gave some indication that this conservatism may have been justified. Farm production had been running higher than the trend projections made in 1947 indicated, while farm prices had declined from a level of 306 in January 1948 to 233 in December 1949.

The parity ratio (the relation between the indexes of prices received and prices paid by farmers) was equal to 100 in both of these reports. Regardless of what one may think of the parity index as a means of determining individual commodity prices in connection with support-price and related farm programs, the parity ratio is a good statistical indicator of the general price position of agriculture relative to that of the rest of the economy of the United States. This ratio tends to fall well below 100 when the economy is operating under conditions of substantially less than full employment, to be fairly close to parity under conditions of full employment, and to move well above parity when there are abnormally large demands for agricultural products, such as developed during World War II and during the postwar period, when the demands arising out of foreign relief and reconstruction programs were added to the full-employment demands of the domestic economy.

I wish to emphasize that parity ratios in the two BAE reports were products of the projection process, rather than governing assumptions used in making the projections. However, the parity ratio used in the Hope Report might well have been anywhere within the range of 100-106 percent of parity. It was the conscious choice of a relatively conservative position with respect to the long-range agricultural price projections that resulted in the use of the lower figure.

In addition to the high or most probable level, this model also analyzes an *average* level and a *depression* level. These were constructed partly in recognition of the fact that a number of agricultural economists are much less optimistic about the long-run economic prospects for agriculture than the BAE, and partly to illustrate the effect of large variations from the high-employment level. The latter constitutes the basic long-run projection of this report.

Projections for the *average* level assume that the economy will perform about as well as it did in the interwar period 1920-40. They assume also that the pattern of employment and prices would affect the basic trends envisioned in the high-employment model. Population and labor force would increase somewhat less rapidly; the annual increase in productivity per worker would drop to 1 percent a year; and agricultural production would expand at a slightly slower rate. Given lower levels of employment and output, prices would be expected to drop. This is illustrated by a decline of 14 percent in the consumer price index below the high-employment level. Agricultural prices and incomes are adjusted downward accordingly, showing their characteristic tendency to decline further than nonagricultural prices and incomes when the general level of economic activity drops. The general relation between this intermediate model and the high-employment level can be seen from the consumer disposable income projections in Chart 2.

This average level is regarded as a highly unstable situation. The *depression* model is designed to illustrate the type of cyclical drop that might occur if the economy lacked the basic strength to maintain itself at the high-employment level. The drastic assumptions used in this model are evident from an examination of the last column in Table 3.

I return now to certain differences between the projections in *What Peace Can Mean to American Farmers* and those in the Hope Report. The first report set out some alternative economic possibilities for agriculture during the postwar period, together with suggestions of national policies that might serve to maintain full employment, and suggestions of appropriate agricultural policies under conditions of both full employment and underemployment. Projections in the Hope Report were focused on a more distant period and represented the Bureau's judgment as to which of the several alternatives was the most probable. The greater definiteness of the Hope Report arose out of the nature of the original request which the House Committee on Agriculture made to the Bureau. As Congressman Hope said in the Foreword to the report, "the committee felt that it would be helpful in its consideration of proposals for a long-time program to have before it the considered judgment of agricultural economists as to the major economic factors which may affect agricultural production, consumption, and prices for the next 25 years."

In some respects the projections in the first report were more complex than those in the second. They involved greater commodity detail, and a considerable effort was made to obtain consistency among all the individual commodity components and the larger aggregates. The second report was basically more aggregative, and contained fewer individual commodity projections. On the other hand, this report represented a greater effort to ascertain the likelihood that long-time trends would be continued or modified. A particular effort was made to arrive at a consensus as to the implication of these trends for the long-run outlook for agriculture.

It is impossible to say how "good" the projections in the Hope Report are. The Bureau has made a number of recalculations assuming a considerably larger population, and a somewhat higher level of total farm output and of prices generally. These adjustments, however, have not caused us to alter our views on the long-run prospects for agriculture, except perhaps in strengthening our conviction that the projection of a relatively high level of farm prices and incomes is justified.

F. CURRENT PROGRESS IN AGRICULTURAL PROJECTIONS

Despite the difficulties and hazards inherent in long-run projections, there are definite needs for them in the field of agriculture. Many programs affecting agriculture must be based on long-run considerations, and some attempt has to be made to formulate a framework of economic expectations. This is particularly true for such programs as flood control, forestry, and valley development, which require large-scale capital investments, and in which comparisons have to be made between current costs of these investments and the economic benefits which are expected to accrue. Projections are also becoming increasingly useful to agencies making repayable loans to farmers on a long-term basis. The abnormal conditions affecting agricultural prices over the past 20 years have rendered historical base periods less and less satisfactory as assumptions to be used in the development of lending standards. As a result there is an increasing tendency to employ projections of alternative future price situations for this purpose.

Because of this interest in long-run projections, the BAE has continued to work in this field. Its efforts have consisted, first, of more detailed projections, particularly for individual commodity prices, within the framework of the Hope Report; and secondly, of further analytic work on the general problem of long-run projections. The rest of this paper will be concerned with the latter.

Daly's study (the next paper in this volume) can properly be regarded as an extension and elaboration of the projection techniques employed in the Hope Report. Apart from the fact that his analyses center on the year 1970, as contrasted with 1955-65 in the earlier study, the principal new features are: (1) the construction of an index of total utilization of farm products, consisting of total domestic use of food plus total domestic use of nonfood commodities; (2) a more integrated analysis of the factors affecting food consumption over time; (3) a more searching analysis of the long-run influences affecting the proportion of gross national product and national income resulting from agricultural output; and (4) an explicit attempt to predict the behavior of the general price level during a prolonged period of full employment.

The construction of the index of total utilization of agricultural products, together with an over-all adjustment for net exports, permits a more direct, simpler comparison between projected total demand for farm products and projected total output than was achieved in the two previous BAE projections.

Daly projects a per capita food consumption index of 117 (1935-39 = 100), compared with 121 in the Hope Report. The analyses underlying this projection bear out the belief that the projected level of per capita food consumption in the Hope Report was somewhat on the high side and that the index of 118 used in *What Peace Can Mean to American Farmers* was closer to the long-time full-employment level. However, the problem of the long-run level of food consumption has not yet been satisfactorily solved. Still in doubt are the effects of new dynamic elements—notably a continuing population shift from rural to urban areas, increased processing and preparation of food outside the home, and a rapidly rising population, bringing marked changes in age distribution.[5] Large changes on the production side, particularly for meat, can have a significant influence on the level of food consumption as a whole. Furthermore, our statistical measures of food consumption and expenditures are still imperfect. Significant discrepancies between the BAE index of per capita food consumption and the estimates of consumer expenditures for food of the Department of Commerce need to be reconciled.

Daly's analysis of trends in trade between agriculture and the rest of the economy represents a more thorough exploration of this problem than was attempted in the Hope Report. It provides a firmer base for the final projection of farm output, prices received by farmers, and farm income than was available at the time when the earlier report was prepared.

The 1950 projections in *What Peace Can Mean to American Farmers* were in terms of the 1943 price level. The Hope Report assumed some contraction from the high prices prevailing in 1947, followed by a gradual downward adjustment in the general price level during the 1950's. Daly has attempted to deal more definitively with the long-run price level problem. Because of space limitations, his approach receives only brief treatment as now printed. It is therefore appropriate to summarize the essential steps involved. The core of his method was to examine trends in prices, total money supply, physical output, and money balances, in relation to gross national product in current dollars. This

[5] For a careful analysis of the postwar demand for food, see Marguerite C. Burk, "A Study of Recent Relationships between Income and Food Expenditures," *Agricultural Economics Research* (Bureau of Agricultural Economics), Vol. III, No. 3, July 1951, pp. 87-97.

analysis indicated a secular rise in the general price level. Daly did not accept the price level projection yielded by the trend analysis until he had examined the long-run relation of money wage rates to output, and had concluded that the economy has become increasingly resistant to severe price deflation. This involved an examination of the influence of political forces and of changes in our financial institutions on the general price level. Projected to 1970, his analysis indicated a price level about 30 percent higher than the one assumed in the Hope Report.

Daly's analysis is like the Hope Report, which attempted to deal explicitly with the long-run price level problem, rather than to follow the traditional method of using constant prices in the construction of a projected economic model. The essential reason for such a bold venture is the fact that the BAE projections have had a strong policy motivation. Demand for such projections has arisen as a result of long-range agricultural programs involving heavy financial commitments and requiring the adoption of assumptions as to the probable level of prices and incomes during the period when the fruits of these commitments will be realized. Despite the careful analysis made by Daly and the general plausibility of his findings, it is impossible to say whether his projected price level has any greater or less validity than the relatively conservative level projected in the Hope Report. I believe that his thesis of a gradual long-time rise in the price level under conditions of full employment is a better one than the assumption of a moderate decline adopted in the Hope Report. However, in view of the erratic behavior of farm prices since World War I, the disposition of the Department of Agriculture to take a relatively cautious position with respect to the long-run price level is understandable.

Although the final projections of the general level of prices, as well as those of prices received and paid by farmers, are considerably higher in Daly's study than in the Hope Report, the relationship between prices received and prices paid (the parity ratio) remains within the Hope Report range of 100 to 105. This indicates that the judgment of the BAE concerning the relative position of agriculture in a future high-level economy has not been fundamentally altered.[6] The projected farm income figures

[6] Since this present paper was written, however, there have been indications that the continuance of rapid technological change in agricultural production, together with the impact of the Korean inflation on the farm cost

in the Daly model are substantially higher than in the Hope Report, due to the assumption of both a rising price level and a larger farm output. However, they represent a somewhat lower share of total national income because of the assumption that the historical decline in the agricultural share will still be characteristic of the economy in 1970, which is considerably further out in time than the dates for the income projections in the Hope Report.

G. CONCLUDING REMARKS

The projection process followed in the Hope Report and carried forward by Daly can be summarized in a general fashion. Attention is first centered on trends that might be regarded as exogenous as far as agriculture is concerned, such as population, labor force, productivity, and the general price level. On the basis of these trends, there is projected a framework for the economy as a whole, consisting of a few large aggregates such as gross national product, national income, and a general price index. Secondly, trends are projected for a considerable number of variables within the agricultural segment, giving weight not only to observable long-time movements in the variables themselves, but also to the influences which the projected framework for the economy as a whole might be expected to exert on these movements. When trend projections for the more important components of the agricultural segment are given, an attempt is made to establish a rough equilibrium between agriculture and the rest of the economy. In establishing this equilibrium, certain historical relationships are utilized (arrived at by single equation methods), but their utilization is subject to modification on the basis of any evident trends in these relationships or on the basis of any other knowledge which appears to indicate that changes can be expected during a lengthy time period. Finally, an attempt is made to establish a more precise equilibrium within agriculture itself, partly by checking projections for individual commodities against projections for aggregates containing these commodities, and partly by analyzing the consistency of the input-output relationships that the agricultural projections imply.

The foregoing process of formulating long-range projections in

---

structure, may result in a ratio of prices received to prices paid closer to 95 than to 100, even under conditions of full employment.

129

agriculture can hardly be described as a method, in the sense of consisting of a definite number of steps, taken in unvarying sequence, and employing a fixed set of statistical relationships. It does, however, involve the use of an enormous amount of quantitative data and scores of statistical relationships. More importantly, it is a synthesis of the economic judgment of a large number of trained and experienced analysts concerned with practically every field within the economics of agriculture.

In concluding, I should like to emphasize again the difference between our projections for the economy as a whole and those for agriculture as such. We feel rather confident that, given a set of over-all projections, we can construct a reasonably good set of projections for agriculture. But unless our framework projections are good, our agricultural projections will be defective. Future progress in our projective efforts will in very large degree depend on the development of satisfactory methods for projecting those large critical components which determine the general level of employment, output, and income. It is relatively easy for us to make agricultural projections under various alternative assumptions of the general level of economic activity, but the payoff comes when one has to indicate which of the several alternatives is the one most likely to prevail. So far, we have leaned in the direction of thinking that our "high employment" projections represent the most probable course of economic development in this country over the next 25 years or so, and we hope that the projectors of population, productivity, capital formation, and the like will bear us out.

SOME CONSIDERATIONS IN APPRAISING THE LONG-RUN PROSPECTS FOR AGRICULTURE

REX F. DALY

AGRICULTURAL MARKETING SERVICE

DEPARTMENT OF AGRICULTURE

A. INTRODUCTION

ALMOST every action taken by an individual, a firm, or a government making a commitment extending over several years— whether it be the purchase of a home or a car, the building of a factory, or the development of a huge irrigation project—involves an explicit or implicit appraisal of the future in relation to the action taken. Much legislation relating to long-run commitments made by the government provides that rather specific cost-benefit computations and repayment schedules be developed for appraising a project or for ranking one project relative to others proposed. Many departments and agencies of the government— the Interior Department, the Army Engineers, the Soil Conservation Service, the Forest Service, and lending agencies of various types—must base their proposed programs on an appraisal of the future. These programs include development of rivers and harbors, flood control, construction of power dams, improvement of waterways, conservation of resources, reforestation, construction of public buildings, river valley development, and others. Appraisals for these purposes often require projections in much

Note: This is not an official report of the Bureau of Agricultural Economics. The views are the author's own. However, the Bureau has a continuing interest in the long-run prospects for agriculture and is called upon from time to time to make such projections as a basis for appraising proposed projects relating to river valley development, flood control, reforestation, and long-term financing. One of the most controversial issues relating to such projections is that of the general price level. Many of the important factors influencing the long-run level of prices are beyond the scope of economics. This paper appraises the prospective level of prices under specific assumptions which may or may not materialize. The analysis and projections relating to prices do not represent an official position of the Bureau, nor has the report, as a whole, been reviewed by the Bureau for publication. Although the author is completely responsible for the content of the paper, he wishes to acknowledge the advice and comments of K. A. Fox, N. M. Koffsky, O. C. Stine, R. O. Been, and many others of the Bureau of Agricultural Economics. Thanks are tendered also to Professors E. J. Working and L. J. Norton of the University of Illinois for their helpful comments and suggestions. This paper is based on a report submitted for a Ph.D. thesis at the University of Illinois.

131

more detail than can be justified in terms of statistical error concepts. Yet such projections are made and will continue to be made.

The purpose of this investigation was to prepare a set of projections for the economy centering on 1970, in which to cast an appraisal of the long-run prospects for agriculture. Specific objectives included projections of the population, the labor force, productivity, total output, the price level, and the relative position of agriculture, i.e., the demand for farm products, farm output, imports and exports, farm income, prices received for major farm products, and prices paid for products used by farmers.

Most economists will agree that forecasting, either short-term or long-run, is a hazardous undertaking. Any appraisal of the future could set in motion the very circumstances that would make it inaccurate. Long-run forecasts are usually "conditional" within a framework of assumptions. Unfortunately, it is often difficult to specify more than the main assumptions. Projections of the population, labor force, productivity, and potential output are usually based on relatively stable patterns of growth and are generally considered to be more accurate than those involving the price level or prices of specific commodities. However, even the more basic trends may vary and may materially influence the accuracy of long-run appraisals. Probably there are no economic forecasting techniques for the long term which are highly accurate or to which a probability calculus can be applied. We cannot determine the probability that a long-term projection will fall within a given range. Informed judgments about the future also differ, as do attempts to make objective forecasts in a framework of assumptions.

Appraisals of the future are influenced to a very large extent by the sum total of social, political, and economic forces characterizing the current era, and these may distort the perspective of the economic forecaster. For example, in the spring of 1929, a report by the Committee on Recent Economic Changes of the President's Conference on Unemployment commented on the health of the nation and the "degree of progress in recent years." These observations were made on the very brink of the 1929-32 depression. It was but a few years later (1934) that Dr. Nourse and his associates in the Brookings Institution were concerned with the distribution of wealth and income in relation to economic progress, to apparent "under-consumption," to reduced outlets for investment, and to the generally inadequate level of demand.[1] And, toward the end of the decade of the 1930's, there developed the "stagnation" or "mature economy" thesis. The mature economy, it was asserted, would lead to long periods of unemployment and continuous deficit spending by the government to maintain investment and employment. Long-run population projections of the late 1930's and early 1940's probably influenced some of the more pessimistic long-run appraisals made in this period for agriculture and the total economy.

Adam Smith, who wrote during the industrial revolution in England (1776), was optimistic about the prospects for innovation and capital accumulation. Schumpeter likewise wrote in a period of growth and development and considered innovation to be the prime mover in economic growth, without much concern for the possibility that demand might be inadequate to maintain a high rate of capital development.[2] On the other hand, Sismondi, Lauderdale, and Malthus wrote during the latter part of England's industrial and social revolution (1776-1850), when a large poverty-stricken laboring class was concentrated in cities without adequate housing, sanitation, or food. These men were concerned about the prospective lack of purchasing power of the common man and the possibility that investment and capital accumulation might result in output greater than could be absorbed in the market.

Most forecasts made in recent years recognize the potentials of the dynamic economy which has characterized the development of the United States, but the specter of war, or the possibility of long periods of semimobilization, overshadow all other considerations.[3] As man's experience is about the only basis for appraising the future, it appears logical to expect that such appraisals will continue to be influenced largely by the economic, political, and social trends of the time.

B. METHODOLOGY

The nature of growth, process, and change in the economy over

[1] E. G. Nourse and associates, *America's Capacity to Produce* (Brookings Institution, 1934), pp. 1-17.

[2] J. A. Schumpeter, *The Theory of Economic Development*, tr. from the German by Redvers Opie (Harvard University Press, 1936).

[3] See H. G. Moulton, *Controlling Factors in Economic Development* (Brookings Institution, 1949); K. E. Boulding, *The Economics of Peace* (Prentice-Hall, 1945).

time does not lend itself to the rigorous type of analysis employed for short-period or static appraisals. Moreover, in most instances, background data for long-period analyses are sketchy and conceptually inconsistent. Refined statistical techniques must be supplemented by judgment.

A long-run appraisal of the economy must be concerned with the very forces which are usually impounded in the static assumption "other things being equal," as used in most modern theory of the firm and of price determination. We are not so much concerned with the "allocation of scarce means among competing ends"[4] as with the growth in the means themselves. For long-run projections, an appraisal must be made of probable "structural changes" which result in trends in coefficients of relationship of one variable to another or to several others. It is quite probable, for example, that price and income elasticities of consumption vary over time as real income per capita grows and modes of living change. In addition, changes in "taste" and "style" and technological developments modify both the demand for and the supply of a commodity over time. The primary problem of supply response is one of growth in productive factors and innovation. Prospective changes in the "state of the arts" become of primary importance in a long-run appraisal. But, for a given industry, transfer of resources from one industry to another—changes in size—probably are as important as changes in efficiency in determining long-run supply response.

In this report, per capita use of food and other farm products was projected on the basis of apparent trends in taste and consumption habits, trends in innovations influencing consumption, the apparent long-run effect on consumption of price and income, and the judgment of commodity men, each familiar with a commodity or group of commodities. The aggregate per capita use of farm products was first appraised in the projected framework, then compared with detailed projections for the individual commodities and groups of commodities that make up the aggregate. The supply response was also appraised in relation to growth in aggregate farm output, interindustry shifts of resources, output per man, and the shift from horse to machine power. These projections were then compared with detailed commodity analyses which were related to demand, past output, acreage, capital and other inputs, and yields.

[4] G. J. Stigler, *The Theory of Price* (Macmillan, 1947), p. 12.

It will be obvious to anyone who has thought about the problem that we cannot expect to make highly accurate 20-year forecasts of production, utilization, and prices for individual commodities. We may feel reasonably certain, for example, that per capita use of food fats and oils, as an aggregate, will continue reasonably stable, as it has in past years. Yet the prospects for butter and lard as compared with margarine and shortening are much less certain. On the supply side, similar problems arise. An appraisal of the prospects for a group of related commodities is surely more reliable than one for a given commodity. The output of soybeans has grown rapidly over the last three decades. Will it continue to grow as it has in the past? An attempted answer would require assumptions regarding innovations that influence the demand and supply prospects for soybeans and the demand and supply prospects for every other commodity related to soybeans on the side of demand or resource use.

Methodology in appraisals such as those undertaken in this report must be primarily historical, insofar as past relationships and trends in economic, social, and political conditions provide the basis for appraising the future. Many trends reflect tides of change in underlying forces that influence the economy. However, projections cannot be simply an extension of trends. Judgments concerning the future and possible technological developments often provide a basis for modification of past trends. Many empirical measurements and statistical analyses were used in this investigation, with varying degrees of success. For the next two to three decades the long-run stability of growth rates and the general inertia of behavior patterns of individuals over time must provide much of the foundation for a framework of projections. No influence can be considered entirely exogenous to the whole system of cause and effect. Growth of population, the size of the labor force, government policy, and foreign demand are all influenced to some extent by underlying trends in economic, social, and political developments.

In appraising the prospects for agriculture, an equilibrium was assumed within agriculture and between agriculture and the rest of the economy. In general, the rate of growth in demand for agricultural products will marshal resources to provide the commodities desired, and the nature of the supply response will largely condition the cost price required to bring supply and demand into equilibrium. The agricultural and nonagricultural segments of the economy are closely interdependent from the standpoint of demand and resource use. And, in a long-run economy of growth, it is assumed that labor and capital will be reasonably mobile so that productivity and income of the commercial farm population relative to the rest of the economy will approach some sort of equilibrium, given time for adjustments to take place. The projected balance within agriculture is based largely on the feed-livestock balance and other complementary relationships with respect to both quantities and prices. Prices of products that compete for the same resources were related to each other and to past and expected future trends in these relationships. In effect, an effort was made to examine the competing and complementary relationships among commodity supplies and prices.

General methodology for the over-all projections for the economy involved the basic premise that potential output of the economy over several decades will depend primarily on the growth, employment, and quality of both labor and capital, and the desires of the people as reflected in the institutional, political, and social framework in which the economy grows. The latter group of factors are often important influences on the rate of innovation, shifts in resource use, incentives, and other forces which affect the economic progress of an economy.

C. MAJOR ASSUMPTIONS

No attempt is made to specify all assumptions explicitly. It is assumed that the economy will continue to grow during the next two to three decades much as it has in the last three or four decades. The projections do not assume wartime conditions or long periods of semimobilization of sufficient magnitude to result in continued inflationary pressure. Although the economy is likely to experience ups and downs, it is assumed that the government will be at least partly effective in its countercyclical measures to maintain full employment and prevent deflations of the magnitude of the depression of the 1930's.

Population and the labor force will continue to grow. Innovation, technological development, and capital accumulation will result in greater output per man-hour, and the length of the work week is expected to decline gradually as it has in the past.

Acreage of crops probably will expand very little and the acre-

136

age that will be released for food production by further declines in the numbers of horses and mules will be small. However, yields per crop acre and per animal unit will continue to rise as a result of new varieties and breeds; new disease, insect, and weed controls; improved livestock nutrition; and use of fertilizer, better cultural practices, and more machinery and equipment. Agricultural policy will affect agricultural growth. But as policy is not planned in advance over long periods, it will be influenced by underlying economic conditions that affect agriculture as well as by the possibility of a politically weaker agriculture.

D. THE PROJECTED ECONOMY

Projections of the population, labor force, capital inputs, and output per man and per man-hour for the United States economy are described at length in this volume. As many of the techniques and considerations used in this study are similar, we report only the projected framework in which agriculture was appraised.

Population projections are somewhat lower than those most recently prepared by the Bureau of the Census. The labor force estimates reflect trends in labor force participation by age and sex groups. Legislation affecting employment and trends in employment by occupation was also considered, as it influences participation of the labor force by age and sex groups. Output per man-hour for the entire economy, approximated on the basis of past growth, was projected at an annual rate of around 2.4 percent per man-hour. This growth assumes, among other things, continued innovation and growth in capital per man, a continuation of inter-industry shifts in employment of resources, a continuation of trends in demand influencing the composition of the gross national product, a shift toward more services and other activities formerly performed in the home, and a continued trend toward a shorter work week. Given the population, labor force, employment, hours worked, and trends in output per man-hour, we can readily compute total output of the economy.

1. The price level

If we are to specify a level of prices for agriculture and for individual commodities, it will be necessary to begin with a projection of the general level of prices. The association of a "price level" or some measure of final-product prices[5] with projected employment and output is a difficult problem, both theoretically and empirically. Some of the factors that affect the level of prices, such as war, private and public controls, administrative determinations, and the influence of political pressure groups, cannot be measured. However, an attempt was made to appraise the past and likely future trends of some of the underlying factors that influence the price level, to indicate a level of prices that might be expected to prevail in the projected framework for 1970. The hazards of such projections are realized and the supporting arguments can be only briefly summarized in this paper.

The general framework of the traditional quantity-of-money theory of the price level is probably about as reasonable a basis as is available for appraising long-run movements in the price level. The quantity theory, if anything, is essentially a tool for long-run appraisals. To begin with, values were assigned to the variables of the Cambridge cash-balance version of the equation of exchange, $M = KPQ$: M refers to the total of money outside banks, demand deposits, government deposits, and time deposits; PQ represents the value of all goods and services produced by the economy—gross national product—where P is the implicit GNP deflator index and Q measures total output; and K is simply the ratio of the means of payment to total expenditures, M/PQ, representing the average turnover period or its reciprocal, the number of times per year that money filters through the economic system.

Each variable depends upon a multitude of factors, many of which cannot be measured, and the subtle system of cause and effect probably changes constantly. The rather persistent long-run growth in the supply of money M suggests that it may have a sort of impetus of its own. It seems logical to expect that the means of payment expands in response to demand for money to service a larger output, changes in cash balances, and those movements in the level of prices which are largely independent of economic and monetary considerations. Thus, although the price level will depend on monetary influences, monetary practices and policies will depend upon a complex of politico-economic forces

---

[5] No attempt is made to define the "price level" concept. In this connection see O. V. Wells, "Significance of the General Price Level and Related Influences to American Agriculture," *Journal of Farm Economics*, Vol. xxxi, No. 4, Part 2, November 1949.

such that the means of payment becomes more a result than an independent cause of change in the price level.[6] A rough approximation of long-run growth indicates that the money supply has tended to expand at a rate almost double that of the growth in output of goods and services.

Individuals and business apparently tend to hold larger cash balances relative to total expenditures, thus contributing to a gradual uptrend in K. This tendency has been observed by several writers.[7] But the reasons advanced for it are not conclusive. Probably there has been a trend toward less barter trading and toward relatively more money going through the market place for such commodities and services as gasoline, transportation, and services of various types formerly carried out in the home. The daily and the weekly payday are probably less common than formerly, and a trend toward a longer pay period would require larger cash balances. The general uptrend in prices and a decline in interest rates also may have encouraged relatively larger cash holdings. A gradual uptrend in K seems plausible if we assume a continuation of past trends in the economic, psychological, and institutional forces that influence the amount of money held relative to total expenditures.

One appraisal for the future assumes a continuation of past trends about as illustrated in Chart 1. Any of a number of different trends might be justified, especially for the price level. Those shown indicate a level for 1970 somewhat below current high levels. The general level of prices may tend upward also if the rise in wage rates during the next two decades is assumed to equal or exceed somewhat the gain in output per man-hour.

As indicated above, prices and costs of many important groups of commodities and services are independent of economic and monetary forces. For example, we have "fair trade" legislation, informal agreements, customary margins and markups, controlled utility rates, milk orders, price supports, minimum wages, and many other arrangements throughout the economy to regulate

[6] E. J. Working, "Internal Stresses as Causes of Price Level Change," chapter in *Explorations in Economics*, notes and essays contributed in honor of F. W. Taussig (McGraw-Hill, 1937), p. 275.

[7] J. M. Keynes, *The General Theory* (Harcourt, Brace, 1935), p. 306; A. H. Hansen, *Monetary Theory and Fiscal Policy* (McGraw-Hill, 1949), pp. 3ff.; E. E. Hagen, *Additional Chapters on the Theory of Price Level and Employment* (unpublished MS, 1949), p. VI-6; and Clark Warburton, "The Secular Trend in Monetary Velocity," *Quarterly Journal of Economics*, Vol. LXIII, No. 1, February 1949, p. 81.

CHART 1

Output, Means of Payment, Relative Cash Balances,
and Price Level, Overlapping Decade Averages,
1869-78 to 1939-48; Projected to 1970

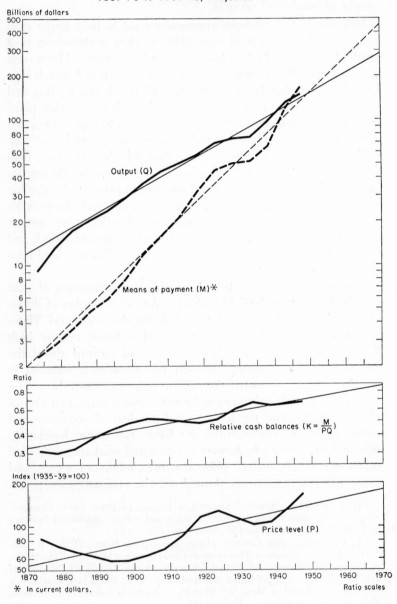

Billions of dollars

Output (Q)

Means of payment (M) ✱

Ratio

Relative cash balances (K = $\frac{M}{PQ}$)

Index (1935-39=100)

Price level (P)

✱ In current dollars.

Ratio scales

140

prices. Strong primary producer groups strive to maintain or to improve their share of total income and, more often than not, political expediency in settling disputes between large producer groups results in higher prices. In the last two decades, labor unions have become strong, well informed, and effective in their bargaining with business.

The debt structure rises in periods of high prices and becomes rather inflexible to downward adjustment. The federal debt is now deeply ingrained in our monetary system and it probably will lend greater stability to the credit base than was the case when credit expansion was based largely on private loans and securities. In addition to these considerations, many governments are more or less committed to a policy of full employment, which may prevent substantial deflations, such as took place in the 1930's. If effective, this policy may contribute to a gradual uptrend in the level of prices. Most of the arguments advanced in support of rather moderate deflations and prospects for a continued gradual rise in the United States price level are probably as applicable to foreign countries and world prices as to the United States.[8]

The projected level for 1970 approximates that of 1949, but it is below current levels. The Korean conflict and defense mobilization may postpone for years any downward adjustment in prices. Because of the upward shift of the entire debt-cost-price structure, the postadjustment level probably will be higher than it would have been.

2. Projected framework for 1970

Projected real output and the price level assumption provide a basis for assigning value to the gross national product. The components of the national product were approximated largely on the basis of historical relationships. No attempt is made to explain in this treatment the specific assumptions regarding tax rates, corporate profits, government revenue and expenditures, consumption, saving, and investment.

The high-employment model assumes about 5 million unemployed with a labor force of around 78 million. Employment, output per man-hour, a reduced workweek, and the projected

[8] In this connection, see *Measures for International Economic Stability* (United Nations Publications, Sales No. 1951, II. A. 2, November 1951), chap. I.

price level for 1970 resulted in a gross national product of around $510 billion, with personal disposable income at approximately $375 billion (Table 1).

TABLE 1

GROSS INCOME, PRICE LEVEL, POPULATION AND EMPLOYMENT,
1935-39 AVERAGE, 1949, AND PROJECTIONS FOR 1970

				1970	
Item	Unit or Base	1935-39 Average	1949	High Employ- ment	Unem- ployment Assumptio
Gross national product	$ billion	84.2	257	510	375
Consumption expenditures	do.	63.6	180	347	290
Personal disposable income	do.	66.2	186	375	310
Consumers' price index	1935-39	100	170	170	145
Wholesale prices of all commodities, index	1926	81	155	160	120
Population[a]	Million	129	150	181	181
Labor force	do.	54.4	63.6	78	77
Employment[b]	do.	45.0	60.2	73	65
Unemployment	do.	9.4	3.4	5	12

[a] Estimated as of July 1.
[b] Including armed forces.
Source: Background data from the *Survey of Current Business* (Department of Commerce)

The unemployment assumptions are not as severe as the depression of the 1930's, when nearly a fourth of the labor force was unemployed. The period of decline was assumed to be about two or three years. Associated with the lower level of employment, a reduction is assumed for money wage rates and the money supply, while the demand for cash reserves is assumed to rise as prices and incomes decline. A considerable reduction in the price level accompanies the rather severe drop in economic activity for the unemployment assumption.

E. LONG-RUN PROSPECTS FOR AGRICULTURE

The general framework within which the prospects for agriculture are appraised was projected in preceding sections of this report. Thus, many of the major factors that affect agriculture are now "given." These include population growth, the labor force, employment, income, the general price level, and an economic system and government organization in which the pricing mechanism is the primary regulator of rates of production and utilization of individual commodities and services.

1. The demand for farm products

Agricultural production consists primarily of food and fibers —two major necessities of life—the total demand for which is rather inelastic with respect to both price and income. As we are primarily interested in an aggregate demand function for agricultural products, changes in taste and consumption habits for individual commodities will be to some extent offsetting and will affect very little the total per capita demand for agricultural products. It is recognized, however, that innovations may expand or reduce the total per capita use of farm products.

Total demand for agricultural products over time can be thought of as a relatively inelastic relationship between consumption and price which shifts rather continuously in response to population growth. Per capita use will depend upon: the effect of growth in per capita real income on the pattern of consumption, as indicated by the varying income elasticities of consumption; price changes and the price elasticity of demand; changes in taste or innovations which influence per capita use independent of the price and income effect; and the supply response which equilibrates price, demand, and supply. Foreign demand probably will continue to depend primarily upon government policy. Long-run changes in underlying economic conditions of different countries—industrial development, new resource development, depletion of resources, and innovations—will cause shifts in the comparative advantage of producing particular commodities and thus, over long periods, will influence the foreign trade policy of the government.

a. SOME CONCEPTS AND EMPIRICAL APPROXIMATIONS

It immediately becomes apparent that for the long-run period we will be concerned with the very forces and structural shifts which are usually impounded in such assumptions as "other things being equal" or "a given state of the arts." In order to specify and discuss some of the problems encountered, suppose per capita consumption to be as expressed in the following equation form:

$$q = k\, p^a\, o^b\, y^c\, t^d \qquad (1)$$

where q refers to quantity utilized per person, p to the price per unit, o to prices of nonagricultural products, y to per capita real income, and t to time or trend influences. Our concern is not only with trends and the relationships among variables as indicated for a given period, but also with the possibility and the probable nature of shifts in these relationships over time, i.e., changes in the coefficients a, b, and c.

Price elasticity of demand is usually represented as the relationship between quantity and price at given levels of the other variables. In the framework of equation 1, it would be represented by a, the partial elasticity, which logically should be negative.

$$E_p = \frac{\partial \log q}{\partial \log p} = a = \frac{\partial q}{\partial p} \cdot \frac{p}{q} \qquad (2)$$

Although price elasticity of demand for farm products in the aggregate is small, demand elasticities for individual agricultural products may vary from virtually zero to unity or higher.[9] Analyses of food consumption per capita relative to retail food prices and per capita income suggest a price elasticity of demand of around –0.25. Although the empirical elasticities varied, all showed per capita use of farm products to be relatively inflexible in response to price changes.[10]

The comprehensive work of Henry Schultz on demand analyses for farm products in different periods of time indicated that price elasticity of demand may decline as real incomes rise over time.[11] For some products this tendency may be a reflection of the effect of trend factors other than price or income. The indi-

---

[9] Karl A. Fox, "Factors Affecting Farm Income, Farm Prices, and Food Consumption," *Agricultural Economics Research*, Vol. III, No. 3, July 1951.

[10] See, for example, M. A. Girshick and T. Haavelmo, *Statistical Analysis of the Demand for Food*, Cowles Commission Papers, New Series, No. 24, 1947, p. 109; G. Tintner, "Multiple Regression for Systems of Equations," *Econometrica*, Vol. 14, No. 1, January 1946, pp. 34-36; *Consumption of Food in the United States, 1909-1948* (Department of Agriculture, Misc. Pub. 691), p. 140; and Marguerite C. Burk, "Changes in the Demand for Food from 1941 to 1950," *Journal of Farm Economics*, Vol. XXXIII, No. 3, August 1951, pp. 281-98. Some unpublished analyses prepared in the Division of Statistical and Historical Research also indicate a retail price elasticity of demand around −0.25. See also J. Tobin, "A Statistical Demand Function for Food in the U.S.A.," *Journal of the Royal Statistical Society*, Vol. CXIII, Part II, 1950, pp. 132, 133, 142; and W. W. Cochrane, "Farm Price Gyrations—An Aggregative Hypothesis," *Journal of Farm Economics*, Vol. XXIX, No. 2, May 1947.

[11] *The Theory and Measurement of Demand* (University of Chicago Press, 1938), pp. 548-49.

cated decline in the price elasticity of demand for farm products, foods in particular, may result because purchases of food represent a declining portion of total expenditures as real incomes rise over time so that price changes tend to become less important. Also, there may be some inertia in the pattern of consumption.

Price elasticity of demand for agricultural products as a whole is very low (inelastic) and it may become somewhat less responsive to changes in price as the economy grows. In a long-run appraisal of the demand for agricultural products, the low price response suggests that growth of population and effects of income on per capita use will be the major factors influencing total utilization of agricultural products.

Income elasticity of consumption refers to the response of per capita use of farm products to changes in per capita income. In terms of equation 1, this elasticity is represented by c when prices are held constant.

$$E_y = \frac{\partial \log q}{\partial \log y} = c = \frac{\partial q}{\partial y} \cdot \frac{y}{q} \qquad (3)$$

For virtually all farm products, this relationship should be positive—consumption increases as real incomes rise. However, for some commodities—the so-called inferior goods—income elasticity is negative. Over time, the influence of income on per capita use is probably inextricably bound up with changes in "taste," which are independent of income. However, the effects on consumption of year-to-year changes in income can be measured much more accurately.

As foods generally represent 80 percent or more of the total utilization of farm products, substantial increases or decreases in the physical volume of per capita use should not be expected, even though prices and incomes vary widely. About 175 years ago (1776), Adam Smith made the frequently quoted observation that ". . . the desire for food is limited in every man by the narrow capacity of the human stomach." He might have enlarged on this statement by observing also that waste may represent a substantial disappearance of food and clothing and, possibly even more important, that the resources required to keep the human stomach full of the commodities desired may vary widely with the pattern of consumption and with techniques of production.

145

A brief review of statistical analyses that attempt empirical measurements of income elasticity makes one hesitant to generalize a coefficient for farm products. Most studies have dealt with foods at the retail or approximately retail level. The list of studies referred to in footnote 10 shows income elasticities varying from approximately 0.2 to around 0.9. They also demonstrate how elasticity may vary depending upon the types of data used. An income elasticity around 0.25 appears reasonable on the basis of the Bureau of Agricultural Economics index of per capita food consumption.[12] Analyses using deflated retail expenditures for food as a measure of consumption are inadequate for the present purpose. Such measures, indicating elasticities from 0.5 to 0.9, reflect marketing and processing services and, possibly, some influence of price.

Budget studies based on a cross section of incomes and expenditures at a given time show the nature and extent of differences in the consumption pattern at different income levels. An examination of 1947 data[13] for various commodities indicates that unit prices rise with income for some commodities, especially for such foods as meats, vegetables, and the highly processed grains, fats and oils, and sugar products. The quantity of livestock products, fruits, and vegetables also increased with income, but consumption of such foods as grains, fats and oils, sugar, dry beans, and potatoes declined as incomes rose. The indicated shifts in the pattern of consumption appear reasonable.

One appraisal of these data indicated an income elasticity for food consumed (quantity) of only 0.14.[14] Elasticities of expenditures for food relative to income for recent years appear to be around 0.3.[15] Although budget and time series data are conceptually different, elasticities based on budget data effectively illustrate that the income elasticity of demand for food tends to

[12] This is an index of per capita disappearance of major foods on an approximate retail weight basis which was weighted by unit retail prices as of 1935-39 and expressed on that base as 100. The index does not reflect variations in the services rendered by restaurants and retailers and, in some instances, it does not reflect processing costs. See *Consumption of Food in the United States*, as cited above.

[13] *Food Consumption of Urban Families in the U.S., Spring 1948* (Bureau of Human Nutrition and Home Economics, Department of Agriculture, Prel. Report No. 5, 1949).

[14] Fox, *op.cit.*, p. 81.

[15] See Marguerite C. Burk, "A Study of Recent Relationships between Income and Food Expenditures," *Agricultural Economics Research*, Vol. III, No. 3, July 1951, p. 89.

decline as real incomes rise. An index of per capita food consumption (BAE) computed on the basis of estimated food use per person by income level suggests larger income elasticities at low than at higher income levels.[16] An elasticity of about 0.25 was computed for the range of incomes from $750 to $4,000. But for average incomes from $750 to $1,250, the income elasticity of consumption was around 0.3; from $1,250 to $1,750, around 0.23; from $1,750 to $2,500, around 0.22; and from $2,500 to $4,000, the elasticity was approximately 0.15.

Available information from time series and budget data, as well as reason, suggests that the income elasticity of consumption (physical volume) of farm products would tend to decline as real incomes rise over time. A very low income elasticity of consumption is implied for the long run on the basis of historical data for the last seven or eight decades. Rough measures of per capita use of agricultural products indicate that, during the 40-year period before 1900, average use of agricultural products per person based on overlapping decade averages ranged between 90 and 100 percent of 1935-39, in 1925-29 just over 100 percent, and during 1940-45, 115 percent. In comparison, per capita real incomes during the last seven decades have increased nearly five times above the average for 1869-78. Prices received for farm products have varied widely during the period, but the trend has been upward.

Several different equation forms were tried to approximate empirically the influence of gradually rising real income on changes in the income elasticity of per capita use of farm products over time. Fairly reasonable results were obtained from a logarithmic relationship between per capita use of farm products and income where it was assumed that the income coefficient, and thus income elasticity, declines gradually as real incomes rise over time. This form was

$$\log q = a + (c - dt) \log y + \cdots \qquad (4)$$

where income elasticity of per capita use is represented by the partial elasticity $(c - dt)$. This form of equation assumes that, as real incomes rise over time, the slope of the relationship between consumption and income becomes flatter—consumption becomes less responsive to changes in income. The analysis was based on some rough approximations of per capita use and total real in-

[16] *Consumption of Food in the United States*, as cited, p. 142.

come per person, using multiple correlation techniques. The results, by no means conclusive, are not unreasonable compared with some other techniques of analysis. Trend factors are, of course, very important. Empirical approximations based on the period 1919 to 1949 are shown in equation 5:

$$\log q = 0.605 + (0.486 - 0.00575t) \log y - 0.000693p + 0.016t \quad (5)$$

where q represents per capita use, y represents per capita real income, p represents the ratio of farm prices to the general price level, and t represents time $(1, 2, \ldots n)$. For period 1 in this equation, income elasticity was 0.48 and declined to around 0.18 for the 1970 projection. Similar results were obtained in several analyses using slightly different variables. In the long-run analysis employed above, price and income coefficients were "statistically significant" by the usual measures.

To digress for a moment: An examination of the *income elasticity of expenditures* for food will give more insight into relationships of elasticities to each other and, in addition, provide information that can be used as a further check on the projected framework. Price variations, as might be expected, are highly correlated with changes in expenditure and income. Variations in quantity contribute relatively less to changes in expenditure for food. Income elasticity of expenditures logically should range somewhere between the coefficient of price flexibility relative to income and the elasticity of quantity with respect to income. In this connection, a study referred to earlier shows an income elasticity of expenditures for food of about 0.8 compared with price flexibility relative to income of 1.0 and income elasticity of demand around 0.24.[17] Variations in expenditure because of price would be expected to approximate the higher elasticity and those because of quantity, the lower elasticity.

The persistent long-run downtrend in the ratio of total expenditures for farm products to gross national income indicates an income elasticity of expenditures of less than unity, though it may be rising gradually over time. Extending the long-run decline observed in the above ratio on the basis of the projected increase in income and the income elasticity of expenditures indicated for recent years provides another basis for appraising total expenditures for farm products in the projected framework. These computations are discussed later in the report.

[17] Burk, "Changes in the Demand for Food from 1941 to 1950," as cited above, p. 297.

b. CONSUMPTION OF FARM PRODUCTS

The major relationships among the variables consumption, income, and price, discussed above, may be illustrated approximately as shown in Chart 2. Changes in per capita use of agri-

CHART 2

Hypothetical Illustration of Relationship of Income, Price, and Consumption of Agricultural Products

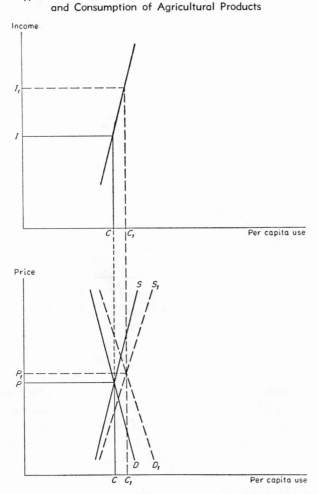

cultural products are very small in relation to changes in income. Likewise, consumption is rather inflexible in relation to price changes. The illustration indicates an increase in per capita real

149

income of approximately 50 percent, which results in a rise in per capita demand of nearly 10 percent at the same relative price for agricultural products. The increase is indicated by the shift in the demand curve from D to D_1. Price, in this context, depends primarily upon the growth in output of agricultural products per person in response to the shifts in per capita demand. The illustration shows a slight increase in relative prices for farm products. The shift in supply response depends primarily upon innovations, with resulting greater output per unit of resources used, and upon the possible diversion of resources away from or to agricultural production.

In the framework of empirical measurements discussed in the preceding section, per capita demand for farm products may be approximated from projected income, a price assumption, and the price and income elasticities approximated from analyses of historical data or from such analyses supplemented by judgment. This relationship is of the general form

$$q = k\, p^a\, y^c \qquad (6)$$

in which a and c are approximations of the price and income elasticities of consumption, respectively. In this case, the per capita income y is given. As a first approximation of per capita consumption, prices for farm products were assumed which appeared reasonably consistent with the general price level assumption. These computations are not shown. They were first approximations until an appraisal of the supply of farm products, exports, and imports determined the per capita domestic supply in this general framework. The final approximations show a slightly higher price for farm products and a little lower per capita consumption than were used in the first approximation. Per capita demand for all farm products under the high-employment assumption, at 115 percent of 1935-39, turned out to be about equal to per capita supply for domestic consumption at an index of prices received by farmers of around 260-265 (1910-14 = 100) and a general price level about 180 percent of 1935-39 (consumers' price index around 170 percent of 1935-39). Per capita use under the unemployment assumption was estimated at 110 percent of 1935-39.

The results of empirical analyses were far from conclusive. Probably there will never be any very conclusive bases for projecting the structural changes that are important in long-run appraisals. Consequently, it was considered desirable, as a basis for projecting consumption, to consider in some detail the trends taking place in the pattern of consumption and to enlist the cooperation of commodity specialists in order to get informed appraisals by persons intimately familiar with each commodity. Commodity specialists were given the broad framework of assumptions for income, growth of population, employment and unemployment, and the general price level. They were requested to estimate, in this framework, the per capita use of their commodity. These estimates were examined for over-all consistency, converted into an index of per capita food consumption (BAE), and combined with projected use of nonfoods to arrive at an estimate of total per capita use of agricultural products.

Per capita consumption of food, projected to 117 percent of 1935-39, in general reflects increased use of meats and livestock products and increased consumption of fresh vegetables and citrus fruits. Lower per capita consumption was projected for potatoes, cereal crops, butter, and sugar. These projections generally reflect trends. But they are not inconsistent with most empirical measurements of income elasticities, which indicate positive coefficients for fresh citrus fruits, other fresh fruits, beef and veal, and livestock products in general. Negative income elasticities were indicated for potatoes and grains, for example (Table 2).

During the last seven to eight decades, per capita consumption of food in total apparently has not fluctuated widely from year to year. But averages for selected five-year periods indicate a gradual uptrend. The shifts mentioned above from low-unit-cost to high-unit-cost foods would cause a price-weighted index to rise without any necessary increase in physical volume of consumption or in calories. However, the price-weighted index is probably a better measure of demands on resources. Use of nonfood agricultural products was projected to around 107 percent of the 1935-39 average, which is about the same as in 1949. Projected higher per capita use of tobacco approximately offsets assumed declines in per capita use of cotton. Competition of synthetic fibers is expected to be important in the demand for cotton. Technological developments in synthetic detergents used for soaps, in synthetic resins, and in chemical developments in the paint industry may moderate trends in per capita demand for industrial fats and oils. As is to be expected, use of nonfood

151

TABLE 2

PER CAPITA USE OF FOOD AND NONFOOD AGRICULTURAL PRODUCTS,
1935-39 AVERAGE, 1949, AND PROJECTIONS FOR 1970

				1970	
				High	
		1935-39		Employ-	Une.
Item	Unit	Average	1949	ment	ploym
Per capita food consumption	Index	100	111	117	11
Meats (carcass weight)a	Pounds	126.2	143.9	156.5	15
Beef	do.	55.2	63.5	67.0	6
Pork, excluding lard	do.	56.1	67.6	75.0	7
Poultry					
Chickens and turkeys	do.	20.5	29.7	34.0	3
Eggs	Number	298	381	375	37
Dairy products (fat-solid basis)	Pounds	801	761	780	77
Fluid milk and cream					
(milk equivalent)	do.	340	384	410	40
Butter (actual weight)	do.	16.7	10.5	9.0	
Fats and oils, including butter					
(fat-content basis)	do.	44.7	42.3	44.2	4
Fruits, fresh and processed on					
fresh-equivalent basis	do.	218	234	273	25
Vegetables					
Fresh	do.	235	249	275	26
Processed (processed weight)	do.	30.6	44.5	53	5
Potatoes, white and sweet	do.	152.4	122.3	99	10
Dry edible beans and peas	do.	9.4	7.4	8.8	
Sugar (refined)	do.	97.0	94.9	93.0	9
Grains					
Wheat	do.	226	193	185	18
Other	do.	68.6	66.4	66.4	6
Nonfood commodities					
Cotton	do.	25.3	25.6	21.0	2
Wool, apparel	do.	2.2	2.3	2.7	
Tobacco	do.	7.1	9.4	11.5	1

a Includes veal, lamb, and mutton.
Sources: Background data from *Consumption of Food in the United States, 1909-1948* partment of Agriculture, Misc. Pub. 691); *The National Food Situation* (Bureau of Agricul Economics); commodity situation reports of the BAE; and estimations by the author.

products fluctuates much more than the food consumption index and thus causes slightly more variation in the indicator of per capita use of all agricultural products.

With a relatively short period of falling employment assumed for the lower projection, farm output probably would be maintained at a high level. Slightly reduced output with substantially lower prices would tend to result in a per capita use of farm products only moderately below the projection for high employment. Exports probably would decline and some net accumulation of stocks would be expected with the reduction in employment and income.

C. EXPORTS AND IMPORTS

Exports and imports of supplementary agricultural products (the similar competing products) were first assumed approximately equal with a relatively high level of trading. Later estimates of imports and exports by commodity and group of commodities were prepared in connection with detailed projections. The projected volume of agricultural exports under the high-employment assumption is nearly 80 percent (1924-29 = 100), compared with 108 for 1949 and 60 in 1935-39 (Table 3). Although reductions from the high levels for 1949 are projected for wheat, flour, and other grains, exports of food grains are expected to be relatively large. Value of exports in this framework is estimated at $2.5 to $3.0 billion under the high- and about $2 billion under the low-employment assumptions. Agricultural exports were valued at $3.6 billion in 1949.

Imports of supplementary agricultural products, projected in some detail by commodity, are 122 percent (1924-29 = 100)

LE 3

XES OF VOLUME OF AGRICULTURAL EXPORTS AND IMPORTS,
CTED PERIODS AND PROJECTIONS FOR 1970
EXES, 1924-29 = 100)

| | | | | | 1970 | |
Item	1925-29 Average	1935-39 Average	1940-42 Average	1949	High Employment	Unemployment
cultural exports	98	60	43	108	79	66
imports	104	101	103	100	137	122
mplementary[a]	105	108	97	110	148	134
pplementary[b]	102	92	110	87	122	106

Complementary agricultural imports include those not considered as supplementary—about ercent of which consist of rubber, coffee, raw silk, cocoa beans, carpet wool, bananas, tea, spices.
upplementary agricultural imports consist of all imports similar to agricultural commodities uced commercially in the United States, together with all other agricultural imports intergeable to any significant extent with domestic production.
urce: Background data from *Foreign Agricultural Trade* (Office of Foreign Agricultural tions, Department of Agriculture).

153

for high employment. This compares with 87 in 1949 and 110 for the 1940-42 average. Complementary imports, representing primarily rubber, coffee, bananas, carpet wool, cocoa beans, tea, and spices, are projected to 148 for high employment compared with 110 in 1949. Total agricultural imports are projected to 137 percent of 1924-29 compared with 100 in 1949. The values of supplementary and complementary imports of agricultural products are each estimated at around $2 billion under the high-employment assumption and $1.4 billion for the unemployment assumption. The projected high-employment value of $4 billion compares with about $2.9 billion for 1949.

d. TOTAL UTILIZATION

The product of projected per capita use of agricultural products and population should approximate total domestic use of farm products. This computation, on the basis of index numbers, is shown in Table 4. Detailed projections indicated that exports above competing supplementary imports may average 1 to 2 percent of total output. Data presented for the 1970 projections represent final approximations after all the pieces of the picture were fitted together—after exports, imports, and output, as well as consumption and prices, were fitted into what appeared to be a reasonably consistent picture for agriculture in the framework of assumptions for the entire economy.

The absolute difference between the estimated index of total utilization and the index of agricultural production for sale and home consumption was expressed as a percentage of total farm output. This difference represents primarily net exports of agricultural products and net stock changes. Since the approximation of total consumption is rather rough, the difference probably is subject to some error. As a basis of comparison, net value of agricultural exports above the competing supplementary imports was expressed as a percentage of "value of farm sales plus farm home consumption." The comparison indicated that, in most periods, the difference between domestic utilization and total production was accounted for by net exports of agricultural products. With a projected increase in imports and some decline in agricultural exports from recent high levels, projected net exports are small. The relatively large residual for the unemployment assumption represents mostly assumed net stock accumulation.

154

.E 4

˧APITA USE OF AGRICULTURAL PRODUCTS, POPULATION, TOTAL CONSUMPTION, AND TOTAL
ᴘUT, SELECTED PERIODS AND PROJECTIONS FOR 1970

						1970	
Item	1915-19 Average	1925-29 Average	1930-34 Average	1940-44 Average	1945-49 Average	High Em- ployment	Unem- ployment
	Indexes, 1935-39 = 100						
consumption							
ː capita[a]	92.6	101.2	99.2	109.0	114.0	117	113
ɔod use							
· capita[b]	113.6	102.0	85.4	134.3	124.9	107	98
utilization							
· capita[b]	100.0	101.4	96.5	113.6	116.0	115	110
ᴧation	80.0	92.2	96.7	104.6	111.6	141	141
utilization[c]	80.0	93.5	93.4	118.8	129.5	162	155
ᴧction for sale and							
ᴨe consumption[d]	87.2	99.2	97.0	122.6	137.0	165	163
	Percent						
ᴋence as a							
ᴦcentage of total							
ɔduction[e]	8.5	5.7	3.7	3.1	5.5	2.0	5.0
℮ of net exports							
a percentage of							
m income[f]	11.0	7.0	4.9	2.5	6.5	1.3	1.0

ᴣonsumption of Food in the United States, 1909-1948 (Department of Agriculture, Misc.
691); and National Food Situation (Bureau of Agricultural Economics).
ᴣomputed for this purpose by the author.
˥otal utilization is a product of population and per capita use.
˥rom 1950 Yearbook of Agricultural Statistics and Farm Income Situation (BAE).
ᴇrcentage points difference between total utilization and total production expressed as a
ᴨtage of total production index.
˥alue of agricultural exports above imports of supplementary agricultural products from
ᴤgn Agricultural Trade (Office of Foreign Agricultural Relations, Department of Agricul-
ᴥ expressed as a percentage of value of farm sales plus home consumption from the Farm
ᴨe Situation (BAE).

2. Supply of agricultural products

The data presented in Table 4 put us ahead of our story, as output is yet to be considered in our framework of assumptions
and in relation to projected demand and relative prices for farm
products. Having considered major demand factors for agricultural products and attempted some empirical generalizations
for the long run, let us examine supply prospects in the light of
projected demand, agricultural productive facilities, possible innovations, and the level of prices received for farm products.
Successive approximations among demand, supply, and price

155

projections for agricultural products were used as a basis for projecting relative prices considered reasonable in relation to demand and supply considerations in the projected framework.

a. GENERAL NATURE OF THE SUPPLY RESPONSE

For several reasons, the long-run supply response for agriculture is difficult to appraise. The inherently involved problems of supply probably account for so few attempts at statistical measurement of agricultural production functions.[18] And, even with approximate empirical measurements, innovations may result, in the long run, in substantial shifts in the use and contribution of each agent. Thus, they may constantly modify the production function. The problem is to appraise probable use of resources in agriculture and possible innovations that affect the output per unit of input. Simply stated, the output of agricultural products depends upon resources used—land, labor, and capital—the quality of these resources, and innovations.

In some respects, the competitive long-run theory of the firm is unrealistic for agriculture, because of the relative immobility of labor and capital within agriculture and, particularly, between agriculture and the rest of the economy. Yet, during long-run periods, resources do move into and out of agriculture. Employment in agriculture has declined moderately during the last four decades. Indexes of volume of farm power, machinery, and equipment indicate that this type of capital has more than doubled since 1890, both in total and per worker, and these indexes probably do not reflect improved quality of capital.[19] Inputs of fertilizer and materials for control of diseases and insects appear to be very responsive to prospective changes in agricultural prices and income. Cropland harvested has varied moderately in the past, primarily because of crop failure for one reason or another and because of variations in general economic conditions. Land in the fringe uses may become profitable under "high" prices, but in periods of low farm prices it will revert to a natural state (dry-farm grain land, for example), and the cropping of pasture land or more intensive types of rotation may

[18] See Cochrane, *op.cit.*, and D. G. Johnson, "The Supply Function for Agricultural Products," *American Economic Review*, Vol. XL, No. 4, September 1950, p. 559, n. 32.

[19] M. R. Cooper, G. T. Barton, and A. P. Brodell, *Progress of Farm Mechanization* (Department of Agriculture, Misc. Pub. 630, 1947), p. 7.

vary the acreage of cropland harvested, depending on economic conditions.

As a basis for long-run appraisals, it seems reasonable to assume that resources used in agriculture will vary in response to changes in both demand and innovations. Acreage of land may vary moderately, depending upon river valley developments, reclamation work, economic conditions, and possible withdrawals of cropland in the interest of conservation, reforestation, recreation, flood control, and urban development. In the long run, it is reasonable to assume some rough equality of returns to "commercial agriculture," compared with the rest of the economy, in order to induce or retard shifts in resource use. Admittedly many institutional and social factors will influence these shifts—government financing of farm capital, financing of education in rural areas, better communication, unemployment services, shifts in industry to rural areas, social prejudices, and many other factors. But continued availability of nonfarm jobs will be of major importance in the shift of labor out of agriculture. Use of capital per man and per acre probably will continue to increase as demand expands and workers continue to shift out of agriculture.

For short-period adjustments, it is reasonable to expect that the agricultural-supply function will be very inelastic to changes in price and especially to downward adjustments in prices. Most agricultural land has practically no alternative uses aside from agriculture, and farm capital equipment has few alternative uses. Mobility of labor is low, for both relatively declining and relatively rising prices of farm products. The bulk of farm labor is classed as "unpaid family labor," so that the supply of labor may actually rise during generally depressed economic conditions.

Over time, we may conceive of an inelastic short-run supply response of the type described above, which shifts as resources move into or out of agriculture and because of innovations. These shifts are usually made in response to a rather continuous growth in total demand for farm products. Under a given "state of the arts," the long-run supply response for agriculture may be expected to rise as more resources are bid away from alternative employment for use in agriculture. The long-run supply curve L is traced out by successive inelastic short-run responses S (Chart 3). Innovations result in similar shifts in the short-run supply curve, but they also tend to shift the entire long-run supply response downward as indicated by L_1 and L_2. Innovations reduce

157

resources required for a given output and thus lower the entire price-output relationship for the long run. Substantial innovations that cause a shift in the supply response, such as that indicated by L_2, may result in relative prices for farm products, at a given level of demand, so low that returns to productive agents will be reduced below what they could command in alternative employment. Under such circumstances, we might expect a withdrawal of resources—labor, capital, and possibly land—from use in agriculture. This would result in some backward shift in the supply response and higher relative prices for farm products.

CHART 3

Long-Run Supply Response of Agriculture
to Resource Shifts and Innovations

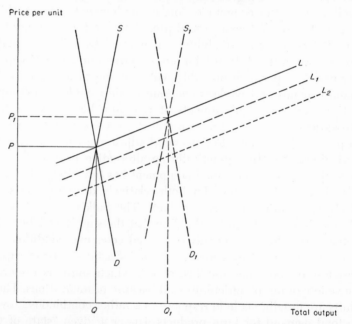

Innovations often result in greater total expenditure and greater output, as well as lower expenditures per unit. For example, fertilizers, weed control, insecticides, and better seed tend to increase total production expenditures. New processes, better transportation, and new machinery in production and marketing may actually reduce total costs by displacing other, less efficient resources. Innovations, also, may involve the introduction of new

158

goods and new methods of production and marketing. They may open new markets, provide new sources of raw material, and make new uses for old goods.

The rate of innovation in agriculture and its effect on output are not easy to anticipate. Increased output per man reflects increased capital used per man, which is not an innovation in itself. However, increased use of machinery frequently results indirectly from innovations. Increased output per man may also reflect shifts in employment from less to more productive lines of work, more land per unit of labor, better management, and many other factors, as well as innovations. Growth in output per man in agriculture has been very rapid, if measured from the middle 1930's. A more generalized trend for the last three to four decades would indicate a rate of growth approaching 1.5 percent per year. This has been accomplished with approximately the same crop acreage; a moderately increasing amount of farm power, machinery, and equipment per man (also, a change in the type and quality of this capital); a declining number of workers; higher expenditures for such variable capital inputs as fertilizer, seed, insect control, disease control, and weed eradication; and the many and varied innovations that have affected the growing, harvesting, and marketing of agricultural products during the last half century.[20]

b. AGRICULTURAL OUTPUT: TRENDS AND PROJECTIONS

Long-run growth in output of agricultural products is examined, first, as a basis for projection. Obviously, several different "answers" might be forthcoming from an examination of trends. Apparently a simple arithmetic trend line fits the long-run rise in farm output reasonably well, but runs above the output level of the 1930's and below that for 1943-49 (Chart 4). This trend, projected out to 1970, indicates an index of physical volume of production for sale and home consumption of around 155 percent (1935-39 = 100). The same slope projected from the 1943-49 level indicates an output of around 165 for 1970. A semilogarith-

[20] An indication of the nature and influence of these innovations is presented by S. E. Johnson, *Changes in American Farming* (Department of Agriculture, Misc. Pub. No. 707, 1949); *Technology on the Farm* (Department of Agriculture, August 1940). See also Dorothy C. Goodwin, "A Brief Chronology of American Agricultural History," *Farmers in a Changing World, Yearbook of Agriculture*, 1940, pp. 1184ff.

mic-growth line, approximating a rate of increase of about 1 percent per year, indicates a level of output around 170.

A generalization of the trend in output per crop acre over the last three decades approximates a growth rate of a little less than 1 percent per year. This trend reflects among other things, higher yields because of new and better seed; more fertilizer and lime;

CHART 4

Agricultural Production for Sale and Home Consumption, 1875-1951; Projected to 1970

Index (1935-39=100)

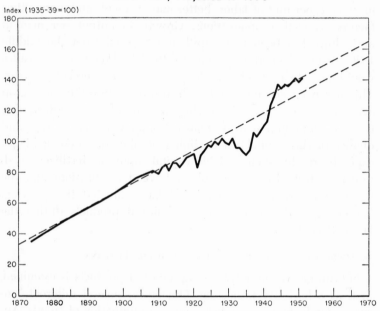

and better control of insects, diseases, and weeds. Per unit output of breeding animals also increased moderately but some of this growth may have been due to expanded feed output, so the two rates are not additive.

The long-run supply of agricultural products may also be considered in relation to past trends in some of the primary agents of production and trends in output per man as a basis for projecting future output. Total land available for crops, as indicated above, probably will not change greatly during the next two decades.[21] An important factor that has influenced land available

[21] See, for example, approximate land use conversions needed on privately owned land as reported in *Probable Impacts of Missouri Basin Pro-*

for production of food and fiber during the last three decades has been the decline in the numbers of horses and mules and the release of that acreage and production for other purposes. It is assumed that the numbers of horses and mules will continue to decline and this may release another 10 to 12 million acres of cropland for other purposes.[22]

Farm employment, as a percentage of the total labor force, declined rather steadily (both series vary little from year to year) until 1940, when the exodus of farm labor reduced the agricultural portion sharply. In view of past trends in employment, productivity, and use of capital, farm employment is projected to around 75 percent (1935-39 = 100) by 1970.

A trend line fitting the long sweep of years reasonably well suggests an increase in output per worker to around 220 to 225 percent (1935-39 = 100) by 1970. Such a projection implicitly assumes, among other things, continued expansion in farm power, machinery, and equipment per man; increased use of fertilizer, lime, and other variable inputs; and continued development of innovations in agriculture. Farm employment around 75 percent and output per man around 220 percent of 1935-39 appear reasonable in relation to past growth. These projections would result in farm output around 165 percent of prewar by 1970.

The long-run supply response for agriculture was also built up from detailed appraisals for each commodity or group of commodities. Each commodity was considered in relation to a first approximation of projected utilization for that commodity. Crop yields and acreage were projected in each case, livestock was related to feed supplies, acreage was considered in relation to all crops and to past performance, and many competitive and complementary relationships were considered both on the supply or resource side and on the demand side in working out the demand-supply-price balance for each commodity. In this connection, considerations for each commodity were discussed with commodity men familiar with each group of farm products. The detailed projections that allow for feed, seed, waste, industrial use, exports, stocks, and consumption came out very close to the 165 projected above.

gram on United States Agricultural Economy, a statement by O. V. Wells (Department of Agriculture, Release No. 1845-50, August 1-2, 1950).

[22] See Progress of Farm Mechanization (Department of Agriculture, Misc. Pub. 630), p. 76.

The livestock projections assume a cattle population of around 100 million head on a sustained basis, with virtually all of the gain in production of beef cattle. Hog slaughter was projected to around 100 million head, assuming a continued trend toward lighter, lean hogs. A sheep enterprise of about 40 million head of stock sheep and feeders was assumed. Some of the data on supply and disposition and on the livestock-feed concentrate balance built up from detailed appraisals are shown in the appendix tables.

Production of meat under the high projection is about 30 percent above 1949, and production of poultry is up 35 percent. Output of dairy products based on detailed demand and supply prospects is projected to about 15 to 20 percent above 1949, and eggs to about 15 percent above 1949. Utilization of grains (corn, oats, and barley) for feed was increased by nearly a fourth from the 1948-49 feeding year. The outputs of fruits and vegetables are projected for 1970 to about 45 and 35 percent, respectively, above 1949 outputs. Detailed projections of supply and demand prospects indicated smaller production for such crops as food grains, potatoes, dry beans and peas, and cotton.

3. Prices received for farm products

Prices and incomes still have considerable influence as regulators of rates of consumption and production. Agriculture will not continue indefinitely to produce and accumulate goods in excess of "effective demand," even though it may do so over a period of several years. Labor and capital can and do flow between agriculture and the nonagricultural segment of the economy. Over the long run, demand for agricultural products will influence the use of resources, the rate of adopting innovations, and probably the rate of innovation itself, and thus direct the use of resources to provide goods in demand. The relative ease or difficulty of meeting this demand—the supply response—will complete the pricing mechanism and determine long-run relative prices for agricultural products. Prices in the long run must cover the supply price of a given output, which represents a payment to all services used in production approximately equal to what they could command in alternative employment. Obviously, many largely noneconomic influences affect the relative prices for farm products. Many controls, by private groups and by the government, affect output and prices for many commodities, both farm and nonfarm. Yet, it is believed that these controls are responsive to changes in underlying economic forces.

The prices of agricultural products, both the absolute and the relative price, contain an element of the general level of all prices. However, prices of farm products may be relatively higher or lower depending upon long-run forces of demand (population growth, growth in real income, innovations that affect the demand for farm products, and exports) in relation to the long-run supply response for agricultural products. It is unlikely that prices for a substantial group of staples, such as food and fibers, will vary widely from past relationships to the general level of prices so long as projections assume a continuation of relative rates of innovation and approximately equal returns to services used in commercial agriculture and the rest of the economy. Assuming considerable mobility of resources, the supply response and relative prices for farm products will depend upon possible limiting resources, such as land and the rate of innovation. Another major factor that is likely to influence relative prices for farm products is the political strength and the price policy of the farm bloc.

a. TERMS OF TRADE: SOME EMPIRICAL APPROXIMATIONS

Suppose the farm output projection to 165 percent of the 1935-39 average is considered reasonable relative to past growth and in relation to projected demand, trends in consumption, and favorable general economic conditions. After accounting for imports and exports, that level of output and projected population provide a per capita supply of all farm products around 115 percent of 1935-39. This supply and projected demand, together with the empirical elasticities approximated from historical data, indicate a price for agricultural products of around 260-265 percent (1910-14 = 100) for the high-employment projection. An index of 190 is indicated under the unemployment framework, if it is assumed that per capita supply (not consumption) may be about the same as that for the high projection. Per capita income and the general level of prices would be lower under the unemployment assumption. As pointed out earlier, empirical approximations may yield a rather wide range of results, especially in a long-run appraisal of this type.[23] However, the level of farm

[23] As an illustration of the type of result we might get under these gen-

product prices indicated does not seem unreasonable in this general framework of assumptions for 1970.

The agricultural share. Over the last seven or eight decades, agricultural output apparently increased nearly 1 percent per year. Total output of the economy, except for depression periods, has tended to increase around 3.5 percent a year. These relative trends have meant that agricultural output necessarily has become a progressively smaller part of the total. It was observed, also, that the ratio of prices received for agricultural products to the general level of prices was inversely related to the ratio of farm output to total output of the economy. This relationship tended to shift to the left (downward) over time. That is, at a given time (or in this case, a given relative level of farm and nonfarm output) when agricultural output represented a relatively larger share of total output, agricultural prices were relatively low; and vice versa. In the depression years, even though farm prices were low, farm output was maintained and represented a relatively large share of total output. In this rather simple framework, the ratio X of prices of farm products to the general price level (GNP deflator index) was expressed as a function of two variables: the ratio P of farm output to total output, and the trend $(t = 1, 2, \ldots n)$, which reflected the tendency for the relationship to shift downward gradually as farm output became a smaller share of total output.

$$X = 2.27 - 8.566P - 0.0084t \qquad (7)$$

R, the multiple correlation coefficient, is 0.92.

If the relative growth in farm output, indicated by the trend line (Chart 5), continues to decline in the projected economy of growth to around 6 percent of the total by 1970, a prices-received index of 260 to 265 is indicated for the high-employment economy. For the unemployment framework in this approach, it may be assumed that farm output will recede little, if any,

---

eral assumptions, suppose prices are estimated on the basis of the following equation, which is sometimes used for shorter-period approximations:

Log (prices-received index) = 2.812 + 1.241 log (disposable income)
+ 0.142 log (value of agricultural exports)
− 1.658 log (volume of farm marketings index)

These relationships indicate an index of prices received under the high assumptions of around 415 percent of 1910-14. The equation was taken from *Some Statistical Relationships Used in Price Analysis and Outlook Work*, working data made available at the 1949 Department of Agriculture Outlook Conference.

from the figure for the high-employment assumption. But a substantially reduced gross national product would tend to increase
the ratio of farm to total output, possibly to around 6.5 percent.
Such a rise in farm output relative to the total and the lower
general price level for the unemployment assumption suggest a

CHART 5

Ratio of Farm Sales plus Farm Home Consumption to
Gross National Product (Both in 1935-39 Dollars),
Overlapping Decade Averages, 1869-78 to 1939-48;
Projected to 1970

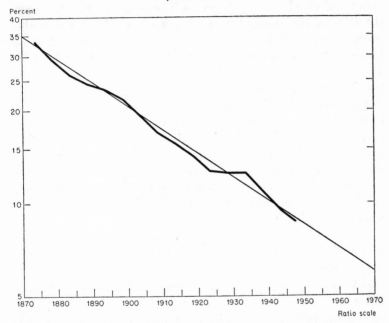

price for farm products of about 200 percent (1910-14 = 100).
The indicated value of farm sales plus home consumption is
around $40 billion for high employment and about $30 billion
under the unemployment assumption.[24] A long-run relationship,

[24] It may be of interest to compare this approach with results obtained
from a forecasting equation which has given reasonably good results for
year-to-year estimates of cash receipts from farm marketings.
Cash receipts = −1.05 + 0.113 (disposable personal income)
+ 1.722 (value of agricultural exports)
This equation, with projected disposable income and agricultural exports,
indicates cash receipts about $10 billion larger than equivalent cash receipts
estimated above. Cash receipts of $46 billion and volume of farm marketings

expressing the value of farm sales plus home consumption as a function of gross national income and time, indicates an elasticity of value of farm products with respect to national income of around 0.6 to 0.7 at the means. The estimated value of farm sales plus farm home consumption, based on projected gross national income and an elasticity of 0.6 to 0.7, comes very near the $40 billion estimated for the high-employment assumption.

A composite of commodity prices. Detailed price appraisals were also prepared for each commodity in an effort to project prices which seemed reasonably consistent with the projected demand and supply prospects for each commodity as well as consistent with the assumed general price level. Each commodity specialist was asked to estimate demand, supply, and prices for his commodity in the general framework of assumptions for 1970. These prices were compared to others through competitive relationships on the demand side and relationships among commodities competing for the same resources on the supply side. Estimates were appraised in relation to each other and to projections prepared independently by the author on the basis of statistical analyses, trends in price relationships, product-feed price ratios, and other techniques. Detailed price projections resulted in an index of prices received of 265 (1910-14 = 100) for the high-employment assumption and 190 under the unemployment assumption (Table 5).

b. THE PROJECTED PICTURE SUMMARIZED

Projections of per capita demand for agricultural products, population, exports, imports, total output, and an over-all price index for farm products are now available for the two employment assumptions. We also have estimates of the value of farm sales plus home consumption. These projections should be tied together. The total value of agricultural production should be approximately equal to the following:

$$R = \left[(qP) + e \right] p$$

where R is cash receipts including value of home consumption, q is per capita use, P is population, e is net exports and net stock

---

projected to around 178 (1935-39 = 100) indicate an index of prices received for farm products of around 340 percent of 1910-14. This compares with 415 percent, computed in the preceding footnote.

TABLE 5

INDEXES OF PRICES RECEIVED FOR FARM PRODUCTS,
SELECTED PERIODS, 1935-49, AND PROJECTIONS FOR 1970
(INDEXES, 1910-14 = 100)

| | | | | | 1970 | |
Item	1935-39 Average	1937-41 Average	1948	1949	High Employment	Unemployment
All farm products	107	107	285	249	265	190
Livestock and livestock products	115	117	314	272	300	218
Meat animals	117	121	361	311	345	252
Dairy products	119	123	300	251	286	207
Poultry products	107	105	235	219	222	159
Wool	134	153	263	273	245	190
All crops	99	96	252	223	224	159
Feed grains and hay	95	87	250	170	216	144
Food grains	94	90	250	219	207	144
Oil-bearing crops	113	112	351	242	309	207
Cotton	87	87	270	245	218	151
Tobacco	172	163	380	398	409	296
Fruit	95	92	174	199	200	144
Truck crops	95	106	214	201	210	173
Other vegetables	99	96	252	222	161	112

Sources: Background data from *Agricultural Prices* (Bureau of Agricultural Economics).

accumulation (may be negative), and p is prices received for farm products. This relationship assumes that net stock accumulation, net exports, and home consumption are valued at the average of prices received. For convenience, these variables were expressed in terms of index numbers. Measuring the change in the computed value of R from both 1949 and 1942 to 1970 and raising the dollar value of farm sales plus farm home consumption for 1949 and 1942 on the basis of the projected percentage change in R suggest a total of around $39 billion under the high projection. If the relative change in the computed value of R from the high-employment to the unemployment assumption is applied to the $39 billion projected for high employment, a value of farm sales plus home consumption of around $28 to $29 billion is indicated for the unemployment assumption. Cash receipts for these projections would total around $36 billion for high employment and $25 billion for the low-employment projection. These receipts and projected farm marketings reflect prices received by farmers of around 265 percent of 1910-14 for the high- and about 190 for the low-employment assumption.

4. *Prices paid by farmers*

The problem of projecting prices for cost items used in farm production is basically the same as that of projecting prices for farm products or any other product. However, no detailed consideration is attempted. The "parity index," which is used to compute parity prices for most farm products, includes nearly 180 cost items for family living, 159 price series for production items, interest payable per acre, taxes payable per acre, and farm wage rates for hired labor. As so many items are involved, a very simple procedure was adopted. The gross national product deflator index—the price component of GNP—and the parity index had closely correlated movements during the last three decades. Both indexes represent a wide range of commodities at retail and wholesale levels. On the basis of this relationship, the parity index was first approximated from the projected general level of prices for the high-employment and unemployment assumptions.

TABLE 6

INDEXES OF PRICES PAID BY FARMERS, INCLUDING INTEREST, TAXES, AND WAGES, SELECTED PERIODS, 1935-49, AND PROJECTIONS FOR 1970
(INDEXES, 1910-14 = 100)

| | | | | | 1970 | |
Prices Paid for Items in:	1935-39 Average	1937-41 Average	1948	1949	High Employment	Unemployment
Family living	124	124	251	243	245	202
Farm production	124	126	250	238	237	195
Family living and production	124	125	250	240	241	201
Interest payable per acre	117	104	72	76	70	70
Taxes payable per acre	182	184	254	275	300	250
Wage rates for hired labor	121	133	442	428	470	350
Prices paid, interest, taxes, and wages	125	127	259	250	256	210
Parity ratio[a]	86	84	110	100	103	90

[a] Ratio of the index of prices received to the index of prices paid, interest, taxes, and wage rates.

Source: Background data from *Agricultural Prices* (Bureau of Agricultural Economics).

As interest, taxes, and wages represent only 15 percent of the total index weight, it is reasonable to expect a very high association between the parity index and the index of prices paid for items used in family living and farm production. Consequently, this relationship was used as a basis for projecting the index of prices paid for living and production items. A similar procedure was followed in projecting major components of the living- and production-cost indexes.

The index of wage rates was projected on the basis of past growth in real wages (the wage rate deflated by the index of prices paid for items used in family living). The projection was then converted to a current-dollar basis, using the projected index of prices paid for items used in family living. This approximation of the wage rate index appeared reasonable in relation to past trends and to other cost items in the parity index. Farm and nonfarm wage rates were not compared, but per capita incomes are shown below. Interest payments per acre were assumed to be at levels around those of 1949. Interest has a very small weight in the index. Taxes payable per acre, also a small part of the total cost index, were assumed to be at levels somewhat higher than the 1949 level (Table 6).

5. Farm income

Many techniques of appraisal used above assumed that wide differences in returns to productive services would not persist during long periods. Although some comparisons are made between farm and nonfarm income, no attempt is made to determine whether equality exists. Almost any type of data will show considerably lower money incomes to farmers than to the nonfarm segment of the economy.

The usual census concept of a farm includes many units which are not primarily in the business of farming. There are some rural residences, estates, institutions, and part-time units of various types. This latter group of farms can be approximated and separated from commercial farms on the basis of the 1945 Census of Agriculture.[25] Economic classes I through IV are primarily "commercial" farms. Data as to number of farms, population, value of farm products sold, and value of products used in the home were tabulated for the commercial and noncommercial groups. About 57 percent of the farms and around 62 percent of the population fall in the "commercial" group. However, commercial farms sold more than 95 percent of all farm products and accounted for 92.5 percent of the total value of products for

[25] See the special report *Sample Census of Agriculture, 1945* (Bureau of the Census).

sale and use in the home. If farm population, production, and income are allocated to commercial farms on the basis of these proportions, per capita incomes of persons on commercial farms are well above the average for all farms.

TABLE 7

INCOME PER PERSON FOR ALL FARMS, COMMERCIAL FARMS, AND THE TOTAL POPULATION, SELECTED PERIODS, 1935-45, AND PROJECTIONS FOR 1970
(IN DOLLARS)

| | | | 1970 | |
Item	1935-39 Average	1949	High Employment	Unemploy- ment
Net income per person on farms from agriculture[a]				
All farms	177	592	927	645
Commercial farms	—	905	1,595	1,105
Agricultural gross product per person on farms				
All farms	226	792	1,190	847
Commercial farms	—	1,190	2,040	1,450
Gross national product per person	653	1,713	2,818	2,070

[a] Includes government payments.
Source: Background data partly from the *Farm Income Situation* (BAE) and partly estimated.

Data in Table 7 are approximations, but they indicate the extent of differences between farm and nonfarm incomes and between all farms and commercial farms. Persons on farms also received an estimated $181 per person in 1949 from nonfarm sources, and nonfarm people averaged around $18 per capita from agriculture. Other differences, such as valuing the estimated rental of farm homes and products used on the farm at "retail" rather than at farm prices, might be approximated. Such an adjustment may account for several hundred dollars of the difference between per capita farm and nonfarm incomes. In addition, the purchasing power of the dollar may be generally higher in the country.[26] There are many nonmonetary considerations, too, that may make individual families prefer the farm (or the urban area), even with a lower real income. Finally, and equally as important, these figures are rough approximations and may be

[26] See N. M. Koffsky, "Comparison of Purchasing Power—Farm and Urban," *Studies in Income and Wealth, Volume Eight* (NBER, 1946).

subject to a considerable range of error. Probably no explanation of absolute differences can ever be conclusive.

6. Some projections under different assumptions

a. AGRICULTURAL OUTPUT AND PRICES

The computations made in this short section are largely mechanical first approximations prepared to indicate variations in farm prices and incomes under rather restricted sets of conditions. The results have not been examined for internal consistency.

Suppose the over-all assumptions as to population, income, prices, and the projected demand for farm products remain unchanged for each of three alternative levels of farm output—160, 165, and 175 percent of 1935-39 (Table 8). In this general framework, the index of per capita supply rises as output increases, resulting in lower prices and lower incomes for high than for low farm output. It is recognized, however, that total real incomes per person would vary somewhat with different levels of farm output, and, also, that output and total utilization would depend upon prices and incomes in agriculture. Thus, for an assumed output of 175, per capita real incomes would probably be a little higher than for a smaller farm output. And, although the influence of price on aggregate per capita use of farm products is small, lower prices would encourage a higher per capita use, particularly if a relatively large part of the greater output consisted of livestock and livestock products. If these successive approximations were made, prices and incomes would tend to be

ABLE 8

RICES AND INCOMES RECEIVED FOR FARM PRODUCTS UNDER GIVEN LEVELS OF TOTAL DEMAND ITH VARYING LEVELS OF FARM OUTPUT AND PER CAPITA SUPPLY

ITEM	LEVELS OF FARM OUTPUT (1935-39 = 100)		
	160	165	175
et exports of farm products (in index points)	3	3	3
omestic supply of farm products	157	162	172
er capita supply of farm products	111	115	122
igh-employment assumption			
Prices received for farm products (1910-14 = 100)	305	264	193
Cash receipts from marketings (in billions of dollars)	40	36	28
nemployment assumption			
Prices received for farm products (1910-14 = 100)	225	191	133
Cash receipts from marketings (in billions of dollars)	30	26	19

somewhat different from those indicated under the alternative assumptions specified for the computations.

b. THE PRICE LEVEL AND AGRICULTURAL PRICES

For purposes of illustration, suppose all real magnitudes remain as projected and only the "price level" is varied so that we can observe its influence on prices received by farmers, on cash receipts from farm marketings, and on the gross national product (Table 9).

TABLE 9

APPROXIMATE INFLUENCE OF DIFFERENT PRICE LEVEL ASSUMPTIONS ON THE GROSS NATIONA PRODUCT, INDEX OF PRICES RECEIVED BY FARMERS, AND CASH RECEIPTS FROM FARM MARKETINGS[a]

ITEM	UNIT OR BASE	ALTERNATIVE PRICE LEVEL ASSUMPTIONS[b]			
		I	II	III	IV
High-employment assumption					
Consumers' price index	1935-39	170	160	145 .	180
Prices received by farmers, index	1910-14	264	246	220	280
Cash receipts from marketings[c]	$ billion	36	33	30	38
Gross national product	do.	510	477	426	542
Unemployment assumption[d]					
Consumers' price index	1935-39	145	136	124	154
Prices received by farmers, index	1910-14	190	178	160	206
Cash receipts from marketings[e]	$ billion	25	24	21	27
Gross national product	do.	375	350	320	405

[a] Only the price level is varied in these calculations. Real income per person, farm outpu exports and imports, and employment are the same for each price level assumption.

[b] Assumption I is the price level projection assumed for most calculations for this report; II simply an alternative; III is the same price level assumed for the "Hope Report" long-rang projections; and IV approximates the January 1951 level of prices. The alternative levels a based on the consumers' price index indicated for each.

[c] Assumes farm production for sale and home consumption at 165 and volume of farm ma ketings at 178, both based on the 1935-39 average.

[d] The unemployment price level alternatives assume the same percentage decline as projecte under price assumption I.

[e] Assumes volume of farm marketings around 175, based on the 1935-39 average.

Price level alternative III, as represented by the consumers' price index, is about the same as that used in the Hope Report— A *Study of Selected Trends and Factors Relating to the Long-Range Prospect for American Agriculture*—made for the House Committee on Agriculture and dated March 10, 1948. Alternative I was used for most projections in this report and alternative IV approximates the level of prices as of January 1951. The importance of the price level assumption as a factor influencing the level of prices and dollar incomes received by farmers is immediately obvious.

C. POPULATION, AGRICULTURAL OUTPUT, AND PRICES

Population growth is the major factor that influences growth in total requirements for farm products. Moreover, growth of population may be a key factor in over-all vigor and expansion in the economy. The rate of population growth will very likely slow down during the next several decades. But prospects for agriculture during the next two to three decades will depend largely on growth of population compared with expansion of agricultural output.

As a basis for examining the importance of population growth on prospects for agriculture, let us assume the same projected level of per capita use of farm products and compute required output under three levels of population. The total product of the economy would vary with growth of population, as would farm output for a specified level of per capita demand. For example, a population of 210 million by 1970—the high census projection —with the same assumptions for rates of labor force participation, unemployment, productivity, and price level used for the high-employment projections in this report, would result in a gross national product of around $600 billion. Assuming no change in relative prices for farm products and no change in per capita demand, a population of 210 million would require a farm output of around 188 percent of 1935-39, even though no net exports of farm products are assumed (Table 10).

As indicated above, with lower prices for farm products, we would expect some increase in per capita use for a specified level of demand. Likewise for a given level of output, as price changes with each population assumption, per capita use would also change and moderate the rise or decline indicated for the specified assumptions.

F. SUMMARY AND CONCLUDING OBSERVATIONS

Long-run projections should be appraised in relation to a framework of assumptions. As anticipations of the future must be based largely on past experience, the framework of assumptions and,

TABLE 10

Indicated Prices Received for Farm Products under Three Population
and Farm Output Assumptions

ITEM	FARM OUTPUT ASSUMPTION (1935-39 = 100)		
	165	175	180
Index of per capita supply under each population assumption (1935-39 = 100)			
165 million people[a]	121	129	133
181 million people[a]	115[b]	122	125
210 million people[a]	101	107	110
Indicated index of prices received for each per capita supply assumption (1910-14 = 100)			
165 million people	202	125	88
181 million people	264[b]	193	163
210 million people	420	351	317

[a] For 165 million people, net exports are assumed as 10 points of the output index; for 18 million, net exports are assumed as 3 points; and for 210 million, zero net exports are assume Per capita real income is assumed to be the same for each combination.
[b] Projections based on assumptions used for the body of this report.

consequently, the projections are, to some extent, products of the times and probably tend to be conservative. War, or an extended period of defense mobilization, accompanied by a high level of economic activity, would tend to raise prices and might stimulate growth in output and incomes sufficiently to make specific quantitative projections obsolete in a matter of several years. In such a period, innovations and the rate at which they are adopted by farmers could result in farm output well in excess of that which might be expected on the basis of past growth.

Total demand for farm products during the next two to three decades will depend primarily upon the growth of population and per capita income. It would be possible to have a large growth of population and a decline in per capita demand for farm products. However, these projections assume substantial increases in per capita real income during the next two decades. Because of the relatively low price and income elasticities of demand for all farm products combined, increases in total utilization per person probably will be small even with much higher incomes or somewhat lower prices. As a result, most of the projected rise in total utilization is due to growth of population. The pattern of consumption, however, will continue to change, and to some extent these shifts will be independent of changes in income and prices. Empirical elasticity measurements as well as a priori

174

reasoning lend economic significance to many changes in per capita use, such as the shift away from grain products and potatoes, and toward more fruits, vegetables, and livestock products in general. It must be recognized, too, that changes in taste, fashion, working conditions, education, advertising, technological developments, and many other factors probably are inseparably bound up with price and income effects on shifts in the pattern of utilization of farm products over a long period of years.

Projected utilization of farm products for 1970, on which most calculations in this study are based, provides for an increase of around one-fourth in total domestic utilization of farm products above the 1945-49 average. This appraisal assumed a population of 181 million by 1970. Per capita utilization of all farm products is about the same as the relatively high 1945-49 average, with a small increase in per capita food consumption and a decline in nonfood use per person. A high level of foreign trade was assumed. But, with some decline in exports and an increase in imports, the estimate of net exports of farm products for 1970 is well below the 1945-49 average. If population expanded to around 210 million—the high projection—the same level of per capita consumption would result in domestic utilization of around 45 percent above the 1945-49 average. The nature of the supply response to an expansion in total demand will largely determine relative prices for farm products and it may also modify the pattern of consumption. That is, heavy pressure of population on available resources could cause a shift back toward more cereals and less livestock products.

The supply response for agriculture is difficult to appraise for several reasons. Even if approximate empirical measurements were available, innovations during the long run might result in substantial shifts in the use and contribution of each agent of production. Given projected demand and approximate relative prices for farm products, the problem becomes one of appraising probable use of resources in agriculture, together with possible innovations, and their effect on unit costs and output per unit of the resources used. There is ample evidence to demonstrate that resources do move into and out of agriculture over the long run in response to changes in demand, shifts in use of resources, and innovations, although probably not rapidly enough to maintain equality of returns for agriculture. Employment on farms has declined during the last four decades, and the use of farm power and machinery has increased rapidly. Tractors on farms rose from around 1,000 in 1910 to more than 4 million in 1951. Much of this gain represents merely a substitution of machine power for horse power, but the shift has released around 65 million acres of cropland for production of foods and fibers. Total crop acres harvested changed little during the last four decades, but land used for food rose by about 100 million acres, or approximately 50 percent.

Yields per crop acre have continued to increase by nearly 1 percent per year reflecting greater inputs per acre and innovations relating to improved seed, insect and disease control, weed control, cropping practices, plant feeding, and other developments contributing to greater output per acre. Use of fertilizer in 1951 was more than 300 percent of the 1935-39 average, and inputs of material for disease, insect, and weed control have also risen substantially. The rate of innovation in agriculture apparently has been relatively rapid, but its effect on output is by no means clear-cut. Production per man or per man-hour is largely a reflection of increased capital inputs as well as innovations, which may result in increased inputs, but also in greater output per unit of resources used.

Total acreage of cropland probably cannot be increased much during the next several decades. In fact, conservation, flood control, and urban development may withdraw more acreage than is made available through reclamation. Acreage that will be released for food production by further declines in numbers of horses and mules will be small. Thus, increased production of food and fiber must come largely from more intensive use of land, which means greater capital inputs and continued innovation. It is conceivable, too, that tillable pasture land may be used for more intensive cropping.

Domestic consumption for 1970, around a fourth larger than the 1945-49 average, probably would not place a heavy strain upon agriculture. Exports were relatively large in the 1945-49 period, and stocks of many farm products had become burdensome by the latter part of that period. Moreover, an examination of trends in yields suggests that an increase of 20 percent in total farm output during the next two decades could be attained with only moderate increases in yields. Such an increase probably will not be difficult under favorable economic conditions and probably would provide for projected utilization at relative prices for farm products around the parity level as now defined. If past growth in farm output is indicative of what can be expected in the future, projected demand for farm products suggests relatively favorable terms of trade for agriculture over the long run.

Preliminary results of a survey by the Land Grant College— Department of Agriculture joint committee on the productive capacity of agriculture are very optimistic and may be instrumental in influencing projections of farm output well above what might have been expected on the basis of long-run growth and well above most projections published in recent years. The assumptions for the capacity study were very favorable, and, for some commodities, productive capacity was well above prospective demand. Under forced draft, agriculture probably could expand rather rapidly during a period of several years. However, such growth would depend upon the expansion of domestic and export demand for farm products and upon the composition of that demand. Substantial increases may be easy for food grains, potatoes, or cotton, for example, but they are not likely to occur if consumers want more livestock and livestock products. It should be pointed out, in this connection, that with prospects for little change in acreage, just a continuation of past growth assumes a rate of innovation and a rate of adoption of innovation somewhat more rapid than those of the last several decades.

A projection well in excess of that indicated on the basis of past growth would reflect a larger expansion in total demand, a very rapid rate of innovation, or probably a combination of both. A very rapid rate of innovation for a given expansion in total demand would contribute to relatively lower prices and incomes for agriculture. A large or short supply of farm products relative to demand probably would also change the pattern of consumption and thus would tend to modify the pressure on resources in agriculture. Farm output will not be expanded rapidly enough relative to growth in demand to result in incomes to resources in agriculture substantially lower than they could earn in alternative employment. A comparison of farm and nonfarm incomes indicated in the projected framework is probably one of the most reasonable checks that can be made on the internal consistency of a set of projections.

The rather optimistic projections for population growth and expansion of the economy during the next 25 years compared with long-run growth in farm output suggest relatively favorable terms of trade for agriculture in the long run. However, if domestic economic activity recedes somewhat and export demand weakens in the next few years, the rapid expansion in farm output in recent years may contribute to surpluses of some farm products following the defense build-up.

STATISTICAL APPENDIX

TABLE A-1

GROSS NATIONAL PRODUCT, MONEY SUPPLY, AND RATIO OF MONEY SUPPLY TO GROSS NATIONAL PRODUCT, UNITED STATES (OVERLAPPING DECADE AVERAGES, 1869-78 TO 1939-48, AND AVERAGE, 1944-51)

Period	GNP in Billions of Current Dollars[a]	Money Supply in Billions of Current Dollars[b]	Ratio of Money Supply to GNP
1869-78	7.5	2.33	0.311
1874-83	9.5	2.85	0.300
1879-88	11.4	3.67	0.322
1884-93	12.7	4.83	0.380
1889-98	13.6	5.87	0.432
1894-1903	16.7	8.03	0.481
1899-1908	23.0	11.84	0.515
1904-13	30.7	15.79	0.514
1909-18	42.8	21.33	0.498
1914-23	66.0	31.95	0.484
1919-28	86.8	44.53	0.512
1924-33	85.1	49.98	0.603
1929-38	77.9	51.43	0.672
1934-43	107.0	65.89	0.636
1939-48	180.8	119.77	0.655
1944-51	249.9	165.78	0.673

[a] See Table A-2.

[b] Money supply includes adjusted demand deposits, time deposits, government deposits, and currency outside banks. Data from *Banking and Monetary Statistics* (Federal Reserve Board), p. 34; *Federal Reserve Bulletin* for recent years; and for years before 1892 from A. G. Hart, *Money, Debt and Economic Activity* (Prentice-Hall, 1948), p. 538.

TABLE A-2

OUTPUT, EMPLOYMENT, TOTAL HOURS WORKED, AND PRODUCTIVITY PER MAN AND PER MAN-HOUR, UNITED STATES

(OVERLAPPING DECADE AVERAGES, 1869-78 TO 1939-48, AND AVERAGE, 1944-51)

Period	GNP in Current Dollars[a] (billions)	Price Deflator Index[b] (1935-39=100)	GNP in 1935-39 Dollars (billions)	Employ-ment[c] (thousands)	Total Hours Worked[d] (millions)	Output per Man 1935-39 (dollars)	Output per Man-Hour 1935-39 (dollars)	Hours per Man-Year	Hours per Week
1869-78	7.5	82.5	9.1	13,430	41,902	678	0.217	3,120	60.0
1874-83	9.5	72.8	13.0	15,400	48,048	844	0.271	3,120	60.0
1879-88	11.4	66.5	17.1	18,750	58,500	912	0.292	3,120	60.0
1884-93	12.7	62.1	20.4	22,050	66,547	925	0.307	3,018	58.0
1889-98	13.6	57.6	23.6	23,530	68,519	1,003	0.344	2,912	56.0
1894-1903	16.7	57.8	28.9	26,330	75,304	1,098	0.384	2,860	55.0
1899-1908	23.0	63.5	36.2	30,200	84,802	1,199	0.427	2,808	54.0
1904-13	30.7	69.9	43.9	34,520	91,547	1,272	0.480	2,652	51.0
1909-18	42.8	86.0	49.8	37,760	94,249	1,319	0.524	2,496	48.0
1914-23	66.0	116.1	56.8	40,040	95,776	1,420	0.594	2,392	46.0
1919-28	86.8	126.8	68.7	42,622	99,656	1,607	0.688	2,338	45.0
1924-33	85.1	114.2	74.0	43,762	99,117	1,686	0.746	2,262	43.5
1929-38	77.9	102.3	75.7	43,406	94,051	1,737	0.803	2,164	41.6
1934-43	107.0	106.5	97.9	48,633	105,845	1,986	0.915	2,167	41.7
1939-48	180.8	134.9	131.1	57,478	128,010	2,268	1.021	2,221	42.7
1944-51	249.9	167.6	149.0	61,769	136,296	2,410	1.094	2,205	42.4

a Department of Commerce official estimates for 1929-51. Data for 1869-78 to 1928 based on S. Kuznets' *National Product since 1869* (NBER, 1946), adjusted to Commerce series by linking in 1929.

b The Kuznets data were presented in current and 1929 dollars. The implicit index was computed from these two series and put on a 1935-39 base. Kuznets' deflated series in 1929 dollars was obtained by deflating components of GNP. The data for 1929-51 are an implicit series based on the deflated Commerce series of GNP related to GNP in current dollars (*Survey of Current Business* [Department of Commerce], January 1951, p. 9). This deflation process was as done by components. The deflator series tends to be more flexible than the consumers' price index and less flexible than wholesale prices.

c Employment for 1869-78 to 1914-23 based on Kuznets' data on gainfully occupied (*National Product since 1869*, p. 120), with employment estimated on basis of E. R. Frickey's series on production (industry and commerce) found in his *Economic Fluctuations in the United States* (Harvard University Press, 1942), and also shown in A. G. Hart's *Money, Debt, and Economic Activity* (Prentice-Hall, 1948), p. 272. The peaks were connected and the deviations from the line connecting these peaks were arbitrarily used as a basis for estimating the average percentage employed by decade. The data for 1919-28 are based on employment data in Senate Committee Print No. 4, *Basic Facts on Employment and Production*, 1945. These data were adjusted upward to the current series on the basis of 1930-39 (divided by 0.9739). Current data for 1929-51 are official estimates of the Bureau of the Census.

d Hours worked per week for 1869-78 to 1914-23 estimated from Colin Clark's estimates of "hours actually worked" for all industry in *Conditions of Economic Progress* (London: Macmillan, 1951), p. 79. Hours worked per week for 1919-28 are composed of estimates for agricultural and nonagricultural employment. The nonagricultural series is based on hours per week for manufacturing industries adjusted to 1929 relationship of total nonagricultural hours per week to manufacturing hours (the hours per week for manufacturing were raised by 1.0153 back of 1929). Missing years in these data were interpolated on the basis of change in other estimates available for those years—Colin Clark's, Paul Douglas's, and others. Hours worked in agriculture are an estimate of total man-hours of work in agriculture from *Gains in Productivity of Farm Labor* by R. W. Hecht and Glen T. Barton (Department of Agriculture Tech. Bul. No. 1020). Hours worked for 1929-49 are a composite of an unpublished estimate for hours worked in the private nonagricultural segment of the economy (this series is a confidential one from the Commerce Department and is not shown separately in the report), total man-hours worked in agriculture (Department of Agriculture Tech. Bul. No. 1020), and an estimate of hours worked in government (40 hours per week during 1929-41 and 1946-49). These series were weighted by employment in each segment to get total hours worked and the average work week for 1929-49.

TABLE A-3

ESTIMATED EMPLOYMENT, GROSS PRODUCTION IN 1935-39 DOLLARS, AND HOURS WORKED IN AGRICULTURE, THE NONFARM SEGMENT, AND THE TOTAL ECONOMY

(DECADE AVERAGES, 1869-78 TO 1939-48)

PERIOD	THE LABOR FORCE[a] (thous.)	EMPLOYMENT			GROSS PRODUCT			HOURS WORKED		
		Total[a] (thous.)	Nonfarm[b] (thous.)	Farm[c] (thous.)	Total[a] ($ bil.)	Nonfarm[d] ($ bil.)	Farm[e] ($ bil.)	Total[a] (millions)	Nonfarm[b] (millions)	Farm[f] (millions)
1869-78	14,440	13,430	5,590	7,840	9.1	6.2	2.9	41,902	17,441	24,461
1874-83	16,740	15,400	6,690	8,710	13.0	9.4	3.6	48,048	20,873	27,175
1879-88	19,528	18,750	9,260	9,490	17.1	13.0	4.1	58,500	28,891	29,609
1884-93	22,729	22,050	11,880	10,170	20.4	15.7	4.7	66,547	34,817	31,730
1889-98	25,580	23,530	12,780	10,750	23.6	18.4	5.2	68,519	36,656	31,863
1894-1903	28,311	26,330	15,110	11,220	28.9	23.3	5.6	75,304	43,798	31,506
1899-1908	31,792	30,200	18,720	11,480	36.2	30.3	5.9	84,802	54,954	29,848
1904-13	35,954	34,520	23,160	11,360	43.9	37.9	6.0	91,547	64,374	27,173
1909-18	39,329	37,760	26,690	11,070	49.8	43.4	6.4	94,249	69,496	24,753
1914-23	41,927	40,040	29,320	10,720	56.8	50.4	6.4	95,776	72,921	22,855
1919-28	45,003	42,622	32,101	10,521	68.7	62.2	6.5	99,656	76,553	23,103
1924-33	48,759	43,762	33,356	10,406	74.0	67.1	6.8	99,117	75,051	23,066
1929-38	52,193	43,406	33,320	10,086	75.6	68.9	6.8	94,051	72,276	21,776
1934-43	56,229	48,633	39,023	9,610	97.9	90.4	7.5	105,845	85,160	20,684
1939-48	60,986	57,478	48,611	8,867	131.1	122.4	8.7	128,010	107,737	20,274

ᵃ See footnotes to Table A-2.

ᵇ Nonfarm employment and nonfarm hours worked were computed by taking the differences between estimates of the total and the farm segment.

ᶜ Employment in agriculture for 1910-28 is based on the old BAE series (*Farm Labor* [BAE], January 14, 1948) for the period linked to the census series in 1929-30 (0.9255 percent of the BAE series). This adjustment was made in order to use census data on farm employment which is considered consistent with the labor force concept. Estimates before 1910 are rough approximations from census data on persons engaged in agricultural pursuits for selected years, as reported in *Progress of Farm Mechanization* (Department of Agriculture, Misc. Pub. No. 630, 1947), p. 5.

ᵈ Nonfarm gross product is the difference between estimated total and estimated farm gross product.

ᵉ Gross product for agriculture was approximated by adding to net income from agriculture, 1910-49 (*Farm Income Situation* [BAE], August 1950, p. 25), the estimated value of maintenance and depreciation (*Net Farm Income and Parity Report* [BAE, 1943], p. 23, for 1910 to 1939; and *Farm Income Situation*, August 1950, p. 30). The decade data were approximated from the long-run relationship of value of farm sales plus home consumption to the gross product of agriculture as estimated above. These estimates follow very closely those published in the *Survey of Current Business* (Department of Commerce), September 1951. There were wider year-to-year variations in the deflated series. Estimates of the gross product for agriculture were then deflated by the index of prices received by farmers (1935-39 = 100). The price series for 1869-1909 is the arithmetic index of prices received by farmers reported in *Gross Farm Income and Indices of Farm Production and Prices in the United States*, 1869-1937, by F. Strauss and L. H. Bean (Department of Agriculture, Tech. Bul. No. 703, December 1940), p. 24; recent data are from *Agricultural Prices* (BAE).

ᶠ Hours worked in agriculture are based on estimates prepared by R. W. Hecht and G. T. Barton for *Gains in Productivity of Farm Labor, 1910 to 1948* (Department of Agriculture, Tech. Bul. No. 1020). Decade data are rough approximations based on assumed hours per week for all labor and are designed to tie into the data for 1910-48.

TABLE A-4

ESTIMATES OF PER CAPITA USE OF FARM PRODUCTS, 1910-49

(INDEXES, 1935-39 = 100)

Year	Per Capita Food Consumption[a]	Per Capita Use of Nonfoods[b]	Per Capita Use of All Farm Products[c]
1910	96	95	96
1911	97	97	97
1912	98	102	99
1913	96	101	97
1914	97	100	98
1915	96	110	99
1916	95	120	100
1917	95	120	101
1918	97	113	100
1919	98	105	99
1920	97	100	98
1921	95	97	95
1922	99	99	99
1923	101	102	101
1924	102	93	100
1925	100	99	100
1926	102	100	102
1927	101	106	102
1928	101	100	101
1929	102	104	102
1930	101	86	98
1931	100	88	97
1932	98	79	94
1933	98	90	97
1934	99	83	96
1935	96	95	96
1936	99	104	100
1937	100	104	101
1938	101	91	99
1939	104	106	104
1940	106	110	107
1941	109	141	115
1942	109	146	116
1943	109	140	114
1944	112	135	116
1945	114	130	117
1946	119	132	121
1947	115	131	118
1948	111	125	114
1949	111	107	110

[a] *Food Consumption in the United States* (Department of Agriculture, Misc. Pub. No. 691) and *National Food Situation* (BAE).

[b] The approximation of per capita nonfood use of agricultural products is based on tobacco, cotton, wool, and industrial oils. The index is price-weighted and based on the period 1935-39. It is a simple combination of available information on per capita use. No attempt was made to investigate and handle some of the conceptual problems involved, particularly for industrial oils. Data are from statistical publications of the Bureau of Agricultural Economics.

[c] Per capita use of all farm products is a combination of the food and nonfood indexes. They were combined by weighting each by the respective food and nonfood aggregates for each year computed for the BAE index of agricultural production for sale and home consumption.

TABLE A-5

Supply and Utilizations: Estimated for Major Commodity Groups, United States, 1935-39 Average, 1949, and Projections for 1970 under High-Employment and Unemployment Conditions

COMMODITY AND YEAR	UNIT	PRODUCTION	IMPORTS	EXPORTS AND SHIPMENTS	CONSUMPTION OR USE Food	Feed and Seed	Other[a]	OTHER UTILIZATION[b]
Meats (carcass weight)[b]								
1935-39 average	Million lbs.	16,182	262	198	16,382	—	—	-136
1949	do.	21,710	242	133	21,853	—	—	-36
1970: High employment	do.	28,193	245	111	28,327	—	—	—
Unemployment	do.	27,332	205	205	27,332	—	—	—
Dairy products (fat-solid basis)								
1935-39	Million lbs.	106,450	741	351	103,992	2,794	—	54
1949	do.	121,962	308	2,581	114,360	3,219	—	2,110
1970: High employment[e]	do.	142,600	1,950	370	141,180	3,000	—	—
Unemployment	do.	140,790	1,950	370	139,370	3,000	—	—
Poultry (dressed weight)								
1935-39	Million lbs.	2,677	2	2	2,670	—	—	7
1949	do.	4,556	18	13	4,456	—	—	130
1970: High employment	do.	6,151	18	15	6,154	—	—	—
Unemployment	do.	5,844	13	15	5,842	—	—	—
Eggs								
1935-39	Million doz.	3,335	18	2	3,225	—	126	—
1949	do.	5,186	2	20	4,755	—	210	185
1970: High employment	do.	5,916	15	15	5,656	—	260	—
Unemployment	do.	5,836	10	15	5,581	—	250	—
Fats and oils (incl. butter on actual-weight basis)								
1937-41	Million lbs.	8,239	1,974	479	6,486	—	3,163	85
1949	do.	11,961	1,093	2,328	6,718	—	3,548	460
1970: High employment	do.	12,424	1,460	1,208	8,026	—	4,650	—
Unemployment	do.	12,155	1,260	1,060	7,830	—	4,353	172

185

TABLE A-5 (continued)

COMMODITY AND YEAR	UNIT	PRODUCTION	IMPORTS	EXPORTS AND SHIPMENTS	CONSUMPTION OR USE			OTHER UTILIZATION[b]
					Food	Feed and Seed	Other[a]	
Fruits (fresh and processed on fresh-equivalent basis)								
1935-39[d]	Million lbs.	25,154	4,840	3,132	26,862	—	—	—
1949[d]	do.	31,752	4,659	2,447	33,964	—	—	—
1970: High employment	do.	45,268	6,220	2,075	49,413	—	—	—
Unemployment	do.	43,810	4,645	1,990	46,465	—	—	—
Vegetables (fresh and processed on fresh-equivalent basis)								
1935-39	Million lbs.	37,577	354	221	37,293	—	133	284
1949	do.	48,725	482	541	48,340	—	165	161
1970: High employment	do.	65,189	629	386	65,232	—	200	—
Unemployment	do.	61,672	521	386	61,607	—	200	—
Potatoes and sweet potatoes								
1935-39	Million bu.	423	1	3	334	92	3	—8
1949	do.	456	10	5	314	111	26	10
1970: High employment	do.	383	5	5	304	69	10	—
Unemployment	do.	400	5	5	313	75	10	—
Dry edible beans and peas								
1935-39	Million lbs.	1,590	46	73	1,216	273	—	74
1949	do.	2,303	46	145	1,287	282	—	635
1970: High employment	do.	1,880	50	65	1,595	275	—	—
Unemployment	do.	1,890	40	65	1,595	275	—	—
Sugar (raw)								
1935-39	Thous. tons	1,948	4,868	108	6,733	—	—	—25
1949	do.	2,112	5,703	60	7,544	—	—	211
1970: High employment	do.	2,500	6,560	100	8,960	—	—	—
Unemployment	do.	2,500	6,470	100	8,870	—	—	—
Wheat, rye, and rice (crop year)								
1935-39	Thous. tons	24,708	464	1,995	14,838	7,140	232	967
1948-49	do.	41,381	250	16,048[e]	14,868	6,844	188	3,594
1970: High employment	do.	34,534	142	8,350	17,384	8,728	224	—
Unemployment	do.	34,224	159	7,550	17,384	7,888	224	1,320

TABLE A-5 (concluded)

COMMODITY AND YEAR	UNIT	PRODUCTION	IMPORTS	EXPORTS AND SHIPMENTS	CONSUMPTION OR USE			OTHER UTILIZATION[b]
					Food	Feed and Seed	Other[a]	
Corn, oats, and barley (crop year)								
1935-39	Thous. tons	87,304	1,000	1,520	4,312	75,712	2,920	3,840
1948-49	do.	134,568	620	4,068	5,572	98,820	4,148	22,580
1970: High employment	do.	132,512	680	980	5,424	120,932	5,856	—
Unemployment	do.	131,640	480	980	5,176	116,812	4,808	4,344
Cotton lint								
1935-39	Thous. bales	13,149	171	5,300			6,938	9,419
1949	do.	16,128	244	5,906			8,870	1,218
1970: High employment	do.	12,030	250	4,500			7,780	—
Unemployment	do.	12,000	250	3,000			7,410	1,790
Wool (scoured basis)								
1935-39	Million lbs.	187	56	7			281	-38
1949	do.	111	155	—			339	-80
1970: High employment	do.	150	350	—			500	—
Unemployment	do.	150	260	—			410	—
Tobacco (crop year; farm sales weight)								
1935-39	Million lbs.	1,460	88	478			969	101
1949	do.	1,980	100	581			1,340	159
1970: High employment	do.	2,580	110	610			2,080	—
Unemployment	do.	2,500	110	500			1,900	210

[a] Includes hatching eggs, fats and oil used in soaps, paints and other industrial uses, shrinkage and waste of vegetables, cotton, wool, tobacco, and nonfood industrial uses for grains.

[b] These are balancing items, including primarily net stock change in most years, and, in 1949, Department of Agriculture net purchases.

[c] Exports of nonfat solids which make up a large part of total milk exports are not reflected on a fat-solid basis.

[d] Projections on basis of total apple crop, while background data are for commercial apple crop only. If an estimate for all apples is included, average production for 1935-39 may be around 26.5 billion pounds and for 1949 would be around 32.8 billion pounds.

[e] Includes military purchases of wheat and rice.

TABLE A-6

FEED CONCENTRATE BALANCE: LIVESTOCK PRODUCTION UNITS AND FEED PER UNIT, UNITED STATES, 1935-39 AVERAGE, 1948-49, 1949-50, AND PROJECTIONS FOR 1970

(IN MILLIONS OF TONS)

| ITEM | YEAR BEGINNING OCTOBER | | | 1970 PROJECTIONS | |
	1935-39 Average	1948-49	1949-50	High Employment	Unemployment
Supply					
Stocks at beginning of year	10.7	7.9	30.8	a	a
Production of feed grains					
Corn	64.9	103.1	94.6	99.68	99.12
Oats	16.7	23.9	21.3	24.48	24.48
Barley	5.7	7.6	5.7	8.35	8.04
Sorghum grains	1.6	3.7	4.3	5.04	5.04
Total	99.5	138.3	125.9	137.55	136.68
Other grains fed[b]	5.1	4.5	5.5	6.86	5.91
By-product feeds fed	14.4	20.0	20.6	23.18	22.29
Total supply	119.0	170.7	182.8	167.59	164.88
Utilizations, October-September					
Concentrates fed					
Corn	75.3	73.3	83.2	91.09	88.35
Oats		20.8	19.3	22.13	21.44
Barley and grain sorghum	4.2	5.7	5.5	9.36	8.80
Wheat and rye	3.3	3.9	4.8	6.17	5.42
Oilseed cake and meal	2.8	7.3	7.8	9.73	9.15
Animal protein feeds		2.4	2.5	2.25	2.29
Other by-product feed	8.3	10.3	10.3	11.20	10.86
Total concentrates fed	93.9	123.7	133.4	151.93	146.31

188

TABLE A-6 (concluded)

| ITEM | YEAR BEGINNING OCTOBER | | | 1970 PROJECTIONS | |
	1935–39 Average	1948–49	1949–50	High Employment	Unemployment
Feed grains for seed, human food, industry, and export	11.2	17.7	17.2	15.66	14.23
Total utilization	105.1	141.4	150.6	167.59	160.54
Utilization adjusted to crop year basis	104.5	139.9	152.6	—	—
Stocks at end of crop year	14.5	30.8	31.2	[a]	4.34[c]
Total supply	119.0	170.7	182.8	167.59	164.88
Livestock production in terms of production units (in millions)	140.2	171.4	176.5	207.0	201.0
Concentrates fed per production unit	0.67	0.72	0.76	0.733	0.728

[a] Stocks are assumed at normal levels with no net accumulation of inventory.
[b] Imported grains and domestic wheat and rye.
[c] Net stock accumulation.
Source: Background data from *Feed Statistics* (Department of Agriculture, Stat. Bul. Nos. 85 and 95).

SPECIFIC INDUSTRY OUTPUT
PROJECTIONS

HAROLD J. BARNETT

RAND CORPORATION

A. ALTERNATIVE PROJECTIONS

LET us assume that the time is the beginning of 1947. We have just completed the first full-scale projections of industrial output employing an input-output matrix to calculate derived demand. Our article, which presents outputs by industries for 1950, has been sent to the publisher.[1]

In the projections we used a matrix about 40 x 40 in size consisting of 1939 input-output coefficients. An attempt was made ". . . to correct the 1939 input ratios for a few clearly discernible changes. . . ."[2] These adjustments were made partly on the basis of past trends, partly in consultation with experts. Clearly, changes in addition to these may occur by 1950, but there is no present basis for estimating even roughly their nature, direction, or magnitude."[3]

After consideration of population size, labor force, productivity changes by industries, and other variables, we estimated that 1950 gross national product (in 1939 prices) would be about 86 percent greater than that for 1939 if final demand represented a *consumption* model, and 79 percent greater if final demand represented an *investment* model.[4] We inserted our alternative final demands in the revised matrix, solved the simultaneous equations, and,

---

Note: I am indebted to a major degree to Ronald Shephard, Russell Nichols, Andrew Marshall, Roland McKean, Sam Schurr, and Alice Hirsch. In addition I have benefited from useful comment from Joseph Kershaw, Marvin Hoffenberg, W. Evans, and E. M. Hoover.

[1] J. Cornfield, W. Evans, and M. Hoffenberg, "Full Employment Patterns, 1950," *Monthly Labor Review*, February and March 1947; reprinted in pamphlet form in 1947 with the same title by the Government Printing Office, Washington. Also Appendix A thereto (mimeographed, May 1946).

[2] "These [were]:
"(1) A 25 percent reduction in unit coal consumption by railroads.
"(2) A 650 percent increase in unit diesel oil consumption by railroads.
"(3) A 20 percent increase in the amount of textile fiber per tire with 60 percent of the fiber supplied by cotton, 40 percent by synthetics.
"(4) A continuation of the prewar trend toward the substitution of synthetic fibers for cotton in apparel."

[3] Cornfield, Evans, and Hoffenberg, *op.cit.*, Appendix A, p. 17.

[4] Percentages furnished by Marvin Hoffenberg.

after a certain amount of recycling to satisfy the assumption of full employment, arrived at two sets of projected 1950 outputs by industries.

At this point we say to ourselves: Let us make projections by alternative techniques using certain basic assumptions identical with those employed for the input-output projections. We shall file them in a folder marked "not to be opened until 1951." In 1951 we shall compare the projections with actual outputs by industries, and discover the deviations from actual of the various projections.

Which alternative techniques shall we use? One technique in general use is multiple correlation. For these individual industry or commodity projections, we shall arbitrarily use the same relationship for all:

$$\text{Specific industry output} = a + b \text{ GNP} + c \text{ time}$$

For the historical periods, we shall arbitrarily use the periods 1922-41 and 1946 for each industry or commodity. The gross national products projected will, of course, be those used in the *Full Employment Patterns, 1950* projections (186 percent and 179 percent of 1939). We will refer to projections derived by this technique as *multiple regression projections*.

Our second alternative technique will be simple. We shall assume that

$$\frac{\text{Projected industry output in 1950}}{\text{Actual industry output in 1939}} = \frac{\text{Projected GNP in 1950}}{\text{Actual GNP in 1939}}$$

With an 86 or 79 percent increase in GNP by 1950, this technique results in projected increases in the output of every specific industry of exactly 86 or 79 percent. We shall refer to these projections as *GNP blowups*.

Our third alternative is also simple. To employ the input-output matrix used in the *Full Employment Patterns, 1950* projections for estimating derived demand, it was necessary to estimate final demand for the output of each industry. These demand estimates reflecting income elasticity were made according to universal estimating practice—regression analysis, budget studies, arbitrary assumption about the government budget, etc.—and had nothing to do with the input-output matrix, beyond uniformity of industry classification. For example, 1950 final demand for agricultural and fishing output was estimated at 52 percent

192

over 1939 for a consumption-oriented economy and at 35 percent over 1939 for an investment-oriented economy. For ferrous metals, the same estimates were 94 and 139 percent, and for chemicals, 89 and 83 percent.[5] For this third alternative technique, we assume an increase in the total output of each industry equal to the percentage increase in final demand for the output of that industry. Thus, using the above examples, we project (with 1939 = 100) the following:

Output by Industry	Consumption Model	Investment Model
Agriculture and fishing	152	135
Ferrous metals	194	239
Chemicals	189	183

Projections by this technique (in which we employ final demand structures identical with those to which the input-output matrix in *Full Employment Patterns, 1950* was hinged) will be called *final demand blowups.*

B. COMPARING 1950 PROJECTIONS WITH ACTUAL

The time is now 1951 and the results of the *Full Employment Patterns, 1950 (FEP)* and alternative projections may be presented and compared with the 1950 actual.[6] Table 1, in millions of 1939 dollars, compares actual 1950 output with the eight output projections produced by the published article and the three alternative techniques. Table 2 presents the same information in index numbers, with 1939 = 100. Tables 3 and 4 present deviations of the eight projections from the actual, in millions of 1939 dollars and in index number points, with 1939 = 100. These tables also present arithmetic means of the errors in the several projections.

[5] Cornfield, Evans, and Hoffenberg, *op.cit.*, table 14, p. 34.
[6] See Appendix for basic data, sources, and details of computation.

TABLE 1

COMPARISON OF EIGHT PROJECTIONS WITH ACTUAL 1950 OUTPUT (IN MILLIONS OF 1939 DOLLARS)

| | | | | Method of Projection | | | | | |
| | | Actual Output, 1950 | FULL EMPLOYMENT PATTERNS | | MULTIPLE REGRESSION | | FINAL-DEMAND BLOWUP | | GNP BLOWUP | |
Line	Industry		C-Model[a]	I-Model[b]	Larger GNP (C-Model)	Smaller GNP (I-Model)	C-Model	I-Model	Larger GNP (C-Model)	Smaller GNP (I-Model)
1.	Agriculture and fishing	13,056	16,937	14,915	13,562	13,259	15,384	13,663	18,825	18,117
2.	Food processing	20,152	22,685	19,263	20,948	20,285	22,008	19,092	24,660	23,732
3.	Ferrous metals	5,212	4,824	5,927	5,523	5,186	5,030	6,197	4,823	4,641
4.	Shipbuilding	481	441	476	2,015	1,892	358	441	813	782
5.	Agricultural machinery	1,242	893	1,276	1,225	1,159	896	1,326	817	786
6.	Machinery	12,865	9,307	11,837	15,388	14,448	9,599	12,865	9,203	8,857
7.	Motor vehicles	6,607	6,157	6,255	6,117	5,756	6,349	6,427	4,801	4,620
8.	Aircraft	1,652	2,030	2,269	2,066	1,735	1,840	2,101	500	482
9.	Transportation equipment, n.e.c.	609	566	722	1,019	920	572	782	495	476
10.	Iron and steel, n.e.c.	4,589	4,066	4,952	4,863	4,566	4,452	5,776	4,246	4,087
11.	Nonferrous metals and their products	2,854	3,124	3,473	3,340	3,152	2,713	2,901	2,916	2,807
12.	Nonmetallic minerals and their products	3,779	3,522	4,748	4,522	4,254	4,605	4,688	3,841	3,696
13.	Petroleum production and refining	7,569	10,067	9,593	7,909	7,715	11,208	10,141	9,025	8,685
14.	Coal mining and manufactured solid fuel	2,059	3,015	3,055	2,716	2,578	2,837	2,699	3,218	3,097
15.	Manufactured gas and electric power	7,131	5,539	5,233	5,528	5,384	5,986	5,298	5,327	5,127

TABLE 1 (concluded)

Line	Industry	Actual Output, 1950	FULL EMPLOYMENT PATTERNS		MULTIPLE REGRESSION		FINAL-DEMAND BLOWUP		GNP BLOWUP	
			C-Model[a]	I-Model[b]	Larger GNP (C-Model)	Smaller GNP (I-Model)	C-Model	I-Model	Larger GNP (C-Model)	Smaller GNP (I-Model)
16.	Communications	3,047	2,713	2,484	2,638	2,562	3,335	2,714	2,820	2,714
17.	Chemicals	8,026	6,411	6,635	8,332	7,992	6,428	6,224	6,326	6,088
18.	Lumber and timber products	1,869	2,022	2,791	2,154	1,993	2,476	3,206	2,303	2,216
19.	Furniture and other wood manufactures	2,030	2,154	2,281	2,267	2,137	2,184	2,338	2,208	2,125
20.	Wood pulp and paper	2,799	3,036	2,914	2,851	2,765	3,107	3,448	3,175	3,056
21.	Printing and publishing	3,624	3,962	3,468	3,420	3,307	4,009	3,488	4,213	4,054
22.	Textile mill products	5,118	5,743	5,199	5,497	5,276	4,739	4,644	5,876	5,655
23.	Apparel and other finished textile products	6,146	6,742	5,645	6,457	6,215	6,664	5,594	6,423	6,181
24.	Leather and leather products	1,055	1,667	1,436	1,311	1,272	1,696	1,509	1,834	1,765
25.	Rubber	1,757	1,725	1,744	2,052	1,962	1,641	1,713	1,659	1,597
26.	All other manufacturing	3,195	3,432	3,217	3,528	3,361	3,744	3,578	3,095	2,979
27.	Construction	16,445	14,889	25,291	19,976	18,261	14,932	25,323	18,766	18,059
28.	Steam railroad transportation	8,361	8,739	8,563	9,180	8,620	13,361	11,077	8,017	7,715
	Gross national product	152,000	170,000	163,000	170,000	163,000	170,000	163,000	170,000	163,000

Method of Projection

[a] Consumption model.
[b] Investment model.

Sources: Full-employment patterns projections are from J. Cornfield, W. Evans, and M. Hoffenberg, *Full Employment Patterns, 1950* (Government Printing Office, 1947). They may be read directly from Table 15, page 35, except in the case of the machinery industry, for which we have lumped five *FEP* classifications.

The other projections were obtained by applying the indexes in Table 2, below, to the 1939 actual outputs for each industry, as given in Table A-3, below.

Actual output, 1950 is from *The Annual Economic Review* of the Council of Economic Advisers (Government Printing Office, 1951), p. 179.

TABLE 2

COMPARISON OF EIGHT PROJECTIONS WITH ACTUAL 1950 OUTPUT[a] (INDEX NUMBERS, 1939 = 100)

				Method of Projection					
		Actual Output, 1950	FULL EMPLOYMENT PATTERNS		MULTIPLE REGRESSION		FINAL-DEMAND BLOWUP		GNP BLOWUP	
Line	Industry		C-Model[b]	I-Model[c]	Larger GNP (C-Model)	Smaller GNP (I-Model)	C-Model	I-Model	Larger GNP (C-Model)	Smaller GNP (I-Model)
1.	Agriculture and fishing	129	167	147	134	131	152	135	186	179
2.	Food processing	152	171	145	158	153	166	144	186	179
3.	Ferrous metals	201	186	229	213	200	194	239	186	179
4.	Shipbuilding	110	101	109	461	433	82	101	186	179
5.	Agricultural machinery	283	203	291	279	264	204	302	186	179
6.	Machinery	260	188	239	311	292	194	260	186	179
7.	Motor vehicles	256	239	242	237	223	246	249	186	179
8.	Aircraft	614	755	843	768	645	684	781	186	179
9.	Transportation equipment, n.e.c.	229	213	271	383	346	215	294	186	179
10.	Iron and steel, n.e.c.	201	178	217	213	200	195	253	186	179
11.	Nonferrous metals and their products	182	199	221	213	201	173	185	186	179
12.	Nonmetallic minerals and their products	183	171	230	219	206	223	227	186	179
13.	Petroleum production and refining	156	207	198	163	159	231	209	186	179
14.	Coal mining and manufactured solid fuel	119	174	177	158	149	164	156	186	179
15.	Manufactured gas and electric power	249	193	183	193	188	209	185	186	179

TABLE 2 (concluded)

| | | FULL EMPLOYMENT PATTERNS | | MULTIPLE REGRESSION | | FINAL-DEMAND BLOWUP | | GNP BLOWUP | |
| | | | | Method of Projection | | | | | |
Line	Industry	Actual Output, 1950	C-Model[b]	I-Model[c]	Larger GNP (C-Model)	Smaller GNP (I-Model)	C-Model	I-Model	Larger GNP (C-Model)	Smaller GNP (I-Model)
16.	Communications	201	179	164	174	169	220	179	186	179
17.	Chemicals	236	189	195	245	235	189	183	186	179
18.	Lumber and timber products	151	163	225	174	161	200	259	186	179
19.	Furniture and other wood manufactures	171	181	192	191	180	184	197	186	179
20.	Wood pulp and paper	164	178	171	167	162	182	202	186	179
21.	Printing and publishing	160	175	153	151	146	177	154	186	179
22.	Textile mill products	162	182	165	174	167	150	147	186	179
23.	Apparel and other finished textile products	178	195	163	187	180	193	162	186	179
24.	Leather and leather products	107	169	146	133	129	172	153	186	179
25.	Rubber	197	193	196	230	220	184	192	186	179
26.	All other manufacturing	192	206	193	212	202	225	215	186	179
27.	Construction	163	148	251	198	181	148	251	186	179
28.	Steam railroad transportation	194	203	199	213	200	310	257	186	179
	Gross national product	167	186	179	186	179	186	186	186	179

[a] See Appendix for notes on sources.
[b] Consumption model.
[c] Investment model.

197

TABLE 3

DEVIATIONS OF EIGHT PROJECTIONS FROM ACTUAL 1950 OUTPUT (IN MILLIONS OF 1939 DOLLARS)

						Method of Projection				
			FULL EMPLOYMENT PATTERNS		MULTIPLE REGRESSION		FINAL-DEMAND BLOWUP		GNP BLOWUP	
Line	Industry	Actual Output, 1950	C-Model[a]	I-Model[b]	Larger GNP (C-Model)	Smaller GNP (I-Model)	C-Model	I-Model	Larger GNP (C-Model)	Smaller GNP (I-Model)
1.	Agriculture and fishing	13,056	+3,881	+1,859	+506	+203	+2,328	+607	+5,769	+5,061
2.	Food processing	20,152	+2,533	−889	+796	+133	+1,856	−1,060	+4,508	+3,580
3.	Ferrous metals	5,212	−388	+715	+311	−26	−182	+985	−389	−571
4.	Shipbuilding	481	−40	−5	+1,534	+1,411	−123	−40	+332	+301
5.	Agricultural machinery	1,242	−349	+34	−17	−83	−346	+84	−425	−456
6.	Machinery	12,865	−3,558	−1,028	+2,523	+1,583	−3,266	0	−3,662	−4,008
7.	Motor vehicles	6,607	−450	−352	−490	−851	−258	−180	−1,806	−1,987
8.	Aircraft	1,652	+378	+617	+414	+83	+188	+449	−1,152	−1,170
9.	Transportation equipment, n.e.c.	609	−43	+113	+410	+311	−37	+173	−114	−133
10.	Iron and steel, n.e.c.	4,589	−523	+363	+274	−23	−137	+1,187	−343	−502
11.	Nonferrous metals and their products	2,854	+270	+619	+486	+298	−141	+47	+62	−47
12.	Nonmetallic minerals and their products	3,779	−257	+969	+743	+475	+826	+909	+62	−83
13.	Petroleum production and refining	7,569	+2,498	+2,024	+340	+146	+3,639	+2,572	+1,456	+1,116
14.	Coal mining and manufactured solid fuel	2,059	+956	+996	+657	+519	+778	+640	+1,159	+1,038
15.	Manufactured gas and electric power	7,131	−1,592	−1,898	−1,603	−1,747	−1,145	−1,833	−1,804	−2,004

TABLE 3 (concluded)

			Method of Projection							
			FULL EMPLOYMENT PATTERNS		MULTIPLE REGRESSION		FINAL-DEMAND BLOWUP		GNP BLOWUP	
Line	Industry	Actual Output, 1950	C-Model[a]	I-Model[b]	Larger GNP (C-Model)	Smaller GNP (I-Model)	C-Model	I-Model	Larger GNP (C-Model)	Smaller GNP (I-Model)
16.	Communications	3,047	−334	−563	−409	−485	+288	−333	−227	−333
17.	Chemicals	8,026	−1,615	−1,391	+306	−34	−1,598	−1,802	−1,700	−1,938
18.	Lumber and timber products	1,869	+153	+922	+285	+124	+607	+1,337	+434	+347
19.	Furniture and other wood manufactures	2,030	+124	+251	+237	+107	+154	+308	+178	+95
20.	Wood pulp and paper	2,799	+237	+115	+52	−34	+308	+649	+376	+257
21.	Printing and publishing	3,624	+338	−156	−204	−317	+385	−136	+589	+430
22.	Textile mill products	5,118	+625	+81	+379	+158	−379	−474	+758	+537
23.	Apparel and other finished textile products	6,146	+596	−501	+311	+69	+518	−552	+277	+35
24.	Leather and leather products	1,055	+612	+381	+256	+217	+641	+454	+779	+710
25.	Rubber	1,757	−32	−13	+295	+205	−116	−44	−98	−160
26.	All other manufacturing	3,195	+237	+22	+333	+166	+549	+383	−100	−216
27.	Construction	16,445	−1,556	+8,846	+3,531	+1,816	−1,513	+8,878	+2,321	+1,614
28.	Steam railroad transportation	8,361	+378	+202	+819	+259	+5,000	+2,716	−344	−646
	Total, ignoring signs		24,553	25,925	18,521	11,883	27,306	28,832	31,224	29,375
	Average		877	926	662	424	975	1,030	1,115	1,049

a Consumption model.
b Investment model.
Source: Data obtained by differencing data from Table 1.

199

TABLE 4

DEVIATIONS OF EIGHT PROJECTIONS FROM ACTUAL 1950 OUTPUT (IN INDEX POINTS, 1939 ACTUAL = 100)

						Method of Projection				
		Actual Output, 1950	FULL EMPLOYMENT PATTERNS		MULTIPLE REGRESSION		FINAL-DEMAND BLOWUP		GNP BLOWUP	
Line	Industry		C-Model[a]	I-Model[b]	Larger GNP (C-Model)	Smaller GNP (I-Model)	C-Model	I-Model	Larger GNP (C-Model)	Smaller GNP (I-Model)
1.	Agriculture and fishing	129	+38	+18	+5	+2	+23	+6	+57	+50
2.	Food processing	152	+19	−7	+6	+1	+14	−8	+34	+27
3.	Ferrous metals	201	−15	+28	+12	−1	−7	+38	−15	−22
4.	Shipbuilding	110	−9	−1	+351	+323	−28	−9	+76	+69
5.	Agricultural machinery	283	−80	+8	−4	−19	−79	+19	−97	−104
6.	Machinery	260	−72	−21	+51	+32	−66	0	−74	−81
7.	Motor vehicles	256	−17	−14	−19	−33	−10	−7	−70	−77
8.	Aircraft	614	+141	+229	+154	+31	+70	+167	−428	−435
9.	Transportation equipment, n.e.c.	229	−16	+42	+154	+117	−14	+65	−43	−50
10.	Iron and steel, n.e.c.	201	−23	+16	+12	−1	−6	+52	−15	−22
11.	Nonferrous metals and their products	182	+17	+39	+31	+19	−9	+3	+4	−3
12.	Nonmetallic minerals and their products	183	−12	+47	+36	+23	+40	+44	+3	−4
13.	Petroleum production and refining	156	+51	+42	+7	+3	+75	+53	+30	+23
14.	Coal mining and manufactured solid fuel	119	+55	+58	+39	+30	+45	+37	+67	+60
15.	Manufactured gas and electric power	249	−56	−66	−56	−61	−40	−64	−63	−70

TABLE 4 (concluded)

		Actual Output, 1950	FULL EMPLOYMENT PATTERNS		MULTIPLE REGRESSION		FINAL-DEMAND BLOWUP		GNP BLOWUP	
			C-Model[a]	I-Model[b]	Larger GNP (C-Model)	Smaller GNP (I-Model)	C-Model	I-Model	Larger GNP (C-Model)	Smaller GNP (I-Model)
Line	Industry									
16.	Communications	201	−22	−37	−27	−32	+19	−22	−15	−22
17.	Chemicals	236	−47	−41	+9	−1	−47	−53	−50	−57
18.	Lumber and timber products	151	+12	+74	+23	+10	+49	+108	+35	+28
19.	Furniture and other wood manufactures	171	+10	+21	+20	+9	+13	+26	+15	+8
20.	Wood pulp and paper	164	+14	+7	+3	−2	+18	+38	+22	+15
21.	Printing and publishing	160	+15	−7	−9	−14	+17	−6	+26	+19
22.	Textile mill products	162	+20	+3	+12	+5	−12	−15	+24	+17
23.	Apparel and other finished textile products	178	+17	−15	+9	+2	+15	−16	+8	+1
24.	Leather and leather products	107	+62	+39	+26	+22	+65	+46	+79	+72
25.	Rubber	197	−4	−1	+33	+23	−13	−5	−11	−18
26.	All other manufacturing	192	+14	+1	+20	+10	+33	+23	−6	−13
27.	Construction	163	−15	+88	+35	+18	−15	+88	+23	+16
28.	Steam railroad transportation	194	+9	+5	+19	+6	+116	+63	−8	−15
	Total, ignoring signs		882	975	1,182	850	958	1,081	1,398	1,398
	Average		32	35	42	30	34	39	50	50

Method of Projection

a Consumption model.
b Investment model.
Source: Data obtained by differencing data from Table 2.

201

The most obvious results are the mean errors. These, expressed as percentages of value of industry output in 1939, are as follows:

PROJECTION TECHNIQUE USED	MODEL	MEAN ERRORS—PERCENT OF VALUE OF INDUSTRY OUTPUT IN 1939 Weighted by Specified Industry Value of Output, 1939	Unweighted
Multiple regression	Investment	14	30
Multiple regression	Consumption	22	42
Full Employment Patterns	Consumption	29	32
Full Employment Patterns	Investment	30	35
Final-demand blowup	Consumption	32	34
Final-demand blowup	Investment	34	39
GNP blowup	Investment	34	50
GNP blowup	Consumption	36	50

Which of the mean errors—weighted or unweighted—is more important depends on one's specific projection interest. If interest centers on individual industries, the unweighted mean comparison is more relevant. But means do not fully describe the error patterns. Frequency distribution charts (1 through 4) and tables (5 and 6) yield additional information on the error patterns. These appear to indicate the following:

1. With respect to dollar projections, equivalent to the weighted mean comparison above, and confirming the results indicated by the means, the descending order of "goodness" of these particular projections is: (a) multiple regression; (b) *Full Employment Patterns, 1950*; (c) final-demand blowup; and (d) GNP blowup.

The horizontal lines on Table 5 indicate the size of error reached by the time the best 23 and 26 cases, respectively, are included. The above order of "goodness" (minimal dispersion) holds when five and two extreme errors in each projection are discarded, as well as when no cases are discarded.

2. For unweighted projections, the results are more equivocal. The horizontal lines on Table 6 are used as they were in Table 5. If five extreme errors in each projection are discarded, multiple regression and *Full Employment Patterns, 1950* projections are somewhat better than final-demand blowup and GNP blowup projections. If two extreme cases are discarded, multiple regression projections become inferior to the others, and FEP projections become best. If all cases are included, errors of FEP and final-demand blowup projections are less dispersed than those

202

of multiple regression and GNP blowup projections. These differing dispersions result in the means indicated above and in Table 4, in which FEP, multiple regression, and final-demand blowup projections are all of approximately equal error, and GNP blowup projections have greater error.

There may be some interest in a classified list of the industries in which each projection was best. In the list below, I have ignored GNP blowups and final-demand blowup projections, in the belief that these are crude approximations of the multiple regression and the FEP projections, respectively. The list is as follows:

Full Employment Patterns (Consumption Model)	Full Employment Patterns (Investment Model)	Regression, Smaller GNP
Transportation equipment, n.e.c.	Shipbuilding	Agriculture & fishing
Nonferrous metals & their products	Machinery	Food processing
Communications	Motor vehicles	Ferrous metals
Construction	Printing & publishing	Aircraft
	Textile mill products	Iron & steel, n.e.c.
	Rubber	Petroleum production & refining
	All other manufacturing	Coal mining
	Steam railroad transportation	Chemicals
		Lumber & timber products
		Furniture & other wood manufactures
		Wood pulp & paper
		Apparel
		Leather

The list excludes manufactured gas and electric power, in which FEP projections (consumption model) and regression projections (larger GNP) were tied; and agricultural machinery, where regression projections (larger GNP) were best. If these are included, regression projections are better in 14 industries, FEP projections are better in 13 industries, and both are equally poor in 1.

C. QUALIFICATIONS

At various times in the preparation of these data, I found myself wondering whether I was testing projections or testing the quality of the index numbers which record the "actual." This problem was aggravated by the fact that I had to match actual 1950 "physical" outputs with the industrial classifications used in *Full Employment Patterns, 1950*, and these classifications are not homogeneous. The first qualification, then, is that the projection

203

CHART 1

Frequency Distribution of Errors in
Consumption-Model Projections, by Dollar Class Intervals

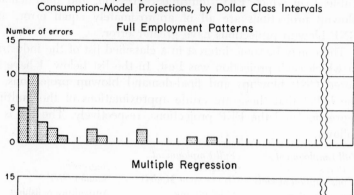

Number of errors   Full Employment Patterns

Multiple Regression

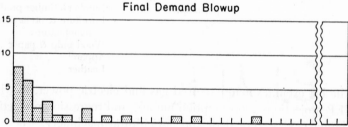

Final Demand Blowup

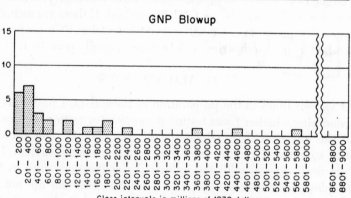

GNP Blowup

Class intervals in millions of 1939 dollars

Source: Table 3.

204

CHART 2

Frequency Distribution of Errors in
Investment-Model Projections, by Dollar Class Intervals

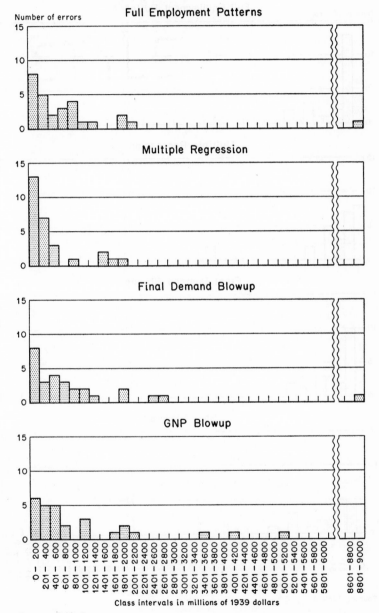

Source: Table 3.

CHART 3

Frequency Distribution of Errors in
Consumption-Model Projections, by Index Points

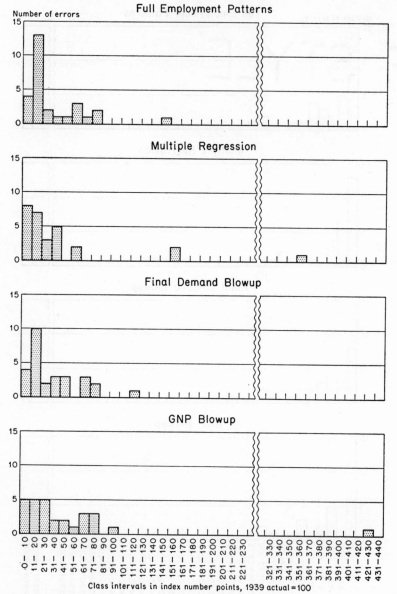

Source: Table 4.

CHART 4

Frequency Distribution of Errors in
Investment-Model Projections, by Index Points

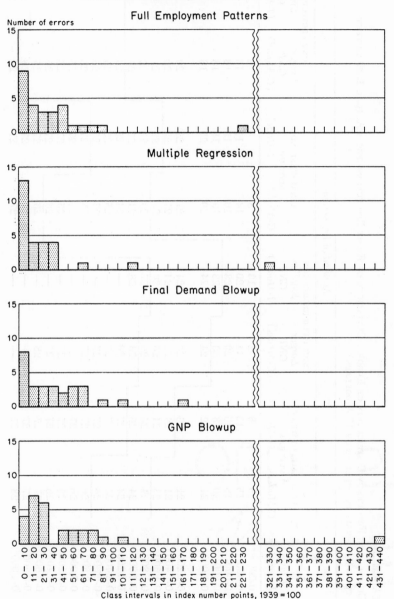

Number of errors

Full Employment Patterns

Multiple Regression

Final Demand Blowup

GNP Blowup

Class intervals in index number points, 1939 = 100

Source: Table 4.

207

TABLE 5

CUMULATIVE FREQUENCY DISTRIBUTION OF ERRORS; DEVIATIONS OF EIGHT PROJECTIONS FROM ACTUAL 1950 OUTPUT
(CLASS INTERVALS IN MILLIONS OF 1939 DOLLARS)

	Method of Projection							
	FULL EMPLOYMENT PATTERNS		MULTIPLE REGRESSION		FINAL-DEMAND BLOWUP		GNP BLOWUP	
Class Interval	C-Model[a]	I-Model[b]	Larger GNP (C-Model)	Smaller GNP (I-Model)	C-Model	I-Model	Larger GNP (C-Model)	Smaller GNP (I-Model)
0-200	5	8	2	13	8	8	6	6
0-400	15	13	14	20	14	11	13	11
0-600	18	15	20	23	16	15	16	16
0-800	20	18	23	23	19	18	18	18
0-1,000	21	22	24	24	20	20	18	18
0-1,200	21	23	24	24	21	22	20	21
0-1,400	21	24	24	24	21	23	20	21
0-1,600	23	24	25	26	23	23	21	21
0-1,800	24	24	26	27	23	23	22	22
0-2,000	24	26	26	28	24	25	24	24
0-2,200	24	27	26	—	24	25	24	25
0-2,400	24	27	26	—	25	25	25	25
0-2,600	26	27	27	—	25	26	25	25
0-2,800	26	27	27	—	25	27	25	25
0-3,000	26	27	27	—	25	27	25	25
0-3,200	26	27	27	—	25	27	25	25
0-3,400	27	27	27	—	26	27	25	25
0-3,600	27	27	28	—	26	27	26	26
0-3,800	27	27	—	—	27	27	26	26
0-4,000	28	27	—	—	27	27	26	26

TABLE 5 (concluded)

| | *Method of Projection* | | | | | | | |
| | FULL EMPLOYMENT PATTERNS | | MULTIPLE REGRESSION | | FINAL-DEMAND BLOWUP | | GNP BLOWUP | |
Class Interval	*C-Model*[a]	*I-Model*[b]	*Larger GNP (C-Model)*	*Smaller GNP (I-Model)*	*C-Model*	*I-Model*	*Larger GNP (C-Model)*	*Smaller GNP (I-Model)*
0-4,200	—	27	—	—	27	27	26	27
0-4,400	—	27	—	—	27	27	26	27
0-4,600	—	27	—	—	27	27	27	27
0-4,800	—	27	—	—	27	27	27	27
0-5,000	—	27	—	—	28	27	27	27
0-5,200	—	27	—	—	—	27	27	28
0-5,400	—	27	—	—	—	27	27	—
0-5,600	—	27	—	—	—	27	27	—
0-5,800	—	27	—	—	—	27	28	—
0-9,000	—	28	—	—	—	28	—	—

[a] Consumption model.
[b] Investment model.
Source: Data obtained from Table 3.

TABLE 6

Cumulative Frequency Distribution of Errors; Deviations of Eight Projections from Actual 1950 Output

(Class intervals in index number points, 1939 = 100)

	Method of Projection							
	FULL EMPLOYMENT PATTERNS		MULTIPLE REGRESSION		FINAL-DEMAND BLOWUP		GNP BLOWUP	
Class Interval	C-Model[a]	I-Model[b]	Larger GNP (C-Model)	Smaller GNP (I-Model)	C-Model	I-Model	Larger GNP (C-Model)	Smaller GNP (I-Model)
0-10	4	9	8	13	4	8	5	4
0-20	17	13	15	17	14	11	10	11
0-30	19	16	18	21	16	14	15	17
0-40	20	19	23	25	19	17	17	17
0-50	21	23	23	25	22	19	19	19
0-60	24	24	25	25	22	22	20	21
0-70	25	25	25	26	25	25	23	23
0-80	27	26	25	26	27	25	26	25
0-90	27	27	25	26	27	26	26	26
0-100	27	27	25	26	27	26	27	26
0-110	27	27	25	26	27	27	27	27
0-120	27	27	25	27	28	27	27	27
0-130	27	27	25	27	—	27	27	27
0-140	27	27	25	27	—	27	27	27
0-150	28	27	25	27	—	27	27	27
0-160	—	27	27	27	—	27	27	27
0-170	—	27	27	27	—	28	27	27
0-230	—	28	27	27	—	—	27	27
0-330	—	—	27	28	—	—	27	27
0-360	—	—	28	—	—	—	27	27
0-430	—	—	—	—	—	—	28	27
0-440	—	—	—	—	—	—	—	28
0-450	—	—	—	—	—	—	—	—

a Consumption model.
b Investment model.

errors depend on the handling of the ever present index number problem.[7] And the second is that the constraint of the input-output-matrix industry classifications was in some cases unkind to regression analysis, which had to combine value weights with heterogeneous physical units which were individually well adapted to correlation analysis and projection (e.g., kilowatt-hours for electricity and British thermal units for manufactured gas). *Full Employment Patterns, 1950* did not directly project commodity outputs in conventional physical units, which regression analysis normally does, and it is relevant that interest in specific industry outputs frequently centers on particular commodities.

A third qualification, related to the above two, is that I did not find it possible to apply the alternative techniques to some of the specific industries covered by the Bureau of Labor Statistics, for lack of output measures from which to determine actual 1950 output in relation to 1939. The deleted industries are trade, business and personal services, eating and drinking places, miscellaneous transportation, and iron and steel foundry products. In addition, I found it necessary to combine five BLS machinery categories (engines and turbines; industrial and heating equipment, n.e.c.; machine tools; merchandising and service machines; and electrical equipment, n.e.c.) in order to approximate the single machinery index of the Federal Reserve Board.

A fourth qualification is that the comparisons cannot be interpreted as generalized evaluations of alternative projection techniques for obvious reasons.

A fifth qualification is that the FEP estimates were not designed to project actual 1950:

"Neither of these models [consumption or investment] is in fact likely to be realized. If full employment is achieved in 1950, it is likely to be as a result of increases in all forms of demand. The

[7] The authors of *Full Employment Patterns, 1950* handled this problem in an arbitrary fashion (*op.cit.*, table 16, p. 427). In most cases they appear to have assumed the percentage increases in their industry aggregations were representative of components of these aggregates. Thus they present the percentage increase in "Manufactured Gas and Electric Power" as the percentage increase applicable to kilowatt-hours; the percentage increase in "Agricultural Machinery" as the percentage increase applicable to tractors; the percentage increase in "Rubber" as the percentage increase in tires; etc. The unsatisfactoriness of this is indicated by the fact that this projects public utility electric power output for 1950 at about 245 billion kilowatt-hours, only 10 percent above 1944-46.

211

two models thus provide extremes; a real full employment situation is likely to occupy an intermediate situation" (p. 421).

In this connection, however, the final-demand blowup projections utilized exactly the same extreme assumptions and resulted in mean errors approximately equal to those of *Full Employment Patterns, 1950*. This connotes that the specific input-output matrix used in the published article to calculate derived demand or intermediate output contributed little, in reducing error, to the conventional-type final-demand estimates on which the input-output matrix was hinged. This, however, is indirect and incomplete evidence of the validity of the underlying matrix used in these projections. More definitive evidence in the form of applying 1950's *actual* final demand is needed. I hope that Evans and Hoffenberg will make this test.

D. RELATIVE ROLES OF FINAL DEMAND
AND DERIVED DEMAND IN
THE FULL EMPLOYMENT PATTERNS,
1950 PROJECTIONS

I have had to attack the question of derived demand in an indirect fashion.

The differences between the investment-model specific industry projections and those of the consumption model are attributable to (1) sharply different conventional-type final-demand projections, and (2) calculations from a single input-output matrix of differences in derived demand, which stem wholly from the differences in the final-demand estimates. I ask this question: For each industry, what part of the difference between investment-model and consumption-model projections was accounted for *directly* by final-demand-estimate differences and what part stemmed *indirectly* from final-demand-estimate differences, in the form of input-output calculations of derived demand? The answers appear in Table 7.

It appears that the major part of the differences between investment-model and consumption-model industry projections resulted from the authors' conventionally estimated final-demand differences, and that a lesser part resulted from the input-output derived-demand shifts incident to the differing final demands.[8]

[8] If construction final demand is visualized as final demand for cement, lumber, and steel, as it could be, then the derived-demand differences be-

ꞮLE 7

ꜰFERENCES BY INDUSTRY BETWEEN TWO MODELS IN *Full Employment Patterns, 1950*
ᴊECTIONS; PORTION ACCOUNTED FOR BY FINAL DEMAND AND BY DERIVED DEMAND
INDEX NUMBER POINTS, 1939 = 100)

ꬲ Industry	Excess of 1950 C-Model[a] over 1950 I-Model[b] (1)	Points in Column 1 Accounted for by Final Demand (2)	Points in Column 1 Accounted for by Derived Demand (3)
Agriculture and fishing	+20	+6	+14
Food processing	+26	+18	+8
Ferrous metals	−43	−3	−40
Shipbuilding	−8	−16	+8
Agricultural machinery	−88	−86	−2
Machinery	−51	−41	−10
Motor vehicles	−3	−3	0
Aircraft	−88	−93	+5
Transportation equipment, n.e.c.	−58	−61	+3
Iron and steel, n.e.c.	−39	−8	−31
Nonferrous metals and their products	−22	−4	−18
Nonmetallic minerals and their products	−59	0	−59
Petroleum production and refining	+9	+11	−2
Coal mining and manufactured solid fuel	−3	+3	−6
Manufactured gas and electric power	+10	+10	0
Communications	+15	+15	0
Chemicals	−6	+2	−8
Lumber and timber products	−62	−2	−60
Furniture and other wood manufactures	−11	−9	−2
Wood pulp and paper	+7	−2	+9
Printing and publishing	+22	+7	+15
Textile mill products	+17	+1	+16
Apparel and other finished textile products	+32	+31	+1
Leather and leather products	+23	+17	+6
Rubber	−3	−3	0
All other manufacturing	+13	+5	+8
Construction	−103	−103	0
Steam railroad transportation	+4	+10	−6
Total, ignoring signs[c]	845	570	337
Columns 2 and 3 as percent of total		63	37

Consumption model.
Investment model.
This total is less than the sum of columns 2 and 3 because of offsets in some cases; see, e.g.,
ꞻstry 4, shipbuilding.
ources: Column 1 was obtained from the *Full Employment Patterns, 1950* projection col-
ꞻs, Table 2.
ꞄColumn 2 was obtained by subtracting the 1950 final-demand estimate for the investment
ꞻel from the 1950 final-demand estimate for the consumption model, and expressing the
ꞻlt as a percentage of 1939 total output. See Table A-3.
ꞄColumn 3 was obtained by subtracting column 2 from column 1.

213

Derived demand from this matrix appears to be less responsive to final-demand variations than I expected. Evans and Hoffenberg have suggested that the matrix used was probably defective in terms of too large an "unallocated sector" (in the neighborhood of 25 percent of output) and too aggregative a set of industry classifications.

E. CRUCIAL IMPORTANCE OF FINAL DEMAND IN SPECIFIC INDUSTRY PROJECTIONS

Let us conceive of industry projections of, say, 10 or 15 years' distance as involving a quantitative determination of how much greater or smaller the increase of an industry's output is than the projected (assumed) change in gross national product.

The *Full Employment Patterns, 1950* approach breaks this determination into two stages: (1) a conventional-type estimate of how much industry output for final demand shifts relative to gross national product; (2) an input-output-matrix estimate of how much intermediate output—demand derived from the final-demand estimates—shifts relative to gross national product. The final-demand estimates thus crucially enter both stages of the projections. They are not only large values in themselves in the first element, but they are also the axes on which derived demand turns. Error in final demand directly contributes error to the projections, and, through the input-output matrix, additional error in the derived-demand calculations.

In this situation it seems to me that it is probably at least as important to answer the questions—How valid are final-demand projections? What specific tendencies toward error do they have? What can be done to improve them? What is being done to improve them?—as to ask these questions about the input-output matrix. While I have not followed the recent literature carefully, my impression is that these final-demand questions have been relatively neglected; and it is possible that more attention to them might be at least as helpful in the problem of final-demand projections by industries as were earlier discussions and measurements in the related consumption function controversy.

---

tween the consumption and investment models become even less. As indicated in Table 7, these construction commodities are the ones for which derived-demand outputs differ very sharply from one model to the other.

In summary, an input-output table is a strenuous and detailed analysis of production functions. It is possible that we need to know a great deal more about analogous detailed consumption (final-demand) functions.

In comparison with the *Full Employment Patterns, 1950* approach, a regression analysis of the type used earlier attacks the problem of industry output change relative to change in gross national product without the two-stage operation indicated above. It simply assumes that future total industry output will change relative to gross national product as it has in the past.

It is quite obvious that there is no a priori basis for knowing which type of projections will turn out to be more accurate in a specific case. The answer depends on the practical matter of data availability for each estimating approach.[9] And since data and classifications are not of uniform quality for various industries and products, the answer depends also on which industries or products are being considered.

APPENDIX

Notes to Table 2

Actual output, 1950 is expressed as an index number, with 1939 = 100. The source of this 1950:1939 ratio is, in most cases, the series shown in Table A-2. In six cases different series were used, for the reasons indicated below:

Industry	Series and Source Used for 1950 Index
Agricultural machinery	The ratio of 1949 to 1939 total domestic shipments of wheel-type tractors (Table 628 in the 1950 *Agricultural Statistics*) was used because census data on farm equipment were not available. M. Hoffenberg of the Bureau of Labor Statistics suggested this alternative as a satisfactory approximation of a farm equipment 1950:1939 ratio.
Petroleum production and refining	I used the Federal Reserve Board petroleum production series in error instead of a production and refining series. These series, which moved together in pre-war years, have diverged since the war. The correct 1950:1939 ratio is 160, as compared with the 156 I show in Table 2.
Manufactured gas and electric power	I used the series prepared by the Council of Economic Advisers. See the *Annual Economic Review, 1951*, p. 186.
Communications	I used the CEA series for the production of telephone and telegraph services. The source does not

[9] As indicated, I suspect that difficulties in estimating final demand for a free enterprise peacetime economy constitute an important obstacle to the *Full Employment Patterns, 1950* approach for such an economy.

215

Industry	Series and Source Used for 1950 Index
	show 1950 production, which I estimated by increasing 1949 production by 2½ percent, the increase from 1948 to 1949. This increase is less than the increase in number of telephones but more than the increase in the number of workers employed in telephone and telegraph industries as shown in the *1951 Survey of Current Business.* I preferred the CEA series to my makeshift "number of telephones" series.
Construction	I used the CEA series, which I preferred to my own series.
Steam railroad transportation	I used the CEA series on transportation services, which I preferred to the Interstate Commerce Commission series.

The actual gross national product for 1950 is in 1939 dollars (page 179 of the CEA document referred to above) converted to the base 1939 = 100.

Full employment patterns projections are from J. Cornfield, W. Evans, and M. Hoffenberg, *Full Employment Patterns, 1950* (Government Printing Office, 1947). They may be read directly from Table 15, except in the case of the machinery industry, which comprises five FEP classifications.

Multiple regression projections are based on historical regressions calculated in the Rand computing laboratory, as indicated in the correspondence quoted in part below:

Mr. Ronald W. Shephard
Economics Division
Rand Corporation

Herewith the series (Table A-2 below). You'll remember the problem is to correlate each of the series with GNP and time. The forms of the functions should be simple—either output $= A$ plus (GNP) plus C (time) or output $= a \cdot b^{\text{GNP}} \cdot c^{\text{time}}$, whichever would appear to be the better fit. If the better fit cannot be determined by inspection, then let them all be fitted by the latter equation. If the latter equation adds substantially to the work, then let them all be fitted by the former equation, except that I will note that there is considerable usefulness in observing the time drift as a constant rate. Please don't bother with lagging any of the variables—in some cases it is a component of GNP that is the proper independent variable, and I haven't introduced this more important improvement. You'll remember that one of the important elements of the test is that it be quite mechanical in order that there be no question of hindsight.

Harold J. Barnett

Mr. Harold J. Barnett
3417 Pendleton Drive
Wheaton, Maryland

I enclose herewith your original data sheets [Table A-2] and a summary of the correlation calculations [Table A-1]. The regression $Y = \bar{A} \cdot \bar{B}^{\text{GNP}} \cdot \bar{C}^{\text{time}}$ is written in logarithmic terms as log $Y =$ $A + B$ GNP $+ C$ time, where $A = \log \bar{A}$, $B = \log \bar{B}$, $C = \log \bar{C}$. But the corresponding standard errors of estimate [(Se) log. est] and correlation coefficients [C.C. log. est] are computed in absolute terms, that is, in terms of the residuals about the nonlog regression $Y = \bar{A} \cdot \bar{B}^{GNP} \bar{C}^{time}$. The coefficients for both regressions (linear for arithmetic Y and linear for log Y) are given, with D, E, F referring to the straight arithmetic regressions—as indicated in the upper left hand corner of the attached sheet. The coefficients $\bar{A}$, $\bar{B}$, $\bar{C}$, of the exponential regression (log. est) are found as anti-logs of A, B, C, respectively.

A word about the equation $Y = D + E(GNP) + F(time)$. The origin of time for this equation is the year 1934, the unit of time is one year, and time is measured positively going forward from 1934 and negatively going backward from 1934. The year 1950 would correspond to a value of T equal to $+16$.

Ronald W. Shephard

The linear relationship $Y = D + E(GNP) + F(time)$, which fitted better in most cases, was chosen for the projections for all industries.

The multiple regression projections were computed by taking $T(time) = 16$, $GNP(gross national product) = 170$ for the consumption model, $GNP = 163$ for the investment model, and by using the appropriate values of D, E, and F for each industry, as given in Table A-1. The results were then converted, where necessary, to the base $1939 = 100$. The GNP figures are in billions of dollars. They were obtained by applying the 1939 percentages furnished by Marvin Hoffenberg, 186 and 179, respectively, to the 1939 actual gross national product of $91.3 billion.

The time series used in the regressions are presented in Table A-2. The correlation period 1922-41, 1946 was used. A few years were omitted because time series data were not available.

Certain 1950 values have been added. These values were not part of the original data series sent to Rand and referred to in the correspondence quoted above.

Final-Demand Blowups. The source of the changes in final demand from (actual) 1939 to (estimated) 1950 is *Full Employment Patterns, 1950,* table 14, p. 34. The blowups may be read directly from this table, except for the machinery industry, which comprises five FEP classifications.

217

TABLE A-1

Correlation of Output with Gross National Product and Time in 28 Industries

Line	Industry	A	B	C	D	E	F	Y	Log Y	Standard Error		Correlation Coefficients	
										Lin. Est.	Log. Est.	Lin. Est.	Log. Est.
1.	Agriculture and fishing	1.85953	0.0017487	0.000492	64.3	0.448	0.11	9.6	0.035	3.72	3.64	0.92	0.93
2.	Food processing	1.75626	0.0027539	0.003217	38.9	0.710	0.67	16.9	0.060	2.56	3.08	0.99	0.98
3.	Ferrous metals	1.09176	0.0104269	−0.016074	−79.4	2.148	−2.68	35.4	0.176	17.89	26.68	0.86	0.66
4.	Shipbuilding	0.94019	0.0127157	0.000038	−300.3	5.118	1.01	114.4	0.249	55.73	69.82	0.87	0.79
5.	Agricultural machinery	1.34184	0.0075823	−0.000868	−88.8	2.241	−0.80	38.5	0.145	10.95	16.89	0.96	0.90
6.	Machinery	1.09272	0.0105814	−0.008473	−126.6	2.763	−1.26	47.8	0.173	10.62	21.15	0.97	0.90
7.	Motor vehicles	1.18093	0.0092325	−0.013349	−62.2	1.894	−2.32	31.2	0.156	15.64	20.83	0.87	0.74
8.	Aircraft	0.47611	0.0176297	0.018628	−2079.8	30.921	−114.52	345.7	0.518	151.50	326.30	0.90	0.33
9.	Transportation equipment, n.e.c.	0.71035	0.0159581	−0.041034	−252.5	4.566	−12.14	74.7	0.244	39.12	42.72	0.85	0.82
10.	Iron and steel, n.e.c.	1.09176	0.0104269	−0.016074	−79.4	2.148	−2.68	35.4	0.176	17.89	26.68	0.86	0.66
11.	Nonferrous metals and their products	1.27978	0.0084767	−0.010962	−60.9	1.961	−2.00	32.9	0.141	14.60	20.76	0.90	0.78
12.	Nonmetallic minerals and their products	1.25528	0.0085885	−0.008651	−68.5	2.011	−1.50	32.0	0.130	4.66	12.80	0.99	0.92
13.	Petroleum production and refining	1.76819	0.0020772	0.012537	42.5	0.572	2.24	23.6	0.114	3.90	6.21	0.99	0.96
14.	Coal mining and manufactured solid fuel	1.61946	0.0049634	−0.014750	3.9	1.268	−3.87	20.1	0.070	8.00	7.99	0.92	0.92
15.	Manufactured gas and electric power	1.86423	0.0020471	0.019584	27.2	1.046	3.87	41.7	0.156	6.16	6.76	0.99	0.99

TABLE A-1 (concluded)

Line	Industry	A	B	C	D	E	F	Y	Log Y	STANDARD ERROR Lin. Est.	STANDARD ERROR Log. Est.	CORRELATION COEFFICIENTS Lin. Est.	CORRELATION COEFFICIENTS Log. Est.
16.	Communications	2.01636	0.0024274	0.008166	61.0	1.297	2.60	39.9	0.094	11.74	11.06	0.96	0.96
17.	Chemicals	1.61349	0.0042840	0.013584	−29.3	1.544	2.56	42.0	0.149	7.60	5.40	0.98	0.99
18.	Lumber and timber products	1.26315	0.0088159	−0.024107	−61.7	1.994	−5.81	31.1	0.139	11.91	14.30	0.92	0.89
19.	Furniture and other wood manufactures	1.31277	0.0080003	−0.014299	−46.8	1.756	−2.93	26.4	0.119	10.51	14.75	0.92	0.83
20.	Wood pulp and paper	1.72256	0.0027042	0.011364	30.9	0.730	2.20	25.8	0.111	6.51	9.16	0.97	0.93
21.	Printing and publishing	1.73105	0.0029159	0.001742	39.8	0.668	0.41	15.4	0.080	5.63	7.17	0.93	0.88
22.	Textile mill products	1.66060	0.0037890	0.003272	14.0	0.995	0.71	23.5	0.088	8.02	8.07	0.94	0.94
23.	Apparel and other finished textile products	1.61180	0.0041737	0.006201	−0.7	1.145	1.34	29.0	0.123	8.59	8.83	0.96	0.95
24.	Leather and leather products	1.80756	0.0020595	0.000386	56.2	0.478	0.11	11.2	0.041	6.03	6.17	0.84	0.84
25.	Rubber	1.53410	0.0052881	0.006144	−35.9	1.621	1.25	37.1	0.132	8.76	7.30	0.97	0.98
26.	All other manufacturing	1.43672	0.0064791	−0.002736	−34.2	1.595	−0.34	29.1	0.109	6.40	10.75	0.98	0.93
27.	Construction	2.50973	0.0117262	−0.033290	−3726.1	84.779	−251.87	1333.3	0.173	547.00	661.40	0.91	0.87
28.	Steam railroad transportation	1.92526	0.0073719	−0.015326	−170.8	6.328	−12.27	84.5	0.107	12.94	14.23	0.99	0.99

Note: Log $Y = A + B(\text{GNP}) + C(T)$ and $Y = D + E(\text{GNP}) + F(T)$.

TABLE A-2

GROSS NATIONAL PRODUCT AND SPECIFIC INDUSTRY TIME SERIES

(DATA IN INDEX POINTS, 1935-39 = 100, EXCEPT WHERE OTHERWISE SPECIFIED)

Year	Gross National Product, in Billions of 1939 Dollars	Agriculture and Fishing	Food Processing	Ferrous Metals	Shipbuilding	Agricultural Machinery (1939 = 100)	Machinery	Motor Vehicles	Aircraft	Transport Equipment, N.e.c.
1950	—	137	165	229	140	—	270	241	1,075	197
1946	143	136	149	150	383	217	240	159	798	243
1941	118	113	127	186	518	165	221	152	1,103	247
1940	100	110	113	147	195	121	136	118	429	141
1939	91	106	108	114	127	100	104	94	175	86
1938	84	103	101	68	98	103	82	67	97	72
1937	88	106	103	123	111	127	126	121	105	162
1936	84	94	98	114	97	100	105	114	76	110
1935	74	91	89	81	68	75	83	104	48	69
1934	68	93	88	61	58	—	69	71	42	74
1933	61	96	83	54	46	—	50	50	35	40
1932	61	96	79	32	58	—	43	36	32	52
1931	72	102	90	61	73	56	66	62	—	66
1930	79	98	100	97	103	110	100	87	—	147
1929	87	99	101	133	98	129	130	139	—	174
1928	83	102	93	121	75	106	106	113	—	127
1927	80	98	88	108	93	99	99	88	—	160
1926	79	100	87	115	85	99	102	112	—	194
1925	76	97	85	108	75	85	89	111	—	184
1924	71	98	81	90	74	67	81	93	—	218
1923	72	94	82	109	85	78	86	105	—	329
1922	62	91	77	85	—	49	—	68	—	—

TABLE A-2 (continued)

Year	Iron and Steel, N.e.c.	Nonferrous Metals and Their Products	Nonmetallic Minerals and Their Products	Petroleum Production and Refining	Coal Mining and Manufactured Solid Fuel	Manufactured Gas and Electric Power (1929 = 100)	Communications (Hundred Thousand Telephones in Service at Dec. 31)	Chemicals	Lumber and Timber Products	Furniture and Other Wood Manufactures
1950	229	206	209	—	119	—	—	264	160	183
1946	150	157	192	148	130	237	300	236	131	147
1941	186	191	162	120	125	168	212	176	134	145
1940	147	139	124	116	113	151	197	130	116	118
1939	114	113	114	108	100	138	186	112	106	107
1938	68	80	92	104	88	126	177	96	90	87
1937	123	122	114	109	110	126	172	112	113	117
1936	114	104	103	94	109	116	162	99	105	106
1935	81	80	77	85	96	105	152	89	85	83
1934	61	62	64	78	94	97	147	83	64	61
1933	54	60	54	77	87	92	144	76	63	60
1932	32	52	51	67	82	93	151	68	51	54
1931	61	83	77	73	99	101	170	78	76	78
1930	97	106	96	77	122	103	172	87	105	95
1929	133	136	110	86	138	100	169	89	146	135
1928	121	118	110	77	130	91	159	78	142	124
1927	108	108	106	77	135	84	149	73	144	126
1926	115	113	105	66	150	77	140	70	148	120
1925	108	104	101	65	129	67	130	63	148	112
1924	90	93	91	61	132	61	122	56	139	100
1923	109	90	87	63	150	56	114	57	143	99
1922	85	—	73	47	106	48	105	—	—	—

221

TABLE A-2 (concluded)

Year	Wood Pulp and Paper	Printing and Publishing	Textile Mill Products	Apparel and Other Finished Textile Products	Leather and Leather Products	Rubber	All Other Manufacturing Industries	Construction (Millions of 1913 Dollars)	Steam Railroad Transportation (Billions of Revenue Freight Ton-Miles)
1950	187	170	182	205	111	223	209	—	—
1946	145	127	162	178	122	225	177	4,086	595
1941	150	127	152	158	123	163	168	5,298	478
1940	123	112	114	118	98	123	126	3,725	375
1939	114	106	112	115	105	113	109	3,356	333
1938	95	96	85	85	93	83	87	2,746	292
1937	107	109	106	105	102	104	113	2,920	363
1936	98	99	104	102	103	107	104	2,704	341
1935	86	89	93	91	99	93	87	1,835	284
1934	75	80	76	73	91	86	74	1,579	270
1933	76	75	88	84	88	77	68	1,460	251
1932	65	74	71	65	76	64	57	1,924	235
1931	74	88	79	72	82	72	75	3,046	311
1930	79	97	74	66	84	78	90	4,020	386
1929	85	104	94	85	95	100	110	4,862	450
1928	79	96	87	79	93	98	99	5,417	436
1927	74	93	92	84	94	83	94	5,535	432
1926	72	92	84	77	90	80	95	5,644	447
1925	66	84	84	78	88	81	90	5,281	417
1924	61	79	72	69	86	66	81	4,728	392
1923	58	74	83	80	99	63	86	4,264	416
1922	—	—	79	—	93	—	—	3,815	342

Notes to Table A-2

Gross national product. That used in Table A-2 is my deflation of published current-dollar gross national product data of the U.S. Department of Commerce and of Simon Kuznets, National Bureau of Economic Research. The official Department of Commerce gross national product series in 1939 dollars was first published in January 1951, and was not available for use when the regressions were computed. It differs somewhat from the gross national product series used in this paper, as indicated below. Both gross national product series are shown, in billions of 1939 dollars.

Year	Department of Commerce Series	Barnett Series
1929	86	87
1930	78	79
1931	72	72
1932	62	61
1933	62	61
1934	68	68
1935	74	74
1936	84	84
1937	88	88
1938	84	84
1939	91	91
1940	100	100
1941	116	118
1946	138	143

Production indexes. Those cited in the list below as being FRB indexes are from the Board of Governors of the Federal Reserve System and may be found in the following publications: for 1922-41, *Federal Reserve Index of Industrial Production* (Board of Governors of the Federal Reserve System, 1943); for 1946 and 1950, *Industrial Production, by Industries, Annual Indexes* (mimeographed release, Division of Research and Statistics, Federal Reserve System, 1951). There is no published source for the 1946 and 1950 FRB indexes for shipbuilding (private yards), aircraft, railroad cars, and locomotives. These indexes were kindly furnished by the Federal Reserve Board.

Item	*Source*
1. Agriculture and fishing	Department of Agriculture, "Index of Volume of Agricultural Production for Sale and for Consumption in the Farm Home, All Commodities," 1946 *Agricultural Statistics*, table 612; 1950 *Agricultural Statistics*, table 655; *Annual Economic Review* of the Council of Economic Advisers, January 1951, p. 186.
2. Food processing	FRB index, "Manufactured Food Products."
3. Ferrous metals	FRB index, "Iron and Steel."
4. Shipbuilding	FRB index, "Shipbuilding (Private Yards)."
5. Agricultural machinery	Department of Agriculture, reprocessed data of the Bureau of the Census on the value of manufacturers' shipments of farm machines and equipment. 1929-46 data from 1950 *Agricultural Statistics*, table 630, deflated by the Department of Agricul-

223

Item	Source
5. Agricultural machinery (cont.)	ture farm machinery price index from *ibid.*, table 677, converted by author to base 1939 = 100.
6. Machinery	FRB index, "Machinery."
7. Motor vehicles	1922-34: FRB index, "Automobile Factory Sales." 1935-50: FRB index, "Automobile Bodies, Parts, and Assembly."
8. Aircraft	FRB index, "Aircraft."
9. Transport equipment, n.e.c.	FRB indexes, "Railroad Cars" and "Locomotives," weighted 4 and 1, respectively; computations by author.
10. Iron and steel, n.e.c.	FRB index, "Iron and Steel."
11. Nonferrous metals and their products	FRB index, "Nonferrous Metals and Products."
12. Nonmetallic minerals and their products	FRB index, "Stone, Clay, and Glass Products."
13. Petroleum production and refining	*Survey of Current Business* (Department of Commerce), "Crude Production" and "Crude Run to Stills," weighted 2 and 1, respectively, by author on basis of values added by manufacturing as given in 1939 Census of Manufactures.
14. Coal mining and manufactured solid fuel	FRB index, "Bituminous Coal" and "Anthracite," weighted by author 4 and 1, respectively.
15. Manufactured gas and electric power	J. M. Gould, *Output and Productivity in the Electric Power and Gas Utilities, 1899-1942* (NBER, 1946). Extensions by the present author.
16. Communications	*Survey of Current Business*, "Hundreds of Thousands of Telephones in Service at December 31."
17. Chemicals	FRB index, "Chemical Products."
18. Lumber and timber products	FRB index, "Lumber and Products."
19. Furniture and other wood manufactures	FRB index, "Furniture."
20. Wood pulp and paper	FRB index, "Paper and Paper Products."
21. Printing and publishing	FRB index, "Printing and Publishing."
22. Textile mill products	FRB index, "Textiles and Products."
23. Apparel and other finished textile products	Special components of the FRB textile group, weighted by value added in the respective apparel industries. Data furnished by the FRB.
24. Leather and leather products	FRB index, "Leather and Products."
25. Rubber	FRB index, "Rubber Products."
26. All other manufacturing	FRB index, "Manufactures Total."
27. Construction	Total new construction in dollars deflated by the Associated General Contractors construction cost index. Both series in the *Survey of Current Business*. Computations by author.
28. Steam railroad transportation	*Statistics of Railways in the United States*, annual reports of the Interstate Commerce Commission.

TABLE A-3

Supporting Data for Table 7

(dollar data in millions of 1939 dollars)

LINE	INDUSTRY	1939 ACTUAL OUTPUT	1950 ESTIMATED FINAL DEMAND			ESTIMATED FINAL DEMAND, C MINUS I, AS PERCENTAGE OF 1939 ACTUAL OUTPUT
			C-Model[a]	I-Model[b]	C minus I	
1.	Agriculture and fishing	10,121	5,841	5,200	641	+6
2.	Food processing	13,258	17,860	15,496	2,364	+18
3.	Ferrous metals	2,593	349	430	−81	−3
4.	Shipbuilding	437	314	383	−69	−16
5.	Agricultural machinery	439	782	1,160	−378	−86
6.	Machinery	4,948	5,952	7,980	−2,028	−41
	Engines and turbines	134	107	145	—	—
	Industrial and heating equipment, n.e.c.	2,216	2,375	3,433	—	—
	Machine tools	439	724	1,058	—	—
	Merchandising and service machines	330	521	707	—	—
	Electrical equipment, n.e.c.	1,829	2,225	2,637	—	—
7.	Motor vehicles	2,581	5,499	5,573	−74	−3
8.	Aircraft	269	1,772	2,022	−250	−93
9.	Transportation equipment, n.e.c.	266	442	605	−163	−61
10.	Iron and steel, n.e.c.	2,283	595	773	−178	−8
11.	Nonferrous metals and their products	1,568	916	975	−59	−4
12.	Nonmetallic minerals and their products	2,065	513	522	−9	0
13.	Petroleum production and refining	4,852	5,579	5,060	519	+11
14.	Coal mining and manufactured solid fuel	1,730	1,104	1,049	55	+3
15.	Manufactured gas and electric power	2,864	2,426	2,141	285	+10
16.	Communications	1,516	1,219	989	230	+15
17.	Chemicals	3,401	2,320	2,242	78	+2
18.	Lumber and timber products	1,238	100	129	−29	−2
19.	Furniture and other wood manufactures	1,187	1,491	1,596	−105	−9
20.	Wood pulp and paper	1,707	356	396	−40	−2

TABLE A-3 (concluded)

LINE	INDUSTRY	1939 ACTUAL OUTPUT	1950 ESTIMATED FINAL DEMAND			ESTIMATED FINAL DEMAND, C MINUS I, AS PERCENTAGE OF 1939 ACTUAL OUTPUT
			C-Model[a]	I-Model[b]	C minus I	
21.	Printing and publishing	2,265	1,291	1,124	167	+7
22.	Textile mill products	3,159	1,438	1,411	27	+1
23.	Apparel and other finished textile products	3,453	6,670	5,598	1,072	+31
24.	Leather and leather products	986	1,565	1,393	172	+17
25.	Rubber	892	592	618	−26	−3
26.	All other manufacturing	1,664	2,084	1,996	88	+5
27.	Construction	10,089	14,889	25,291	−10,402	−103
28.	Steam railroad transportation	4,310	2,442	2,024	418	+10
	Other industries not here accounted for		59,973	51,675	8,298	
	Total		146,376	145,851	525	

a Consumption model.
b Investment model.

Sources: 1939 actual output: J. Cornfield, W. Evans, and M. Hoffenberg, *Full Employment Patterns, 1950* (Government Printing Office, 1947), table 15, p. 35.
1950 estimated final demands: *ibid.*, table 14, p. 34.

COMMENT

A. W. MARSHALL, *Rand Corporation*

Two comments arise with regard to Dr. Barnett's paper. The first concerns the appropriateness of comparisons made in the paper for decisions as to the acceptance or rejection of proposed forecasting methods. The second comment concerns a suggested alternative method of measuring the forecasting errors.

Given the comparisons in Tables 3 and 4 based upon the mean deviations of actual from predicted industry outputs, it appears that projection methods using input-output tables are not very much better than quite elementary "naïve" model methods. Indeed, the multiple regression forecasts seem to be somewhat better than those based, in part, upon input-output relations. In situations such as this, where "naïve" models have in some sense to be taken seriously (e.g., if asked to forecast output by industry for, say, 1956, I would prefer Barnett's multiple regression forecasts), it is well to keep in mind their purpose and character. They are not intended to be legitimate alternatives to the model or procedure being tested, but rather are designedly crude and inefficient things, almost *reductio ad absurdum* constructions of economic models and forecasting procedures. They represent a level of efficiency so low and so easily attained that any forecasting procedure proposed for operational use which cannot almost uniformly do better than they can must be rejected as unacceptable.

Two warnings are needed here. First, Barnett's multiple regression model must be conceded to be "seminaïve," in the sense that even if we were to add additional variables to the equations which we felt had a special relevance for the output of some specific industry, it is unlikely, due to the correlation between most economic time series, that continued large reductions in the sum of squares about the regression line could be obtained. Second, the kinds of comparison made in Barnett's paper are very appropriate to decisions as to whether a certain method of forecasting should be used in practice, given its current stage of development, but are often of minor importance with regard to decisions concerning the advisability of continuing development of these methods. Thus, this type of competitive trial of serious, though perhaps immature, models and forecasting methods against "naïve" models should not lead anyone to discard, or

227

neglect the development of, really promising techniques.

I should also like to suggest an alternative and more natural, at least to a mathematician, measure of the error of prediction of the various methods of projecting or estimating specific industry outputs in some future year. In Tables 3 and 4, Barnett has used as his measure of error

$$\sum_{i=1}^{28} \left| X_i \left(\text{GNP}^* \right) - X_i \left(A \right) \right|$$

where $X_i \left(\text{GNP}^* \right)$ denotes the estimated output, in terms of an index number of dollar value, of the ith industry based upon the estimate GNP^* of GNP, and $X_i \left(A \right)$ denotes the actual output of the ith industry. All of the above, of course, refers to some fixed year and method of forecasting. As an alternative, it is appealing to think of the observed production by industry and the projected productions as vectors in n-dimensional Euclidean space, and to think of the error of the projection as being the distance between the two points. Each vector then has 28 components and the distance between the two points (vectors) is

$$d = \left\{ \sum_{i=1}^{28} \left[X_i \left(\text{GNP}^* \right) - X_i \left(A \right) \right]^2 \right\}^{\frac{1}{2}}$$

Not only is this the more usual definition of the distance between two vectors, but it is also a measure which fits in with what would seem to be, from the statistical point of view, the aim of research in forecasting methods, i.e., the finding of minimum variance estimates of the future values of economic variables. From this point of view, once we decide what to forecast, all questions of further disaggregation resolve themselves into questions as to whether a particular disaggregation reduces the variance of our forecasts.

One additional comment may be made. Since it seems to be almost certain that, in the future, we will have estimates of GNP which have considerably smaller errors than the estimates used in the present paper, some separation of the total error of the various forecasting techniques into its component parts is desirable. Errors of the order of magnitude made in the GNP estimates are so bad that none of the methods obtained a fair trial in an absolute sense. It is in general desirable to be able to factor out the errors contributed by the separate steps in the forecasting methods, since one method may be much more sensitive than another to errors in some common component, say, the first component in all of the forecasting methods in Barnett's paper, the estimate of GNP. This factorization is easily carried out in principle as follows: Let us denote by X_i (GNP) the estimated output of the ith industry, which we would have made if we had known the true value of GNP. Then we have

$$d_1 = \left\{ \sum_{i=1}^{28} \left[X_i (\text{GNP}) - X_i (A) \right]^2 \right\}^{\frac{1}{2}}$$

as a measure of the error we would have made, even if we had had the best possible knowledge of the value of GNP. Also, we have

$$d_2 = \left\{ \sum_{i=1}^{28} \left[X_i (\text{GNP}^*) - X_i (\text{GNP}) \right]^2 \right\}^{\frac{1}{2}}$$

and thus the total error d is separated into two factors of which it is the vector resultant.

As an example, I have performed this factorization for Barnett's multiple regression method, where one can easily obtain the X_i (GNP) from the equation

$$X_i (\text{GNP}) = a_i + b_i \, \text{GNP} + c_i \, t$$

by substituting the correct value of GNP rather than the estimate GNP* used to obtain the values in Barnett's Tables 3 and 4. To do a similar factorization for the input-output method would entail much more work. Working with the consumption model (GNP* = 170,000) and the dollar value figures in millions of 1939 dollars, we obtain these components of error:

Error Components	Multiple Regression	Input-Output
d (total error)	5,325	7,178
d_1 (error, given exact GNP estimate)	3,354	—
d_2 (GNP* component of error)	6,052	—

Thus, using an estimate of GNP which is too large by 11.5 percent leads to an over-all increase in the error of forecast of 59.0 percent. The reader will also notice that the distance between the two estimates, one based upon GNP and the other upon GNP*, is greater than the distance of each estimate from the true value. If we were concerned with a two-industry world, this situation could be depicted as in Chart 1.

Chart 1

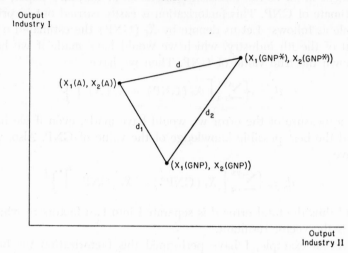

Output
Industry I

$(X_1(A), X_2(A))$

d

$(X_1(GNP^*), X_2(GNP^*))$

d_2

d_1

$(X_1(GNP), X_2(GNP))$

Output
Industry II

STANLEY LEBERGOTT, *Bureau of the Budget*

Mr. Barnett's paper represents an excellent departure from previous, a priori criticisms in the direction of an empirical evaluation of the input-output technique. It sets a course toward a richer understanding of what this technique offers for economic programming. It suggests the following lines of comment, among others:

1. By making one essential modification in Barnett's procedure, we find that the regression method produces estimates which are markedly better for these particular projections than those derived by the input-output approach.

Barnett's regression-estimating equation is based on 1922-41 and 1946 data. Since he is projecting to a peacetime year (*Full Employment Patterns, 1950* assumed no war, a small army), he properly excludes the war years in making his equation. However, for aircraft, shipbuilding, and transportation, n.e.c., the years 1939-41 should also have been excluded. These were years of war preparation—first for the Allies and then for this country. Unless we exclude them, what do we do? For shipbuilding, we derive an estimating equation which tells us that the more ships we build, the more we have to build—this, because the 1939-41 values are so far above those for the first 25 years.[1] For aircraft the infer-

[1] This arises, of course, because no allowance is made in this model for

230

ences are even more anomalous: the equation indicates that by 1960 (or earlier) no aircraft will be produced in the United States.[2] The aircraft estimate has a sizable negative trend term, resulting from a combination of (a) a time series with few observations (1932-41 and 1946) and (b) a terminal value—for 1946—some 40 percent below the previous 1941 value. The same general consideration is applicable to each transport industry: Years of extensive war preparation, like years of war output, should be excluded in projecting a peacetime level of production.

By excluding the three industries, we at once reduce the unweighted mean error of estimate for the regression technique to half the error for the input-output investment model and to three-quarters of that for the input-output consumption model. (The weighted mean errors for the regression estimate were smaller than those for the input-output estimate even before this exclusion.)[3]

2. The fact that the input-output estimate of production in agriculture and fishing was too great while its estimate for agricultural machinery was too small indicates one of those contradictions which the technique is designed to avoid. Moreover, for industries like petroleum production, coal, gas, and steam railroads—where the input-output contribution to the analysis of derived demand should be greatest—the input-output estimates were not better. In most instances they were worse. These facts suggest the importance of making all reasonable adjustments in the technical coefficients before using them for projecting—a possibility which time did not permit when the *Full Employment Patterns, 1950* estimates were being made.

3. Regression estimating is not necessarily an alternative to the input-output approach. It may very well supplement that procedure. For by regression analysis we may be able to estimate the proper coefficients to use in input-output projections. For certain industries, the sales and production data are already sound enough; for others, crude attempts can be made. Such attempts deserve more attention than they have hitherto received as a

---

inventory accumulation. An additional term for this item would likewise have improved the estimate for motor vehicles.

[2] Barnett's trend term is negative 114.52, while the 1950 aircraft index is 614. His coefficient for GNP is likewise negative.

[3] Such hand tailoring is parallel to the procedure of revising the 1939 coal and diesel consumption coefficients for railroads in making the 1950 input-output projections.

means of securing coefficients which will subsume in a non-mechanical way the joint effects of social change, of shifts in distribution patterns, and of shifts in production procedures which, interacting with more obvious technical and economic factors, bring about changes in the technical coefficients.

4. Mr. Barnett rightly emphasizes the role of sound guesswork —it can hardly deserve a more dignified name—in stipulating the final-demand figures. For this purpose, we do not need so much *more* as *more current* data on consumption patterns by income level, occupation, and/or class of worker. To the extent that we can secure monthly, quarterly, or even annual data on such patterns, and tabulate them with reasonable speed, we will have a much sounder basis for estimation than is possible given our current reliance on comprehensive, but outdated, survey results.

PRODUCTIVE CAPACITY, INDUSTRIAL PRODUCTION, AND STEEL REQUIREMENTS

PAUL BOSCHAN

ECONOMETRIC INSTITUTE, INC.

A. INTRODUCTION

THIS paper will attempt to analyze the factors controlling the demand for steel and to suggest a method of estimating steel requirements based on separating total industrial production into a capacity-determined, or long-term, and an output-determined, or short-term, component.

This approach should be especially useful for making long-term projections. The method is applied to data for the years 1919-40. The usefulness of the relationships is tested by extrapolating them into the postwar period to project the demand for steel in 1950 and neighboring years.

Analyses of steel demand have been attempted both to develop economic theory and to answer questions of economic policy. Early analysts of the general supply and demand relationship used the price of a commodity as the sole determinant of its demand. This emphasis on the "level of the price" was modified a quarter of a century ago by G. C. Evans, who introduced the "change in price" as another factor.[1]

The fact that the level of the price, the change in price, and even the relative prices of other commodities do not sufficiently explain demand was stressed by C. F. Roos in 1929.[2] In 1936, R. W. Whitman applied this general demand theory to the steel industry in particular.[3]

Note: This paper was prepared with the assistance of Todd May, Jr. and Charlotte Boschan. The analysis presented has profited greatly from the spirited advice given by Franco Modigliani and the constructive suggestions of George G. Garvy and others. Comments by various industry analysts have provided a better insight into the problems discussed.

[1] G. C. Evans, "The Dynamics of Monopoly," *American Mathematical Monthly*, Vol. 31, No. 2, February 1924.

[2] ". . . in some cases it [demand] may even depend upon the rate of production, the acceleration of the rate of production, and upon the cumulation of these effects. . . ." C. F. Roos, "Dynamical Theory of Economics," *Journal of Political Economy*, Vol. 35, 1929.

[3] R. W. Whitman, "The Statistical Law of Demand for a Producer's Good as Illustrated by Demand for Steel," *Econometrica*, Vol. 4, No. 2, pp. 138-52.

This movement away from the classical concept of a demand function was not without controversy. The question of the influence of price on steel demand developed into political argument. Several studies were submitted for both sides in the *Hearings before the Temporary National Economic Committee* in 1940.[4] One of the most useful of these was a study of over-all steel consumption by various major industry groups.

A continuation of the trend away from using price as a determinant of steel demand and toward introducing production, or some measure of general business activity, is shown in L. J. Paradiso's study for the National Resources Planning Board.[5] The price factor was also ignored in a study by L. H. Bean.[6]

The starting point for this analysis is the comparison of steel production for ingots and castings with total industrial production as measured by the Federal Reserve Index of Industrial Production. Chart 1 clearly reveals that in the period from 1919 to 1940, fluctuations in the demand for the production of steel can be accounted for largely by fluctuations in the level of industrial activity. Correlating steel output with total industrial production for the years 1919-40 leads to a correlation coefficient of 0.897 and the following regression equation:

Formula I

$$S_T = -17.49 + 0.697\,P_T = 0.697(P_T - 25.1)$$
$$[6.25] \qquad [6.90] \quad [0.077]$$

S_T: Annual production of steel for ingots and castings, in millions of net tons.

P_T: Total industrial production (Federal Reserve Index, 1935-39 = 100).

In brackets: Standard error of estimate and standard error of regression coefficients.

[4] H. G. Lewis under the direction of T. O. Yntema, *United States Steel Corporation, A Statistical Analysis of the Demand for Steel, 1919-1938*, TNEC papers, Pamphlet No. 5.

[5] L. J. Paradiso, *Capital Requirements, A Study in Methods as Applied to the Iron and Steel Industry* (Government Printing Office, 1940). On page 25, Dr. Paradiso presents an estimate of steel demand for 1941 based on an extrapolation of a trend line through the peaks of steel production during the period 1899-1929. Actual steel production in 1941 exceeded his estimated level by less than 1 percent.

[6] *The Dependence of Industrial-Agricultural Prosperity on Steel Requirements for Full Employment*, statement by Louis H. Bean, Office of the Secretary, Department of Agriculture, before the Steel Subcommittee of the Senate Committee to Study Problems of American Small Business, June 19, 1947 (mimeographed).

CHART 1

Relation of Steel Output (Ingots and Castings)
to Industrial Production

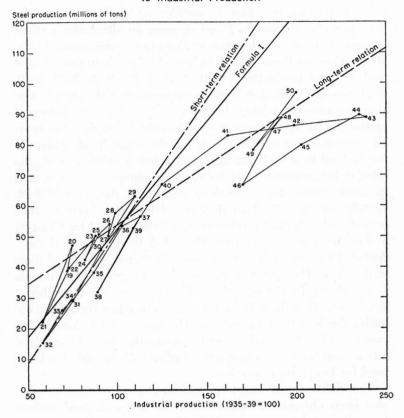

Steel production (millions of tons)

Industrial production (1935-39 = 100)

The regression line corresponding to Formula I is indicated by
the solid black line on Chart 1 and in Table B-3, column 1 (see
Appendix B). Although the line provides a well-fitting general
description of the conditions during the period of observation,
its use for projecting the demand for steel in the postwar period,
when industrial production was far beyond prewar bench marks,
would have resulted in substantial overestimates of steel demand.
For the five postwar years 1947-51 in particular, when the index
of total industrial production averaged 195, or 122 percent above
the average for 1919-40, Formula I yields an estimate of the demand for steel of 118.4 million net tons, 31 percent above the
actual production of 90.7 million tons. Obviously Formula I
does not provide a suitable basis for long-run projections.

235

B. THE BASIC APPROACH
OF THIS ANALYSIS

Close inspection of Chart 1 provides an explanation for the shortcomings of Formula I and suggests an alternative method of estimation, more adequate for long-term projections. If the observations for those years which established an unprecedented peak in total production (1920, 1923, 1925, 1926, 1928, 1929, 1940) are emphasized, it becomes apparent that the straight line approximating the relation between steel demand and industrial production for those years is considerably flatter than the over-all regression line of Formula I. On the other hand, whenever the Federal Reserve Index fluctuates below a previous peak, the relation between steel and industrial production is represented by much steeper lines, like those marked by the years 1920-22, 1929-36, or 1937-39. Two distinct relationships between steel output and industrial production are thus revealed by Chart 1: a short-term or cyclical one, illustrated by the steep dashed-dotted line, and a long-term one, illustrated by the shallow dashed line. The apparent prewar relation expressed in Formula I—and shown by the solid line falling between the two others— is a hybrid of both. It is for this reason that this formula is un-usable for long-term projections. The apparent relationship be-tween steel output and industrial production must be resolved into a short-term and a long-term component, and only the latter used for long-term projections.

This difference in long-term and short-term relationships has also been observed in other economic series. Several authors have discussed its nature and significance, especially in connec-tion with the problem of estimating an aggregate consumption function for purposes of long-run forecasting.[7] We shall attempt to apply to the steel problem a variant of a general method sug-gested by Modigliani for separating cyclical and secular com-ponents in the relation between two variables.

Modigliani was concerned with the relation between income and consumption. He suggested that, for a number of reasons, aggregate consumption depends not only on the current level of

[7] Franco Modigliani, "Fluctuations in the Savings-Income Ratio: A Prob-lem in Economic Forecasting," *Studies in Income and Wealth, Volume Eleven* (NBER, 1949), pp. 371-443. James S. Duesenberry, *Income, Saving, and the Theory of Consumer Behavior*, Harvard Economic Studies, No. 87 (Harvard University Press, 1949).

income, but also on the "cyclical position of income." He measured the cyclical position of income by relating current income to the highest previous peak of disposable income. The previous income peak serves as a moving bench mark, and we can consider it an "associated secular function" of current income. In Modigliani's approach, therefore, consumption was ultimately expressed as a function of both current disposable income and the highest previous peak of disposable income.

Modigliani himself has suggested various modifications of this kind of function, according to the requirements of the problem at hand. Following his general method, we shall express the demand for steel as a function of the current level of industrial production and of the "cyclical position" of industrial production. We propose to measure the "cyclical position" of a given level of production by relating it to the highest previous peak or, more generally, to an "associated secular function."

Before applying this technique, let us consider the theoretical justification for its use in this case.

Nearly all major steel-consuming industries are represented by the components of the production index. Cyclical sensitivity as well as consumption of steel per unit of product vary from industry to industry. A simple demonstration suggests that these conditions lead to cyclical sensitivity of steel consumption.

Suppose two industries, $i = 1$ and 2, make up total industrial production. The production index is, therefore, the sum of the absolute contribution P_i to total output P_T:

$$P_1 + P_2 = P_T \qquad (1)$$

The absolute contribution P_i to production index P_T is the level of activity in that particular industry, in terms of its base period activity, multiplied by the weight of the industry in the base period. Multiplication by the base period weight is a scale transformation which permits us to express the level of activity in each industry in terms of a common denominator, that is, in units of total industrial production. Suppose aggregate steel requirements of industry i, at a level of activity P_i, are S_i; then the average rate of steel requirements per unit of production for industry i is

$$s_i = S_i/P_i \qquad (2)$$

Total steel requirements, at a level of total production of $P_T = P_1 + P_2$, will therefore amount to $S_T = s_1 \cdot P_1 + s_2 \cdot P_2$.

The average rate of steel consumption, s_T, can then be expressed in terms which will reflect the relative composition of total production:

$$s_T = S_T/P_T = s_1 \cdot (P_1/P_T) + s_2 \cdot (P_2/P_T)$$
$$= s_2 + (s_1 - s_2) (P_1/P_T) \qquad (3)$$

If the cycle sensitivity is not the same for both industries 1 and 2, then it follows from the identity

$$(P_1/P_T) + (P_2/P_T) \equiv 1 \qquad (4)$$

that the relative contribution of industry 2 will vary inversely to that of industry 1 at any time during the business cycle. Suppose now that industry 1 is not only the heavier steel consumer per unit of production, or $s_1 - s_2 > 0$, but that it is cyclically more sensitive than total production. Given two positions in the course of the cycle, marked by superscripts ′ and ″, it follows, in the case of a decline,

$$1 > P''_T/P'_T > P''_1/P'_1 \qquad (5)$$

that as the relative importance of industry 1 declines, that of industry 2 increases, or

$$P'_1/P'_T > P''_1/P''_T \quad \text{and} \quad P'_2/P'_T < P''_2/P''_T \qquad (6)$$

From (6) it follows that average consumption of steel will be lower for the second position:

$$s'_T = s_2 + (s_1 - s_2) (P'_1/P'_T) >$$
$$s''_T = s_2 + (s_1 - s_2) (P''_1/P''_T) \qquad (7)$$

since s_2 is inherently positive and $(s_1 - s_2)$ is positive by assumption.

The rate of average steel consumption $s_T = s_T(t)$ is thus cyclically sensitive, that is, it depends upon the cyclical position of P_1/P_T. An obvious example for an industry which is not only a heavy consumer of steel per unit of production, but also cyclically more sensitive than total production, is the behavior of the metal-fabricating industries: machinery and transportation equipment manufactures. Their behavior in the short run and in the long run is shown in the following table with the average rate of steel consumption:

238

Year or Period	Relative Importance of Metal Fabricating in Total Industrial Production, in Percent	Rate of Steel Consumption per Point of the Index of Total Industrial Production, S_T, in Thousands of Tons
1929	20	575
1932	12	264
1937	18.5	501
1938	14.7	357
1923-25	17.3	552
1935-39	16.7	466

If we now explicitly introduce a bench mark for measuring the cyclical position, such as the highest previous peak of total industrial production (more generally, the "associated secular function"), P_T^0, then the rate P_T^0/P_T can be used as a measure of the cyclical position of total industrial production. The simplest form for stating the cyclical sensitivity of the industry i is the linear relationship of the two rates:

$$P_i/P_T = c_i - d_i \,(P_T^0/P_T) \quad (d > 0; i = 1, 2) \qquad (8)$$

All the measures entering (8) must be considered as functions of time t, that is, $P_i = P_i(t)$, $P_T = P_T(t)$, and $P_T^0 = P_T^0(t)$. Because of the identity (4), which holds for any time t, the parameters c_i and d_i are subject to the condition that the c_i's add up to unity, the d_i's to zero.

The presentation of average steel requirements as a function of the relative importance of the component industries, (3), can now be transformed with the help of (8) into a presentation of average steel requirements as a function of the cycle position of total industrial production:

$$s_T = S_T/P_T = s_1 \,[c_1 - d_1 \,(P_T^0/P_T)] + s_2[c_2 - d_2 \,(P_T^0/P_T)]$$

$$= 1/P_T \,[(s_1c_1 + s_2c_2)P_T - (s_1d_1 + s_2d_2)P_T^0]$$

$$= 1/P_T \,[\qquad p \cdot P_T - \qquad q \cdot P_T^0] \qquad (9)$$

Aggregate steel requirements will, therefore, be of the general form

$$S_T = s_T \cdot P_T = p \cdot P_T - q \cdot P_T^0 = -p(P_T^0 - P_T) + (p - q)\,P_T^0 \qquad (G)$$

From the fact that all the s_i's, c_i's, and d_i's are positive, it follows that p and q are also positive. For a given level of indus-

239

trial production, P_T, steel requirements will tend to be lower the higher the bench mark value P_T^0 is, and they will, in general, also tend to be lower the lower P_T is relative to the bench mark P_T^0. The derivation of Formula G holds, not only for the case $n = 2$, but, in general, for any number of industries.

In addition to the "product-mix" effect in the case where cyclical sensitivity is correlated with unit requirements of steel, another factor contributes to the cyclical sensitivity of steel consumption: working-inventory requirements. Working inventories are built up or depleted according to whether a given level of production is reached on the upswing or on the downturn. This is true for every component industry and *ipso facto* for total industrial production itself. When, in the gradual long-run expansion of production, a level of 90 on the Federal Reserve Index was reached from below—as in 1925—working-inventory requirements expanded, as reflected by a rate of 564,000 tons of steel per point on the Index. But when total industrial production, after having reached a high of 110, fell off to a level of 91 on the Index—as in 1930—inventories previously geared to higher production levels became excessive as working inventories and thus depressed the demand for new steel below the level indicated by the long-run expansion of production. Steel requirements in 1930 amounted to 501,000 tons per point on the Index.

Thus the working-inventory factor alone would be able to cause both a moderate rate of increase in steel consumption in a gradual long-run expansion of industrial activity and a much sharper backsliding of steel demand during a recession of production. This is shown by the pattern of successive cycle swings in Chart 1. Since two factors are operative, one might ask whether their effects can be separated. The results of a test introducing the annual rate of change in production as an additional factor in the analysis are reported in Section F-3.

First, however, the general hypothesis embodied in Formula G will be tested.

C. THE ASSOCIATED SECULAR FUNCTION
OF INDUSTRIAL PRODUCTION

In order to test Formula G, it is necessary to develop a suitable measure for the "associated secular function" of the index of industrial production corresponding to the variable P_T^0 of this formula. This series must, in some sense, represent a measure of "normal" production, so that the relation of actual industrial production to it will provide a reasonable measure of cyclical slack or strain.

Such a series could be derived in various ways. One could, for instance, apply directly the specific technique used by Modigliani and define the associated series in the year t, $P_T^0(t)$, as the highest level of total industrial production preceding the year t. Another simple method has been used by A. G. Hart.[8] According to this method, the associated function would consist of a time series of annual points including the successive peaks of industrial production and points interpolated annually between them leading in geometric progression from one peak to the next.

While any of these methods would probably yield a reasonable approximation, a somewhat different approach will be used here, which, at least conceptually, appears more suitable for the purpose on hand. The associated function in any given year will be expressed as an estimate of productive capacity for that year, measured—like production itself—in points of the Index; in other words, as a series measuring the highest level that total industrial production could reach on the basis of productive capacity in existence in that year.

The relation of production to productive capacity is a reasonable over-all measure of cyclical position. Indeed, the difference between actual production and productive capacity seems to be a very good operational measure of the notion of cyclical slack or strain. In addition, such a relation may be expected to indicate the effect of cyclical strain on the activity of producers' equipment industries. These industries are heavy users of steel, the main raw material for producers' equipment. Such a relationship for manufacturing and mining equipment is illustrated in Chart A-1 and Table B-2 (see Appendix B).

The task of developing a measure for over-all productive capacity obviously presents some serious problems, both conceptually and statistically. Some of these problems are mentioned in Appendix A, in which an estimate of productive capacity for every year from 1919 to date is developed. This estimate was constructed on the basis of yearly data on the flow of equipment installed and on yearly estimates of retirements of existing ca-

[8] A. G. Hart, *Money, Debt, and Economic Activity* (Prentice-Hall, 1948), pp. 260ff.

pacity.[9] The estimate represents no more than a rather crude, though useful, over-all approximation of the theoretically relevant concepts. There has been considerable interest in the general problem of developing, both conceptually and statistically, suitable measures of productive capacity. Such measures have a number of important potential applications, of which the present is but one. It is to be hoped that the work now in progress will yield more refined methods of estimation and improved estimates for the past.

D. STATISTICAL TESTS OF
THE HYPOTHESIS

In order to test the hypothesis and to estimate the coefficients of the general formula G, total steel production S_T is correlated with total industrial production P_T (Federal Reserve Index) and with the measure of productive capacity P_{CAP}. The conditions of the period 1919-40 are then summarized as follows:

Formula II

$$S_T = k + p \cdot P_T - q \cdot P_{CAP}$$
$$= 15.40 + 0.857P_T - 0.403P_{CAP}$$
$$[5.48] \quad [0.044] \quad [0.052] \quad R = 0.969$$

The resulting parameters are obviously quite favorable to the hypothesis. The coefficient of P_{CAP} is negative, as expected, and is highly significant by standard statistical tests, being 7.75 times as large as its standard error. The multiple correlation coefficient rises to 0.969, as against a simple correlation of 0.897 for Formula I.

In order to see fully the implications of Formula II, it will be useful to perform certain algebraic transformations. In the first place, it must be remembered that the variable P_{CAP} denotes the maximum level consistent with existing capacity. In general, however, a level of production equal to capacity, that is, a 100 percent rate of use, can hardly be considered normal. Ideally

---

[9] It is likely that installation of equipment is highly sensitive cyclically. Thus, when the surviving annual equipment installations of preceding years (or their capacity equivalents) are cumulated, it must be expected that the series of productive capacity will show an echo effect, that is, ripples of the damped and lagged effect of the business cycle. As far as these ripples are still present, productive capacity is only an approximation of the "associated secular function." The series on productive capacity was originally developed for the Econometric Institute, Inc. It is described in Appendix A. It forms part of the copyrighted service of the Institute, and is presented here by permission of its president, C. F. Roos.

the "normal" rate of use might be defined as that rate at which firms, in the aggregate, do not wish either to expand or to contract their capacity. In general, such a rate of use will be significantly less than 100 percent of P_{CAP}, especially since the measure of capacity is a ceiling for the production during any month of the year and enough slack capacity must be allowed to take care of seasonal fluctuations in production. We assume that 85 percent of capacity represents a normal rate of use. In fact, this assumption is implicit in the method of estimating the capacity series.

On the basis of this assumption, the "normal level of production" for the year t, or $P_N(t)$ would not equal 100 percent of $P_{CAP}(t)$, but only 0.85 $P_{CAP}(t)$ or

$$P_N = P_N(t) = 0.85 P_{CAP}(t) \qquad (10)$$

In the following reformulation of Formula II, P_N, the "normal" level, will be used as the "associated secular function." The qualifications which apply to P_{CAP} (see footnote 9) apply also to P_N. Production, P_T, will not only fall short of capacity, P_{CAP}, but more often than not, of the normal rate of production, $P_N = 0.85 \cdot P_{CAP}$. This was the case in 15 out of 22 prewar observations. Only in 5 cases did P_T exceed P_N. Thus it appeared advisable to introduce the cyclical position of production not as a cyclical strain, $P_T - P_N$, but as a cyclical slack, $P_N - P_T$. It should be noted that the substitution of P_N for P_{CAP}, while logically desirable, does not affect the results substantively.

Substituting (10) into the general formula G and into the formula with numerical parameters (II) leads to

$$
\begin{aligned}
S_T = k & \quad + p \cdot P_T & - (q/0.85) \cdot (0.85 P_{CAP}) & \\
= k & \quad + p \cdot P_T & - \quad q' \quad \cdot \quad P_N & \text{(G-a)} \\
= 15.40 & + 0.857 P_T & - 0.474 \quad \cdot \quad P_N & \text{(II-a)}
\end{aligned}
$$

These formulae may be rewritten in the following forms, which will be used in the following discussion:

$$
\begin{aligned}
S_T = & \quad k \quad + (p - q') \cdot P_T - \quad q'(P_N - P_T) & \text{(G-b)} \\
= & \ 15.40 + \quad\quad 0.383 P_T - 0.474 (P_N - P_T) & \text{(II-b)}
\end{aligned}
$$

or also:

$$
\begin{aligned}
S_T = & \quad k \quad - \quad p \cdot (P_N - P_T) + (p - q') \cdot P_N & \text{(G-c)} \\
= & \ 15.40 - 0.857 (P_N - P_T) + 0.383 \quad \cdot P_N & \text{(II-c)}
\end{aligned}
$$

From the expression on the right-hand side of Formula II-a,

243

it is apparent that as long as P_N remains constant, S_T will tend to change by 857,000 tons per point of the Federal Reserve Index. In the short run, P_N will be relatively stable compared with P_T. Indeed, especially if P_T fluctuates below P_N (this has been called a "cyclical fluctuation" in production), P_N is likely to change very little, if at all. Hence, given a stable value $\overline{P}_N$, the relation between steel output and industrial production during any given cycle may be approximately described by

$$S_T = \quad (k - q' \cdot \overline{P}_N) + \quad p \cdot P_T \qquad \text{(G-d)}$$

$$= (15.40 - 0.474\overline{P}_N) + 0.857 \, P_T \qquad \text{(II-d)}$$

This is a line with considerably steeper slope than the slope of 0.697 million tons per point on the Federal Reserve Index indicated by the "hybrid" Formula I. It is indicated by the dashed-dotted line on Chart 1. As P_N changes—that is, increases from one cycle to the next—this line will shift to the right as indicated by the configurations on Chart 1 for the years 1919-22, 1929-36, and 1937-39.

Alternative statements of Formula G—(G-b) and (G-c)—are designed to bring out the long-run aspects of the demand for steel more clearly.

A long-run change in the demand for steel may now be operationally defined as a change in demand S, associated with a change in the over-all level of production P, when enough time has been allowed for the level of capacity to adjust itself to the new level of production. Clearly this definition of "long run" is basically consistent with the traditional Marshallian notion. By means of Formula II-b, the long-run change in the demand for steel which is associated with a change in production can be computed. Suppose the starting point is the year 0 with a level of production $P_T(0)$. Suppose now the level of capacity is fully adjusted; then

$$P_T(0) - P_N(0) = 0$$

and therefore

$$S_T(0) = 15.40 + 0.383 \, P_T(0)$$

Suppose that production rises to a new level

$$P_T(1) = P_T(0) + \Delta P_T(0)$$

If, as has been assumed, capacity is fully adjusted to this new level, or

$$P_T(1) - P_N(1) = 0$$

244

and hence

$$S_T(1) = 15.40 + 0.383\,P_T(1)$$

then the change in demand will be given by

$$\Delta S_T = 0.383\,\Delta P_T$$

Thus Formula II implies that, in the long run, the demand for steel would tend to change only 0.383 million tons per point of the production index, as contrasted with a rate of 0.857 million tons per point of the production index in the short run and a rate of 0.697 million tons on the production index in the hybrid Formula I. The equation obtained for the vanishing cyclical slack $(P_N - P_T) = 0$ is

$$\begin{aligned}S_T = k + (p - q')P_T &= k + (p - q')P_N = k + n \cdot P_N \\ &= 15.40 + 0.383\,P_N \end{aligned} \qquad \text{(G-e)}$$

This equation may thus be considered an estimate of the long-run relation between the demand for steel and industrial production. The coefficient $n = p - q'$ is an estimate of the long-run marginal steel requirements per unit of change in the production index. The long-run relation is indicated by the slope of the dashed line in Chart 1 and by column 1 of Table B-4 (see Appendix B).

E. EXTRAPOLATION TESTS

The introduction of the variable P_N in addition to P_T resulted in a substantial reduction in the variance which was not explained by Formula I. A more significant test of Formulae I and II, because the parameters are based on prewar observations only, is to use these equations for an estimate of the demand for steel for the postwar period, say, around 1950, when production was at much higher levels. Since the change in production between 1940 and 1950 can be regarded largely as a long-run change, Formula II should be expected to yield somewhat more accurate results than Formula I. At the same time a margin of error considerably larger than in the period of observation must be expected, since the stretch of years between 1940 and 1950 is substantial, and some changes in the basic relation between production and steel requirements might have occurred.

If Formula II is used to estimate the demand for steel at the 1950 level of production (200), it is also necessary to specify the assumption about the associated secular function, or its ap-

245

proximation P_N. An assumption of no cyclical slack, that is, complete adjustment of capacity to this production level, yields the estimate $S_T(1950) = 15.40 + 0.383(200) = 92$ million net tons of steel. The actual level of production in 1950 was 96.8 million net tons, so that this long-run projection represents an underestimate of about 5 percent. For the year 1951, the underestimate is of the same order of magnitude, with an estimated level of 99.6 million tons and an actual level of steel output of 105.1 million tons. This represents a striking improvement over Formula I, the use of which leads to overestimates in the order of 25 and 30 percent, respectively, for these two years. (See Table B-3, column 2, in Appendix B.) With a value for $P_T(1948)$ of 192, the long-run projection of steel demand is 88.9 million net tons; with a value for $P_T(1949)$ of 176, it turns out to be 82.8 million net tons. These estimates compare with actual levels of steel output of $S_T(1948) = 88.6$ million net tons and $S_T(1949) = 78$ million net tons. In every case the error is in the order of 5 percent or less. These results can also be obtained from Chart 1, by reading the projected long-run steel demand at each level of total industrial production from the dashed line showing this long-term projection. The vertical excess of actual steel output from each of these levels gives the extent of the deviation in millions of net tons.

Actually it is possible to develop some supplementary, though tentative, information on P_N for the postwar period. It is shown in Table B-2, column 4. Substituting these values in Formula II leads to a more accurate extrapolation, shown in column 3 of Table B-3 and in column 1 of Table B-4. For the five-year period 1947-51, actual steel production averaged 90.7 million net tons, estimated steel production derived by Formula II amounted to 92.5 million net tons. The absolute average error is 7.4 million net tons.

At this point it may suffice to point out that Formula II performs far better than Formula I and that its use for long-run projections is reasonably satisfactory. Before further extrapolation tests are undertaken, some refinements of the hypothesis must be introduced.

F. SOME REFINEMENTS OF THE HYPOTHESIS

1. Changes in rates of consumption of steel within the period of observation, 1919-40

The period 1919-40 is a long one, in the course of which some changes in the underlying relation between steel output and total industrial production might have occurred. To test this hypothesis, two sets of coefficients, p and n, one for the period 1919-29, the other for the period 1930-40, were simultaneously reestimated. We call the analysis of total production of steel for ingots and castings with different levels of p and n Formula III. To distinguish the reestimated coefficients and the constant from those derived for the period as a whole in Formulae G-a—e, the number of the formula is introduced as a subscript of the parameter, e.g., p_{II}, p_{III}, etc. refer to the coefficients of total industrial production in the general formula G-a or to that of the cyclical slack $(P_N - P_T)$ in Formula G-c, while n_{II}, n_{III} refer to the coefficient of P_T in (G-b). Finally k_{II}, k_{III} refer to the constant term, which covers the entire period 1919-40 in each of these formulae.

A comparison of the coefficient p_{III} for the two separate periods (see Table 1) reveals a substantial decline from the twenties to the thirties in the short-term rate of steel consumption and a less pronounced decline in the long-term rate n_{III}. There are good reasons for these declines in steel requirements per unit of production. It is probable, in the short term, that improvements in the control of flow and the stocking up of raw materials for operating inventories took place. The cooperation of some steel producers with automobile manufacturers in an effort to tighten up steel delivery schedules is one of several examples. In the long run, use of better-grade steel and more elaborate end-use specifications reduced the requirement per unit of output. How closely Formula III fits the data can be seen from Chart 2. In this chart, actual steel production is shown as a heavy solid line, while steel production as estimated from Formula III is represented by a thin line. (For all other lines see Section H.)

2. Demand for steel for the domestic market

Not all finished steel produced from the output of steel ingots

TABLE 1

Comparison of Three Alternative Estimates of Coefficients for the General Formula $S = k + n \cdot p_N - p \cdot (P_N - P_T)$

Parameter	Period				
	1919-40	1919-28	1929	1930	1931-40
Constant					
k_{II}	15.40(5.48)	—	—	—	—
k_{III}	5.575(10.7669)	—	—	—	—
k_{IV}	0.744(10.4623)	—	—	—	—
Coefficient for the normal rate of production					
n_{II}	0.383(0.076)	—	—	—	—
n_{III}	—	0.5073(0.2372)	0.4922	0.4719	0.4568(0.1227)
n_{IV}	—	0.5225(0.2216)	0.4986	0.4668	0.4429(0.1191)
Coefficient for the cyclical strain, $P_N - P_T$					
p_{II}	0.857(0.044)	—	—	—	—
p_{III}	—	0.9916(0.1491)	0.9323	0.8532	0.7939(0.0486)
p_{IV}	—	1.0705(0.1448)	0.9413	0.7690	0.6398(0.0471)

Note: Standard errors of regression coefficients are given in parentheses. The transition between the twenties and the thirties has been derived heuristically. Various types of splicing were tested and the one with the least error of estimate selected. This particular form of splicing does not jump immediately from the higher level of the parameters in the twenties to the lower level of the parameters for the thirties, but provides for two intermediate stages in the transition: the year 1928 is the last year of the higher level, the year 1931 the first year of the lower level for the parameters. In descending from the higher level, the year 1929 is placed 0 of the total jump below the higher level; 1930 is placed 0.3 of the total jump above the lower level for the parameters.

and castings is consumed in the domestic market.[10] While United States business cycles may affect the rest of the world, factors other than industrial production in the United States also have been determinants of foreign demand for American steel. For instance, the shortage of steel in other countries after each of the two world wars caused exports of steel to rise more sharply than domestic consumption. The proportion of United States domestic raw steel production ultimately shipped abroad as finished steel has varied from 3 percent to 18 percent during the last thirty years. For this reason the coefficients of Formula III were reestimated and only the domestic supply of steel was used as a dependent variable.

[10] In order to estimate this portion, it was necessary to translate the exports of rolled steel (*Metal Statistics, 1951* [American Metal Market, 1951], p. 260) into the equivalent steel for ingots and castings. The conversion factors were derived by comparing total rolled steel for sale with total ingot production, assuming a one-month lag of rolled steel shipments after the production of ingots.

CHART 2

Steel Output and Capacity and Estimated Demand
for Steel at Various Levels of Industrial Production

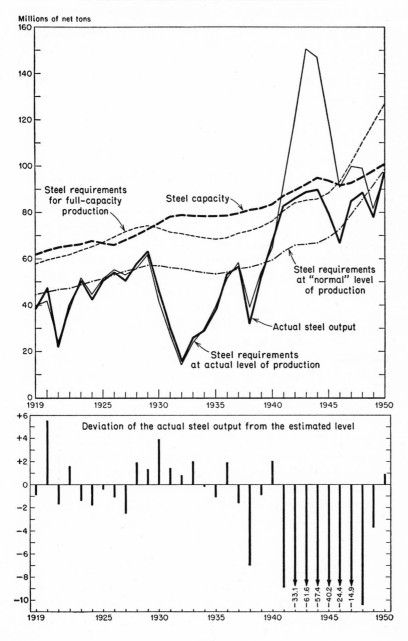

Millions of net tons

Steel requirements
for full-capacity
production

Steel capacity

Steel requirements
at "normal" level
of production

Actual steel output

Steel requirements
at actual level of production

Deviation of the actual steel output from the estimated level

−33.1 −61.6 −57.4 −40.2 −24.4 −14.9

249

The estimates thus obtained are denoted, k_{IV}, n_{IV}, and p_{IV}. They are compared in Table 1 with the various estimates discussed previously.

An interesting result of the successive refinements of the analysis is the progressive fall in the constant term from 15.40 million net tons for Formula II to less than 1 million net tons for Formula IV.

It should be noted that the original hypothesis, as expressed in Formula G, lacked a constant term. There is no reason to expect that this condition would be exactly satisfied by a regression equation fitted to the data. The measure of total production is not only directly representative of manufacturing and mining industries consuming steel, but it acts also as an indirect measure of the variations in the demand of nonmanufacturing steel consumers, such as railroads or public utilities. Nonetheless the constant term of 15.40 million net tons was uncomfortably large. It had to absorb the effect of averaging over the entire period 1919-40 in the determination of the value of n_{II}. Inspection of n_{III} indicates that while the rate for the thirties was 10 percent below that of the twenties, it was still 16 percent above the "average" rate of n_{II} for the entire period. The latter is, therefore, not a pure average of the two rates 0.5073 and 0.4568, which ought to be around 0.48, but contains also the slurring effect of moving from the higher long-run relation to the lower long-run relation for the later years. The difference in the amount of variation, explained by an average of the long-run parameters of Formula III and by that of Formula II, appears as a difference of about 10 million net tons between the constants of the two formulae.

Formula IV not only confirms the decline in the rate of steel requirements, but suggests that the difference in this respect between the thirties and the twenties is even greater than that indicated by Formula III: for p, the drop amounts to 20 percent in the case of Formula III and 40 percent in the case of Formula IV; for n to 10 percent and 15 percent. An analysis of these shifts from the viewpoint of technology would be desirable. The Formula III estimates of 95.9 million net tons for 1950 and 104.6 million net tons for 1951 come closer to the actual performance of 96.8 and 105.1 million net tons than the Formula IV estimates of 92.8 and 102.4 million net tons.

The mean square deviation for the period 1947-51 amounts to

7.6 million net tons in the case of Formula IV, 8.3 million net tons in the case of Formula III, 8.5 million net tons in the case of Formula II, and to 27.8 million net tons in the case of Formula I.

As stated earlier, it should be noted that there are other segments of steel consumption in addition to exports which are not measured by the Federal Reserve Index of Industrial Production. A certain portion of steel is shipped directly to railroads, utilities, waterworks, farmers, government, etc., and thus does not pass through any manufacturing stage outside the steel industry. To this extent the parameter of Formula IV contains an indirect weight for such steel consumers.

3. The rate of change of industrial production as a factor in the demand for steel

In the theoretical discussion of the basic approach to the general Formula G, the product-mix change was given as one reason why the cyclical position of industrial production ought to be considered as well as the rate of production. The working-inventory requirements for steel were given as another factor. Working-inventory changes resulting from changes in the level of production are not necessarily cyclical in nature. It may, therefore, be asked whether we can substitute the change in the *level* of production for the cyclical slack of production and reach an equally satisfactory explanation of steel requirements. Will the introduction of the change in the level of production as a third supplementary variable contribute to a sharpening of the analysis and to a separation of the "product-mix" from the "working-inventory" effect?

In order to obviate, at least partially, the inadequacy of annual data on production changes as indicators of inventory movements, two different forms of the annual change in production have been tested, both by use of Formula II.

a. The change from the last year—which amounts roughly to the change during the preceding fiscal year—has shown a positive effect. At maximum it amounted in 1938 to 4.8 million tons, if used as a substitute for the cyclical slack in production, and to 1.8 million tons, if used as a supplementary third variable. In general, a change of one point on the production index is accompanied by a change in steel output of nearly 200,000 tons and 75,000 tons, respectively. The reduction in unexplained variation resulting from the introduction of the change during the fiscal year is, however, insignificant.

b. The change during the calendar year—which points further into the future—has a negative effect of 46,000 tons per point on the production index, if used as a substitute, and of 39,000 tons if used as a supplementary variable. Its introduction scarcely reduces the unexplained variation.

If an analysis of inventory changes based only on annual data can be considered fair evidence, the effect of these annual changes is minor, or insignificant, and an *ex post* adjustment, rather than an immediate adjustment or anticipation.

G. EXTRAPOLATIVE VALUE

1. *Wartime conditions*

The formulae cannot be applied to steel requirements under wartime conditions: P_{CAP} is a measure of peacetime civilian capacity. Total military and civilian production exceeded peacetime capacity in the two main war years 1943 and 1944 by about 80 points. The measure of production expanded by 137 points over 1935-39, while peacetime civilian capacity, which excludes the capacity of ordnance and similar plants, advanced only 28 points. Peacetime capacity also does not allow for multiple-shift use of a plant if normally it is used only in single-shift operations. It also excludes the obsolete or obsolescent stand-by equipment returned temporarily to operation under emergency conditions.[11] The development of a properly calibrated measure of wartime additions to capacity, which would take all the distortions into account and allow for the shifts in the composition of production, has not been undertaken. A proper test of the formulae by extrapolation is, therefore, confined to the postwar period.

[11] The war period was characterized by a rapid expansion of the machinery and transportation equipment industries. This can be explained, in part, by the greater amount of fabrication and inspection actually required for the output of combat material, and, in part, statistically, by the use of labor input as a measure of output. During the prewar period, 1919-40, the metal-fabricating segment of the production index amounted to 1.1 times its basic metal segment plus 1 point on the index. The equivalent for the postwar period was about 11 points higher than the prewar relation. During the height of the war, 1943 and 1944, the metal-fabricating segment actually rose 90 points above the prewar relation. In 1951, it rose 4 points above the postwar relation.

2. The postwar period

Formulae II, III, and IV overestimate steel requirements in the first few years of the postwar period. This result emphasizes the temporary effect of wartime demand and suggests that steel requirements per unit of production may have declined. On the other hand, these overestimates decline from year to year until they change into underestimates either in 1949 or in 1950. Such a pattern would point to the existence of real steel shortages, especially in the strike years 1946 and 1949. On the whole, it seems not unlikely that the truth is somewhere between the two extremes: part of the overestimate from 1946 to 1949 may reflect a true shortage of steel, while part of it may reflect a genuine overestimate. Formula IV would result in a gross overestimate of about 40.7 million net tons for the three years 1946 to 1948. If—by way of an illustration—this gross overestimate is formally segregated into a "genuine" steel shortage of 25 million net tons and a "genuine" overestimate of about 15 million net tons, the effect on the parameters of Formula III or IV can be expressed as a drop of 8 percent in the short-term parameter, as compared with a drop of 40 percent in the same parameter between the twenties and the thirties; and a drop of 3 percent in the long-run parameter n_{IV} as compared with a drop of 15 percent between the twenties and the thirties. Thus the formal assumption of a steel shortage of about 25 million net tons during 1946-48 would suggest that a further drop of unit requirements for steel has occurred, amounting to about one-fifth of that which characterized the transition from the twenties to the thirties. Further evidence will be needed before a definite statement can be made.

H. STEEL CAPACITY AND STEEL REQUIREMENTS FOR FULL-CAPACITY PRODUCTION

One interesting application of Formula G is its use in estimating "steel requirements at capacity operations," that is, steel requirements for a level of industrial production equal to capacity. This represents an estimate of the maximum steel requirements in any given year.

The original formula

$$S(P_{\text{T}}, P_{\text{CAP}}) = k + p \cdot P_{\text{T}} - q \cdot P_{\text{CAP}}$$

is a convenient starting point for estimating "steel requirements at capacity operations." Substitution of $P_T = P_{CAP}$ leads to

$$S(P_{CAP}) = S(P_{CAP}, P_{CAP}) = k + (p - q)P_{CAP}$$
$$= k + (n + q' - q) P_{CAP} = k + (n + q' - 0.85q')P_{CAP}$$
$$= k + [n + 0.15(p - n)]P_{CAP} \qquad (11)$$

Using the values $n_{III} = 0.5073$ to 0.4568 and $p_{III} = 0.9916$ to 0.7939, the coefficients of P_{CAP} assume the following values: for 1919-28, 0.580; for 1929, 0.558; for 1930, 0.529; and for 1931-40, 0.507.

These estimates of "steel requirements at capacity operations" are shown as a time series in Chart 2 and compared with steel capacity, actual and estimated steel production, and steel requirements at the "normal" level of production (that is, 85 percent of capacity). "Steel requirements" according to Formulae II, III, and IV are shown for the "normal" level of production in columns 1, 2, and 3 and for capacity industrial operations in columns 4 and 5 of Table B-4 (see Appendix B).

An inspection of Chart 2 reveals the relative closeness of actual steel capacity and "steel requirements at capacity operations" as estimated from Formula III. During the thirties—as a result of the decline and the slow recovery of industrial capacity—"steel requirements at capacity operations" fell below actual steel capacity, which remained relatively constant. If the rate of short-term, or output-determined, and the rate of long-term, or capacity-determined, steel requirements are applied to the postwar period without any further reduction, it appears that industrial capacity has expanded much faster than steel capacity. During 1946, when existing steel capacity dropped nearly 5 percent as a result of writing off obsolete facilities, "steel requirements at capacity operations" started to exceed actual steel capacity. In fact, steel capacity fell so far behind that it was only 2 million tons above the steel requirements for the normal level of activity (85 percent of capacity) for the year 1950, thus leaving little leeway for the expansion of activity beyond this level. Since steel capacity was so much lower in 1950 than the steel requirements indicated by estimates of peacetime production capacity, one might expect it to have had a limiting effect on the expansion of industrial production in recent years.

I. STEEL CAPACITY AS A LIMIT TO THE TOTAL LEVEL OF INDUSTRIAL PRODUCTION

An estimate of the ceiling imposed on the possible level of total industrial production by the available capacity for producing steel can be derived by inverting Formula G and solving it for total industrial production P_T. From

$$S_T = k + p \cdot P_T - q \cdot P_{CAP} \qquad (12)$$

it follows that

$$P_T = (q/p)P_{CAP} - (1/p)(S - k) \qquad (13)$$

Substituting first $q = 0.85 \cdot q'$ and then $q' = p - n$ into the formula leads to

Formula V

$$P_T = 0.85(1 - n/p)P_{CAP} + (1/p)(S - k)$$

Formula V is to be regarded as measuring the amount of industrial production that can be supported by a given supply of steel, S. Introduction of estimates of the parameters n, p, and k and of the level of steel capacity S_{CAP} in Formula V yields an estimate of the maximum level of industrial production consistent with the available capacity to produce steel. If the values assumed by the coefficients for the period after 1930 ($n_{III} = 0.4568$, $p_{III} = 0.7939$, and $k_{III} = 5.575$) are used, and if the values prevailing in 1952 are approximated by P_{CAP} (1952) $= 286$ and S_{CAP} (1952) $= 111.5$ million net tons, the production potential can be estimated at

$$0.4246 \cdot 243 + 1.2596(111.5 - 0.0 - 5.6) = 237 \text{ points} \qquad (14)$$

The ceiling for total industrial production is determined by the steel supply for the domestic market, or $111.5 - 3.8$ million net tons, rather than the total steel supply. Using the comparable parameters of Formula IV for the period after 1930 results in

$$0.3078 \cdot 243 + 1.5630(111.5 - 3.8 - 0.7) = 239 \qquad (15)$$

Introducing the tentative reduction of steel requirements developed in Section G-2 would increase the industrial production potential to about 245 points, or 6 points above the results based on 1930-40 parameters.

J. SUMMARY

Earlier investigations have demonstrated that price alone is not a major determinant of changes in steel demand. More and more emphasis has been placed upon the shift of the demand function itself. Steel constitutes a unique raw material for many durable goods. The area where substitutions are technologically or economically feasible comprises only a minor fraction of aggregate steel demand. This being the case, how will the steel consumer who wants to stay in business react to an increase in steel prices? He will ask whether it is possible to shift the whole cost increase to his customers without impairing the size of the market for his product and he will consider whether his profits permit him to absorb the price increase. Only in a few cases will he find it possible to use a substitute or to reduce his unit demand for steel on short notice. In the long run, one must expect steel savings to result more from the continual striving for efficiency and general cost reduction rather than in response to isolated shocks of increases in the price of steel. Thus, using the language of the classical demand and supply analysis, it is necessary to explain the shifts in the demand function itself. The extent of the shifts of the demand function will make shifts along the demand curve due to price changes appear unimportant.

An attempt at explaining shifts in the demand function might be expected to consider industrial production as such or the activity of an individual steel-consuming industry. But this approach can be refined. Our method refines it by taking into account not only the over-all level of production, but also its cyclical position. The cyclical variation in the "product-mix" of industrial output and variation in the "working-inventory requirements" will be reflected in the short-term component. This refinement of the approach leads to Formula II, which provides not only an improved explanation of the demand for steel during the period of observation, 1919-40, but also leads to radically different and far more accurate results when used for long-run extrapolation. A further attempt at estimating the effect of technological progress in steel consumption within the 22 years under consideration resulted in Formula III.

There was an indication that the output destined for the foreign market was often distorted substantially by exogenous factors not related to the level of domestic industrial activity. Since foreign demand accounted for a fluctuating share of the total steel output, varying from 3 percent to 18 percent, the output for the domestic market was investigated separately. This relation is described by Formula IV.

Finally, it seemed useful to explore the relation of steel capacity to over-all industrial capacity, both to gauge the adequacy of steel capacity during the period of observation as well as thereafter and to gain a better understanding of the concept and statistical construction of industrial capacity. Formula V expresses industrial peacetime capacity in terms of steel requirements. An inversion of the process could be used to determine the cyclical expansion permitted by the level of rated steel capacity, but this is subject to the qualification that the estimate of steel requirements per unit of output is based on peacetime goods. If industrial production comprises a large portion of combat material other than ships, unit steel requirements are lowered and allow a considerable extension of the area of cyclical expansion. This happened during World War II when more intensive use of facilities also caused industrial activity to exceed the peacetime level of industrial capacity.

The successive steps of this analysis are: (1) distinguishing between the long-term and short-term components of demand, (2) distinguishing between conditions of steel demand in the twenties and the thirties, and (3) distinguishing between export and domestic demand. Some of the procedures as well as some tools of the analysis are of a tentative character and subject to further improvements, but it is hoped that the general outline of the procedure will be useful for a similar analysis of raw materials or finished products.

APPENDIX A

Peacetime Civilian Capacity for Industrial Production

The series on peacetime civilian capacity for industrial production used in the analysis of steel requirements is a revision of an earlier series, developed by C. F. Roos, V. V. Szeliski, and F. L. Alt before World War II.[12] A more detailed account of the conceptual problems, construction, and limitations of this series will be found in a forthcoming paper. The description presented here is confined to the essential elements.

[12] The series forms an integral part of the copyrighted service of the Econometric Institute, Inc. The data and the series are presented here by permission of C. F. Roos, president of the Institute.

The basic principles of the capacity series were used by Roos in somewhat cruder form in 1937 in order to point out that in spite of an army of nearly 8 million unemployed, the mechanical facilities were becoming scarce and that, therefore, demand for investment goods would take a sharp upturn.

257

The series is constructed on the basis of annual data on installation of equipment in manufacturing and mining given in 1935-39 prices (column 1, Table A-1). It is essentially a portion of the producers' equipment data of the gross national product account of the Department of Commerce[13] deflated by H. Shavell's price indexes for capital equipment.[14] The series has been carried back with the help of data developed by S. Kuznets and W. H. Shaw.[15] Data after 1945 have been derived from subsidiary information and are only tentative.

The efficiency factor shown in column 2 of Table A-1 converts the dollar volume of equipment installed (column 1) into terms of gross addition to capacity (column 3). A gradual linear increase in initial efficiency has been assumed. This increase is implicitly given once the bench marks for capacity are set, and the pattern and length of retirement assumed. The retirement pattern applied to gross addition to capacity assumes a full life of 16 years before 1939 and 14 years for the later period. It is a compromise between a straight-line retirement for 16 years and an 8-year step function dropping from 100 to 0 percent survival. A one-parametric sequence of such retirement has been developed by B. F. Kimball.[16] The first eight years of the symmetric retirement pattern for 16 years indicate the following survival values: 1.000, 1.000, 0.994, 0.977, 0.933, 0.841, 0.692, 0.500. Column 4 of Table A-1 represents the portion of capacity retired during calendar year t. If column 4 is subtracted from the gross addition for the same year (column 3), the net addition to capacity (column 5) is derived. Going forward and backward from the bench mark level of 126 for the end of 1929, the annual capacity series is computed (column 6). Interpolating the midyear capacity, together with total industrial production for the calendar year (column 8), determines the rate of capacity use (column 9).

[13] "National Income Supplements" to the *Survey of Current Business*, July 1947, table 32, p. 45; and July 1950, p. 26.

[14] Henry Shavell, "Price Deflators for Consumer Commodities and Capital Equipment, 1929-1942," *Survey of Current Business*, May 1943, pp. 13ff. The deflation of producers' equipment by segments was undertaken before the appearance of "Estimates of Gross National Product in Constant Dollars, 1929-1949," *Survey of Current Business*, January 1951, p. 9.

[15] Simon Kuznets, *Commodity Flow and Capital Formation*, Vol. I (NBER, 1938); William H. Shaw, *Value of Commodity Output since 1869* (NBER, 1947).

[16] Bradford F. Kimball, "A System of Life Tables for Physical Property," *Econometrica*, September 1947.

The capacity series presented here is an over-all series. It is not an aggregation of capacities in individual industries, which, by necessity, must be higher than the over-all series so long as imbalances between consuming and supplying industries exist. Its bench marks have been developed for years of peak production. Assuming that "normal" production is characterized by 15 percent unused, stand-by capacity to take care of seasonal and other peaks during the year or to meet emergencies, the "peak" rate of operations was set halfway between the 85 percent "normal" rate of operations and the 100 percent capacity rate of operations.

Paralleling the analysis of steel demand is an estimate of the relative importance of equipment for manufacturing and mining in total industrial production, based on the rate of operations during the preceding fiscal year. Introducing P_{EMM} for producers' equipment for manufacturing and mining in points of the total production index, and

$$r_{\overline{t-\frac{1}{2}}} = [P_T(t-\tfrac{1}{2})]/[P_{CAP}(t-1)]$$

the rate of operations in percent of capacity, we have

Formula VI

$$P_{EMM}/R_T = P_{EMM}(t)/P_T(t) = 1.794 + 0.479 \cdot r_{\overline{t-\frac{1}{2}}}$$

The volume of equipment for manufacturing and mining is translated from constant 1935-39 dollars into terms of the production index by a conversion factor of $315.8 million (1935-39 dollars) per point on the index developed for the output of capital goods as a whole. Table A-2 contains the necessary annual data and indicates the computations. Except for 1937, the war years 1944-45, when investment anticipated reconversion, and 1950, the year in which defense investment was accentuated by fears of material shortages, the actual observations differ from the calculated relative importance of producers' equipment by not more than 0.7 percent of the production index. These limits are shown in Chart A-1, which compares the output of equipment for manufacturing and mining industries (in percent of total industrial production) with the rate of operations during the preceding fiscal year (in percent of capacity).

This is rather remarkable, since the dollar volume of new equipment installed is stated in nondescript constant dollars: it does not say whether $100 worth of equipment is for a steel mill or a candy factory. It cannot be expected that the output po-

TABLE A-1

CAPACITY IN MANUFACTURING AND MINING, 1918-1950

Year	Equipment Installed (in Millions of Dollars, 1935-39 Prices) (1)	Efficiency, (t − 1900) × 0.170787 (2)	Gross Capacity Added (IN POINTS OF THE FRB INDEX) (3)	Gross Capacity Retired (4)	Net Capacity Added (5)	Capacity at End of Year, 1935-39=100 (6)	Capacity as of July 1 (1935-39=100) (7)	FRB Index of Production (1935-39=100) (8)	Rate of Operation, (8) ÷ (7) (in Percent) (9)
1918	1,597	3.074	4.91	1.49	3.42	88.34			
1919	1,398	3.245	4.53	1.68	2.86	91.20	89.77	72	80.2
1920	1,541	3.416	5.26	1.88	3.38	94.58	92.89	75	80.7
1921	889	3.587	3.19	2.11	1.08	95.66	95.12	58	61.0
1922	1,259	3.757	4.73	2.41	2.32	97.98	96.82	73	75.4
1923	1,675	3.928	6.58	2.80	3.78	101.76	99.87	88	88.1
1924	1,468	4.099	6.02	3.28	2.74	104.50	103.13	82	79.5
1925	1,697	4.270	7.25	3.77	3.48	107.98	106.24	90	84.7
1926	1,827	4.440	8.11	4.18	3.93	111.91	109.95	96	87.3
1927	1,672	4.611	7.71	4.45	3.26	115.17	113.54	95	83.7
1928	1,892	4.782	9.05	4.61	4.44	119.61	117.39	99	84.3
1929	2,256	4.953	11.17	4.78	6.39	126.00	122.80	110	89.6
1930	1,647	5.124	8.44	5.08	3.36	129.36	127.68	91	71.3
1931	1,181	5.294	6.25	5.55	0.70	130.06	129.71	75	57.8
1932	772	5.465	4.22	6.14	−1.92	128.14	129.10	58	44.9
1933	755	5.636	4.26	6.77	−2.51	125.63	126.88	69	54.4
1934	967	5.807	5.61	7.39	−1.77	123.86	124.75	75	60.1
1935	1,307	5.978	7.81	7.94	−0.13	123.73	123.79	87	70.3
1936	1,906	6.148	11.72	8.32	3.40	127.13	125.43	103	82.1
1937	1,918	6.319	12.12	8.36	3.76	130.89	129.01	113	87.6
1938	1,407	6.490	9.13	7.99	1.14	132.03	131.46	89	67.7
1939	1,635	6.661	10.89	7.31	3.58	135.61	133.82	109	81.5

TABLE A-1 (concluded)

Year	Equipment Installed (in Millions of Dollars, 1935-39 Prices) (1)	Efficiency, (t − 1900) × 0.170787 (2)	Gross Capacity Added (3)	Gross Capacity Retired (4)	Net Capacity Added (5)	Capacity at End of Year, 1935-39 = 100 (6)	Capacity as of July 1, 1935-39 = 100 (7)	FRB Index of Production (1935-39 = 100) (8)	Rate of Operation, (8) ÷ (7) (in Percent) (9)
			(IN POINTS OF THE FRB INDEX)						
1940	2,146	6.831	14.66	7.48	7.18	142.79	139.20	125	89.8
1941	2,560	7.002	17.93	7.48	10.45	153.25	148.02	162	109.5
1942	1,586	7.173	11.38	7.98	3.40	156.65	154.95	199	128.4
1943	1,278	7.343	9.38	9.35	0.03	156.68	156.67	239	152.5
1944	1,794	7.515	13.48	10.99	2.49	159.17	157.93	235	148.8
1945	2,436	7.685	18.72	11.77	6.95	166.12	162.65	203	124.8
1946	3,400	7.856	26.71	12.68	14.03	180.15	173.14	170	98.2
1947	3,800	8.027	30.50	13.11	17.39	197.54	188.85	187	99.0
1948	3,700	8.198	30.33	13.45	16.88	214.42	205.98	192	93.2
1949	3,500	8.369	29.29	13.62	15.67	230.09	222.26	176	79.2
1950	4,150	8.539	35.43	16.08	19.35	249.45	238.6	200	83.8

TABLE A-2

THE RECURSION FOR THE RENEWAL AND GROWTH OF PRODUCTION CAPACITY, 1919-1950

Year	Peacetime Civilian Capacity (Beginning of Calendar Year), $P_{CAP}(t-1)$ (1)	Total Civilian Industrial Production (Fiscal Year), $P_T(t-\frac{1}{2})$ (2)	Rate of Operations (Fiscal Year, Percent), $r_{t-\frac{1}{2}}$ (3)	Share of Equipment for Manufacturing and Mining in Civilian Industrial Production (Percent)		Civilian Industrial Production (Calendar Year) $P_T(t)$ (6)	Output of Equipment for Manufacturing and Mining in Points of Total Industrial Production		
				Calculated, $s_t(r_{t-\frac{1}{2}}) = 1.794 + 0.0479\, r_{t-\frac{1}{2}}$ (4)	Actual, s_t $(8) \div (6)$ (5)		Calculated, $(4) \times (6)$ (7)	Actual, $P_{EMM}(t)$ (8)	Deviation, $(8)-(7)$ (9)
1919	—	71	80.4	5.65	6.15	72	4.07	4.43	+0.36
1920	91.2	77	84.4	5.84	6.51	75	4.38	4.88	+0.50
1921	94.6	64	67.7	5.04	4.85	58	2.92	2.81	-0.11
1922	95.7	64	66.9	5.00	5.47	73	3.65	3.99	+0.34
1923	98.0	84	85.7	5.90	6.02	88	5.19	5.30	+0.11
1924	101.8	85	83.5	5.79	5.67	82	4.75	4.65	-0.10
1925	104.5	85	81.3	5.69	5.96	90	5.12	5.36	+0.24
1926	108.0	93	86.1	5.92	6.03	96	5.68	5.79	+0.11
1927	111.9	97	86.7	5.95	5.56	95	5.65	5.29	-0.36
1928	115.2	95	82.5	5.75	6.09	99	5.69	5.99	+0.30
1929	119.6	107	89.5	6.08	6.49	110	6.69	7.14	+0.45
1930	126.0	103	81.7	5.71	5.73	91	5.20	5.22	+0.02
1931	129.4	82	63.4	4.83	4.98	75	3.62	3.74	+0.12
1932	130.1	65	50.0	4.19	4.21	58	2.43	2.44	+0.01
1933	128.1	60	46.8	4.04	3.46	69	2.79	2.39	-0.40
1934	125.6	76	60.5	4.69	4.08	75	3.52	3.06	-0.46
1935	123.9	78	63.0	4.81	4.75	87	4.18	4.14	-0.04
1936	123.7	94	76.0	5.43	5.85	103	5.59	6.03	+0.44
1937	127.1	114	89.7	6.09	5.36	113	6.88	6.07	-0.81
1938	130.9	95	72.6	5.27	5.02	89	4.69	4.46	-0.23
1939a	132.0	98	74.2	5.35	4.80	108	5.78	5.18	-0.60

TABLE A-2 (concluded)

Year	Peacetime Civilian Capacity (Beginning of Calendar Year -1), $P_{CAP}(t-1)$ (1)	Total Civilian Industrial Production (Fiscal Year), $P_T(t-\frac{1}{2})$ (2)	Rate of Operations (Fiscal Year), Percent, $r_{t-\frac{1}{2}}$ (3)	Share of Equipment for Manufacturing and Mining in Civilian Industrial Production (Percent)		Civilian Industrial Production (Calendar Year) $P_T(t)$ (6)	Output of Equipment for Manufacturing and Mining in Points of the Index of Total Industrial Production		
				Calculated, $s_t(r_{t-\frac{1}{2}})$ $= 1.794 +$ 0.0479 $r_{t-\frac{1}{2}}$ (4)	Actual, s_t $(8) \div (6)$ (5)		Calculated, $(4) \times (6)$ (7)	Actual, $P_{EMM}(t)$ (8)	Deviation, $(8) - (7)$ (9)
1940[a]	135.6	113.5	83.7	5.80	5.71	119	6.90	6.79	-0.11
1941[a]	142.8	124.5	87.2	5.97	6.23	130	7.76	8.10	$+0.34$
1942[a]	153.2	111	72.5	5.27	5.46	92	4.85	5.03	$+0.18$
1943[a]	156.7	86	54.9	4.42	5.06	80	3.54	4.05	$+0.51$
1944[a]	156.7	80	51.1	4.24	7.10	80	3.39	5.68	$+2.29$
1945[a]	159.2	81	50.9	4.23	7.89	90	3.81	7.71	$+3.90$
1946	166.1	137	82.5	5.75	6.34	170	9.78	10.76	$+0.98$
1947	180.2	183	101.6	6.66	6.44	187	12.45	12.04	-0.41
1948	197.5	189	95.7	6.38	6.10	192	12.25	11.71	-0.54
1949	214.4	186	86.8	5.95	6.35	175	10.41	11.09	$+0.68$
1950	230.1	180	78.2	5.54	6.60	200	11.08	13.20	$+2.12$

[a] Civilian production as indicated in table on page 852 of the *Federal Reserve Bulletin*, September 1945, for the calendar years 1939 through 1945.

CHART A-1

Output of Manufacturing and Mining Equipment Compared
with Rate of Operation of Total Industrial Capacity

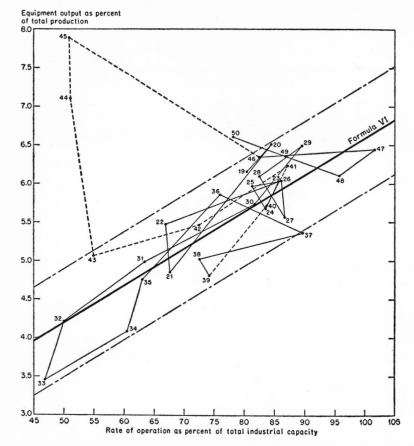

Equipment output as percent
of total production

Rate of operation as percent of total industrial capacity

Output of equipment for manufacturing and mining is measured as a share of total industrial production during the calendar year.

Rate of operation is measured as the portion of peacetime civilian capacity used by total industrial production during the preceding fiscal year.

Estimates for the years 1939-45 cover only nonwar industrial production and are indicated by the dashed line (figures from the Federal Reserve Bulletin, September 1945).

The Formula VI estimate of manufacturing and mining equipment output compared with rate of operation is indicated by the heavy line. Note that in most years the range of variation of actual data from this estimate is not more than ±0.7 of 1 percent (indicated by the dot-dashed lines).

tential will be the same in each case. The same holds for capacity itself. The set of conditions accompanying the capacity levels in bench mark years is not necessarily duplicated in the unknown composition of annual gross addition to capacity. Thus, developing capacity levels only on the basis of a nondescript constant-dollar volume of installed new equipment may lead at times to an unattainable level of capacity. This was demonstrated by the constraint imposed by steel capacity shown in Formula V, in Section H. However, it must be assumed that such deviations are more or less short-term in character. Thus, given a long-term projection of industrial production, Formula VI permits a recursive development of a long-term projection of capacity. This provides, in turn, a partial test of the long-term projection of industrial production itself, since the changes in the internal structure of industrial production during the business cycle are of a fairly definite character. They will permit a check of the estimates of producers' equipment for consistency.

APPENDIX B

TABLE B-1

STEEL PRODUCTION, CAPACITY, AND REQUIREMENT RATES IN THE UNITED STATES, 1919-1951

YEAR	PRODUCTION OF INGOTS AND STEEL FOR CASTINGS DESTINED FOR VARIOUS MARKETS (MILLIONS OF NET TONS)			PRODUCTION CAPACITY FOR INGOTS AND STEEL FOR CASTINGS, MIDYEAR (MILLIONS OF NET TONS)	APPARENT RATE OF STEEL REQUIREMENTS[a]	
	Total, S_T (1)	Domestic, S_D (2)	Foreign, S_E (3)	S_{CAP} (4)	Total, S_T/P_T (5)	Domestic, S_D/P_T (6)
1919	38.8	31.7	7.1	61.7	539	440
1920	47.2	39.7	7.5	63.3	629	529
1921	22.2	19.0	3.2	64.9	383	328
1922	39.9	36.8	3.1	65.6	547	504
1923	50.3	47.1	3.2	66.2	572	535
1924	42.5	39.8	2.7	67.6	518	485
1925	50.8	48.0	2.8	66.7	564	533
1926	54.1	50.7	3.4	66.0	564	528
1927	50.3	47.1	3.2	68.0	529	496
1928	57.7	53.9	3.8	70.1	583	544
1929	63.2	59.2	4.0	72.7	575	538
1930	45.6	43.0	2.6	75.2	501	473
1931	29.1	27.7	1.4	78.1	388	369
1932	15.3	14.7	.6	78.7	264	253
1933	26.0	25.1	.9	78.4	377	364
1934	29.2	27.6	1.6	78.3	389	368
1935	38.2	36.6	1.6	78.3	439	421
1936	53.5	51.1	2.4	78.4	519	496
1937	56.6	50.8	5.8	79.4	501	450
1938	31.8	28.4	3.4	81.0	357	319
1939	52.8	48.1	4.7	81.7	484	441

266

TABLE B-1 (concluded)

YEAR	PRODUCTION OF INGOTS AND STEEL FOR CASTINGS DESTINED FOR VARIOUS MARKETS (MILLIONS OF NET TONS)			PRODUCTION CAPACITY FOR INGOTS AND STEEL FOR CASTINGS, MIDYEAR (MILLIONS OF NET TONS)	APPARENT RATE OF STEEL REQUIREMENTS[a]	
	Total, S_T (1)	Domestic, S_D (2)	Foreign, S_E (3)	S_{CAP} (4)	Total, S_T/P_T (5)	Domestic, S_D/P_T (6)
1940	67.0	54.8	12.2	83.4	536	438
1941	82.8	73.4	9.4	87.0	511	453
1942	86.0	75.7	10.3	89.4	432	380
1943	88.8	78.3	10.5	91.9	372	328
1944	89.6	81.3	8.3	94.7	381	346
1945	79.7	72.4	7.3	93.7	393	357
1946	66.6	59.7	6.9	91.6	392	351
1947	84.9	75.9	9.0	92.7	454	406
1948	88.6	82.2	6.4	95.2	461	428
1949	78.0	70.6	7.4	97.8	443	401
1950	96.8	92.7	4.1	100.6	484	463
1951	105.1	100.5	4.6		478	457
Average, 1919-40			3.7	72.9	43.7	40.0

[a] In thousands of net tons annually per point on the Federal Reserve Index of Industrial Production.

Column

1 Source: American Iron and Steel Institute, *Metal Statistics, 1950*, p. 119.

2 ($S_T - S_E$)

3 This is an estimate based on the percentage which "Iron and Steel Exports Other than Scrap" (Department of Commerce, *Metal Statistics, 1950*, p. 260) is of "Rolled Steel Products for Sale" (American Iron and Steel Institute, *op.cit.*, p. 135) applied to column 1. Both series are stated for the 12-month period ending January 31. The comparison of rolled steel for sale with production of ingots and steel for castings implicit in this procedure accounts (a) for the rate of scrap and (b) for the share of rolled steel not for sale (but for reconversion). Both rates vary over time.

4 Reported or estimated for midyear as an approximation for the annual average. Source: Same as column 1.

5 Column 1 ÷ column 1 of Table A-2.

6 Column 2 ÷ column 1 of Table A-2.

TABLE B-2

TOTAL INDUSTRIAL AND SELECTED METAL PRODUCTION, 1919-1951 (1935-39 = 100)

Year	Production			Industrial Production		
	Total Industrial, P_T (1)	Metal and Metal Products, P_{MET} (2)	Iron and Steel Products, $P_{I\&S}$ (3)	Normal Level, $0.85(P_{CAP})$ or P_N (4)	Cyclical Slack, P_{CY} (5)	Peacetime Civilian Capacity (Midyear), P_{CAP} (6)
1919	72	24.2	9.2	77	5	90
1920	75	27.3	11.2	79	4	93
1921	58	13.6	5.3	81	23	95
1922	73	22.9	9.4	82	9	97
1923	88	30.2	12.0	85	−3	100
1924	82	27.2	9.9	88	6	103
1925	90	31.1	11.9	90	0	106
1926	96	33.6	12.7	94	−2	110
1927	95	31.1	11.9	97	2	114
1928	99	34.9	13.3	99	0	117
1929	110	40.4	14.6	105	−5	123
1930	91	29.7	10.7	109	18	128
1931	75	19.8	6.7	111	36	130
1932	58	11.8	3.5	110	52	129
1933	69	16.1	5.9	108	39	127
1934	75	19.9	6.7	106	31	125

TABLE B-2 (concluded)

| Year | Production | | | Industrial Production | | Peacetime |
	Total Industrial, P_T (1)	Metal and Metal Products, P_{MET} (2)	Iron and Steel Products, $P_{I\&S}$ (3)	Normal Level, $0.85(P_{CAP})$ or P_N (4)	Cyclical Slack, P_{CY} (5)	Civilian Capacity (Midyear), P_{CAP} (6)
1935	87	25.4	8.9	105	18	124
1936	103	33.3	12.6	106	3	125
1937	113	37.9	13.5	110	−3	129
1938	89	22.9	7.5	111	22	131
1939	109	33.1	12.5	114	5	134
1940	125	43.8	16.2	118	−7	139
1941	162	65.5	20.5	126	−36	148
1942	199	94.8	21.9	132	−67	155
1943	239	125.6	22.9	133	−106	157
1944	235	123.5	22.7	134	−101	158
1945	203	94.2	20.1	139	−64	163
1946	170	61.4	16.6	147	−23	173
1947	187	70.9	21.5	161	−26	189
1948	192	72.8	22.9	175	−17	206
1949	176	64.9	20.6	189	13	222
1950	200	77.0	24.8	203	3	238.6
1951	220	88.8	28.5	222	2	261.7
Average 1919-40	87.8	27.7	10.3	99.3	11.5	116.8

Column
1 Source: Board of Governors of the Federal Reserve System, *Federal Reserve Bulletin*, October 1943.
2 Source: Same as column 1.
3 Source: Same as column 1.
4 Source: See Appendix A.
5 Because of the prevalence of slack rather than strain ($-P_{CY} = P_T - P_N$) during the period 1919-40, cyclical slack has been used as the short-term variable.
6 Source: See Appendix A.

TABLE B-3

Estimates of Total Steel Production and of Production of Steel for the Domestic Market Based on Industrial Production and Its Normal Rate, 1919-1939 (in millions of tons)

Year	Formula I		Formula II		Formula III		Formula IV		
	$S_T(P_T)$ (1)	Residuals, $S_T - (1)$ (2)	$S_T(P_T, P_N)$ (3)	Residuals, $S_T - (3)$ (4)	$S_T(P_T, P_N)$ (5)	Residuals, $S_T - (5)$ (6)	$S_D(P_T, P_N)$ (7)	$S_E + S_D(P_T, P_N)$ (8)	Residuals, $S_T - (8)$ (9)
1919	32.7	+6.1	40.6	−1.8	39.7	−0.9	35.6	42.7	−3.9
1920	34.8	+12.4	42.3	+4.9	41.7	+5.5	37.7	45.2	+2.0
1921	22.9	−0.7	26.7	−4.5	23.9	−1.7	18.5	21.7	+0.5
1922	33.4	+6.5	39.1	+0.8	38.3	+1.6	34.0	37.1	+2.8
1923	43.8	+6.5	50.6	−0.3	51.7	−1.4	48.4	51.6	−0.7
1924	40.0	+2.5	44.0	−1.5	44.3	−1.8	40.3	43.0	−0.5
1925	45.2	+5.6	49.9	+0.9	51.2	−0.4	47.8	50.6	+0.2
1926	49.4	+4.7	53.1	+1.0	55.2	−1.1	52.0	55.4	−1.3
1927	48.7	+1.6	50.9	−0.6	52.8	−2.5	49.3	52.5	−2.2
1928	51.5	+6.2	53.3	+4.4	55.8	+1.9	52.5	56.3	+1.4
1929	59.2	+4.0	59.9	+3.3	61.9	+1.3	57.8	61.8	+1.4
1930	45.9	−0.3	41.7	+3.9	41.7	+3.9	37.8	40.4	+5.2
1931	34.8	−5.7	27.0	+2.1	27.7	+1.4	26.9	28.3	+0.8
1932	22.9	−7.6	12.9	+2.4	14.5	+0.8	16.2	16.8	−1.5
1933	30.6	−4.6	23.4	+2.6	24.0	+2.0	23.6	24.5	+1.5
1934	34.8	−5.6	29.4	−0.2	29.4	−0.2	27.9	29.5	−0.3
1935	43.1	−4.9	40.2	−2.0	39.3	−1.1	35.7	37.3	+0.9
1936	54.3	−0.8	53.4	+0.1	51.6	+1.9	45.8	48.2	+5.3
1937	61.3	−4.7	60.1	−3.5	58.2	−1.6	51.4	57.2	−0.6
1938	44.5	−12.7	39.0	−7.2	38.8	−7.0	35.8	39.2	−7.4
1939	58.5	−5.7	54.8	−2.0	53.7	−0.9	48.0	52.7	+0.1

TABLE B-3 (concluded)

Year	Formula I		Formula II		Formula III		Formula IV		
	$S_T(P_T)$ (1)	Residuals, $S_T - (1)$ (2)	$S_T(P_T,P_N)$ (3)	Residuals, $S_T - (3)$ (4)	$S_T(P_T,P_N)$ (5)	Residuals, $S_T - (5)$ (6)	$S_D(P_T,P_N)$ (7)	$S_E + S_D(P_T,P_N)$ (8)	Residuals, $S_T - (8)$ (9)
1940	69.6	−2.6	66.6	+0.4	65.0	+2.0	57.5	69.7	−2.7
1941	93.4	−12.6	94.6	−11.8	91.7	−8.9	79.5	88.9	−6.1
1942	121.2	−35.2	123.4	−37.4	119.1	−33.1	102.1	112.4	−26.4
1943	149.1	−60.3	157.1	−68.3	150.5	−61.6	127.4	137.9	−49.0
1944	146.3	−56.7	153.3	−63.7	147.0	−57.4	124.7	133.0	−43.4
1945	124.0	−44.3	123.4	−43.7	119.9	−40.2	103.2	110.5	−30.8
1946	101.0	−34.4	91.4	−24.8	91.0	−24.4	80.6	87.5	−20.9
1947	112.8	−27.9	99.4	−14.5	99.8	−14.9	88.7	97.7	−12.8
1948	116.3	−27.7	97.0	−8.4	99.0	−10.4	89.2	95.6	−7.0
1949	105.2	−27.2	76.7	+1.3	81.6	−3.7	76.2	83.6	−5.7
1950	121.9	−25.2	90.6	+6.2	95.9	+0.9	88.7	92.8	+4.0
1951	135.9	−30.8	98.7	+6.4	104.6	+0.5	97.8	102.4	+2.7

TABLE B-4

ESTIMATES OF STEEL REQUIREMENTS AT NORMAL LONG-RUN AND CAPACITY
RATES OF TOTAL INDUSTRIAL PRODUCTION BASED ON VARIOUS FORMULAE,
1919-1951 (IN MILLIONS OF TONS)

| | NORMAL LONG-RUN RATES BASED ON FORMULA | | | CAPACITY RATES BASED ON FORMULA | |
| | II | III | IV | II | III |
YEAR	$S_T(P_N)$ (1)	$S_T(P_N)$ (2)	$S_D(P_N)$ (3)	$S_T(P_{CAP})$ (4)	$S_T(P_{CAP})$ (5)
1919	44.9	44.6	41.0	56.3	57.8
1920	45.7	45.7	42.0	57.6	59.5
1921	46.4	46.7	43.1	58.5	60.7
1922	46.8	47.2	43.6	59.4	61.8
1923	48.0	48.7	45.2	60.8	63.6
1924	49.1	50.2	46.7	62.2	65.3
1925	49.9	51.2	47.8	63.5	67.0
1926	51.4	53.3	49.9	65.3	69.3
1927	52.6	54.8	51.4	67.2	71.7
1928	53.3	55.8	52.5	68.5	73.4
1929	55.6	57.3	53.1	71.2	74.2
1930	57.1	57.0	51.6	73.5	73.3
1931	57.9	56.3	49.9	74.4	71.5
1932	57.5	55.8	49.5	74.0	71.0
1933	56.8	54.9	48.6	73.1	70.0
1934	56.0	54.0	47.7	72.2	69.0
1935	55.6	53.5	47.2	71.7	68.5
1936	56.0	54.0	47.7	72.2	69.0
1937	57.5	55.8	49.5	74.0	71.0
1938	57.9	56.3	49.9	74.9	72.0
1939	59.1	57.7	51.2	76.2	73.6
1940	60.6	59.5	53.0	78.5	76.1
1941	63.7	63.1	56.5	82.6	80.7
1942	66.0	65.9	59.2	85.8	84.2
1943	66.3	66.3	59.6	86.7	85.2
1944	66.7	66.8	60.1	87.1	85.7
1945	68.6	69.1	62.3	89.4	88.3
1946	71.7	72.7	65.9	93.9	93.4
1947	77.1	79.1	72.1	101.2	101.5
1948	82.4	85.5	78.3	108.9	110.1
1949	87.8	91.9	84.5	116.2	118.2
1950	93.1	98.3	90.7	123.7	126.6
1951	100.4	106.9	99.1	134.5	138.5

PART III

LONG-TERM TENDENCIES
IN PRIVATE CAPITAL FORMATION

The Rate of Growth and Capital Coefficients

WILLIAM FELLNER

YALE UNIVERSITY

A. INTRODUCTION

THE first four sections of this study lead to an appraisal of the "rate of growth and capital coefficients" approach to the aggregative theory of investment. A brief statement of the approach itself is found in Section C-4.

Sections F and H apply this approach to the problem of long-term investment projection as it presented itself prior to the outbreak of hostilities in Korea. "Long run" will here mean roughly a period extending from the "present" to a comparable phase of a future business cycle, some years ahead. However, comments on longer-range problems will also be included, involving statistical data for several past decades.

Not all economic theory is directly connected with the objective of prediction. It takes professional analysis to derive *specific criteria of evaluation* applicable to economic processes from *given general principles* considered significant in a social system. Theories performing this function are important and they are at best indirectly related to prediction. They are linked to prediction merely by their ability to disclose the consistency or inconsistency of specific economic results with the survival of some social system which is defined by certain general principles. However, a large part of modern economic theory is much more directly oriented to the objective of making informed guesses. This study is concerned with theories of the latter type.

The justification for developing theories of this sort is not that they perform particularly well as measured by their own standards. The justification is that it frequently is necessary to make

Note: The writer is indebted to Professor Simon Kuznets of the University of Pennsylvania and to Messrs. E. M. Hoover and B. H. Klein of the research staff of the Council of Economic Advisers for valuable suggestions and for unpublished materials which they kindly placed at his disposal. He is indebted to Professor Clarence Long of The Johns Hopkins University for detailed and helpful comments.

up our minds on the probable course of future events in circumstances that preclude dependable prediction. In our everyday lives as in the social sciences, it is impossible to do this without some kind of theory, although the "theories" we use in our everyday lives to decide what is likely to happen in the future are usually too crude and unsystematic to warrant the term.

B. THE MEANING OF PROJECTABILITY IN ECONOMICS

At the present stage, we cannot expect to develop a theory of investment which could be used for prediction in a more or less mechanical fashion. All economic theory is based on *ceteris paribus* assumptions and all economic theory requires informal appraisal of how reality is likely to accord with, or deviate from, these assumptions. Alternatively we may say that our theories are established for given "environments." Their logical structure is valid for a specific environment, and the functions of this structure shift when the environment changes. Appraisal of the likelihood and of the consequences of environmental change remains largely a matter of subjective or quasi-intuitive judgment.[1]

Given these limitations, the predictive usefulness of an economic theory depends in a large measure on whether it implies a useful separation of "formal framework" from "environment." The formal framework must enable the economist to collect information and to draw rigorous conclusions for given environmental conditions (i.e., on definite *ceteris paribus* assumptions). At the same time the environment in which the logical structure operates must be defined in such a way that the problem of environmental change appears as an articulate, meaningful problem. The appraisal of the likelihood of environmental change (in this sense) will remain a matter of individual judgment, but not every environmental problem constitutes an articulate complex on which individuals are capable of using their subjective judgment.

A useful theory must separate internal structural elements from environmental elements in a convenient way. More cannot at present be expected. In economics, true projectability is at

---

[1] These judgments can be characterized by an analogy. They are like feeling an imperfect die and then forming an opinion of roughly how the frequency distribution for a series of throws is likely to be influenced by the imperfections.

present a utopian goal. Any number of predictive theories will hold on the corresponding *ceteris paribus* assumptions, and no theory will hold aside from such assumptions (i.e., no theory is sufficiently complete to incorporate all causal factors into the logical structure itself). We must try to select theories with fruitful *ceteris paribus* assumptions.

Unfortunately, realism is not the criterion of the fruitfulness of these *ceteris paribus* assumptions. They are certain to be unrealistic. Our ability to arrive at objectively justifiable appraisals of the environmental factors is also not an acceptable criterion, because if this criterion were satisfied, the environmental factors could be worked into the logical framework itself. They would then cease to be environmental factors in this sense. The main criterion of fruitfulness with respect to the environmental factors (or *ceteris paribus* assumptions) is our ability to arrive at some kind of quasi-intuitive judgment concerning them. It is helpful if reasonably independent judgments of individuals do not differ too radically from one another, or if most persons forced to make judgments of this sort fall into a small number of groups. This condition cannot always be satisfied. But we should always try to select theories which separate the logical apparatus from the environment in such a way that (a) information is available for drawing inferences from the logical apparatus on definite environmental assumptions, and (b) the problem of environmental change constitutes an articulate complex capable of provoking an answer from the typical individual who is forced to make a judgment. Condition b should probably be labeled "genuinely psychological." The present writer knows of no helpful discussion (explicit treatment) of this problem, but he feels convinced that fruitful theorizing requires awareness of its significance.

This paper is concerned, not just with predictive implications of economic theory in general, but with the question of the usefulness of specific kinds of theory for a definite problem of qualified prediction. We shall be concerned with long-run projections of private capital formation. The difficulties of long-run projection are partly different from those of making informed guesses for the near future. Some errors tend to cancel in the long run. More can be said about average relationships over a longer past period than about individual instances belonging in a universe. Hence, if the appraisal of the *ceteris paribus* assumptions (environmental factors) gave rise to the same difficulties for a short as for a long future period, long-run projection should be considerably more dependable than short-run projection. However, the appraisal of the environmental factors usually becomes more difficult when the period is extended.

C. PRELIMINARY COMMENTS ON ALTERNATIVE METHODS OF PROJECTION

1. The current textbook proposition

The amount of investment is said to equate the marginal efficiency of capital to the rate of interest. This proposition can be worded in several alternative ways and has its equivalents in pre-Keynesian terminology. All propositions of this kind are elaborations on the profit-maximization principle. They form the counterpart of the utility-maximization principle and its applications in the theory of consumer demand.

These propositions are important because they disclose the specific economic corollaries of general principles which play a significant role in contemporary social systems. However, these propositions are not at present directly applicable to microeconomic projection.[2] It is not easy to conceive of statistical techniques which would measure the highly volatile marginal efficiency schedule (or, in general, the investment-vs.-interest-rate schedule, regardless of whether this implies strict profit maximization). It seems to us that the empirical approach to the theory of investment requires keeping some sort of qualified profit-maximization principle in the background of the analysis without losing sight of it. However, lack of data makes it impossible to place the principle in the center of empirical investigation. Whatever relationships may become "established" empirically between investment and other observable variables, it is necessary to stay aware of the fact that these relationships imply something with respect to the profitability to individual firms of the pattern of behavior under consideration. A valid pattern of behavior must be compatible with individual profit objectives, although not necessarily with the all too simple principle of strict profit maximization. In other words, the methods with which we will be concerned are one or more steps removed

---

[2] On the microeconomic level, predicting the behavior of the firm requires a framework which is largely built around profit objectives.

from the usual textbook propositions, but an attempt should be made to see what the links are.

2. The questionnaire method

In recent years data have become available on planned plant and equipment expenditures of business. The so-called SEC-Commerce data, which are based on direct inquiries to a sample of firms accounting for a substantial proportion of total investment, apply to periods ahead ranging from a few months to a year. The McGraw-Hill survey is an example of the attempt to obtain information about long-range plans by similar methods. It seems to us that the questionnaire method is more promising for short-run than for long-run projection.

This does not mean that long-range data of this sort are useless. However, their potential usefulness does not derive from the reliability of the planned investment-outlay figures. Investment plans for several years ahead are very tentative and are almost certain to be changed with the passage of time. Direct information concerning long-run plans may prove to be revealing, not because the planned investment outlays are likely to be realized, but because the relationship between different planned magnitudes or changes may be indicative of how much of something may be expected to go with how much of something else. The answers of firms may disclose the fact that they intend to increase their capacity by a certain number of output units and that they expect to spend a certain amount on such a program. The ratio of these figures contains a more useful piece of information than do the two figures in isolation. Moreover, this piece of information—the planned investment outlay associated with a unit increase of capacity—must be obtained from long-run relationships, if it is to be useful as supplementary information for long-run projections based on other methods. Therefore, answers of firms to questions concerning long-run investment plans may contain valuable information. But the planned total outlays bear no easily understandable relationship to the total outlays the investigator should expect over a longer period.

The planned total outlays may be quite different from those realized, even in shorter periods. But considering the fact that it is wasteful to stop halfway in the realization of short-run plans, and that commitments are entered before outlays are actually made, it is conceivable that appropriate interpretation of planned outlays will prove to be of direct help for the short-run projection of private investment. It is possible that sufficiently inclusive inquiries will lead to the collecting of planned data which, without further manipulation, will give tolerably good approximations to realized data over sufficiently short periods. This result could scarcely be achieved for total private investment including inventory accumulation, because inventories are partly determined by daily fluctuations of demand. But it is not inconceivable that, for short periods, a good approximation to realized plant and equipment outlays could be obtained by collecting data on planned outlays. Short-run GNP (gross national product) projection would still remain a thorny problem, because additional information would be required on income-consumption relationships, on government expenditures, and on planned inventory accumulation to appraise the level toward which output is moving. Subsequently, it would be necessary to allow for the fact that a rise (so obtained) may be somewhat counteracted by an unplanned reduction of inventories, and that a fall (so obtained) may be counteracted by an unplanned increase of inventories. Yet, it is worth while to make an effort to obtain reliable information on plant and equipment outlays for a period ending a few months ahead. Even if businessmen should change their minds very frequently, and if, therefore, data of this kind should never become good approximations to the subsequently realized magnitudes, it is conceivable that valuable information could be derived by comparing the planned magnitudes with the subsequently realized ones for a succession of short periods. Some property of the planned series may become an advance indicator of some subsequent property of the realized series.[3]

In summary, we feel that the survey method may in due time become significant, but that its significance is likely to be greater for short-run than for long-run projection. However, the method may yield valuable supplementary information even for long-run projection, because the estimates of firms concerning the long-run relationship between different magnitudes may be subject to less severe limitations than their estimates of what they are going to spend in the course of a period of considerable duration.

[3] For example, it is conceivable that a sufficiently great decrease in the rate of increase in the planned series goes with a fall in the realized series.

3. *Projecting investment from profits*

Methods based on observed relationships between profits and subsequent private investment are but one step removed from textbook propositions of the "marginal efficiency vs. rate of interest" variety. This is especially true if some allowance is made for the availability of funds for investment. In a sense, it is true even aside from this. Any reasonable interpretation of the effect of present profits on future investment must imply that present profits have something to do with profit expectations for the future. Consequently, if future investment is said to depend on present profits and some magnitude related to the availability of funds, we come close to the "marginal efficiency and interest rate" proposition. Even if, technically, no separate allowance is made for funds, we may be interpreted as using the same general kind of approach on the further assumption of given expectations concerning the availability of funds. If only profits and lagged investment are included in the technical approach, it is necessary to keep in mind the dependence of the observed relationship on the liquidity position of firms and to make informal allowances for possible changes. If the technical apparatus is rendered more complete by the inclusion of some measure of the availability of funds (and possibly by the inclusion of further variables), then these informal allowances pertain to a different complex of "outside" (environmental) factors, but they still will have to be made. In statistical work, some investigators have found consistent relationships between profits and lagged investment outlays. Some statistical business cycle models rely heavily on this relationship.[4]

The same statistical relationships do not bear directly on long-run projection. One reason for this—but perhaps not the ultimately significant one—is that the lagged profit-investment relationship must be assumed to depend on the nature of cyclical development. In a long period of typically high output with moderate cyclical swings, a given rate and amount of profit may call forth more investment than in a less satisfactory (more insecure) period. Most of our statistical experience relates to decades during which cyclical instability was greater than we hope

---

[4] Cf., e.g., Lawrence R. Klein, *Economic Fluctuations in the United States, 1921-1941*, Cowles Commission for Research in Economics, Monograph No. 11 (Wiley, 1950), chap. 3. Cf. also *Factors Affecting Volume and Stability of Private Investment*, Joint Committee Print (Government Printing Office, 1949).

it will be in the future periods with which we are concerned. This is especially true if we disregard the first half of the 1940's as untypical from the point of view of the profit-investment relation. On the other hand, we have had several postwar years of high employment and of little instability. In general it may be argued that it has been possible to observe lagged profit-investment relations during subperiods with markedly different characteristics, and that the difficulties of making up our minds on the relevance of the one or the other of these experiences for projection are not fundamentally different from a great many other difficulties with which long-run projection is fraught.

What really destroys the usefulness of this type of analysis for long-term projection is the shortness of the lag between profits and investment outlays. Whether this lag is in the order of six months or of a year, its short duration excludes the possibility of reaching the average investment outlays of a long period ahead from profit data now available. Profit-investment relations may still retain a good deal of indirect usefulness for long-term projection because they point to the likelihood that sustaining a given amount of investment in some future period of longer duration will require profits of some magnitude during approximately the same period. This piece of knowledge in itself tells us nothing about how to project future investment from data now observable, for it contains no indication concerning the dependence of future profits on present data. However, propositions of the sort here considered do possess indirect usefulness for long-run projection, in the sense of telling us something about certain conditions which will have to be met in the future if projections derived by other methods are to be trustworthy. Projections resulting from other methods will, of course, have to be interpreted as implying certain *ceteris paribus* assumptions, or qualifying clauses, pertaining to the environmental factors not included in the theory. One group of significant environmental factors is connected with the profit problem considered. For long-term projection, this group of factors will have to remain "environmental," because we have no way of projecting distant future investment from present profits, or distant future profits directly from now observable variables.

4. Projecting the rate of increase in output and the capital requirement for achieving it

In the present essay, this kind of approach will receive more attention than those previously discussed, although our conclusions will take account of supplementary considerations based on the preceding discussion.

The dominant trait of the theory and the method in question is that they imply our ability to appraise crudely (in part, quasi-intuitively) whether certain observed relationships between stock and output are likely to change and, if so, what the nature of this change might be. It would be unfair to the theory, and to the method of projection based on it, to maintain that it implies constancy of some property of the capital-output relationship, let alone constancy of the capital coefficients themselves. Crude statements of the theory may lead one to believe that it implies just this, but such a theory would be clearly unacceptable. The general limitations of economic theory and of methods of projection must be kept in mind here as elsewhere. At the present stage, we cannot expect to develop a complete theory of investment which would incorporate into its formal structure all factors influencing the outcome. We can merely place in the foreground of our analysis a formal relationship which holds on *ceteris paribus* assumptions (i.e., given the "environment" in which the logical structure operates), and then try to allow in a quasi-intuitive fashion for changes in the environmental factors. No general agreement can be expected on the appropriateness of these allowances, but the problem of these environmental changes (that is, of the deviations from *ceteris paribus* assumptions) may or may not be posed in a meaningful way. Individuals—and perhaps groups of individuals similarly inclined—may or may not feel that they have tentative answers to these environmental questions. What the method to which we now turn implies is that certain aspects of the capital-output relationship lend themselves to reasonable generalizations on given "environmental" assumptions, and that the question of environmental change so posed is an articulate (i.e., meaningful) question in the sense here described. In the opinion of the present writer these conditions are better satisfied for the approach now under discussion than for the approaches previously considered.

In this introductory section, only the broad characteristics of

283

the approach will be described. More detailed analysis will be made in subsequent sections.

We may begin by stating a truistic relationship and by inquiring into the circumstances in which the relationship acquires more meaning. It follows from the *ex post* savings-investment identity that the product of the percentage rate of growth of output times the incremental (i.e., marginal) capital-output ratio must always equal the percentage of output which is absorbed by investment. Hence we may write

$$\frac{\Delta V}{\Delta O} \cdot \frac{\Delta O/\Delta t}{O} = a \tag{1}$$

where V means the stock of wealth, O the rate of output, t time, and a the ratio of savings to output (i.e., one possible definition of the "average propensity to save"). This follows from the fact that the foregoing expression is a slightly changed version of $\Delta V/\Delta t = aO$, that is to say, of aggregate investment equals aggregate savings. If we want to have on the right-hand side the average propensity to save in a now more usual sense, that is, in the sense of the ratio of individual savings to the disposable income of individuals, then the expression becomes somewhat more complicated. It then takes the form

$$\frac{\Delta V}{\Delta O} \cdot \frac{\Delta O}{\Delta t} + G_n = a(O - \text{NBS} - \text{TP} + \text{TR}) + \text{NBS} + \text{TP} \tag{2}$$

where O (output) is interpreted as the net national product, NBS means net business savings, TP tax payments, TR government transfer payments, and G_n that part of the government output which does not increase the capital stock and also is not included in consumption. Considering the nature of the data which will be used in this study, we shall mainly be using (1), but it must be remembered that in (1) G_n equals zero, and hence all government output is interpreted either as consumption or as capital formation (see Section F).

Purely logical relations do not in themselves solve empirical problems. A useful relationship is obtained only if the values of the magnitudes entering into these equations are capable of being interpreted in a reasonable way. This means that it must be possible *to appraise the conditions under which the values in question would tend to repeat themselves and also to appraise, in a general way, the nature of the change in these values which may be produced by changes in the surrounding conditions.* Short-run values of the variables of our equation do not, in themselves, satisfy this condition. Long-run average values may come closer to satisfying it and, if they do, comparisons of the long-run average values with the fluctuating short-run values may prove revealing for short-run (i.e., business cycle) analysis.

Changes in the rate of growth of output from one short period to the next are quite erratic in the sense of disclosing no orderly pattern. The truism that the rate of change would be the same in each short period if all properties of the environment repeated themselves is completely sterile, because we are incapable of forming a judgment on the relevance of the various environmental factors and on the likelihood of their repeating themselves. Similar statements may be made of the short-run behavior of $\Delta V/\Delta O$ and of a. But it is hoped that the same misgivings apply to long-run average data merely in an attenuated form, so that investigators may find it useful to study the past behavior of the long-run data and to try to appraise by general judgment the likelihood of outside changes which may alter the values in question for future periods. The cycle (or cycles) may then be represented in terms of deviations from long-run values, although interrelations between the trend and cyclical deviations must not be overlooked. A theory corresponding to the long-run interpretation of our equations leads into questions of this sort: For what reasons and in what way is the future average rate of growth of output likely to be different from the typical past rate of growth, as observed over a period of several decades? For what reasons and in what way is the behavior of the marginal capital-output relationship likely to deviate from its past behavior? And that of the saving ratio a? Opinions will differ on these matters, but it nevertheless seems to us that these questions are posed in an articulate and useful fashion.

The method of projection corresponding to this approach is one that is intended to find consistent future values for the variables entering into the equation used, with the proviso that they must bear a plausible relation to the past behavior of these variables. By the consistency of values, we mean that the equation must be satisfied. By plausible relation to past behavior, we mean that the investigator must be able to "make a case" for the assumption that the past values will repeat themselves or that they will change in one way or another. This "case" must be made in terms of properties of the "environment," that is to say, in terms of factors external to the formal apparatus itself. The reader, if he is dissatisfied with these environmental assumptions, may then substitute his own for those developed in any particular analysis.

In the treatment of the "environmental" problem (or *ceteris paribus* problem), the influence of government policy on these variables must not be overlooked. This influence is quite direct on government expenditures in general and it is direct on a, too (especially as defined in [1], where it expresses government capital formation as well as savings in the ordinary sense). The influence of policy on $\Delta V/\Delta O$ and on $(\Delta O/\Delta t)/O$ is perhaps less "direct," but it is also significant. Relative prices (scarcity and abundance in specific areas) and the state of the credit market are likely to have an influence on $\Delta V/\Delta O$, because there is no reason to assume extreme insensitivity of coefficients of production in the long run. These same factors are almost certain to influence the rate of growth of output, which, at the same time, may obviously be affected by tax policy and also by wage policy.

Treatment of the problem in terms of the equation formulated has the advantage of avoiding unnecessary restrictive assumptions with respect to the sequence of causation. The various magnitudes included in the equation interact. The significant questions are those relating to the level of activity at which the equation becomes satisfied and to the nature of the adjustments by which the two sides are made equal. Obviously, there exists a great deal of difference between an automatic adjustment in a, expressing itself in the lowering of its value through underemployment, and an automatic adjustment of the rate of growth of output to the available resources. If analysis of this sort is to be useful, it is necessary to make up one's mind as to what is likely to adjust under different conditions, and as to what the nature of the process of adjustment is likely to be. But, it is not necessary to develop a sweeping general hypothesis which explains investment as being caused by the rate of growth of output, via the capital-output relation; or an alternative general hypothesis explaining the growth of output as being caused by investment, via the capital-output relation. Interactions may be recognized. The requirement is merely that of the consistency of various changes.

The foregoing discussion was deliberately held in very general terms. Subsequently, it will be made more specific in two respects. The problem of the environmental factors (or "outside" factors, *ceteris paribus* assumptions) will be discussed explicitly, and the question will be raised as to what really is involved in appraising these by general judgment. Secondly, some methods of obtaining information on the past behavior of the relevant magnitudes will be discussed. However, before turning to these problems, we shall compare the present approach with more or less closely related ones which received attention in the recent literature.

D. SOME NEWER VARIANTS OF THE ACCELERATION PRINCIPLE

If we interpret the term broadly enough, the approach just considered is a variant of the "acceleration principle." This is because it conceives of the amount of investment as the product of the rate of growth of output and of a relationship $(\Delta V/\Delta O)$ by which the rate of growth is linked to investment. But most presentations of the acceleration principle are based on more specific or restrictive assumptions which are not expressed in our general equations (Section C-4) and which will also not be introduced into our subsequent specific discussion. In some recent expositions of the acceleration principle, investment is linked to the rate of increase in consumption rather than output. In most expositions of the principle, high rigidity of $\Delta V/\Delta O$ (or at least of the $\Delta V/\Delta O$ compatible with dynamic equilibrium) is assumed. In some cases this may be a consequence of the fact that the principle is used in the framework of business cycle analysis, i.e., for the discussion of short-run change. But even where the short-run analysis proceeds by way of contrasting long-run relationships (observable along trend lines) with the fluctuating relations of cyclical development, it is not unusual to imply rigid capital-output relations throughout the analysis. Furthermore, the causal sequence is frequently represented as running unequivocally from the rate of increase in output, or in consumption, to investment, rather than possibly the other way around, or both ways. This is an unnecessarily restrictive assumption even for short-run analysis. If one or more of these restrictive assumptions are considered essential to the acceleration principle,

287

then the more flexible approach to be adopted here should not be called a variant of this principle. Nor should it be called a variant of this principle if the latter is limited to business cycle analysis. The equations of Section C-4 can be interpreted as expressing the acceleration principle only in the very general sense that they emphasize a consistency requirement between the rate of increase in output and output itself according to equation 2:

$$O = \frac{\Delta O}{\Delta t} \cdot \frac{\Delta V}{\Delta O} + G_n$$

This analogy makes it desirable briefly to survey some recent treatments of the acceleration principle and also to attempt to make explicit the most essential differences.

1. The Samuelson analysis[5]

Professor Samuelson's well-known presentation of a multiplier-acceleration model is of an essentially short-run character; at least one of the magnitudes $(\Delta O / \Delta t)$ shows a behavior which is not found in long-run average values and discloses disturbances (incorrect expectations) of the sort encountered in various phases of cyclical development. The corresponding long-run system (pertaining to trend values) could be characterized by

$$\frac{\Delta V}{\Delta C} \cdot \frac{\Delta C}{\Delta t} = a \cdot O \qquad (3)$$

where C stands for consumption. Otherwise, the notation of our equation 1 is used. Equation 3 differs from ours merely in that the capital stock is conceived of as producing consumer goods, rather than output (i.e., consumer goods *and* investment goods). There is no need for introducing an assumption of this kind, unless it simplifies the exposition and is otherwise unimportant for the purpose of a specific piece of analysis. No simplifications would be achieved by writing ΔC instead of ΔO in the long-run equation just considered. Samuelson uses no equation of such long-run variety but he uses dated, short-run relationships by which investment is derived from the rate of change of consumption rather than output. To the investment so derived (I) there is added a constant flow of "autonomous" investment.

[5] Paul A. Samuelson, "Interaction between the Multiplier Analysis and the Principle of Acceleration," *Readings in Business Cycle Theory*, American Economic Association (Blakiston, 1944).

(It may therefore be appropriate to add a term for autonomous investment on the left-hand side of Equation 3, too, and to interpret ΔV as applying merely to induced investment, that is, to Samuelson's I.)

Whether the results are affected by using ΔC instead of ΔO is a question which could be answered in different ways. It is true that the Samuelson system can be rewritten with ΔO in the place of ΔC; in *his* notation, with

$$I_t = \beta \left(C_t - C_{t-1} + I_t - I_{t-1} \right)$$

in the place of his

$$I_t = \beta \left(C_t - C_{t-1} \right)^6$$

and that the broad characteristics of the formal apparatus remain the same after this change. But the change brings out the fact that a sufficient degree of optimism is self-justifying as long as the economy does not run into specific scarcities. For in the broadened model characterized by

$$I_t = \beta \left(C_t - C_{t-1} + I_t - I_{t-1} \right)$$

there exists no good reason for assuming that the value of β and that of I_t are technologically determined by the capital-depleting effect of a past increase in consumer income such as results in a rise in consumer demand. The *justified* values of β and of I_t (the values which will create no excess capacity) become dependent upon how much will be invested in subsequent periods. With no scarcities and no uncertainty in the model, there is nothing to limit investment in the successive periods. This is an essential characteristic of such a system. A similar conclusion could be read even from a model using ΔC rather than ΔO, although the treatment would then have to include a discussion of the significance of changes in the so-called autonomous investment of private producers.

If we link the endogenous or induced investment to movements *in consumption alone*, then our proposition relating to the self-

---

[6] C = consumption; I = investment; β corresponds to $\Delta V/\Delta O$ or to $\Delta V/\Delta C$, depending on whether, in the model we use, investment depends on the change in output or on that in consumption (that is, whether it corresponds to $\Delta V/\Delta C$ in the Samuelson model proper). Subscripts relate to time periods. Samuelson also has $C_t = \alpha Y_{t-1}$, where α stands for the marginal propensity to consume and Y for income. This fully describes the system, except that there is a constant amount of autonomous investment, in addition to $I_t = \beta \left(C_t - C_{t-1} \right)$. Hence, in addition to this last equation for I_t and in addition to $C_t = \alpha Y_{t-1}$, the model assumes $Y_t = 1 + C_t + I_t$.

justification of investment aside from specific scarcities and uncertainty must be developed with reference to an unexplained flow of "autonomous" investment. For not even from the viewpoint of purely aggregative theory is investment justified *by consumption alone*, except to the extent that a rise in consumption which is occasioned by a past rise in consumer income has already depleted the capital stock or currently tends to deplete it. Aside from this, investment must justify itself partly by future consumption and partly by future investment, provided that the marginal propensity to consume is less than 1. In a growing economy, investment must become justified partly by subsequent future investment because the income created by investment is only partly consumed. In a model linking investment to an increase in consumption alone, only that part of the investment can be explained which is called forth by the fact that a preceding rise in income may, via the propensity to consume, be exerting a capital-depleting influence. If investment is linked to ΔC rather than ΔO, then it must be pointed out that, in addition to the investment in question, any amount of autonomous investment would be self-justifying in the foregoing sense, and that the nature of a purely aggregative cycle model so developed depends ultimately on what is postulated concerning the behavior of autonomous investment. This is not very satisfactory. The same is true if we link endogenous or induced investment to movement in output ΔO but limit the concept of this investment to what is technologically justified by the *past* ΔO (as if no further ΔO were expected). This is what Professor Hicks has done. In this case, too, we have to deal separately with an unexplained and self-justifying flow of autonomous investment, because not all investment can be related to the *past* ΔO in a purely technological way. The outcome will again depend on our postulates concerning autonomous investment. However, *all investment may be said to bear some reasonable relation to expected movements in output.* A system stressing this relationship does not have to exclude part of the investment flow by labeling it autonomous. Only if some constituent of total investment can be explained more satisfactorily by a definite relationship of a different sort, is it advisable to distinguish between flows of investment induced in different ways. The distinction between induced and autonomous does not seem fruitful and it can be avoided if we relate investment to movements in output, without implying that the relevant relation-

ship links past changes to present investment in a purely technological way. Specific scarcities and uncertainty then become the
limiting factors. Even the question of how completely the long-
run "tendency" toward diminishing returns must be offset in each
period by improvements depends on the appraisal of uncertainty
(that is, on required risk premiums). However, this question does
not arise in the Samuelson system, in which investment does not
appear to be subject to a tendency toward diminishing returns.
The "tendency" toward diminishing returns, of course, is also a
matter of relative resource scarcities, although not of scarcities
in specialized resources.

In the present paper we shall relate investment to output
trends and we shall not limit the concept of the "induced" to what
is technologically justified by past rates of increase. The attempt
will be made to deal with the magnitudes involved in equation 1
in terms of long-run average values with the underlying assumption that errors may have largely cancelled over these periods,
and hence that the realized magnitudes disclose planned expected
relationships, except where there exist specific indications to the
contrary. Over these longer periods all terms of our basic equation tend to adjust. Obviously adjustments are far more limited
in the short run, and the general suggestion will be made that
comparison of the fluctuating short-run values of these variables
with their average long-run values may contribute to the understanding of the business cycle. This paper will not be concerned
with the interpretation of cyclical developments. But the kind
of cycle theory by which the present approach may be supplemented is one that develops cyclical errors and their consequences by contrasting short-run with long-run values. Such a
treatment focuses attention, not on the unexplained size of autonomous investment, but on the question of how and with what
lags the internal structure of the economy can adjust to the requirements that were expressed in aggregative terms.

2. The Harrod-Domar analysis

If the type of analysis developed by Mr. Harrod in England and
by Professor Domar in the United States is characterized broadly
enough, it may be considered identical with that underlying the
present approach.[7] Similar views have been expressed by other

[7] Cf. R. F. Harrod, "An Essay in Dynamic Theory," *Economic Journal*,
March 1939, and *Towards a Dynamic Economics* (London: St. Martins,

authors, including the present writer.[8] However, specific differences must also be pointed out.

Harrod uses the equation $G \cdot C = s$, where G stands for our $(\Delta O / \Delta t)/O$, C stands for our $\Delta V / \Delta O$, and s for our a. In elaborating upon this relationship, he later writes $G \cdot C = s - k$, where k expresses capital formation such as is "not deemed to have any immediate relation to current requirements." We prefer not to include such a term because consistent treatment of it would require the kind of period analysis suitable for short-run analysis and employed neither by Harrod nor in the present approach. Sooner or later all additions to capital must prove to be justified by "requirements," if no disturbance is to develop. Harrod's k is not intended to explain disturbances, but merely the lag that may arise between investment and its justification by "requirements."

Domar's apparatus is of a similar kind. The "equilibrium" rate of growth is defined as $a\sigma$, where a is the average propensity to save and σ is the reciprocal of our $\Delta V / \Delta O$ (or, more precisely, of our V/O, with explicit recognition of the fact that if the incremental ratio should be different from the average ratio, then the incremental ratio must be used). The resulting equation is identical with ours. It is not quite clear to us how much flexibility Domar attributes to σ (or to a) in the long run. Extreme rigidity is not assumed, but it seems to us that the present analysis places more emphasis on long-run adjustments of all variables to equilibrium requirements than does that of Domar. Our way of handling the matter is to find the long-run average values of these variables, recognizing the fact that they are likely to result from (usually incomplete) internal adjustments to changing conditions and that their long-run values may change considerably from one long period to another. We suggest that short-run disturbances may be analyzed in terms of deviations from these long-run values. Domar's way of handling the matter is that of finding the theoretical long-run rate of growth compatible with a more or less *given* (perhaps somewhat adjustable) $\Delta O / \Delta V$, and with a more or less *given* (perhaps somewhat adjustable) a. Economic conditions depend on whether this theoretical rate can

1948), lecture 3; E. D. Domar, "Expansion and Employment," *American Economic Review*, March 1947, and "The Problem of Capital Accumulation," *ibid.*, December 1948.

[8] William Fellner, *Monetary Policies and Full Employment* (University of California Press, 1946-47), pp. 27-45, 73-83.

be achieved in reality. However, some adjustability is assumed by him; and on the other hand, we do not postulate that the long-run values always express complete adjustment to equlibrium requirements.

The Harrod analysis possesses a specific characteristic which will not be incorporated into the present approach. When analyzing the equation

$$\frac{\Delta O/\Delta t}{O} \cdot \frac{\Delta V}{\Delta O} = a$$

(or, in his symbols, $GC = s$), Harrod describes three possible ways of interpreting $(\Delta O/\Delta t)/O$, and his theory consists largely of contrasting the values obtained on these three different interpretations. The *actual* rate of growth and the actual values of the other terms are the *ex post* magnitudes found for any period, i.e., the values by which this tautological relationship becomes always satisfied. *Warranted* values are those compatible with the equilibrium requirements of the system, so that the warranted rate of growth is that which is compatible with a true incremental capital requirement (leaving producers satisfied with what they have done), and compatible with the true or intended value of the propensity to save. The *natural* rate of growth is the maximum rate compatible with the underlying real factors, such as population growth, new resources, technological progress, etc. Only for a short while can the actual rate of growth exceed the natural. This limited possibility, whenever it exists, is a consequence of excess capacity. Aside from this, the actual rate can be no greater than the natural rate of growth. The analysis is based on the idea that the natural rate of growth may be lower than the warranted rate, in which case the actual rate will also become lower than the warranted and hence a deflationary tendency will develop. Later, given enough excess capacity, expansion again becomes possible, because, for a while, the actual rate of growth may exceed the natural. But if the natural rate falls short of the warranted, the *trend* is unfavorable. If, on the other hand, the natural rate of growth exceeds the warranted, the trend is likely to be favorable (even inflationary?), because there is no lasting reason for the actual rate to fall short of the warranted rate. In general, comparison of the natural rate with the warranted rate leads to an appraisal of the long-run tendency, while comparison of the warranted rate with the actual rate characterizes the framework in which the cycle problem may be approached.

In the analysis of the present paper, the existence of a definite "natural rate of growth" will not be assumed. This is because the marginal capital-output ratio depends on the methods of production selected, and these may adjust, especially in the longer run. With the appropriate capital-output ratio, the economy *could* always grow at the warranted rate (see Section D-1, supra). We will be concerned with observable long-run values involved in Harrod's $GC = s$, and we will assume that these tend to be the "warranted" values at the same time, except in periods where some disturbance was so long-lasting (or so repetitive in one and the same direction) that the values of the variables could not adjust during these periods. But even in these chronically disturbed periods, the trouble should not be attributed to the existence of some well-defined natural rate of growth. It should be attributed to the inability of G, C, and s,—or, in our terminology, of $(\Delta O/\Delta t)/O$, $\Delta V/\Delta O$, and a—to find their "equilibrium values" in relation to one another. In the short run, they can scarcely be assumed to hit their "equilibrium values" (or warranted values), except by accident. The observable values of any short period, selected at random, are practically certain to be different from the warranted values of Harrod. Hence we also suggest that the comparison of *warranted* with *short-run actual* values may prove to be a fruitful avenue of cycle research. But we will assume that the *long-run actual* values may be interpreted as first approximations to the warranted values and that, when they cannot be so interpreted, the reason is the same as that producing short-run discrepancies (namely, failure of these values to settle down at the appropriate level *in relation to each other* during the period of observation). We will not build on the concept of the natural rate of growth.

The rate of growth and the capital-output ratio may well show, and in many periods have shown, a tendency toward long-run adjustment at warranted levels. Furthermore, the propensity to save may also show such a tendency in the long run, because the saving habits of a society need not be independent of its investment opportunities. The rate of growth, taken in isolation, could always be great enough to absorb the available resources, were it not for the possibility of specific scarcities, which are frequently overlooked in purely aggregative analysis. But even though the rate of growth, taken in isolation, could always be sufficient (aside from specific scarcities), it is not always, in reality. Each investor is faced with uncertainty concerning the willingness of other investors to invest, and hence each investor is faced with uncertainty concerning aggregate effective demand. *Furthermore, each investor is faced with uncertainty concerning the specific composition of the aggregate demand which will be forthcoming.* Specific scarcities *or* these varieties of uncertainty may prevent the rate of growth from reaching "warranted" levels. Even aside from scarcities in specialized resources, the amount of new investment required for matching savings may, of course, give rise to gradually diminishing returns. This is because the relative scarcity in one of the broad factor categories may not be fully offset by improvements. But gradually diminishing returns could not limit the investment process were it not for uncertainty, which in each period sets *some* limit to the downward flexibility of the interest-plus-profit level. The concept of a definite natural rate of growth implies that the yield of investment, as well as relative income shares, is completely unadjustable to the equilibrium requirements of the system. Thereby the concept significantly overstates a limitation which is imposed by uncertainty.

The piece of truth overstated by the concept of a natural rate of growth is that the growth process could not continue in the face of a consistent and secular decline of returns. A "tendency" toward such a decline develops from a rate of increase in the capital stock which far exceeds the rate of increase in the supply of cooperating factors. The growth process requires that the tendency toward a consistent secular decline of returns should be counteracted by improvements the character of which must adjust to relative factor scarcities in the framework of a response mechanism. This is because the adjustability of interest rates, of relative income shares, and of saving habits to available investment opportunities is *limited.* Consequently, the adjustability of V/O and of $\Delta V/\Delta O$ to equilibrium requirements is also limited.

3. The Hicks analysis

Professor Hicks' recent statement of the relationship between the variables here considered brings out the point which we raised in connection with the extension of Samuelson's analysis.[9] Hicks views the "accelerator"—his v, which corresponds to Samuelson's β—as expressing the relationship between the rate of increase in

[9] J. R. Hicks, *A Contribution to the Theory of the Trade Cycle* (Oxford University Press, 1950).

output, on the one hand, and the amount of investment, on the other. It is the increase in output, not merely that in consumption, which induces investment. We pointed out earlier that, in such a broadened model, it becomes very clear that more investment justifies more investment, unless the economy runs into scarcities. With a given "accelerator"—a given v in Hicks' terminology, or a given $\Delta V/\Delta O$ in ours—economic activity may fluctuate and underutilization may develop. But whenever resources are available for expansion, producers *could* make the variable $(\Delta O/\Delta t)/O$ and the variable $\Delta V/\Delta O$ assume values which would result in an amount of investment such as absorbs savings at a higher level of output. Hence, when a cycle model is derived from such assumptions, the analysis rests essentially on the implied psychological attitudes (insufficient optimism) of investors.

In fact, the Hicks analysis makes this rather explicit, although the proposition is not stated in these terms. For the analysis proceeds on the assumption that the "accelerator" links the output increase of the past "period" (or sometimes of several past periods) to the "present" amount of investment, where, if no further assumption were added, one would have to conclude that such an "accelerator" is as much a psychological as a technological coefficient. This is because, given the past increase in output, more present and future investment will justify itself through future increases in output. But Hicks adds a further assumption. The "accelerator" determines merely the technologically "induced" investment from the *past increase in output*. In other words, it determines the investment which would be *technologically* justified if output were now stabilized at the level just achieved. In addition to this induced investment, there is "autonomous" investment, which, as long as resources are available, will justify itself in the future, provided that, in the future, enough of it is again undertaken. A cycle model can be obtained only on specific assumptions pertaining to some limited amount of autonomous investment which producers are "willing" to undertake. This is precisely what Hicks does. In his theory, the psychological assumption in question is "ultimate." It is given, and is incapable of being further explained, just like the technological or institutional data of the system.

We have seen that Harrod also introduces a term relating to investment undertaken with a long view. Harrod does not use the period analysis and consequently we did not find it easy to interpret his expression for this far-forward-looking investment with much precision. No such difficulty arises in the conceptual interpretation of Hicks' autonomous investment, since Hicks' analysis is developed in terms of functional periods. In Hicks' model, the difference between induced and autonomous investment is well defined. But, is it possible to form an opinion of the realism of an assumption concerning the relative amounts of "induced" and "autonomous" investment so defined? Such a distinction is an absolutely essential property of the Hicks model. In contrast to Harrod's analysis, the Hicks theory cannot be presented without stressing the distinction between autonomous and induced investment, and no opinion can be formed of the validity of this theory without the appraisal of quantitative assumptions concerning the two.

The analysis results in fluctuations that would tend to become explosive, were it not for the fact that, in the upper regions, the rise becomes slowed down significantly due to the increasingly full utilization of the available resources. The accelerator transforms this slowing down of the expansion into contraction, which, in the low regions, becomes slowed down (and hence, via the accelerator, becomes reversed) through the fact that under-maintenance determines a floor level for net disinvestment per period. This outcome of the Hicks analysis depends on the author's quantitative assumptions concerning the relationship between the numerical coefficients, that is, between the "accelerator" (linking the past output increase to the present induced investment), the propensity to save, and the amount of autonomous investment. A judgment on the plausibility of any such assumption involves appraisal of how much investment is continuously induced by "past" increases in output (i.e., would be technologically justified if, after a rise, output were to continue at "present" levels), and how much investment is forward-looking in the sense of not meeting this test.

It seems to us preferable to bypass this difficulty. For long periods the distinction between "induced" and "autonomous" investment is not fruitful because all justified investment must bear a reasonable relation to output trends. Unless restrictive psychological assumptions are introduced, purely aggregative analysis cannot discover the reasons why the proper relation is not always satisfied at full employment. In a cycle study the relevant question would seem to pertain to the deviations of all coefficients from their long-run values. This is a question of lagging internal adjustments, in specific sectors, to aggregative requirements and of uncertainty. It is not a question implying a distinction between investment *induced by past output increases alone* and a postulated rate of "autonomous" investment. We prefer not to build on such a distinction, although at the present stage of this kind of theory one should not purport to have very categorical views on what avenues will ultimately prove fruitful and what avenues will not.

E. THE *CETERIS PARIBUS* ASSUMPTIONS OF PROJECTIONS BASED ON THE RATE OF GROWTH AND THE MARGINAL CAPITAL-OUTPUT RATIO

We shall now return to that version of the "rate of growth and capital coefficients" approach which was broadly outlined in Section C-4. What is involved in using that version as an instrument of "projection"?

From past long-run experience we may obtain an idea of the likely future rate of growth of output, on certain *ceteris paribus* assumptions. The investigator will presumably not try to project the growth of output directly, but he will project population trends (or, more specifically, growth trends of the labor force), trends concerning the length of the working week, and trends in output per man-hour. These three types of projection, each interpreted on its own *ceteris paribus* assumptions, add up to a tentative projection of the rate of growth of output, provided that some further assumption is made concerning the future degree of "fullness" of employment. Wherever the investigator feels that he can (crudely) appraise the likelihood of deviations from the implied *ceteris paribus* assumptions, he can either try to make adjustments, carefully indicating what he has done, or he can simply call attention to the likelihood of these deviations and let the persons responsible for the ultimate decisions make the adjustments. No one is a "professional expert" in making adjustments of this sort.

From the long-run behavior of data, the investigator may also derive projections concerning the future marginal capital-output ratio. These also imply *ceteris paribus* assumptions, and the likelihood of deviations from these must again be appraised informally.

298

One element in the picture which calls for informal appraisal, and requires special attention at this point, is the consistency of the assumptions underlying the output-growth projection with the assumptions underlying the capital-output-ratio projection. For example, if the output trend is projected on the assumption of (practically) full use of capacity, the question arises as to how the past capital-output-ratio experience is affected by the fact that (practically) full use did not exist all the time. If, on the other hand, the output trend is projected on the assumption of a degree of utilization such as existed in the past, the future likelihood of more effective employment policies and perhaps primarily the likelihood of considerably higher government expenditures call for the same kind of supplementary appraisal.

The investigator now has a more or less "informed" guess of future private capital formation, on several corrected *ceteris paribus* assumptions and on some specific assumption concerning the degree of utilization. The consistency of this must be tested against a similarly "informed" guess of government expenditures and of tax payments plus individual and business savings. For, at the levels of output so projected, the planned private capital formation plus the government expenditures on goods and services must absorb the tax payments and the voluntary savings. The contrary assumption implies the kinds of disequilibrium and disturbances which are inconsistent with the method of approach here envisaged. The past experience which we have consulted is one relating to *average* conditions over longer periods, and it is implied that the observed magnitudes express habits and plans, i.e., that they do not to any substantial extent contain haphazard and irregular components such as unintentional savings (or dissavings) and unplanned accumulations (or shortages) of capital. If the data of some specific "long period" seem to be significantly affected by such unintentional components (e.g., if a decade was one of protracted depression or of chronic inflationary pressures), then it is advisable either to disregard this part of the experience, or at least to "correct" it by some method of informal appraisal. Projections so derived should be made to apply to average conditions over longer future periods, with similar implications. An entirely different kind of apparatus would be required to try to trace the "cyclical" consequences of a discrepancy between planned savings and investments. We are concerned with long-run projections, and even the most self-confident "forecaster" of cyclical developments would presumably shy away from saying anything about cyclical impacts several cycles ahead.

The method here considered implies that the projected trend expresses conditions in which the plus and minus differences between planned and realized magnitudes have cancelled out, so to speak.[10] This, in turn, requires that the planned private investment plus the government expenditure should balance with the tax payments plus voluntary savings. It is possible, of course, to postulate that government expenditures and tax rates will be set in such a way as to accomplish this balance. This means deriving a private investment projection on the assumption of some definite degree of employment (for example, practically full employment), and adding that one condition of this amount's becoming "attainable" is that government expenditures and tax rates be set in a fashion such that voluntary savings plus tax revenues at the levels of activity in question should equal the estimated private investment plus the government expenditure. However, any agency (or individual) interested in such a projection would like to know what its probable quantitative implications are for taxation and government spending. Moreover, not every spending and taxing policy is feasible, and not every amount of taxation (let alone every kind of taxation) is compatible with the incentives required to call forth the projected output trends. Consequently, a satisfactory treatment of this problem requires an analysis of what voluntary savings may be expected at the output levels implied, and also of the feasibility of the fiscal policy which would produce monetary equilibrium at those levels. The projected investment figure is attainable only if these fiscal policies are feasible, and if the other assumptions of the individual projection (the "corrected *ceteris paribus* assumptions" of each component of the projection) turn out to be realistic.

Appraisal of these various assumptions by general "judgment" is a highly involved matter. Consequently, the logical case that can be made for using such a method for projection is not particularly strong. But this is true of economic projection in general. It is true of all attempts (including the attempts we make in our

---

[10] But the method does *not* imply that the plans themselves, and hence the long-run averages realized, or trends, were uninfluenced by cyclical fluctuations and the ensuing uncertainties (cf. footnote 25).

everyday lives) at analyzing highly incomplete experience with the purpose of basing our decisions on it. In all these cases, informal correction of essential *ceteris paribus* assumptions is required. The result depends just as much on these quasi-intuitive corrections as on the rigorous part of the logical analysis. In all these cases it is easy to ridicule the method, if it is measured by the standards of some highly developed natural science. But it remains a fact that we are compelled to make up our minds on a great many matters where the best we can do is to combine the analysis of experience with essential supplementary judgments of an informal kind. The general type of approach here envisaged poses very complex problems to this faculty of appraisal, and different persons are very likely to arrive at different conclusions with respect to the appropriateness of alternative appraisals. But we submit that, on the whole, the problems so posed are fairly articulate, and that the *type of analysis* of which the projections now discussed are the "engineering" equivalents has the merit of throwing light on the mechanism underlying the process of capital formation.

However, it is necessary to emphasize one consideration which is frequently overlooked in connection with the requirement of consistency between the estimate of future capital formation and hence of real saving, *as a constituent of an output estimate* (via the propensity to save), on the one hand, and the capital formation estimate derived from output trends and capital coefficients, on the other. In an automatically and fully adjusting economy, this consistency requirement would always be met. It would not have to be created by fiscal policy. This is because, in such an economy, the capital-output ratio would always assume the value corresponding to the postulate that all voluntary savings (plus whatever tax payments there are) must be absorbed by the planned private capital formation (plus whatever government expenditures are made). A given amount of savings will result in more output growth if investment opportunities are available at a low capital-output ratio than if absorption of all savings requires increasing capital-output ratios. But investment opportunities are always available at some capital-output ratio, and these opportunities would always be seized upon in a fully adjusting economy. Moreover, if all investors acted on the expectation that these investment opportunities would prove profitable, and if, in each subsequent period, they again absorbed all savings, then these expectations would justify themselves, except in the event of specific scarcities which might preclude the completion of investment projects.[11] We all know that the economy is not fully adjusting in this sense. But it should not be assumed that the economy is fully nonadjusting in the same sense.

In other words, any inconsistency that may be found between the resulting capital formation estimate (as a constituent of an output estimate) and the output trend plus capital coefficients initially implied in the derivation of the capital formation estimate should give rise to the question of whether, in the given circumstances, some or all of the inconsistency is likely to become eliminated by the internal flexibility of the system. Short-run flexibility may be very limited, but we are here concerned with long-run trends. Long-run flexibility cannot simply be assumed away, especially if major short-run disturbances are effectively counteracted. The possibility that inconsistencies of this sort may be partly eliminated by the internal flexibility of the system should lead the investigator to pose to himself the question whether his "corrected *ceteris paribus* assumptions" should not be corrected once more, after provisional completion of his estimate (i.e., whether the first round of estimating should not be followed by a second). *This is because elimination of inconsistencies by internal adjustments is in itself a possible source of deviations from ceteris paribus assumptions.* Growth trends and trends in the capital-output ratios may become different from what they were because they partially adjust to the requirements of the system.

The problem now considered may give rise to a substantial dilemma on the policy level, because the policies appropriate to promoting internal adjustments are not, in general, identical with those suitable for eliminating inconsistencies by "compensatory fiscal policy." It is possible to overemphasize this conflict of objectives, because in some important respects the two types of policy overlap. For example, the use of monetary and fiscal policy for counteracting cumulative contractionary disturbances (to the extent that this is compatible with a reasonably stable price level) presumably promotes internal adjustments in addition to having desirable direct effects. But, if we are faced with a secular imbalance between saving and investment at desirable levels of employment, the policy suitable for the direct filling

[11] See comments on this point in Section D-1.

of gaps *may* differ from the policy appropriate to promoting balance through internal adjustments. The one may call for undertaking government investment, even if this is somewhat competitive with private investment; the other may lead to suppressing projects of this kind. The two objectives may also call for different degrees of tax graduation. These are matters which must ultimately be decided by policy makers rather than "professional persons," but economic analysis is required for describing the alternative sets of policy decisions and for weighing the likelihood of their success as measured by their own standards. As we shall see later, there is reason to believe that long-run internal adjustments have played an important part in shaping the course of events over many decades.

It follows that the internal adjustments of the system need to be taken into account *not merely* when the question is raised whether there exists an automatic tendency toward the elimination of possible inconsistencies between investment projections (as constituents of output projections) and the output projections implied in the investment projections. Even if the results are consistent, it must be remembered that the past experience so projected already reflects adjustment processes, and that this experience might have been quite different if the behavior of the cost-price data on which individual firms partly base their investment decisions had been different from those actually observable. If there exist reasons to expect differences between the past and the future with respect to price-wage relations, relative prices, the amount and the kind of taxation, the state of liquidity, the state of the capital market, international relations, and so forth, then allowances must be made for these. Only in exceptionally fortunate circumstances could there exist a satisfactory *technical* (statistical) method of measuring them.

It is impossible not to be impressed by what is involved in the quasi-intuitive allowances which were discussed in the present section. The method of approach with which we are concerned in this paper certainly does not qualify as a method of "projection" in any true sense. But as a method of guidance toward informed analysis—and, if necessary, toward informed guesswork—it still seems superior to its potential alternatives. Mechanical projections based on the equations of Section C-4 may create much confusion and they may do much harm. But an investigator who analyzes the relationships expressed in the

303

equations and supplements such analysis by proper discussion of the factors that stay in the background of the equations—that is, an investigator who pays proper attention to the nature of the underlying *ceteris paribus* assumptions and to possible ways of correcting these—may contribute to the understanding of the investment process. Occasionally he may also prove helpful to persons who are compelled to base decisions on highly incomplete evidence.

F. ESTIMATES OF AGGREGATIVE DATA: KUZNETS' DECADE AVERAGES FROM 1869 TO 1929 AND ROUGH SUPPLEMENTARY COMPUTATIONS FOR THE PAST TWO DECADES

The estimates published in Simon Kuznets' *National Product since 1869*[12] will here be used for computing the decade averages of the magnitudes entering into the equation

$$\frac{\Delta O/\Delta t}{O} \cdot \frac{\Delta V}{\Delta O} -$$

The ΔV term excludes the value of unimproved land and consumers' stocks and it includes government expenditures resulting in tangible assets.[13] Other government expenditures, if included in O (that is, if not interpreted as instrumental services or mere transfers), are regarded as part of consumption. O will stand for net national product, unless otherwise explained.

A few introductory comments are necessary.

1. If the equation above is used $(\Delta O/\Delta t)/O$ must mean $\Delta O/\Delta t$ divided by the O of the second of the two periods used in computing ΔO; and $\Delta V/\Delta O$ must mean the ΔV between end-dates of two periods, divided by the change in output between these two periods. This can most easily be seen if we write the equation in the following form (with the subscripts standing for periods, such as decades):

$$\frac{O_n - O_{n-1}}{O_n} \cdot \frac{V_n - V_{n-1}}{O_n - O_{n-1}} = a_n$$

This reduces to

$$V_n - V_{n-1} = a_n O_n$$

[12] (NBER, 1946).

[13] Therefore, the "capital" concept in question includes land improvements, building, durable producers' goods, business inventories, and claims against foreign countries. Cf. *ibid.*, particularly tables II-16 and IV-10.

an equation which is correct if V_n applies to the end-date of period n, and V_{n-1} to the end-date of period $n-1$. If we want to trace through the mutual adjustments of the data in the framework of this kind of equation, then the dating must be such as is just described. But for certain purposes we may prefer to have an estimate of $\Delta V / \Delta O$ in the sense of the change between capital stock at the *midpoint* of output periods divided by the change of output between the two periods. What we want for some purposes is better approximated by

$$\frac{V_{1889} - V_{1879}}{O_{1884\text{-}93} - O_{1874\text{-}83}} \text{ than by } \frac{V_{1889} - V_{1879}}{O_{1879\text{-}88} - O_{1869\text{-}78}}$$

where the subscripts stand for years and decades, respectively. This is because the output of a longer period was more nearly produced (in some average sense) by the factors of production available at the midpoint of the decade than by the stock of the end-date. The equation will not come out right with such dating, and hence this dating does not provide a consistent framework for investigating the mutual adjustments of the terms appearing in our equation. But if we are interested in a question such as "What does experience show with respect to the relationship between capital and output?" midpoint stock estimates are more pertinent. It is not very desirable to try to answer this question in a framework which cannot be broadened into one suitable for tracing mutual adjustments. Hence we are faced here with a limitation, provided that the behavior of $\Delta V / \Delta O$ depends *very much* on whether we use midpoint or end-date data for the capital stock. All data of the first six columns of Table 1 are dated consistently with the requirements of equation 1 of Section C-4, and hence the $\Delta V / \Delta O$ data of column 4 are based on V data for the end-dates of the output periods, for example,

$$\frac{V_{1889} - V_{1879}}{O_{1879\text{-}88} - O_{1869\text{-}78}}$$

The columns following column 6 contain supplementary information not pressed into the framework of the equation, and one of these columns (7) includes $\Delta V / \Delta O$ data computed from capital stock changes at midpoints, for example,

$$\frac{V_{1889} - V_{1879}}{O_{1884\text{-}93} - O_{1874\text{-}83}}$$

305

TABLE 1

CAPITAL-OUTPUT AND INVESTMENT-OUTPUT (SAVING-OUTPUT) RATIOS (IN PERCENT) BASED ON CAPITAL AND OUTPUT FIGURES IN BILLIONS OF 1929 DOLLARS

Decades	(1)	(2)	(3)	(4)	(5)	(6)	Decades	(7)	(8)	(9)	(10)
1869-78	9.5	46.9	26.8	3.19	15.0	14.5	1874-83	3.67	3.22	2.98	2.85
1879-88	17.9	26.0	39.3	6.24	16.2	16.2	1884-93	4.46	4.38	3.20	2.98
1889-98	24.2	35.3	51.5	3.90	13.8	13.6	1894-1903	3.37	3.38	3.58	3.39
1899-1908	37.4	24.3	54.4	4.53	11.0	13.0	1904-13	5.18	5.08	3.50	3.39
1909-18	49.4	27.7	62.5	3.31	9.1	10.2	1914-23	2.01	2.30	3.82	3.75
1919-28	68.3						1929ᵃ			3.18	3.26

Explanation of Title

Column	Title	Explanation of Title
1	O	Average yearly output, in the sense of "net national product, peacetime concept." Net change in claims against foreign countries is excluded. Inclusive of this, the figures would be the following, from top to bottom: 9.3, 17.9, 24.2, 37.3, 50.6, and 69.0.
2	$\Delta O/\Delta t$	Change in total output from preceding decade to decade in question divided by output of decade in question.
3	ΔV	Change in capital stock, excluding foreign claims, from end of preceding decade to end of decade in question. Stocks in possession of households and unimproved land are excluded here and in all subsequent columns.
4	$\dfrac{\Delta V}{\Delta O}$	Column 3 divided by change in column 1 from preceding decade to decade in question.
5	α	Increment of capital stock excluding foreign claims divided by column 1.
6	α_1	Increment of capital stock, including foreign claims, divided by output including change in foreign claims.
7	$\dfrac{\Delta V}{\Delta O}$	Like column 4, except that change in capital stock is computed from *middle* of preceding decade to *middle* of decade in question.
8	$\dfrac{\Delta V}{\Delta O}$	Like column 7, except that capital stock includes foreign claims and output includes the change in foreign claims.
9	$\dfrac{V}{O}$	Capital stock of middle of decade excluding foreign claims divided by output excluding the change in foreign claims.
10	$\dfrac{V}{O}$	Like column 8, except that capital stock includes foreign claims and output includes the change in foreign claims.

ᵃ The decade of 1924-33 is significantly affected by the Great Depression, which is not "smoothed out" effectively by decade

The type of behavior shown by the data of column 7 seems sufficiently similar to that shown by those of column 4 not to rule out this kind of approach on these grounds alone.

2. The capital stock estimates from which the V figures of column 3 were computed exclude the claims of the United States against foreign countries. This is because we had to take those stock estimates which Kuznets made comparable with his capital formation estimates, so that increments of the stock equal Kuznets' net capital formation. The Kuznets series, which in this sense was made comparable with capital formation estimates, does not include foreign claims. Such stock estimates are meaningful. However, the figures of column 5 (a) computed in this fashion are not directly meaningful because the savings going into foreign claims cannot be distinguished meaningfully from other savings. It was necessary to give in column 5 the a figures computed by omitting the increment of foreign claims from capital formation. The first five columns contain data that, in conjunction with each other, satisfy equation 1 of Section C-4, and hence the figures of column 5 could not include foreign claims. Column 6 contains figures which differ from the a figures in that they do include increments of foreign claims. Again it may be submitted that the difference between the behavior of the two series is not so great as to rule out this type of approach.

For the reason just indicated, the $\Delta V/\Delta O$ figures of columns 4 and 7 are based on ΔV estimates which exclude changes in the claims against foreign countries. In column 8 we give $\Delta V/\Delta O$ estimates which include these changes. This correction was made only for the "midpoint of the period" method and not for the "end-date" method. In other words, column 8 is like column 7, not like column 4, so far as dating is concerned.

3. In the framework of which this analysis is developed, equation 1 of Section C-4 does not require reliance on stock estimates (V), but merely reliance on capital formation estimates (ΔV). Absolute stock (V) estimates are affected not merely by all the sources of error which inevitably render the capital formation (ΔV) estimates unprecise, but they are affected also by further sources of error. This is because V estimates imply knowledge of the stock at the beginning of the period of analysis. Estimates of this initial stock are very unreliable. However, in column 9, we give estimates of "stock per unit of output" (V/O) which were computed from the stock and the output estimates pub-

lished in Kuznets' *National Product since 1869.* The stock estimates on which column 9 is based are like those from which
the increments appearing in column 2 were derived, except that
we used the stock estimates applying to the midpoint of each
output decade rather than those applying to the end-date. Column 9 is not required for tracing adjustments in the framework
of our equation, and for all other purposes midpoint dating
seems more desirable. The V figures, which constitute the numerators of the data of column 9, are those made comparable with
Kuznets' direct estimates of net capital formation. Hence, they
exclude claims against foreign countries.

From decade to decade there was a considerable amount of
variation in all magnitudes entering into our equation. The rate
of growth of output, the marginal capital-output ratio, and a
(also a_1) varied a good deal during this period. There is no
justification for interpreting the figures of the table as equilibrium magnitudes in any strict sense because short-run instability
influences the planned as well as the realized long-run magnitudes of the economy. Average values over the cycle do not
show what would have happened in the absence of cyclical disturbances. Trend values are not equilibrium values. But there
surely exist strong reasons for believing that plus and minus
differences between planned and realized magnitudes partly "cancel" in the long run. Realized data tend to come closer to planned
data in the long run than in the short run, even though the long-
run planned data themselves (e.g., decade averages) may be
significantly influenced by the fact that everybody is aware of
the uncertainties connected with cyclical fluctuations.[14] The data
included in Table 1 may be interpreted as expressing this partial
realization of error-cancelling tendencies. In this limited sense it
is permissible to speak of mutual adjustments, rather than merely
of changes from period to period, in the basic data of the table.

The main change in the rate of growth of output (column 2)
appears to be retardation, if the first figure—that pertaining to
the transition from the seventies to the eighties—is included in
the comparisons. If the first figure (46.9 percent) is disregarded—
that is, if the comparison is limited to the subsequent four figures—no clear case can be made for retardation, but there still
remain oscillations of some significance. The a and a_1 figures
show a downward tendency beginning with the turn of century.

[14] See footnote 25.

The marginal capital-output ratio shows considerable fluctuations, only part of which can be explained away with reference to special circumstances. The abnormally high figure for the transition from the eighties to the nineties (especially in column 4) may be partly a consequence of the chronically depressed character of the nineties. That is to say, for the present purpose, decade averaging, which so very obviously does not smooth out the Great Depression of the 1930's, may be more inadequate for the 1890's than for the other decades included in the table (although less inadequate for all these decades than for the 1930's). Furthermore, it may be argued that the very high figures obtained in columns 7 and 8 for the transition from 1904-13 to 1914-23 result partly from the circumstance that the decade output of 1914-23 is affected by the postwar depression, while the corresponding capital stock estimate for 1919 is not. This, however, is not a completely convincing argument in itself, because, aside from this, one would expect to get a low $\Delta V/\Delta O$ figure for the incremental ratio leading into the World War I period, while we obtain a somewhat high (rather than a somewhat low) figure even in column 4, where the output is not affected by the postwar depression. It is conceivable that the remaining difference could be accounted for adequately by excluding from ΔV that part of the government investment which did not increase the "normal" capital stock of the economy. Finally the very low last figure in column 7 (also in column 8) may result partly from the arbitrariness of using the data of a single year (in order to avoid bringing in years of the Great Depression). Tentative calculations made for other years of the late 1920's lead us to believe that the choice, for the sake of symmetry, of 1929 as the relevant single year somewhat lowers the figure as compared with possible alternative choices. But, regardless of how much can or cannot be explained away if enough skill is used, the $\Delta V/\Delta O$ columns must be said to show considerable variation.

The table has not been brought up to date because decade averaging clearly does not perform adequately for our purpose in the 1930's or in the 1940's. Yet, it seems justified to add a few comments on the behavior of the capital-output relationship in the course of the past two decades.

During the Great Depression there existed substantial excess capacity, and spuriously high figures would be obtained for the average capital-output ratio. These could be used only as rough indicators of idle capital. In the late thirties—in years such as 1937 and 1939—both real output and the aggregate stock were approximately at their predepression levels. This is true if we compute the stock (as we have done throughout this analysis) by adding the price-deflated market value of net capital formation to the "initial stock." In efficiency units the real capital of 1937 or 1939 may well have been greater than that of 1929. But this is irrelevant for the purpose of V/O (or $\Delta V/\Delta O$) computations because measurement in efficiency units necessarily (tautologically) results in unitary ratios. If we measure the stock by the method employed in the present analysis, the average capital-output ratio of the late thirties must have been similar to that of 1929. During World War II, output rose very substantially and capital stock increased in a much smaller proportion. The capital stock of the economy was abnormally "fully" utilized. Since the beginning of the postwar period, the capital stock has risen more rapidly than the output flow, but computations of the sort here used would undoubtedly show that, at present, the *average* capital-output ratio is still well below the prewar figure. The use of Department of Commerce estimates for recent additions to the capital stock leads to this conclusion. Similar conclusions could be based on preliminary estimates by Mr. Raymond W. Goldsmith.[15]

In a crude appraisal of general orders of magnitude, we may say that the stock of the late twenties can be valued at about $280 billion in 1929 prices,[16] or at close to $500 billion in the prices ruling at the outbreak of the Korean war in 1950. The net private capital increment of the period 1929-49 corresponds to roughly $100-120 billion in mid-1950 prices, with allowance for reconversion of wartime capital. In contrast to approximately a 20-25 percent increase in the stock, there has occurred from 1929 to the Korean outbreak approximately a 75 percent increase in the national product deflated for price changes. The V/O so computed comes close to 2.7 with foreign claims included, as in column 10 of Table 1. Inclusion of the postwar capital formation in the government sector might raise the ratio to perhaps 2.8.[17]

[15] International Association for Research in Income and Wealth, *Income and Wealth in the United States*, Income and Wealth Series II (Cambridge, England: Bowes and Bowes, 1952).
[16] On the basis of the Kuznets series from which the data of columns 9 and 10 of our table were computed.
[17] The ratio approximating 2.7 results from a stock valued at close to

In the *immediate* postwar period, the ratio was much lower because the bulk of the 1929-49 capital formation occurred in the postwar years. For a comparison of the late thirties with the first half of 1950, the $\Delta V/\Delta O$ is about 1.0-1.2, the numerator being $100-120 billion and the denominator about $100 billion in prices obtaining immediately prior to the Korean war. Here, again, an upward correction should be made for the postwar capital formation in the government sector. Consequently, 1.2-1.5 would seem to be a reasonable estimate for $\Delta V/\Delta O$.

An aggregative marginal capital-output ratio of such small size implies one of two things. One possible implication is that at the end of the forties there still existed a significant backlog of capital in the American economy. The $\Delta V/\Delta O$ figures obtained from a comparison of capital and output in successive postwar years (or subperiods) during the second half of the forties are very high, because the economy was obviously making up for a backlog at that time. It is quite possible that at the end of the decade there still existed an important backlog and that this explains why the $\Delta V/\Delta O$ ratio computed from the late thirties to mid-1950 is 1.5 or less. This would mean that producers were aiming at higher capital-output ratios than those statistically observable, but that they had had no time to realize these ratios (or to catch up with the output trend, so to speak). They were merely on their way toward more desirable capital-output ratios.

This interpretation could be based on the fact that past experience points to a considerably higher ΔV requirement per unit of ΔO than the $\Delta V/\Delta O$ observable for a direct transition from the late twenties to the end of the forties. Among the $\Delta V/\Delta O$ figures leading into the decade of the twenties, the last figure of column 8 of our table would seem to be most nearly suitable for contrasting with the unitary $\Delta V/\Delta O$ now considered. This figure is 2.3. It is less influenced by the inevitable arbitrariness of price deflation techniques than are the data for the earlier decades, since all data are expressed in 1929 prices. Furthermore, recent Kuznets estimates which relate to various in-

---

$620 billion and a net output of about $230 billion. The 1929-49 capital formation estimate of $100-120 billion does not include the postwar government (public) investment. In the period 1919-39, between 15 and 20 percent of the total gross capital formation was in the government sector. The share in net capital formation must have been greater, but if this relationship has not become entirely different for the postwar years, the average capital-output ratio so corrected can scarcely exceed about 2.8.

311

dividual sectors of the economy make it appear likely that the $\Delta V/\Delta O$ figures leading into the twenties are not significantly influenced by changes in the relative weights of these sectors. Therefore, we may say that as we move into the twenties, the observable over-all $\Delta V/\Delta O$ ratios express pretty well the then "normal" tendencies manifesting themselves in the individual sectors of the economy, and that these tendencies would have had to change radically if the more recent ratio of about 1.5 or less were to be interpreted as being "normal" now. If no radical departure from observed *past* tendencies is assumed, the conclusion would be that at the end of the forties the economy was still making up for a capital backlog.

We are inclined to the view that this inference is realistic, but the foregoing reasoning is inconclusive. It is conceivable that the experience of the twenties, and of earlier decades, should be interpreted as indicating a gradual fall in $\Delta V/\Delta O$. This interpretation, too, is compatible with the data of the table. Moreover, it is conceivable that, since the late twenties or thirties, we have been experiencing shifts in the composition of output such as would result in the lowering of the "normal" over-all $\Delta V/\Delta O$, even if the "normal" $\Delta V/\Delta O$ of the individual sectors should not be declining. It is, therefore, not obvious from what has been said so far that past experience points to the likelihood of a $\Delta V/\Delta O$ ratio exceeding 1.5, and, hence, that it points to the existence of a considerable capital backlog at the end of the forties.

Yet we believe that the hypothesis of a backlog is supported, although not proved, by data concerning individual sectors of the economy. Professor Kuznets made these data available to the writer in the form of preliminary estimates. Recently some of these were published.[18] These estimates show a markedly rising long-run tendency for the ratio of fixed capital to output in manufacturing and agriculture, sectors having comparatively low ratios (lower than that applying to the economy as a whole).[19] The data show no appreciable trend for the other sectors with comparatively low ratios, and a markedly falling

---

[18] International Association for Research in Income and Wealth, *op.cit.*, pp. 117ff.

[19] The estimates for 1938 (*ibid.*, pp. 122 and 127) should probably be disregarded because the corresponding output period (1934-43) includes a period of substantial "overutilization" of the capital stock. However, if not disregarded, the 1938 figures point to a reversal of the trend.

trend for the ratios in several sectors with high ratios (higher than that applying to the economy as a whole). One possible explanation would seem to be that in the high sectors cost saving largely *means* reducing the ratio of capital to output, while in the low sectors innovations may pay even if they go with some increase in the capital-output ratio provided they reduce the labor-output ratio sufficiently. At any rate the ratios for manufacturing and agriculture have been rising. If our aggregative $\Delta V/\Delta O$ ratio were to become stabilized at a "normal" level of 1.5 or less, then our aggregative V/O ratio would also have to tend gradually toward this level. This would imply an unlikely rearrangement by which the ratios for typically high sectors (utilities, transportation, construction) fall below the ratios for manufacturing and agriculture, *unless* of course the rising trend for these low sectors also should give way to a falling trend. At present, these sectors have ratios which exceed 1.5.

In our judgment, the argument pointing to the abnormality of a $\Delta V/\Delta O$ ratio of 1.5 or less—that is, the argument pointing to a pre-Korean capital backlog—is fairly strong. Nevertheless, we shall consider 1.5-1.0 the lower limit of the range of the $\Delta V/\Delta O$ values, the implications of which are still worth examining.

G. THE PROBLEM OF PROJECTION

What conclusions could have been drawn from these data, if in the summer of 1950 the war in Korea had not created a new situation?

Roughly speaking, past experience points to an average yearly increase in man-hour output of about 2.5 percent. Considering that the labor force is rising at a yearly rate of more than 1 percent, but that (aside from acute emergencies) yearly hours of work per man may perhaps be expected to show a mildly declining tendency, let us initially assume an average yearly rise in output of 3 percent. This is a very rough guess, but, with qualifications to be added later, adequate as a point of departure for the present purpose.[20] In the "long run," more pretentiously in-

[20] Preliminary estimates point to the following rates of increase of output per man-hour in the American economy as a whole: from 1890 to 1900, 25 percent; from 1900 to 1920 (20 years), 66 percent; from 1920 to 1930, 30 percent; from 1930 to 1940, 33 percent; from 1940 to 1949 (nine years), 24 percent. In the writer's opinion, preliminary estimates point to the likelihood that hours per week would tend to fall by a smaller percentage

terpreted (in the secular long run, so to speak), the main question would be that of the fundamental continuity of Western socio-economic institutional development and of the continued ability of the economic system to produce the structural and technological changes which have given rise to the observed trends. But, at present, we are concerned with a shorter "long run." We shall assume no break in the basic trends. In fact, some of these have proved very resistant to considerable environmental change.

The GNP (gross national product) of the first half of 1950 was about $270 billion at an annual rate, so that even a $\Delta V/\Delta O$ ratio of 1.0-1.5 would have corresponded to net private capital formation of roughly $10 billion[21] and hence to gross private capital formation of about $30 billion. It would have been reasonable to project government expenditures on goods and services at a yearly rate of about $40 billion (the rate immediately prior to the Korean war), and initially to assume that these will be tax-financed. The experience of the late forties and of the first half of 1950 points to the likelihood that, in such circumstances, reasonably full employment would have required a greater amount of gross private capital formation than the $30 billion resulting from the foregoing calculations. It probably would have required about $10-15 billion more than the figure at which we have arrived.[22]

Crude as this calculation is, it points to the likelihood that, aside from disturbances so far disregarded, the system would have tended to operate at high capacity. Waiving at first the question of whether the initial $\Delta V/\Delta O$ figure is not too low—that is, of whether the figure of 1.0-1.5 should not be replaced by a higher figure *even before* adjustments of the system to

---

than that by which the labor force was expected to rise during the next few years.

[21] Being here concerned merely with *private* capital formation, the argument of Section F would make the lower limit fall in the range 1.0-1.2 rather than 1.0-1.5. The figure of $10 billion corresponds to 1.2.

[22] In the inflationary peak year 1948, personal consumption expenditure was $177.9 billion; gross private domestic investment, $42.7 billion; net foreign investment, $1.9 billion; and the government purchase of goods and services, $36.6 billion. In the mild recession year 1949, personal consumption expenditure was $180.2 billion; gross private domestic investment, $33.0 billion; net foreign investment, $0.5 billion; and the government purchase, $43.6 billion. In the first half of 1950, personal consumption expenditure was $186.7 billion at an annual rate; gross private domestic investment, $44.0 billion; net foreign investment, $—1.6 billion; and the government purchase, $40.7 billion.

equilibrium requirements are considered—the conclusion would seem to be that it would have taken a government deficit of perhaps $15 billion to raise total expenditure by the amount of the deficiency. However, if probable internal adjustments are taken into account, the deficit (tax reduction or deficit-financed additional expenditure) required for reasonably full utilization would presumably have been smaller (*perhaps* even zero). In the first place, it seems very unlikely that, under conditions characterized by a tendency toward insufficiency of investment opportunities, the accumulation of undistributed corporate profits would have continued at an unchanging rate. Distribution of all profits might have eliminated much the greater part of a $10-15 billion deficiency, because, in the periods of high activity immediately prior to the Korean war, undistributed corporate profits were accruing at an average yearly rate of $13 billion. Even considerable reduction of the undistributed percentage of all profits would have brought the deficiency below the $10 billion level.

Furthermore, other internal adjustments might also have taken place. Even if the $\Delta V/\Delta O$ ratio of 1.0-1.5 were an adequate point of departure, this marginal ratio might well have shown a tendency to rise in response to unused investment opportunities requiring higher ratios; or the growth-rate of output could have become correspondingly higher, with the reduced capital-requirement per unit of growth. After all, past experience does not point to rigid behavior of this ratio. It points more to mutual adjustments of the variables included in our basic equation. It is impossible to tell whether these various adjustments would have merely reduced a $10 billion deficiency, thus reducing the need for a deficit, or whether they would have practically eliminated it. This would have depended partly on factors such as credit policies, wage policies, and tax policies, and, in general, on how successfully the proper balance would have been reached between the stimulating effect of mass purchasing power (high propensity to consume), on the one hand, and the required incentive effect of inequality, on the other. Assuming reasonably favorable surrounding circumstances, the order of magnitude of the deficiency might well have declined far below $10 billion per year, even with a balanced budget. Moreover, as a consequence of rising productivity, an average yearly budget deficit of about $7 billion might have merely prevented the public debt from falling in relation to the national income; and an average yearly deficit of somewhat more than this might still not have raised the debt burden in a higher proportion than that in which the tax revenue would have tended to rise at unchanging tax rates and constant prices. This is not to say that stabilizing the proportion of the debt burden to the (rising) national income at its pre-Korean relative level would have been desirable. But it is submitted that even the highly "pessimistic" (in the sense of low) assumption of a $\Delta V/\Delta O$ ratio of 1.0-1.5 would not have pointed to a seriously deflationary long-run problem.

Considering that the relevant data for this argument are percentage rates and ratios, and that their relative magnitudes in question would not seem to depend *much* on the absolute level of output (within reasonable limits), the outcome is not *appreciably* affected by using the initial rather than the terminal data of (say) a five-year period.

In an analysis aiming at numerical precision, this statement would have to be made subject to qualifications of which only one will be explicit here. If, aside from the war in Korea, the aggregate government expenditure had remained numerically stable, or had risen less than output, then, with consumption and private investment accounting for a stable proportion of output, the "deficiency" would have tended to be greater at the end of a longer period than at its beginning. While, on the assumption of balanced budgets, tax revenues like government expenditures would have risen less than output, this in itself would have been an incomplete offset to the decline in government expenditures relative to output because part of the tax saving would have tended to go into private savings rather than consumption. But qualifications of this kind are of small consequence in an appraisal of rough orders of magnitude over a period of (say) five years.

If the initially assumed $\Delta V/\Delta O$ is raised, then it becomes necessary to distinguish between a prospective period of gradually diminishing backlog and a subsequent "normal" period. Even without "internal adjustments," the $10-15 billion initial deficiency resulting from the foregoing calculation is eliminated for a normal period if we assume an over-all $\Delta V/\Delta O$ ratio of about 2.5. On the basis of the past experience here discussed, it is readily conceivable that there has been a tendency in this direction and that, after making up for the backlog, the economy would have operated in such circumstances. If the "normal" $\Delta V/\Delta O$ actually was in this order, then a neatly balanced picture may be drawn by the aggregative method here employed. But the picture would become balanced only for a more distant period in which the economy would have already made up the backlog. In the meantime, the economy would have had to go through an inflationary period. This is because, on this assumption, the economy did not in the late forties possess the capital normally corresponding to the simultaneous output. It would have had this capital if the net capital formation of the preceding two decades had been about twice as great as was actually the case. The tendency to catch up would have continued well into the fifties. The length of time it would have taken to eliminate the backlog would have depended partly on the nature and the effectiveness of the anti-inflationary policies adopted. These policies might have slowed down the speed of the catching up process. It is also conceivable, however, that the existence of the backlog would have reduced the secular rate of increase in productivity and output, and that more of the capital formation compatible with reasonably stable prices could have been devoted to the gradual elimination of the backlog.

So far we have considered the possibility that the "normal" marginal capital-output ratio was in the order of 1.0-1.5, i.e., that it was equal to the actual ratio computed from a comparison of the late thirties with the late forties, and we have also considered the possibility that the normal ratio was at the level of about 2.5 (the actual ratio of the twenties or slightly higher). On the first assumption, the crude, aggregative method employed led to deflationary initial results, but the deficiency was of a size suggesting the likelihood of gradual internal adjustments (especially with a moderate budgetary deficit). This assumption is definitely pessimistic with respect to the normal $\Delta V/\Delta O$. On the higher assumption concerning this ratio, which might be somewhat "optimistic" in this special sense of the word, the calculations pointed to an inflationary basic tendency over a transitional period of several years and subsequently to a balanced situation. Given the crudeness of these computations, it is not necessary to develop the consequences of specific intermediate assumptions concerning $\Delta V/\Delta O$ or of specific assumptions placing $\Delta V/\Delta O$ beyond 2.5. At some level between the 1.0-1.5 range and the 2.5 level, this kind of analysis would point to a transitionally balanced situation (owing to the backlog), and subsequently to a mildly deflationary initial tendency calling for internal adjustments or, in the absence of these, for a deficit. At levels higher than 2.5, these same calculations point to a strongly inflationary tendency during the backlog period and to an inflationary tendency even thereafter. Such inflationary tendencies may also call forth internal adjustments (increased corporate savings, a lowering of the increase in productivity owing to shortages, etc.), and, in the event of the insufficiency of these, they would secularly justify more deflationary monetary and fiscal policies than those on which the initial projection is based.

We do not believe that it is possible to arrive at more definite conclusions without relying heavily on subjective appraisal and judgment. In cautious and general terms, our own appraisal of these results of aggregative saving-investment analysis is that the so-called long-run outlook (over, say, a period of five years) was not deflationary, even aside from the Korean war. More specifically, our own "best guess" would have been that the inflationary period of backlog demands would have continued for some time, and that subsequently the economy might have approached a rather balanced situation. But at any rate, from the materials so far used, *it would be difficult to substantiate a heavily deflationary projection unless consistently "low" assumptions are combined with great pessimism concerning the ability of the system to adjust to rather moderate disturbances.*

Before turning to a brief discussion of the general assumptions which underlie these conclusions, we shall merely raise—rather than analyze—a question and we shall refer to the later context where an analysis follows. Are the foregoing conjectures very much influenced by the size of the depreciation allowances which are implicit in the numerators of our $\Delta V/\Delta O$ ratios? This is an important question because depreciation allowances are inevitably arbitrary. Later, in a discussion of the methods employed by the Council of Economic Advisers, a presumption will be established that the preceding results are not decisively affected by this arbitrariness. But, before considering this matter, we shall first cast a critical eye on the nature of the theorizing in which we have engaged.

It can scarcely be overemphasized that these conclusions share all the shortcomings of trend analysis which disregards the cyclical path "around the trend."[23] They also are subject to the sig-

[23] Although it does not disregard the fact that plans, and hence long-run average realized values (trends), are influenced by cyclical fluctuations and

nificant qualifications of all aggregative, saving-investment analysis which disregards (or hides behind a *ceteris paribus* clause) the problems of specific resource requirements and of relative prices. We shall now briefly turn to the necessary qualifying considerations.

As for the qualifications necessary in consequence of the "abstract" character of the trend concept, these express themselves in the fact that cyclical disturbances may become self-reinforcing and may seriously impede the adjustment of the system to the long-run requirements of balanced development. The kind of analysis contained in the preceding pages assumes, not only that random disturbances become smoothed out into a trend line the basic properties of which are independently meaningful (rather than simply the resultants of cyclical forces), but also that, along the trend line itself, threatening discrepancies and gaps tend to call forth certain adjustments (rather than to grow cumulatively).

One could try to take care of this problem by simply stating that a reasonable cycle policy is implied. To be sure, opinions differ on the details of a reasonable cycle policy. But no one would expect this kind of analysis to try to answer all questions encountered on the way and there exists workable consensus on the desirability of counteracting cumulative inflationary and deflationary movements by means of monetary and fiscal policy. However, the problem now posed is not fully met by such references to reasonable cycle policy. This is mainly because the absence of a reasonable cycle policy in this sense may have appreciably affected our past trend data in some periods. In fact, the reason for treating the data for the 1930's and 1940's on a different footing from those of the preceding decades is precisely that, in the sense here relevant, decade averaging does not smooth out the cycle for the past two decades. The thirties were a decade of chronic excess capacity and the forties a decade dominated by the capacity shortages of the war and postwar years. But in what way was the cycle smoothed out during the earlier decades? Certainly not in the same way in each of these. Do we want to imply that, in future decades, the relationship between trend and cycle will be the same as in any one of the past decades

by uncertainty. What the method does imply is that *long-run* average, realized values approximate the planned magnitudes. In other words "plus and minus" errors are assumed to show a tendency to offset each other, but they are not assumed to leave the plan uninfluenced. Uncertainty affects the plans of the public.

or similar to what it was in certain past decades "on the average"? We scarcely want to imply this. The problem is of considerable significance because the trend and the cycle do not live independent lives. They interact.

If cycle policy should become much more successful than was the case in the past, then this would presumably lower the V/O and $\Delta V/\Delta O$ ratios as compared with the pre-1929 observations. It is reasonable to assume that, on the average, there existed varying degrees of excess capacity during those decades, and that the average degree of excess capacity was not negligible in any one of the decades in question. Moreover, it seems reasonable to assume that, from decade to decade, the additions to required capital were associated with additions to the (absolute) amount of excess capacity, since excesses of this sort should be looked upon in terms of proportions (relative sizes) rather than as absolute magnitudes. Hence, excess capacity probably affects the earlier findings concerning $\Delta V/\Delta O$ as well as V/O. Projecting less excess capacity for the future may imply reducing the projected $\Delta V/\Delta O$. It would be difficult indeed to make "proper allowances" for this.

Moreover, if such allowances were made, it would also become necessary to make allowances for the increased rate of output expansion, which is another likely by-product of successful cycle policy. This other by-product depends very much on the methods of policy. Certain kinds of "stabilizing" policy might weaken incentives and thereby might result in a reduced rate of secular growth. However, in the writer's view, this is not likely to prove true of stabilization policy in general, and *if no specific discouraging effects emanate directly from the methods of interference*, then the consequences of the *results* of these policies—namely of greater stability itself—are likely to be trend-raising (rather than -lowering).[24] In this case, uncertainty is diminished and uncertainty is a factor tending to reduce the rate of expansion. In other words, truly successful stabilization policy might tend to reduce $\Delta V/\Delta O$ and to raise $\Delta O/\Delta t$. Whether it would therefore tend to leave the product of these two terms (the rate of investment) approximately unchanged, or whether

[24] In other words, given the characteristics of past full-employment periods, high-employment expectations without much dispersion are likely to induce more secular growth than strongly fluctuating expectations.

it would tend to change it up or down, is a question about which no definite conclusion is suggested.

Another problem disregarded in our crude aggregative approach is that of specific scarcities and of the cost structure. The statistical technique by which projections may be obtained of the composition of output at rising levels of the aggregate is that of the input-output analysis. Any version of this technique has its inevitable *ceteris paribus* assumptions, as do all other types of predictive analysis in economics. Here, as elsewhere, this calls for corrections based on general information and judgment. But the input-output approach leads *toward* forming an opinion of the specific composition of output while the methods so far considered simply bypass this question. Whether the specific commodity and service requirements of projected aggregate outputs can be met by specific dates is a problem that must be subjected to analysis of its own kind before the results of aggregative analysis can be definitively accepted. The present paper is not concerned with this problem, and consequently the analysis must be made subject to an "if" clause with respect to the availability of specific resources. As viewed from the pre-Korean angle, it seems to us that no difficulty that might have tended to arise in connection with specific resource requirements would have seriously interfered with the normal growth trends of the American economy over several years. But this is a distinctly subjective statement and it is no substitute for detailed analysis.

Relative price and cost structure problems enter not merely as a consequence of possible scarcities in the ordinary sense (natural scarcities), but, also, in view of changing degrees of monopoly and of bargaining power (institutional scarcities). It is a well-known weakness of the contemporary aggregative theories that they have little to say on the interaction between relative prices, on the one hand, and aggregate output and employment, on the other. For example, changes in labor cost per unit of output value probably exert two influences which go in opposite directions, but need not always (or even ordinarily) cancel. They change profit margins per unit of output and thus, *ceteris paribus*, they tend to change the willingness to produce. But the *ceteris paribus* condition is not satisfied, because these same changes also tend to change the propensity to consume in the opposite direction, and the likelihood of high employment depends to some extent on the height of the propensity to consume (i.e., on what share of the full-employment output would be consumption and what share would have to be investment).[25] It is necessary to be acquainted with the distinctive characteristics of the *ad hoc* situation in which this problem develops to venture even a very tentative judgment on how the intensity of these two opposing effects may compare. The same is true of the effects of changes in the (relative) commodity price structure. The vague implication of the aggregative method is that the factors pertaining to relative costs will continue to affect the aggregates approximately in the same way as was the case in the past. In some respects, this may not be a bad assumption, in view of the rather stable long-run behavior of certain relationships, e.g., of the share of employee compensation in national income. And yet *ad hoc* problems of wage policy, farm price policy, and perhaps especially of tax policy call for current appraisal in terms of the opposing effects just considered. It is easy to describe these effects qualitatively, but they cannot be gauged by scientific methods.

As for the problem of financing the necessary amount of investment, the deviations from the *ceteris paribus* conditions of aggregative projections are in the upward direction. Comparisons of recent liquidity ratios with those pertaining to the pre-1929 period quite generally lead to the conclusion that during the past decade the economy reached a very high degree of liquidity. This is true regardless of whether we examine the ratios of liquid assets to liabilities of enterprise (corporate and other), or whether we turn our attention to ratios of income to private debt. Given the Federal Reserve support-price policy, the ability of the banking system to acquire reserves for additional loans is also a well-known expansionary factor (inflationary or counterdeflationary factor, as the case may be). Furthermore, any projection of undistributed profit ratios resembling those of recent years would lead to the further conclusion that a considerable proportion of the expansion could be currently financed out of profits.

In the foregoing pages we looked at the problem of long-run projection from the vantage point of the pre-Korean scene. An armament program such as that which has emerged under the changed conditions gives rise to problems to which the present approach is inapplicable. The success of an armament program of this sort depends on specific resource requirements, and on the

[25] Consumption is a more stable (dependable, predictable) constituent of output than is investment.

322

ability of the market forces and of regulations to mobilize the available specific resources. The result expresses itself in aggregate data and aggregative relationships, but there exists no reason to assume that these will bear resemblance to the data derived from the analysis of past long-run trends, or that, in a study of the economic war potential, it is profitable to use long-run aggregative experience concerning capital-output ratios even as a point of departure.

We know from the last war that it was possible to force the capital-output ratios to exceedingly low levels. However, it is scarcely possible to express these results of the war economy in numerical terms. One might argue that the wartime ratios were considerably lower than even the abnormally low postwar ratios, because in no postwar year was the GNP as high in constant prices as at the peak of the war effort, while there was a great deal of net capital formation during the postwar period. But, on the other hand, wartime goods and services are produced partly with the aid of tools and supplies which are not taken into account in the usual estimates of the capital stock. The "productivity" of these does not outlive the wars during which they were used.

H. COMPARISON WITH CONCLUSIONS REACHED BY THE COUNCIL OF ECONOMIC ADVISERS

1. Similarities and differences

The *Annual Economic Review* of January 1950 presented a full-employment model for the year 1954. This pioneering study, which was undertaken prior to the Korean crisis, arrived at a GNP figure of $300-310 billion, at consumption expenditures of $210-225 billion, and at gross private domestic investment (excluding inventory accumulation) of $38-43 billion. All dollar figures were expressed in 1949 prices. The model was developed for the year 1954, but it should presumably be interpreted as applying to average conditions over a number of years; or to 1954 itself, on the hypothesis that that year turns out to possess the average characteristics of the period by which it is surrounded. The underlying estimates of the Council "came out right" (i.e., satisfied the internal consistency requirements) at a GNP of $305 billion, with $217.5 billion of personal consumption expenditures, $42.5 billion of gross private domestic investment (including $2.5 billion of inventory accumulation), $3 billion of net foreign investment, and $42 billion of government purchases of goods and services.

The Council called this a goal based in many respects on hypothetical forecasts. It did not call it simply a forecast, because the Council wished to emphasize the fact that its estimates did not directly lead to these figures satisfying the internal consistency requirements at the prospective full-employment level. The estimates resulted in figures that were several billions lower, and, in the Council's view, called for certain policies by which private investment and consumption could be increased to these prospective full-employment levels, where "full employment" means a frictional, seasonal, etc. unemployment of about 3.5 percent of the labor force. On the assumption that these policies will be adopted, the Council would presumably have been willing to call these projections "forecasts," although with due emphasis on the tentative character of forecasts of this sort. The Council suggested that increasing the amount of residential construction by means of a housing program would be required to bring private investment to the appropriate level of $42-43 billion, and that the propensity to consume would have to be increased by raising the share of employee compensation in national income to bring personal consumption expenditure to the required level of $217-218 billion. The implied rise in the relative share of the compensation of employees is between 3 and 4 percentage points (from 62-63 percent of national income in the period when the computations were made to about 66 percent).

In what respects are these results similar to ours and in what respects are they different?

The main difference is that the Council arrives at a more definite level of future output than we did, thereby also implying definite views on the effect of the recommended policies, which include measures directed at the redistribution of income. In the absence of these policies, the Council expects underutilization. No allowance is made for the possibility of internal adjustments of the system by which this initial tendency might be counteracted or eliminated. The analysis of the present paper, on the other hand, points to the conclusion that the level of the future output which will tend to become established depends largely on whether the projected $\Delta V/\Delta O$ lies nearer the lower or the upper end of a plausible range for this ratio; and that, in the neighborhood of the lower end (but only in that neighborhood), we get an initial tendency toward underutilization *which may very well become offset by automatic internal adjustments of the economic system.* Nor do we believe that it is possible to make statements of general validity on the total effect of redistribution for a long period ahead. In our view, categorical statements on the relative strengths of the favorable "propensity to consume effect" of redistribution vs. its unfavorable "profit margin (incentive) effect" cannot be adequately supported. Given all characteristics of a specific period, a person may suggest partly intuitive conclusions on the relative weight of these two effects *hic* and *nunc.* Even the qualified validity of statements of this sort is apt to vanish, if they are projected into the more distant future.

The differences so far considered may be expressed by saying that the Council foresaw the necessity of antideflationary, long-range, full-employment policies (quite aside from cycle policies) and placed trust in the effectiveness of the specific kind of long-range policy which it recommended. The present analysis places more emphasis on the possibility of automatic internal adjustments *within the ranges in which these are likely to be required* (if the initial tendency should be toward chronic underutilization). It should be added that the Council does not seem to have felt that there was an appreciable capital backlog at the end of the forties, while we are inclined to believe that there still was a backlog of some significance. However, the *lower end* of our "plausible" range for the future $\Delta V/\Delta O$ implies no backlog. Projections based on these low $\Delta V/\Delta O$ ratios lead to an initial underemployment tendency in our framework, too, and the size of this tendency does not seem to be very different from that which would have been obtained by the Council without its policy recommendations. Our conclusion was that internal adjustments may very well turn out to take care of this tendency, although we did not exclude the possibility of a situation calling for upward trend correction by means of fiscal policy.

The methods of projection used by the Council are different from those applied in the present paper. It is impossible to prove the statement that, aside from its policy recommendations, the Council would have arrived at a gap which is not very different from that obtained in the low ranges of our own projections. Yet this is likely for reasons to be considered.

The Council projected domestic investment by alternative

techniques. One of these was based on the McGraw-Hill survey.[26] The answers obtained from the firms included in the survey made it possible to indicate the planned investment outlays per (planned) percentage point increase in manufacturing capacity, and also the planned replacement and modernization outlays per unit of existing capacity. On the assumption of a 3.2 percent yearly increase in manufacturing capacity (which, according to input-output-study estimates of the Council, corresponds to a 2.4 percent yearly increase in GNP), the sum total of manufacturing gross investment outlays was estimated and it was assumed that the other constituents of nonfarm plant and equipment outlays would rise beyond 1949 in the same proportion as the manufacturing outlays.

Another technique used by the Council was based on a statistical relationship between the *increment* in the cumulated sum of gross nonfarm plant and equipment outlays and the *increment* in privately produced nonfarm GNP (both in 1939 prices). The *ratio* of these two increments seems to have oscillated around a "normal" value during the 1920's. In other words, if the cumulated total of gross nonfarm plant and equipment outlays is measured on the ordinate, and the privately produced nonfarm GNP on the abscissa, then a linear relationship is obtained for the 1920's, and the line connecting the point for 1919 with that for 1929 is very nearly the same line as that expressing the best fit for all points of the decade. (The ratio of increments described in the first sentence of this paragraph is the slope of such a line.) It was found that the points for 1941, 1949, and 1950 lie very close to the line going through 1919 and 1929, while the thirties lie above the line, thereby indicating excess capacity, and the forties (after 1941) below the line, thereby indicating capital shortages. If, for this reason, it is assumed that by the end of the forties the economy had arrived back to the normal relationship and would stay on it in the predictable future, then, for the projected long-run rate of increase in output, an estimate is obtained of gross investment outlays. This estimate is not affected by where (from what year on) we start cumulating the nonfarm plant and equipment outlays to obtain the "normal" line expressing the relationship between cumulated investment outlays and private nonfarm GNP. Nor does this arbitrary de-

[26] *Business Plans for New Plants and Equipment*, published annually in February by Department of Economics, McGraw-Hill Publishing Company.

cision affect the finding that at the end of the forties we were back at the normal line. The relevant conclusions depend merely on the slope of the line and not on the constant in its equation.

The techniques based on the McGraw-Hill surveys and the regression technique just discussed lead to practically identical estimates of yearly nonfarm plant and equipment outlays in 1954. These estimates lie between 22 and 25 billions of 1949 dollars. The total gross private domestic investment requirement for full employment is estimated at around $42-43 billion, a figure which includes residential construction (as well as inventory accumulation and farm investment).[27] The Council believes that the $42-43 billion will be forthcoming in the event of a successful housing program. How much less would be forthcoming in the absence of such a program cannot be read conclusively from the computations. But the computations do show that the residential construction which, according to the Council, is required to reach the total of $42-43 billion is no more than about $3-4 billion greater than the actual yearly residential construction of the late forties. Consequently, we have a strong indication that, in the absence of the housing program, the Council's investment deficiency would be *much* smaller than $10-15 billion (which is our initial deficiency obtained by using the $\Delta V/\Delta O$ ratio corresponding to the lower end of our range).

The total investment requirement of the Council is about the same as ours. We assumed a requirement of about $40-45 billion in the late forties (Section I) and we adopted the working hypothesis that over the years the requirement would rise in the same proportion as output (implying roughly that if government expenditures did not rise in the same proportion, then taxes also would not, and hence private outlays would rise in a higher proportion). The Council's full-employment GNP for 1954 is roughly 15 percent greater in constant prices than was the GNP at the end of the forties. In these circumstances our 1954 requirement is about $45-50 billion. The Council's total investment requirement is $45 billion, including foreign investment. This is a very similar figure. The Council believes that there will be a deficiency as compared with this figure, unless a housing program is adopted, and it is a safe guess that this deficiency is much less than $10-15 billion (perhaps one-half of this figure or less). We

[27] In addition to the nonfarm plant and equipment outlays previously considered.

obtained a \$10-15 billion deficiency with the lowest $\Delta V/\Delta O$, before the possibility of internal adjustments was taken into account. We obtained no initial deficiency when a $\Delta V/\Delta O$ ratio of about 2.5 was assumed. It follows that the techniques of the Council are equivalent to a $\Delta V/\Delta O$ assumption of perhaps 2 *in our terms*. This is somewhat, but not very much, smaller than the full-employment requirement (again, in our terms).

It is true that the Council also states the need for income redistribution to obtain the full-employment level of output in 1954. But this is because, in the Council's model (unlike ours), consumption would otherwise not rise sufficiently to compensate for the failure of government expenditure to rise with output. The explanation is partly that the Council does not let tax revenues fall in relation to output in the same proportion as government expenditures are expected to fall: the Council's goals include a cash surplus of \$2-3 billion for 1954. The total consumption deficiency which, according to the Council, would develop in the absence of redistribution is probably in the general order of \$5 billion, because the Council wants to raise the share of employee compensation in national income from 62-63 percent to about 66 percent, that is to say, by about 3 to 4 percentage points. This implies shifting about \$8 to 10 billion of non-labor income to employees whose propensity to consume is greater. Therefore the total would-be deficiency of the Council (in the absence of offsetting policies) may not be very different from our would-be deficiency (in the absence of internal adjustments), if we use the lowest $\Delta V/\Delta O$ in our calculations. But only part of the Council's would-be deficiency is a deficiency of gross private capital formation, while all of ours is. Judging from the supporting argument, this part is unlikely to be more than (very roughly) \$5 billion. It is likely to be less than this figure. In other words, the Council's techniques of *investment* projection yield a figure that seems to be somewhat lower than the full-employment requirement, but not very much lower; and its results are those which our calculations would have yielded, if we had assumed a $\Delta V/\Delta O$ ratio of somewhat less than 2.

2. *Gross or net capital formation?*

This question possesses interesting implications concerning a variant of the method we used in our previous calculations. As was seen, one of the techniques employed by the Council is similar to our $\Delta V/\Delta O$ technique, except that ΔV is replaced by the cumulated total of gross investment outlays. In other words, this technique of the Council is like a $\Delta V/\Delta O$ technique, with the additional assumption that depreciation is proportionate to the absolute increase in output (ΔO).

If depreciation were equal to ΔO multiplied by a constant ($D = K \cdot \Delta O$), then a linear relationship between V and O (i.e., constancy of $\Delta V/\Delta O$) would imply constancy of a slope defined as the *ratio* of the increment of cumulated *gross* investment outlays to ΔO. This latter slope is that underlying the Council's method. It differs from $\Delta V/\Delta O$ in that the numerator includes all current depreciation, that is, the Council's slope may be written as $(\Delta V + D)/\Delta O$. But if $D = K \cdot \Delta O$, then this slope is $(\Delta V/\Delta O) + K$, and hence this slope is constant (the underlying relationship is linear) if, and only if, $\Delta V/\Delta O$ is constant. The statement holds vice versa, too. When the questions are raised whether, at the end of the forties, there existed a capital shortage, and what the prospective level of capital formation is for given values of ΔO, the constant K does not influence the answers. Therefore, one would expect that the Council's method and ours would lead to identical results if $D = K \cdot \Delta O$. This is not necessarily a bad assumption for all periods with which we were concerned, because, in some periods, conceivably $D = K_1 V$, $V = K_2 O$, and $\Delta O = K_3 O$, where all K factors are constants (approximately). This would mean that $D = K \cdot \Delta O$. But for a comparison of capital-output relationships in the past two decades, this is not a very adequate assumption.

The implied assumption $D = K \cdot \Delta O$ slants the analysis in the deflationary direction. This is because, during the 1920's, depreciation was a very much higher proportion of gross capital formation than during the preceding decades. In some years of the thirties, there undoubtedly was undermaintenance of capital, with the result that the 1939 stock seems to have been no greater than that of 1929. The yearly *gross* capital formation figures on which the Council's computations are based did not reach the 1929 level (in constant prices) before 1946, and even the average yearly gross capital formation of the entire period 1930-49 is smaller than that of the twenties. Depreciation must, therefore, have accounted for a considerably higher proportion of gross investment outlays in the two recent decades than in the preceding ones. Hence, if from 1929 to 1949 a unit increase in output was as-

329

sociated with the same amount of gross investment outlay as during the twenties, then this implies that it was associated with a smaller net increment in the capital stock (ΔV). If the "gross method" of the Council points to no appreciable backlog at the end of the forties, then any "net" method would, provided the relationship of the twenties is considered normal (as in the Council's reasoning). For the same reason, if the gross method of the Council points to a future capital formation which is *not quite sufficient* for full employment, then net methods must be expected to show less insufficient or fully sufficient capital formation (or inflation).

Introducing depreciation in the Council's regression analysis (and assuming, as the Council did, that the economy is going to continue on the capital-output slope of the twenties) would have tended to raise the investment projection for 1954, and it would probably have pointed to a shortage as of 1949. The method of the Council actually led to an investment projection which was somewhat too low for full employment in 1954, and the same method led the Council to conclude that there was no appreciable capital shortage in 1949. The analysis of the present paper made it appear likely that there still was a shortage at the end of the decade, and that even without internal adjustments under the influence of a threatening deflationary gap, investment would have been almost sufficient, if we had continued on the $\Delta V/\Delta O$ slope of the 1920's (i.e., on a slope of between 2 and 2.5). Considering that we made substantial allowances for depreciation while the Council's vaguely comparable method made none, one would expect that the two results would deviate *in the direction* in which they actually do. However, *quantitative* reconciliation of the two results is not possible along these lines, because the Council's regression analysis—the second of the two Council techniques here surveyed—applies only to part of the total capital formation, and the results are extended to the total by certain *ceteris paribus* assumptions concerning the relationship between the constituents of the total. The constituent to which the regression analysis is applied—the sum of nonfarm plant and equipment outlays—is a very significant constituent and, hence, one of the two methods of the Council is similar (although not quite identical) to a gross variant of the method used in the present paper.

This comparison of results creates a presumption that the main conclusions of our analysis, in Section G, are not decisively influenced by the depreciation allowances. These may conceivably be too large in the time series we have used. But if *some* allowances were made, the Council's regression analysis would point to a more sufficient (perhaps fully sufficient) private investment even if automatic internal adjustments were disregarded.

However, the main point to be emphasized is that, in the past, the economic system seems to have had quite a bit of flexibility expressing itself in mutual adjustments of the variables included in our basic equations (Section C-4). The estimate of a future "initial" deficiency of private investment as compared with full-employment requirements, which results from the Council's methods (without adjustments for depreciation), cannot be very different from the "initial" deficiency of about $10-15 billion per year obtained by our analysis if this is based on consistently "low" assumptions. In fact, it is likely to be smaller. We do not believe that an initial deficiency of such magnitude warrants the prediction of underemployment. As was argued in the preceding pages, adjustments in more than one variable may well tend to eliminate initial deficiencies of such size. If, instead of these low assumptions, we make assumptions lying in the higher regions of the plausible range, the conclusion is that, for some time to come, internal adjustments as well as monetary fiscal policy might have to cope with inflationary pressures. Neither our analysis nor the computations of the Council made it appear safe to gear long-run government policy to a deflationary gap.

PROBLEMS OF ESTIMATING SPENDING AND SAVING IN LONG-RANGE PROJECTIONS

MARY W. SMELKER

RENYX, FIELD & COMPANY, INC.

A. INTRODUCTION

UNDER the Employment Act of 1946, the government of the United States obligated itself to adopt policies leading to "maximum employment, production and purchasing power." This involves the attempt to reduce cyclical fluctuations in magnitude, either through long-range policies or short-term devices. One important objective of a long-range projection is to find those dynamic relations which will promote fairly smooth economic development and minimize the necessity for short-term, arbitrary intervention in the economic system.

The use of the term "projection" rather than prediction or forecast indicates that the estimates are governed by some basic assumptions which may or may not be realized. In this case the assumption is that of relatively full employment and gradually rising real incomes. The price level may be assumed to be constant or gradually rising; a gradually rising price level being, in the opinion of some, more conducive to steady economic expansion.

A full-employment projection is an ambitious undertaking at this stage of the development of economic analysis. Such an undertaking implies that at a minimum we have a fairly firm grasp of the historical causes of economic growth and cyclical downturns, whereas in actuality we are reminded every day of our inability to penetrate the subtleties and complexities of economic processes. Only the necessity, or at least the advisability, of providing a basic quantitative framework to guide public policies justifies the erection of such a superstructure upon our present foundation of knowledge. Further, if we are "projecting" a future of peaceful, sustained economic growth, this is a different environment than prevailed during most of the period in which

Note: At the time this paper was prepared, the author was a staff member of the Council of Economic Advisers, but bears full responsibility for the views expressed. The author wishes to express her appreciation to Mrs. Selma Goldsmith and Mrs. Rosalie Epstein for assistance and to Mr. Daniel Creamer for helpful criticism.

333

fairly detailed economic observation has been possible. Since the turn of the century, the behavior of income, spending, and saving has been profoundly influenced by business cycles and wars. Consequently, a large element of subjective judgment must enter in adapting any information from recent periods to the conditions which are presumed or "assumed" to prevail in a more stable and peaceable future.

A further complication in projecting saving is introduced by the fact that it is almost impossible to make estimates of one segment of an economy without some fairly detailed assumptions about other areas. For example, the incurrence of a government surplus or deficit will affect consumer behavior. The government maintains, contracts, or enlarges its surplus by some positive action which affects directly or indirectly the household sector of the economy. The effects of tax changes or of increases in transfer payments on the distribution of consumer disposable income are cases in point. In addition, long-range government policies affecting social consumption, personal security, etc. are certain to have effects on consumer behavior of significant magnitude, while programs regarding slum clearance, public housing, and aid and support of private housing, price support programs, and even aid to small business may not be negligible.

The analysis of spending and saving in a long-range projection presents itself in two phases: (1) the selection of basic historic determinants of consumer behavior, and (2) the introduction of modifications, necessary because of the novelty of the assumption of continuous full employment.

It is appropriate to neglect those factors affecting consumer behavior which emanate from cyclical changes elsewhere in the economy. However, tendencies toward self-generating cycles, such as would be provided by excessive accumulations of stocks of consumer durable goods or liquid assets, are of the essence of the inquiry.

The principal problem about consumer behavior that has concerned analysts is the basis of the personal decision to spend or to save. The distribution of expenditures among different types of goods and the distribution of saving among assets of greater or less liquidity have received considerably less attention, although these questions are of scarcely less importance. In posing a sharp dichotomy between spending and saving, a distinction is made which appears to be critical for the analysis of business

334

cycles, yet the point at which the distinction is drawn is somewhat arbitrary and may not be the best one from the standpoint of studying consumer behavior. Definitions of saving in current use in statistical inquiries may not correspond to the consumers' own concept of what saving is, and consequently may not be closely related to the bases of consumer choice, which in turn may cause behavior to appear more erratic, or even irrational, than it is. The distribution of funds at the command of consumers represents a continuum from expenditures which have only a small element of saving, such as those for clothing, through long-lived durable goods, to liquid assets. A moving equilibrium at full employment involves the whole distribution of expenditures, or, rather, the whole pattern of personal sources and uses of funds. Not only does the accumulation of stocks which may be presumed to occur under high incomes pose problems of the maintenance of a high spending rate, but an economy with a high ratio of durable goods to total consumer expenditure will be a very different economy from one in which nondurables or, say, personal services are high. An economy where consumers invest most of their savings directly in homes or businesses may be more stable (but less "manageable") than one in which liquidity has a high premium and the services of financial intermediaries are required.

At the present time there is no theoretical structure regarding consumer behavior which is sufficiently general to provide for simultaneous determination of the whole pattern of consumer outlay. While we do have many of the elements of a theory of consumer behavior, contributed by the work of researchers in this field in the last 10 to 20 years, too much time has been directed to attempting to define, by empirical investigation of time series, regularities in the relation between some aggregation of saving components and a very limited number of other economic variables. Of this type of activity there is no end—the consumption functions which have been "fitted" to time series of inadequate length, often with little regard to the appropriateness of the definitions of income and saving underlying the inquiry, have already been numerous enough for special bibliographies.

The difficulties of discovering any stable or "projectable" relations by correlations of aggregates of income, other variables, and saving rest not only on the technical deficiencies of multicorrelation analysis, but also on the fact that the factors in the particular complex which is represented by movements in the independent variables throughout some observational periods may not be stable in their relations to each other. Thus, we often have no way of knowing whether we have observations on the same consumption function for successive years, or a new function. This is particularly true after a series of years punctuated by wars and depressions. On this score, cross section analyses of consumer budgets, using different types of families, different areas, etc., seem more likely to discover the fundamental regularities rooted in the psychological make-up of the consumer. Drawing inferences from relations between income and other variables discovered to exist at a moment in time and applying them to a situation involving changes through time is nevertheless beset with numerous pitfalls. The classic example of a fallacy resulting from mixing statics with dynamics was the conclusion that since income and the rate of saving are always positively correlated in consumer budgets, the secular growth in real incomes must be accompanied by a continually rising saving rate.

At the present time, out of a great surge of activity in the area of exploration of the "consumption function," following the rise to popularity of Keynesian economics, two propositions concerning consumer behavior have emerged which may be first discussed briefly as a taking off point for the discussion of projections. These propositions are singled out for special treatment because for a time it appeared that the two taken together formed an almost complete explanation of the course of spending and saving over the last 50 or 75 years, including both secular trends and cyclical deviations in the average rate of saving. The two are on quite different levels, the first having the character of a psychological law, at least in our culture, and the second being a matter of empirical observation, although the regularities observed are susceptible to plausible explanation. The first proposition is that the ratio of household saving to household income depends on the relative position of the family in the income scale of the community. Therefore, changes in the saving rate depend on changes in income distribution. The second is that the rate of saving has in this country been secularly constant despite pronounced year-to-year deviations arising from cyclical influences.

B. INFLUENCE OF RELATIVE INCOME POSITION
ON THE RATE OF SAVING

The ability to save, for most families, depends on the current flow of income. Nevertheless, empirical analysis of consumer budgets for a number of types of families in different years for which data are available indicates that the proportion of household income saved depends not on the income level of the family, but on the relative status of the family with respect to other families higher or lower in the income scale.[1] Emulation of the spending habits of higher income groups, rather than the real standard of family living, determines the percent of income which will be saved. Thus, aside from transitory effects, an increase in real income will not affect family saving if other families in the community receive a proportional increase.

By aggregating the saving of households, according to this view, we arrive at an over-all national rate of saving which is directly related to the size distribution of income and changes in this distribution, but is independent of changes in real income. Other factors more or less unrelated to income may influence consumption over the business cycle, or its secular trend, but these are secondary and can be independently evaluated.

C. SECULAR CONSTANCY OF THE
SAVING RATIO

When it was believed that saving depended on the level of real income, it followed that the growth in real income over the decades would lead to a secular growth in saving in relation to income. No such inherent tendency for saving to increase is implicit in the notion that saving depends on relative position in the income scale. Such data as have been available on long-run trends in investment, notably those of Simon Kuznets shown below, failed to indicate a secular growth in saving, casting doubt

[1] The pioneering work in this area was done by Dorothy S. Brady and Rose D. Friedman. See their "Savings and the Income Distribution," in *Studies in Income and Wealth, Volume Ten* (NBER, 1947). Independent work was also done by James S. Duesenberry, who developed the dynamic implications of the theory. See his *Income, Saving, and the Theory of Consumer Behavior,* Harvard Economic Studies, No. 87 (Harvard University Press, 1949).

on the validity of the former theory, if not exactly confirming the latter.[2]

Actually, the Kuznets data cannot establish anything very positive about trends in personal saving because of the changing external factors affecting consumer behavior over the observation period. The thirties must be omitted from consideration because of the magnitude and length of the depression. The period of the First World War is also irrelevant because the federal government ran a large deficit for several years. Thus the three decades previous to the First World War and the twenties are left for observation of the trend. While the rate of saving for the economy as a whole during these decades shows no clear relation to time, a change in the contribution of corporate and government saving to the total national saving might have obscured an upward trend. Furthermore, there may be more or less random shifts in the consumption function from time to time, which, although not inconsistent with long-range constancy in the saving ratio, are of a magnitude which is fairly crucial for the maintenance of employment in the short run.

Although direct statistical evidence for the secular constancy of the ratio of saving to income is not very satisfactory, an ingenious argument may be made resting the conclusion on the better-established proposition that variations in saving depend on variations in the concentration of income. If the rate of saving is determined by the distribution of income and, in fact, the distribution of income has been constant, the rate of saving in relation to income would tend to be constant also. (The influence of an increasing degree of urbanization and a changing age distribution of the population, both long-term secular trends affecting saving, will be discussed later.)

The long-term constancy of the income distribution is not a matter of historical evidence, however. Data are scanty, and even for interwar periods relate mostly to the upper segments of the population. One conclusion that seems fairly well verified is that a significant shift toward lesser concentration of income (as measured by the Lorenz curve) has taken place since the twenties. A priori, there seems no reason to believe that the process

---

[2] This fact was independently observed by Modigliani and Duesenberry at about the same time. See Franco Modigliani, "Fluctuations in the Savings Ratio: A Problem in Economic Forecasting," *Studies in Income and Wealth, Volume Eleven* (NBER, 1949); and Duesenberry, *op.cit.*

DECADE	CURRENT PRICES		1929 PRICES	
	Flow of Goods to Consumers (1)	Net Capital Formation (2)	Flow of Goods to Consumers (3)	Net Capital Formation (4)
1869-78	87.9	12.1	86.3	13.7
1874-83	87.0	13.0	85.6	14.4
1879-88	86.8	13.2	85.4	14.6
1884-93	85.9	14.1	83.9	16.1
1889-98	85.9	14.1	83.8	16.2
1894-1903	86.4	13.6	85.2	14.8
1899-1908	87.4	12.6	86.4	13.6
1904-13	87.9	12.1	86.9	13.1
1909-18	87.5	12.5	87.0	13.0
1914-23	87.6	12.4	88.6	11.4
1919-28	89.1	10.9	89.8	10.2
1924-33	93.3	6.7	94.0	6.0
1929-38	98.0	2.0	98.6	1.4
	Averages			
Lines 1-5	86.7	13.3	85.0	15.0
5-9	87.0	13.0	85.9	14.1
9-13	91.1	8.9	91.6	8.4
1-5	86.7	13.3	85.0	15.0
4-8	86.7	13.3	85.3	14.7
7-11	87.9	12.1	87.8	12.2

urce: Simon Kuznets, *National Income: A Summary of Findings* (NBER, 1946), p. 53.

of industrialization and urbanization which took place over the last century did not produce significant shifts in the distribution of income in earlier decades.

In addition, it is doubtful whether the income distribution theory of saving is a theory of economic dynamics which could be expected to explain long-term changes. The behavior described in the theory rests on patterns of social and economic emulation. "What a family spends depends on what it sees others possess; new products are bought first by upper income groups, and later by those lower down on the income scale."

Emulation and competitive living are deeply imbedded in our social structure; but the influence of these factors might be expected to have varied a good deal as the economy and the culture have passed through successive historical phases.[3] The same objection (namely, that other things cannot be assumed to remain equal) which applies to the now discarded view that saving depends on the level of real income applies, though with less force, to the "relative income" theory, if it is used to explain events widely separated in time. A general reduction in the extremes of income would not only change the rate of saving, but probably also the pattern of emulation. The process of cultural diffusion in a society in which income is concentrated around the mode would undoubtedly be very different from that in a society in which the income distribution is more unequal.[4] Other unrelated historical factors may be thought of which would tend to alter the general structure of social emulation, such as the trends toward greater leisure and toward ease and rapidity of movement from town to country.

If it were possible to construct a system encompassing all possible influences on the consumer psyche, we could then speak of the "consumption function" as though it were immutable. When variables affecting spending are reduced to a manageable number, the possibility of short-term shifts, or even trends, in a statistically determined saving function cannot be excluded. The view that the saving ratio remains constant from cycle to cycle won ready acceptance because of the dilemma involved in projecting a rising saving rate as real income increases secularly. The alternative to a rising rate may be, however, not constancy, but upward or downward shifts from period to period in the consumption function, which over a period of years may be largely offsetting. Since historical shifts in the "propensity to consume" cannot be ruled out, a projection of saving in a full-employment economy should give more weight to the pattern of spending and saving in recent years of full employment, with such qualitative adjustments as may be indicated by the special circumstances of those years, than to secular averages or trends.

[3] Brady and Friedman found that the pattern of spending by relative income level did vary considerably from 1901 to 1935-36 and 1941. Sample differences may have affected this conclusion.

[4] This fact was recognized by those analyzing the data collected in 1935-36 on family budgets who remarked that "the number of families at each income level is, in itself, one factor influencing spending patterns. Keeping-up-with-the-Joneses might take on new and unprecedented forms if the distribution of income should approach much more nearly to equality." *Consumer Expenditures in the United States* (National Resources Committee, March 1939), p. 163.

D. SAVING IN RECENT YEARS
OF FULL EMPLOYMENT

Although the best guide to what consumers will do if full employment and rising incomes are maintained for 5 to 10 years probably lies in recent experience, the question arises whether saving patterns in past years of "full employment," when such years fall at the peak of a business cycle, can be relied on in making estimates of what would happen were full employment to be continuously maintained. The rate of saving is always high in relation to current income in prosperous years, which fact may reflect, among other things, a lag in expenditures behind rising incomes, shifts in the degree of income concentration, or shifts of income to occupational groups with high average or marginal rates of saving. An appraisal of those cyclical influences might lead to the conclusion that in peak years of the cycle the rate of saving is forced above the level it would tend to attain if the same levels of income could be continuously maintained.

On the other hand, there is one factor which tends to make saving during the peak years of a business cycle lower than it might be under conditions of continued prosperity. This factor is the bunching of durable goods expenditures in these years. Changes in the rate of purchases of durable goods involve an increase in the rate of credit utilization, which, other things being equal, causes net saving to decline temporarily—until the higher rate of repayments catches up with the rate of new credit utilization. Dipping into liquid assets to purchase durables has a somewhat similar effect. Such changes act as a depressant of the rate of saving in peak years of the business cycle, and, to some extent, offset other factors which might cause the rate of saving to be unusually high in these years.

The maintenance of general expansion in an economy would require as a condition (and tend to achieve as a result) a smoothing out of not only the rate of capital formation, but also the production of consumer durable goods. For this reason, and also, as will be discussed later, because the lag of expenditures behind incomes in years of rising income is probably small, it seems reasonable that the saving rate under continued full employment would not be substantially below that in past years of full employment.

Until 1951, observations of saving rates in years of relatively

341

full employment in the last 20 years have shown remarkably little dispersion, especially considering that errors in estimating personal saving are relatively large. In 1948 the ratio of saving to income was about 5.6 percent, compared with 4.9 percent in 1940, 5.5 percent in 1937, and 4.5 percent in 1929. If farm inventory changes are excluded from income and saving, the ratio between saving and disposable income was just about 5 percent in 1929, 1937, 1940, 1948, and 1950 (Table 2).[5]

TABLE 2

RELATION BETWEEN PERSONAL SAVING AND INCOME IN
YEARS OF HIGH EMPLOYMENT, 1929-51
(IN PERCENT)

Year	National Income Concept	National Income Concept Excluding Increase in Farm Inventory[a]
1929	4.5	4.8
1937	5.5	4.8
1940	4.9	4.6
1946	7.6	7.7
1947	2.3	3.6
1948	5.6	5.1
1949	3.4	3.9
1950	5.2	5.1
1951	8.3	7.7

a The net increase in farm inventories has been subtracted from disposable income and saving.
Source: Department of Commerce.

In 1951, there was an abrupt upward shift in the saving rate beginning in the second quarter. On the basis of preliminary estimates, it appears that saving may have amounted to over 9 percent of disposable personal income in the last three quarters of the year. The suddenness and magnitude of the shift (which was largely an increase in liquid saving) occasioned great surprise, although a gradual rise in saving appeared probable as postwar backlogs of durables were exhausted.

A number of special factors may have operated to cause a temporary bulge in the rate of saving in 1951, such as adverse reactions to the rise in prices and the buying waves which characterized late 1950 and early 1951. The loss of liquidity in the

5 The exclusion of farm inventories is based on the supposition that accretions to farm inventories are largely involuntary, and that if the inventory had been sold, only part of the proceeds would have been saved.

personal economy which had been going on since the end of the war may have been an important reason for a temporary increase in financial types of saving. In addition to these factors, however, it is impossible to dismiss the hypothesis that there may have been a downward shift in the consumption function, and that this shift may be of considerable duration. And if, indeed, the full-employment saving ratio is now higher than it was prewar, the level of real income can no longer be ruled out as a major determinant of saving. More weight is given to this possibility of a shift in the consumption function by the fact that in the period 1946 through 1950 the saving rate was not especially low, though there were important factors, such as backlog demands for durable goods and high liquidity, which should have depressed it. A downward shift may have been concealed by the satisfaction of backlog demands in the earlier postwar years, only to show up in 1951 as these demands decreased in intensity.

If present high levels of per capita real income are maintained and increased, on the other hand, it is quite possible that increasing family security and confidence in economic stability will weaken the motive for accumulation.

E. FACTORS TENDING TO INFLUENCE
THE RATE OF SAVING

On the following pages some of the factors which might cause the saving rate to change from the pattern of recent years are examined. These are: changes in the concentration of income, changes in the age distribution of the population, changes in income level, a changing degree of urbanization, changes in price level, changes in stocks of financial assets, and changes in stocks of consumer durables.

1. Changes in the concentration of income

Over a considerable span of years it is likely not only that the distribution of income by size will change, but also that the significance of a given relative status in the distribution, so far as it affects consumption, will also change. On the other hand, over the shorter run of 5, 10, or perhaps 20 years, assuming the social and psychological climate is not greatly altered, it seems plausible to suppose that a changing concentration of income will be related to the saving rate in a systematic way. For example, it is reasonable to suppose that if a higher proportion of total income is received by the "poorer" half of the population (in terms of income), a decline in the average over-all saving rate will ensue.[6]

Nevertheless, data drawn from recent sample studies do not encourage the belief that there is a very stable relation between income position and saving. Table 3 shows savings ratios by quintiles of the total population of spending units for the years 1946 through 1950 drawn from the annual *Survey of Consumer Finances.* These were years of marked stability in the income distribution. All were years of rising income except 1949, when, despite general stability of income, farm income dipped substantially.

TABLE 3

DISTRIBUTION OF INCOME AND SAVING AMONG INCOME FIFTHS, 1946-50

SPENDING UNITS	PERCENT OF TOTAL INCOME					PERCENT OF PERSONAL SAVING				
	1946	1947	1948	1949	1950	1946	1947	1948	1949	195
Lowest fifth	4.5	4.3	4.7	3.9	4.1	−8.1	−12.6	−22.2	−40.9	−17.
Second fifth	10.7	10.2	11.3	10.9	11.2	3.4	0.9	−3.3	−12.2	0.
Third fifth	16.1	15.6	16.3	16.8	17.1	5.5	7.7	7.5	1.2	3.
Fourth fifth	22.3	21.6	22.0	23.1	23.5	20.7	10.9	20.8	21.3	20.
Highest fifth	46.4	48.3	45.6	45.3	44.1	78.5	93.1	97.2	130.6	92.
All units	100.0	100.0	100.0	100.0	100.0	100.0	100.0	100.0	100.0	100.

Details may not add to totals because of rounding.
Source: *Survey of Consumer Finances* (Board of Governors of the Federal Reserve System

The shifts in the proportion of saving performed by each fifth of the population in the period 1946 through 1950 were much greater than the shifts in the income distribution. This suggests that the basic relation between relative income and expenditures

[6] This is a "common sense" proposition, which could only be verified by assuming "other things equal" under circumstances where this assumption would hardly be justified. A test was made of the effects of income redistribution, on the hypothesis that the saving rate depends exclusively on relative income, by applying 1949 saving rates per decile (as estimated in the *Survey of Consumer Finances*) to the 1941 size distribution of income by deciles, and secondly to the 1949 distribution. The somewhat more concentrated income distribution in 1941 gave a 6 percent over-all saving rate, compared with 5 percent in 1949. Less significant results would have been obtained had there been less negative saving in the lower deciles of the income distribution in 1949. In any case, the relations between saving and income which have been observed historically can be applied only to relatively small changes in income concentration.

344

which is reflected in budgetary studies is overlaid by a network of dynamic influences, which in the short run are more important than shifts in income distribution in causing variations in the saving rate. The distribution of income may remain quite stable from year to year while the degree to which individuals and families are shifting up or down the income scale may be much larger in some years than in others. For example, there was no marked change in the income distribution from 1948 to 1949, or from 1949 to 1950, but 1949 may have been characterized by much more "displacement" of individual families from their usual position in the income scale. It is known that much of the dissaving at the lower end of the income scale was performed by farmers with large declines in income.

In general, the income distribution alone supplies little information concerning the causes of changing saving rates. Some sort of index of the degree of internal "displacement" or migration of families up or down the income scale would probably be much more useful. While we have become accustomed to the fact that the lower income segments always contain disproportionately large numbers of families who are experiencing a decline in income, we have little notion of how much dissaving, year after year, could take place, or is likely to take place, because of the regular infiltration of the lower income groups by families with reserves of assets. The rate of dissaving in the lower income groups which could be sustained year after year by drawing on accumulated assets or future income may on the average be much smaller than the rate in the post-World War II period. One method of determining whether dissaving represents exhaustion of resources by units normally in a given income class, or merely reduces the new assets being brought into an income class by units with declines in income, would be the preparation of financial balance sheets by income class at intervals of a year or more.

Notwithstanding the inconclusiveness of the evidence thus far, there is still a presumption that a shift in the distribution of income toward reduced concentration will result in a lowering of the saving rate. The assumption chosen with regard to the distribution of income in any model or projection must, of course, be consistent with other aspects of the model, particularly with the distribution of the national income by functional shares and the tax structure.[7]

[7] While the relationship between changes in the relative proportions of

345

2. Changes in the age distribution of the population

It has long been recognized that saving may be affected by changing proportions of the elderly and retired to total population. Dorothy Brady observes, "In the longer run, the general aging of our population promises to alter the relationships of national income, expenditures, saving, and investment significantly."[8] The *Survey of Consumer Finances* has provided considerable data of a type not previously available relating saving to the cycle of marriage, purchase of home and household equipment, provision for old age, and retirement.

These data suggest that the saving behavior of the 18-24 age group varies as much from that of the middle age groups as does that of the over-65 group. The older people have an exceptionally high frequency of zero savings, but the frequency of negative savings was greatest in the younger age groups in 1948 and 1949. In those years, the 18-24 age group (which contained about the same proportion of total consumer units as the over-65 group) had significant negative net savings, whereas the over-65 group had significant positive savings. In 1950, on the other hand, the 18-24 age group accounted for a slightly higher fraction of total net savings (2 percent) than did the oldest age group.[9]

The high frequency of dissaving among the 18-24 age group, and to a lesser extent among the 25-34 age group, reflects in many cases purchases of durable goods incident to setting up a household. As is shown in the *1950 Survey of Consumer Finances*, the purchase of durable goods has a clear relation to the number of years a couple has been married.

It is sometimes remarked that an increasing proportion of aged in the population may lead to a lower over-all rate of saving. During the next 10 to 15 years, however, a changing age distribu-

---

the distributive shares of national income and in the distribution of income by size are not known in detail, it is likely that an increase in the ratio of farm income and/or wages and salaries to dividends, profits, and rent will produce a decrease in the inequality of the size distribution. Aspects of this problem were discussed in my paper "Shifts in the Concentration of Income," in *Review of Economics and Statistics*, Vol. xxx, No. 3, August 1948.

[8] Dorothy S. Brady, "Influence of Age on Family Savings," *Current Economic Comment*, Vol. 11, No. 4 (University of Illinois, 1949), p. 51.

[9] "1951 Survey of Consumer Finances," *Federal Reserve Bulletin*, September 1951, part iv, table 16. Also published as a separate report, *1951 Survey of Consumer Finances*.

tion of population should work in the opposite direction. For example, as shown in Table 4, it is likely that by 1960 the increase in the proportion of aged to total adult population will be largely offset, as far as saving is concerned, by a drop in the proportion of young people. The 20-24 age group, who tend to be dissavers, and the 25-34 age group, who are only moderate savers, will decline in absolute numbers. The heavy savers, the 35-64 age group, will represent a larger proportion of the adult population than at present.

It would be a mistake, however, to concentrate on age to the exclusion of factors which change the saving significance of a given age group, such as earlier retirement or a change in the age of marriage. Early marriage seems to be a feature of a full-employment economy, but retirement may actually be postponed when times are good and jobs plentiful.

TABLE 4

U.S. POPULATION, INCLUDING ARMED FORCES OVERSEAS, ACTUAL 1950 AND PROJECTED 1960

Age Groups	1950, Actual	1960, Projected[a]
	(thousands)	
Under 19 years	52,480	61,796
20-24 years	11,732	11,426
25-34 years	23,717	22,629
35-64 years	52,160	59,746
65 and over	11,600	15,578
Total population	151,689	171,176
Total population over 20 years	99,209	109,380
	(percent of population over 20)	
Population aged 65 and over	11.7	14.2
Population over 65 and between 20 and 25	23.5	24.7
Population 35-64	52.6	54.6

[a] Medium assumptions with regard to rates of fertility, mortality, and net immigration.
Source: Bureau of the Census.

3. Changes in income level

In addition to income level, changes in income have long been recognized as a factor having considerable importance in determining spending or saving. J. R. Hicks, in his recent book on the trade cycle,[10] suggests that the true relation between income and

[10] J. R. Hicks, *A Contribution to the Theory of the Trade Cycle* (Oxford University Press, 1950).

saving is a lagged relation (i.e., current income determines saving in the next period) and that the use of current income and saving in a regression over- or underestimates the marginal propensity to save.

The proposition that the aggregates should be related on a lagged basis rests on the view that families whose incomes have recently increased to a given level will spend less than families whose incomes have been stable at that level, and that, in turn, families with incomes that have been stable at a given level will spend less than families whose incomes have recently declined to that level.

The use of a lagged relation between income and saving has the advantage of getting around the ambiguity of the term "marginal propensity to save." While income increases or decreases may give rise to variations in saving which are temporarily disproportionate to the change in income (and this is important for the business cycle), this phenomenon is not very adequately described by saying that the marginal rate of saving is rising. Once the new income level has become well established, the saving rate may revert to its former level.

The ability to compute even the short-run "marginal propensity to save," particularly in the postwar period, is complicated by shifts in the consumption function. However, the presence of large numbers of families with incomes which tend to fluctuate cyclically indicates that the saving rate will rise in years in which income rises generally. Families with fluctuating incomes, such as entrepreneurial groups and farmers, tend to stabilize their consumption and let the impact of income variations fall on saving. Changes in the incomes of these groups are synchronized with changes in the general income level, but are more extreme. It thus appears that a change in the level of income, even aside from lags, will cause a more than proportional variation in saving. Aside from this, of course, there may be lags in the adjustment of expenditure patterns among the more stable income groups.

The existence of a lag in expenditures has been confirmed by various studies, but it has also been found that there is an asymmetry between the effects of income increases and decreases on family saving. In 1948 Ruth Mack found that the lag of expenditures behind income for families with declining income was more pronounced than in the case of those with rising income.[11] Data from the *Survey of Consumer Finances* also suggest this asymmetry. On the average, people with income decreases dissave more than people with constant incomes, and, on the average, dissave a higher percent of income.[12] Families with income increases are more often savers than families with constant incomes, but income increases may also result in a high frequency of dissavers. In both 1948 and 1949, units with increases in income dissaved (as well as saved) more frequently than units with constant income (Table 5).[13]

TABLE 5

PERCENTAGE OF SPENDING UNITS WITH SPECIFIC CHANGES IN INCOME HAVING POSITIVE, ZERO, AND NEGATIVE SAVINGS, 1948, 1949, AND 1950

CHANGE IN INCOME	POSITIVE SAVINGS			ZERO SAVINGS[a]			NEGATIVE SAVINGS		
	1948	*1949*	*1950*	*1948*	*1949*	*1950*	*1948*	*1949*	*1950*
Large increase	63	62	68	5	2	4	32	31	28
Small increase	67	66	64	5	4	5	28	30	31
No change	64	61	59	9	12	9	27	27	32
Decline	56	48	53	4	8	8	40	44	39

[a] Obtained as a residual.
Source: *Survey of Consumer Finances* (Board of Governors of the Federal Reserve System).

This suggests that families with changes in income may be divided into two groups: those who regard the change as temporary, and those who regard it as permanent. The latter may dissave when income rises, feeling that they can now afford the new car or other item of expenditure which requires temporary credit, while the former may save an unusually large amount. When incomes in general have an upward trend, the former group will assume increased importance.

Modigliani and Duesenberry have suggested that it is the income of the previous peak year, rather than last year's income, which has a significant effect, in addition to current income, on

[11] Ruth P. Mack, "The Direction of Change of Income and the Consumption Function," *Review of Economics and Statistics*, Vol. xxx, No. 4, 1948.
[12] See George Katona, "Effect of Income Changes on the Rate of Saving," *Review of Economics and Statistics*, Vol. xxxi, No. 2, May 1949.
[13] There may be a bias in the survey results in that all of the years (except 1949) were years of generally rising incomes. The response of families with increases in income during years of generally declining incomes might be different.

spending of the current years.[14] The argument seems to be that the peak year of a business cycle establishes a living standard toward which people aspire in subsequent years of lower income. It thus tends to sustain the spending rate in those years. However, if income is moving up gradually and steadily, it soon overtakes the crest of the previous cycle, and from then on previous peak income is merely the income of the preceding year. Since, under the assumptions of this paper, income differences between successive years would be small, in the neighborhood of 2-3 percent in real terms, or 5-6 percent in money terms, the influence of the previous peak would be trivial.

4. Degree of urbanization

Since it has been generally observed that at the same levels of income, farm families save more than nonfarm families, continued migration from farms throughout this century is supposed to have lowered the saving ratio. (While there has been no observable secular decline in the national savings ratio, as has been previously pointed out, the effect of a declining farm population might have been offset by some other factor tending to raise the average.)

The decrease in the percent of population occupied with farming is indeed one of the most spectacular of secular economic changes. The relative decline in numbers of unskilled workers is also arresting, however, as shown in Table 6. The proportion of farmers (owners and tenants) fell from 16.5 percent of the "experienced labor force" in 1910 to 10.1 percent in 1940. This decline was matched, however, by a fall in the proportion of unskilled workers (excluding unpaid family workers on farms) of equivalent size. Although data are not available on an exactly comparable basis for 1940 and 1950, we know that these downward trends were accelerated by the war.[15]

[14] The relation, as presented by Franco Modigliani, is of the following form: $S_t = a + bY_t + c(Y-Y_o)$, in which Y_t is the income of the current period, and Y_o the income in the previous peak period. (All variables are in constant dollars per capita.) At present, we do not have data for a sufficient number of business cycles to test this proposition empirically. Fitted to the years 1923-40 (using rough estimates of income and saving for the years 1923-28), coefficients are obtained which give a gradually rising secular trend to the saving ratio.

[15] Preliminary data from the 1950 census give the following percents of employed persons in these occupational groups: farmers and farm managers, 1940, 11.5 percent, and 1950, 8 percent; laborers (except unpaid family workers and mine workers), 1940, 11.2 percent, and 1950, 8.8 percent.

TABLE 6

Socio-Economic Classification of the Experienced Labor Force,
1940, and Gainful Workers, 1910-30
(persons 14 years of age and over)

WORKER CLASSIFICATION	PERCENT DISTRIBUTION			
	1910	*1920*	*1930*	*1940*
Total	100.0	100.0	100.0	100.0
Professional persons	4.4	5.0	6.1	6.5
Proprietors, managers, and officials—total	23.0	22.3	19.9	17.8
Farmers (owners and tenants)	16.5	15.5	12.4	10.1
Wholesale and retail dealers	3.3	3.4	3.7	3.9
Other proprietors, managers, and officials	3.2	3.4	3.8	3.7
Clerks and kindred workers	10.2	13.8	16.3	17.2
Skilled workers and foremen	11.7	13.5	12.9	11.7
Semiskilled workers	14.7	16.1	16.4	21.0
Unskilled workers—total	36.0	29.4	28.4	25.9
Farm laborers	14.5	9.4	8.6	7.1
Unpaid family workers	6.4	4.1	3.0	2.3
Others	8.1	5.2	5.6	4.8
Laborers, except farm	14.7	14.6	12.9	10.7
Servant classes	6.8	5.4	6.9	8.0

The experienced labor force consists of the labor force excluding new workers. The latter are unemployed persons who had not previously worked full-time for one month or more. These concepts do not correspond exactly to those used in the *Monthly Report on the Labor Force*.

Source: *Statistical Abstract of the United States, 1951* (Bureau of the Census).

Much more is known about the saving habits of farm operators than about those of unskilled workers. However, data from the *1949 Survey of Consumer Finances*, shown below, indicate that in 1948 the average percent of income saved by unskilled and service workers (including farm laborers) was a fraction of that of farm operators, and considerably below that of the population as a whole. In 1944 and 1950, the frequency of positive savers in this group was lower than that for any other group except retired persons. The ratio of saving to income in 1948 by selected occupational groups, in percent, are as follows:

Professional, managerial, and self-employed	12
Clerical and sales	2
Skilled and semiskilled	5
Unskilled and service	3
Farm operators	16
All spending units	6

The year 1948 was chosen for computing saving rates, since it seemed as normal from the point of view of farm income as any other in the postwar period. Although the very high saving rate of farmers in comparison with other groups is in large part due to the omission of nonmoney income, it would undoubtedly be above that for any other group even if nonmoney income were included. (In 1941, the percent saved by farm operators was 26 computed on the basis of money income and 18 on the basis of total income.)[16]

Both migrating farm operators and migrating farm laborers presumably left the farms to enter occupational pursuits where income was higher. Farm operators, however, probably moved into groups with lower average and marginal propensities to save, so that even with higher incomes their rate of saving may have declined. Saving considered as a ratio to money income may have declined drastically. Unskilled workers, on the other hand, probably moved into groups with higher incomes *and* higher propensities to save. Secular shifts in occupational groupings may, therefore, have been to some extent compensating as regards saving.

In order to arrive at the effects on saving of changes in the proportion of earners in different occupations, it would be desirable to know not only from what occupations people come, but what occupations they enter. Secondly, migration may be concentrated at certain income levels. For example, while most agricultural projections assume that under conditions of general prosperity there will be a continued movement of farm populations into towns or cities, these movements will include disproportionately large numbers of low income or marginal farmers. The in-

[16] The ratio in percent of saving to income for farm operator and other groups, including and excluding nonmoney income, as derived from the 1935-36 and 1941 studies, is shown below:

	1935-36[a]		1941[b]	
	Including Nonmoney Income	Money Income Only	Including Nonmoney Income	Money Income Only
Farm operators and tenants	11	18	18	26
Rural nonfarm	11	12	8	9
Urban	10	10	9	10
All	10	11	10	11

[a] Excludes single-person families.
[b] Includes single-person families.

Sources: For 1935-36, *Family Expenditures in the United States* (National Resources Planning Board, 1941), table 40; for 1941, "Spending and Saving in Wartime," *Bureau of Labor Statistics Bulletin 822*, table 16.

come of those leaving, and to some extent, those remaining, will presumably be improved by the process. Under these conditions, the net effect is likely to be a rise in the saving rate of these groups.

The effect of community size on saving may be due in large part to the occupational composition which tends to prevail in a community of a given size. Size itself, or degree of urbanization, is probably also important. However, since general economic changes tend to reflect themselves in cyclical variations in the proportion of income received by various occupational groups, and in secular changes in the numbers in these groups, occupational classifications have some advantage over community size classifications as a basis for analysis.

5. *Changes in price level*

It is assumed that, under conditions of continuous full employment, extreme or rapid fluctuations in the price level are excluded. The alternatives are a gradually rising, stable, or gradually declining price level. Despite the fact that a falling price level offers advantages in the way of a more general and perhaps more equitable distribution of the gains of rising productivity, the present trend is for gains in productivity to be shared between wages and profits. Since the difficulties involved in preventing a mild fall in prices from initiating a recessionary movement are great, this alternative will not be discussed here. The difference between an assumption of constant prices and that of gradually but steadily rising prices would probably not affect the rate of saving so much as the type of asset which people would wish to hold.

The effects on saving of a continuing though small rise in prices—say 2 or 3 percent a year—depend mainly on whether the trend is expected to continue. The anticipation of a continued rise in prices of even moderate proportions would reduce the attractiveness of liquid assets and increase the proportion of income placed in personal businesses, corporate equities, homes, and consumer durable equipment. At the same time, the attempt to dispose of liquid assets would put upward pressure on the interest rate.

The interest rate is not entirely the result of free market influences, however. Particularly in an economy committed to the maintenance of high employment, manipulation of the interest rate would be one of several instruments available to the government for controlling the level of activity. Thus, a rise in prices might not result in an equilibrating upward movement in interest rates. Under these conditions, gradually rising prices would provide a permanent stimulus to the economy.

The price trends which are embodied in a projection thus emerge, not as a more or less neutral assumption, but as one of the pivotal elements in employment policy.

6. Changes in stocks of financial assets

Since a large part of personal saving is not invested directly, but is entrusted to financial institutions or corporations, and since personal saving is generally positive, with asset accumulation exceeding the growth in debt, there has been a secular increase in personal financial assets having varying degrees of liquidity. This growth in liquidity tends to be moderate, but in war years it receives a tremendous impetus from government deficits.

The failure of the ratio of saving to income to rise secularly with the growth in real income has been attributed by some to the compensating effect of the growth in financial assets, which presumably weakens the motive for further accumulation. This hypothesis requires more careful testing after reliable long-term data become available, but it seems unlikely that the net growth in financial assets has much more than kept pace with price increases and the requirements of a higher volume of transactions. If the theory that liquid asset accumulation depresses the rate of saving is true, then the rapid growth in liquidity during wars should be followed by a sharp drop in saving after wars. After World War II, when fixed money value assets rose from $80 billion at the close of 1941 to $198 billion at the end of 1945, we should theoretically have had a drop in saving to below the prewar rate. But this did not occur. What did occur was a drop in liquid saving, or a net decline in the liquidity position of the personal economy. In each year, 1947 through 1950, liquid saving (addition to financial assets less growth in debt) was negative. Funds were supplied to individuals from the rest of the economy. Only in 1951 was there a reversion to the more normal pattern of net liquid saving on the part of individuals.

The experience of recent years suggests that a period of abnormally high liquid saving is indeed likely to be followed by one in which liquid saving is much reduced, or even negative,

354

but that the total rate of saving may not be similarly affected. Saving may rather be shifted into equities and tangible investments. This shift from financial instruments to direct investments may be as stimulating to the economy as a fall in the rate of personal saving.

7. Changes in stocks of consumer durables

In order not to generate cyclical movements, investment must proceed at a rate at which additions to capacity, or the increased flow of output, attain a moving equilibrium with the increased flow of income and demand for output. Expenditures for consumer durable goods are in many respects similar to investment, and give rise to similar problems of attaining equilibrium between flows of expenditure and accretions to stocks. The cyclical behavior of expenditure for consumer durables is closer to that for producer durables than to other types of consumer expenditure. Both are affected by price anticipations which scarcely affect expenditures for perishable commodities or services. While there is nothing in the consumer durable goods area which corresponds exactly to "overcapacity" in producer goods, the market may at times approach temporary saturation.

The "consumption function" has usually been interpreted to mean the relation between income and consumption expenditures, including expenditures for consumer durables (but not for residences). Consumer expenditures are always the passive, dependent variable. Thus, the consumer is either the beneficiary or the victim of the economic drama, but never the hero or villain.

This conception of things is a gross oversimplification, as is indicated by a conspicuous failure in the ability to predict quarterly changes in consumption.[17] Data from consumer surveys have shown the complexities of consumer behavior, complexities which can only originate in the psychology of the consumers themselves. In the last year or so, the consumer has even appeared to be a speculator, along with the businessman. His "innocence" has disappeared, and, with it, the hope of easy predictions of his behavior.

Nevertheless, we may have to be content for some time with estimating expenditures for perishable goods and services as a function of the flow of current income. Durable and even semi-

---

[17] See Robert V. Rosa, "Use of the Consumption Function in Short-Run Forecasting," *Review of Economics and Statistics*, Vol. xxx, 1948, p. 97.

CHART 1

Expenditures for Consumer Nondurable Goods and Services,
Consumer Durables, and Producer Durables, 1929-51

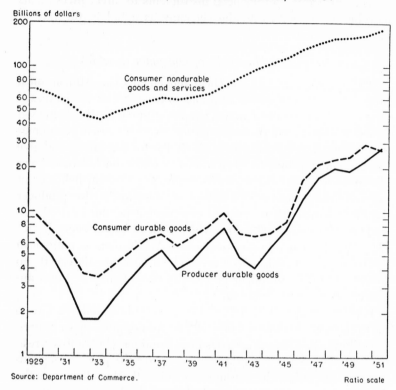

Source: Department of Commerce.   Ratio scale

durable goods expenditures, on the other hand, must be classed
with investments as variables which are often responsive to
changes in income, but may be more vitally affected by stocks
on hand and speculative influences.[18]

[18] This statement will be no surprise to persons working on current estimates of gross national product, or projections for the next 6 to 18 months.
In such projections it has become customary to "move" nondurables and
services with wage and salary and transfer incomes, and to estimate durable
goods expenditures independently, along with investment and government
expenditures. On the other hand, the level of wage and salary incomes
(which theoretically should be estimated from the multiplier after the
exogenous variables have been determined) now is determined to a very
considerable extent by wage bargaining, and the spread of the current wage
pattern, considering the expected strength of demand for labor, is an important additional consideration. The number of exogenous variables considered in short-range models is gradually being enlarged.

356

The accumulation of stocks of durable goods may tend to slow down the rate of expenditure on durable goods while income is yet stable or expanding. At some times, moreover, expenditures for consumer durable goods represent a rearrangement of accumulated savings among different types of assets, rather than an increase in consumption. There was a large element of this type of activity in consumer behavior during the nine months following the Korean invasion. The wave of spending for durable goods did not represent an increase in the propensity to consume so much as the desire to exchange assets which were expected to depreciate in value for assets which would rise in value. In this context, a distinction between "expenditures" and "consumption" is useful. "Expenditures" are influenced by fluctuations in prices and speculative considerations to a much greater extent than "consumption."

One reason that the difference in the characters of durable and nondurable goods expenditures has been overlooked in determining the consumption function is the implicit assumption that a reduction of durable goods expenditures would mean an equivalent increase in demand for other, less durable goods or services.[19] To some extent, this compensating effect undoubtedly does occur. Nevertheless, to assume that there is complete "spill-over," or one-to-one substitution, overlooks the large element of saving in expenditures for durable goods. A spontaneous decline in durable goods demand will in the main be associated with a tendency to save more in other ways. At a minimum, dissaving will decrease. Although the relations between changing durable goods expenditures and saving are difficult to observe in time series, due to simultaneous changes in income, data on individual spending units confirm the fact that durable goods purchases are an important cause of dissaving. The 1950 *Survey of Consumer Finances* says: "In 1949, although a year of some downward economic readjustments, purchases of automobiles and other durable goods reached record levels. These increased purchases, although apparent among both savers and dissavers, were more numerous in the latter group. Almost two-thirds of all dissavers purchased some type of durable good, while less than one-half of all positive savers made such purchases. These purchases apparently moved many spending units into the dissaving category."[20]

[19] See, for example, Lawrence Klein, "Post-Mortem on Transition Predictions of National Product," *Journal of Political Economy*, August 1946.
[20] Part IV, page 50.

A projection which is merely a spot picture of the economy at some time in the future, say, 10 or 20 years hence, need not concern itself with the effects of present stocks on the future stream of purchases. If the objective, on the other hand, is to indicate the rate of expenditure on durable goods conducive to continuous full employment, both present stocks and equilibrium rates of accumulation must be considered. Determining an equilibrium rate of accumulation for consumer durables is probably about as difficult as determining it for producer goods; with a given income and range of products, relative saturation is indeed possible, but changes in the style and type of durable goods available cause the rate of obsolescence on existing durable equipment to vary unpredictably. Data problems are also important. While there is considerable information on stocks and the age distribution of automobiles, and on the number and condition of homes, little is known about other consumer durables or semidurables.

Housing is the one area where demographic factors and consumption standards provide a somewhat more adequate definition of the problem. Estimates of the number of additional housing units required by a given date to take care of the formation of new families and families currently "doubled up" can be derived from population forecasts. To this must be added an estimate of the number of substandard units which should be replaced in a given time interval.[21] The numbers here depend mainly on the content of government programs providing assistance for slum clearance and urban redevelopment. Under any assumptions, however, there is a fairly definite ceiling to the rate of new housing construction which can be sustained, even with rising income, as well as a lower limit as to what "should" take place within a given time span.

Assigning a horizon to additions to stocks of consumer durables is somewhat more of an uncharted enterprise. Automobiles, of course, are the major item of concern. The age distribution of stocks of automobiles is known approximately, but the importance of this knowledge is impaired by the fact that the age at which automobiles are retired is fairly elastic, and depends upon economic conditions as well as technological factors. Still, an ap-

[21] Official estimates of the size and scope of the housing problem can be found in *How Big Is the Housing Job?* issued by the Housing and Home Finance Agency, October 1951.

358

praisal of the feasibility of continuing a given rate of production of automobiles can be made by considering such factors as population growth, population movements, trends toward urbanization, and the number of cars owned by wealthier income classes. In the Council of Economic Advisers projection for 1958, a cursory analysis indicated that an annual addition of between 4 and 5 million automobiles (after the postwar backlog is worked off) would be a reasonable estimate for the next 10 years. Stocks of furniture and household appliance expenditures are related to new family formation and to new housing construction, as well as to technological advance. The extension of electricity to rural areas and the number of localities which can receive television are further pertinent data.

F. PROBLEMS OF PROJECTING SPENDING AND SAVING

Part of the deficiencies of both the analysis of consumer behavior and attempts at projections has been that both have been cast largely in terms of the national income and product accounts, which are not entirely appropriate either to the study of consumer behavior or to economic models. Secondly, the decision to save has been interpreted as depending on the psychology of the consumer, and on economic changes which affect consumers' incomes and expectations without consideration of the role that financial institutions play in determining the pattern of consumer outlays. The effect of changes in terms on which credit is available and in the types of instruments available for saving has been largely ignored. Some modifications in the approach to "projecting" consumer behavior, and to economic projections in general, are discussed below.

1. Concepts of spending and saving and consumer behavior

In the analysis of spending patterns of consumers, through budget data, the proper definition of income has received considerable attention, both in relation to the items which should be included and the time period over which income should be reckoned. As has frequently been pointed out, the relation between a family's income and its consumption pattern may depend less on actual income over some more or less arbitrary period than on what the family regards as its income or its "normal" income.

It is equally essential to know what the family regards as saving. While the behavior of a consumer may not always be rational, even in terms of his own concepts and objectives, the study of motivations must at least start with a knowledge of what these objectives are, and how a given expenditure or asset acquisition fits into the scheme the consumer has in mind.

Questions thus suggest themselves as to what concept of saving is most closely related to consumers' motivations. Should such items as depreciation on homes and cars, additions to equities in life insurance, contributions to private and public pension plans be included in saving?

Probably there is no way of answering these questions except by consumer surveys, directly addressed to finding out how consumers themselves define saving (which may be different from the way they *say* they define it). An alternative approach would be to experiment with several different definitions of saving. A beginning was made in this direction in the *1950 Survey of Consumer Finances*. The "standard" definition used in these surveys does not include additions to stocks of any type of consumer durable goods. Computations for 1949 were made on an alternative basis, including purchases of new automobiles (less depreciation) as saving. The alternative also included an item for depreciation on homes not carried in the "standard" computations.

The importance of knowing what the spending unit itself regards as its saving stems partly from the fact that the institutions through which saving takes place are changing. Private industrial pension plans are becoming of increasing importance, and are currently adding over a billion dollars a year to personal saving. If the consumer regards contributions to these funds as saving (or, more importantly, if he considers that the sum of both employer and employee contributions are the equivalent of his own saving), this will affect his decisions regarding the proportion of income he wishes to place in other types of assets. Since a predominant motive for saving on the part of families of low and moderate means is provision for old age, social arrangements which provide more or less automatically for old age security will have the effect of diminishing those types of saving subject to voluntary control.

Attitudes toward life insurance are also worth exploring. The *1950 Survey of Consumer Finances* uncovered the fact that 77 percent of all spending units in 1949 had some form of life insurance, compared with only 69 percent owning liquid assets, and 55 percent owning automobiles. However, since it was also found that few units owning life insurance have any idea of the annual change in their equity, it seems likely that many regard their total premium as saving, and may thus tend to overestimate their current saving rate, while others probably regard insurance entirely as current expense.

Imputed items of expenditure, now included in the income and product accounts, raise similar definitional problems. For example, failure on the part of home owners to consider depreciation or undermaintenance as dissaving may not be important from the point of view of long-range analysis, but it would be important in causing spending for repair at various stages of the business cycle to deviate from that which might be expected were an annual allowance for repair and maintenance carried in the householder's personal accounting.

2. Personal saving and sources and uses of funds

The neglect of such factors as changes in the terms on which consumers can attain credit for homes or durable goods probably stems mainly from the lack of a systematic set of historical estimates incorporating the components of saving and expenditures into a complete distribution of sources and uses of personal funds. Such a series of estimates would appear to be a requisite first step for an analysis of the effects of changes originating in agencies supplying or absorbing funds. A second reason for the neglect of adequate study of financial institutions is that much of the analysis of consumer behavior has proceeded from cross-section studies of consumer budgets collected at intervals of several years and without explicit comparison of the financial environments in the different sampling periods.

It can scarcely be doubted, however, that changes in methods of financing have had important consequences modifying the pattern of personal expenditures—consequences which have by no means been confined to that group of consumers who own and operate farms or personal businesses. The most far-reaching modification in financing methods in recent experience lies in changes in the character of home mortgages and mortgage institutions since the Home Owners' Loan Corporation began operations in the thirties. Previous to that time the unamortized home loan was the exceptional case. While mortgage renewals might be contingent upon satisfactory reductions in principal, the records of the HOLC indicate that many lending institutions renewed mortgages time after time in the amount of the original loan. In the postwar period government guarantees were of course extended only to loans with amortization provisions, and this became the accepted practice for all mortgage contracts. However, lower interest rates and lengthened maturities in recent years have brought down the monthly cost of the amortized loan to a level within the reach of middle income groups, and often to the level of the unamortized loan of 20 years earlier. This has stimulated home purchases, as has the extension of government guarantees to mortgages involving little (or no) owner equity. For these and other reasons, there has been a sharp swing to home ownership since the war, and almost every mortgage has carried with it a contract for stipulated annual saving. The rate of contractual saving, and probably of total personal saving, will be affected by these developments for years to come.

The growth of facilities for consumer instalment credit is a second important institutional development affecting saving and consumption patterns. Its main effect may be to move forward in time expenditures that would have been made later, and at a somewhat lower cost. It would also seem a priori that the availability of ready credit would increase the proportion of income used for purchase of durable goods and other relatively expensive items. The use of instalment credit also appears to increase the amplitude of cyclical swings in consumption, since, when income drops, the rise of new credit declines, while contractual repayments continue.

The effectiveness of credit mechanisms and their growing pervasiveness indicate that while national income accounts can measure the increase in wealth due to saving, or changes in personal net worth, the analysis of saving must rest in a more comprehensive framework.

Fortunately, the deficiency of historical statistics on sources and uses of funds is now being at least partially rectified by the preparation of a series of estimates by the Federal Reserve Board covering the years 1939 to date. The logic of this series naturally requires that the sources and uses of funds of the financial institutions through which savings flow be presented separately. In addition, the accounts of consumers are being separated from those of personal businesses through estimates of entrepreneurial investments and withdrawals.

The separation of insurance agencies, banks, trust funds, etc. from natural persons and nonfinancial corporations permits study of the effects of the policies of these institutions on the flow and distribution of saving. The separation of the accounts of households from those of personal businesses or farm enterprises is also desirable, but statistically very difficult. Since the assets and liabilities of a household are interchangeable with those of a personally owned business, in many cases it is difficult to tell whether a given financial change originates in the producer or the consumer area.

Budgetary data disclose that families owning businesses have special characteristics, such as fluctuating incomes and high propensities to save.[22] Setting forth and studying in more detail the financing of private businesses may disclose the types of change that originate in the business and affect the household secondarily.

3. Conclusions

If academic economists have erred on the side of neglecting the effect of institutions on saving, government economists may err in the opposite direction, losing sight of the fact that to some unknown, but significant, extent, there are psychological laws or "propensities" dictating the division of income between "spending" and "saving." Government or institutional policy usually deals not with saving, as such, but with some specific component of saving. The effects of policies focused on some institution or credit arrangement on the over-all rate of personal saving may sometimes be disregarded as negligible, but at other times an implicit assumption is involved that an expansion or contraction in some component of saving will cause a similar movement in

[22] Entrepreneurial groups have higher average, and probably higher marginal, propensities to save, although, as was pointed out by Ruth Mack in her article in the *Review of Economics and Statistics* previously cited, part of observed differences between the marginal propensities to save of various occupational groups may be due to the fact that the modal income and the income range vary among different occupations. Thus, at a given income level, different occupational groups will not be comparable with respect to the proportion of units having income increases or declines.

A priori, one would expect saving to be higher at a given income level for entrepreneurial groups, because in addition to the ordinary motives for saving, the businessman or farmer has the incentive that new equipment may mean not only profits but more pleasant ways of performing his tasks and more pleasant work surroundings. In this respect, investment in farm equipment resembles investment in consumer durables, which not only saves the housewife's time, but changes the character of her work.

total personal saving. For example, the restrictions embodied in Regulation W, governing the terms of instalment credit, rested partly on the belief that a curtailment of dissaving in this area would lead to a temporary increase in total saving. Only on this basis could the measure be described as anti-inflationary.

The operational, or policy, approach suggests that research could most fruitfully be centered on those aspects of personal behavior which are most variable and responsive to general economic movements. For example, it may be more important to know the extent to which saving responds to changes in farm income and prices, which are volatile, than to know how it is related to the size distribution of income, which seems very stable.

Intensive study of the entrepreneurial group is especially important. Whatever may be the relation of the saving patterns of this group to other segments of the population at a given time, shifts in saving as economic fluctuations occur are undoubtedly more extreme among entrepreneurs than among other occupational groups. Further, changes in credit policy and financial institutions probably have their maximum impact on farmers and businessmen.

The relation between economic changes and shifting of families between income groups is also important in saving analysis. The stability of the size distribution of income from year to year conceals the high degree of income variability among families comprised in the distribution. An index of the degree of shifting within the income distribution by reason of migrations of families up or down the income scale is needed to supplement our indexes of the change in aggregate money and real income. The variability of income for individual families is known to be a major determinant of saving behavior, but at present we do not know how much shifting about occurs under normal conditions, or the amount of saving or dissaving in each income group which can be attributed to this factor. Consequently, we are ignorant of the extent to which wealth is redistributed through adjustments in saving (or dissaving) in response to fluctuations in family income. We do not even know whether the extreme concentration of saving at upper income levels is causing an increase in the concentration of wealth. This is an important gap in the economics of welfare, as well as in our understanding of the degree to which the normal operation of the economy tends to maintain or restore conditions of equilibrium.

LONG-RUN PROJECTIONS AND GOVERNMENT REVENUE AND EXPENDITURE POLICIES

ARTHUR SMITHIES
HARVARD UNIVERSITY

"PROJECTIONS" involve the extension into the future of observed or inferred economic trends of production, consumption, investment, and employment. These projections are not necessarily forecasts, since their validity depends on the fulfillment of certain conditions which it is the purpose of economic analysis to investigate. It is necessary to speak of inferred trends since many projections deal with continued "full-employment" conditions, and we have no record of such conditions in the past. We must, therefore, attempt to infer from a record of cyclical experience what the trend would have been had full employment been maintained in the past.

From the point of view of fiscal policy, projections have been used and are held to be useful for three distinct purposes:

1. To indicate the fiscal policies that are necessary to maintain short-run stability and the long-run trends of economic growth. Without appropriate fiscal (and other) policies, the original trend projections may not be valid.

2. To serve as a guide as to the feasibility of particular expenditure and revenue programs. The present defense program, for example, can only be realistically discussed in the light of the prospects for economic growth.

3. To serve as a basis for the projection of fiscal policies themselves. With given political conditions, the process of economic growth is likely to influence the nature of the fiscal programs that are adopted, and these may or may not be consistent with continued growth at the projected rate. This most difficult and least explored use of economic projections may turn out to be the most fruitful.

A. FISCAL PROGRAMS FOR STABILITY AND GROWTH

Projections designed to determine appropriate fiscal policies came into vogue with calculations of the inflationary gap during the war and, despite a checkered record, have retained their popularity in the postwar period. The procedure usually involves an estimate of full-employment GNP (gross national product) derived from estimates of the labor force and productivity changes, and estimates of demand for the national product by consumers, businesses, foreigners, and government assuming that existing expenditure and revenue programs will be continued. If the estimate of expenditures exceeds or falls short of the product estimate, deflationary or expansionary government action is supposed to be required. After 10 years' experience, my attitude toward such calculations has changed from optimism to pessimism.

The difficulties I find with the method are discussed briefly below.

1. An overriding difficulty is that the error in the estimates of expenditure is likely to be far larger than any fiscal program that is likely to be undertaken to *forestall* inflation or deflation. Leaving aside the possibility of errors in the observed data, I do not believe that our knowledge of the behavior relations of the economy is sufficient to permit the estimation of anything more precise than a range of values, each of which must be regarded as equally probable. For instance, if the full-employment national product is $300 billion, estimated expenditures may range between, say, $280 billion and $310 billion. Any attempt at greater precision is likely to be spurious. In this example, the conclusion is that there are both inflationary and deflationary possibilities, with a greater likelihood of deflation.

Depending on the relative importance attached to avoiding deflation as compared with inflation, the government can use the projection as a guide to the *general direction* of its policy. If it decides that expansionary measures are appropriate, it may decide on a tax reduction of, say, $5 billion. A greater reduction may be unwise unless the government is indifferent to inflation. I do not believe that this example overstates the case in practice; and, if I am correct, it follows that neither long- nor short-run projections can furnish any guide to the precise changes in fiscal policy that it is desirable or feasible to make. The most they can do is to provide a general guide. If the authors of projections would make their computations in ranges, all this would be obvious at a glance. As it is, the use of single-figure estimates gives the erroneous impression that economists have a technique for devising fiscal policies that will forestall economic fluctuations.

2. We know very little about the relation of fiscal policies to

economic growth. It is usually assumed that future productivity trends will be unaffected by the nature of the fiscal policy followed, provided (a) that the policy is consistent with the generation of sufficient purchasing power to take the full-employment output off the market, and (b) that sufficient savings are generated to finance the investment required to permit growth trends to continue. We know little about the relation of government expenditure and taxation to entrepreneurial incentive or the inducement to invest. We have no adequate information on the effect of government, as compared with private, procurement on productivity; and we cannot answer the vital question whether the increase in the progressiveness of the personal income tax over the last 20 years has affected the rate of economic growth. Yet in making projections, we are forced by our ignorance to assume that these questions are irrelevant.

3. To project productivity trends under full-employment conditions involves difficult questions with respect to incentives and the effects of economic controls.

It is argued by some that the relative scarcity of labor implied by full employment will prove a powerful incentive to technological improvement. On the other hand, full-employment policies are likely, in practice, to include redistributive measures designed to reduce the relative share of profits in the national income. If incentives have anything to do with the increase in productivity, projected trends of full-employment output must be subject to a wide margin of uncertainty.

At the present time, it seems likely that full-employment policies will be associated with a more extensive use of direct controls over prices and wages than has previously been considered necessary. Some countries may deliberately choose a suppressed inflation route to full employment. In fact, if no appreciable fluctuations in employment are permitted, a policy of mild inflation suppressed by direct controls may be the only feasible course of action. We know very little about productivity trends in a controlled economy and still less about the extent to which the experience of a relatively free economy can be used to project economic growth under controlled conditions.

I know it is easy to get carried away by skepticism in this field, and that important economic trends and relationships have exhibited remarkable stability in the face of institutional change. Nevertheless, if projections are to be used to determine specific policies rather than to serve as a guide to the general direction of policy, a high degree of accuracy is required. If we project the improvement in our knowledge over the last 20 years, it seems to me unlikely that sufficient accuracy will be achieved in the foreseeable future.

I am afraid that economists and statisticians have retarded progress toward a satisfactory policy by overstating the predictive power of their projections and by being overoptimistic about the possibilities of improvement in their techniques. The impression that we have within our grasp a device that will show how the business cycle can be forestalled has diverted attention from the need to construct remedial mechanisms that will counteract unemployment or inflation after it has appeared. My present point of view is that fiscal policy should normally follow well-defined rules, such as the principle of the Committee on Economic Development of balancing the budget at the full-employment level of income or the "marginal balanced budget principle."[1] Special preventive action should be taken only in the event of major, foreseeable changes, such as mobilization. But apart from that, economists should admit the limitations on their power to forecast and direct their attention to remedial measures that will come into effect as promptly as possible after it has become clear that there is something to be remedied.[2]

B. THE FEASIBILITY OF PARTICULAR FISCAL PROGRAMS

The difficulties I have mentioned limit the usefulness of projections for considering the feasibility of new programs of expenditure and taxation, but it nevertheless remains essential that long-run programs be considered in the context of a growing economy. If that were done, much of the alarmist literature about the burdensomeness of old-age pensions would appear exaggerated unless it could be demonstrated that the payment of old-age pensions, and the methods used for raising the money, would impede the increase in productivity. Similarly, the feasibility of a long-run mobilization program depends not so much on its initial impact as on the prospect for increased living standards that it permits in the long run. A program that permits no increase is

[1] "Economists' Statement on Revenue and Expenditure Policy," *American Economic Review*, December 1949.

[2] This is the point of view of the United Nations Report on *National and International Measures for Full Employment*, December 1949.

in serious danger of losing support as time goes on; and one that demands successive cuts in living standards is likely to be rejected at the outset.

This point of view has been adopted in the United States and other countries that are now in the process of rearmament, but many of the projections that have been made to support the military programs can be regarded as little more than wishful thinking. The rate of productivity increase has been put at a figure, within the range of possibilities, that will produce the desired results. Such projections represent one plausible outcome, but there may be many others that are equally probable.

If the projections of potential national product were submitted as ranges of possibilities, the policy issues would be revealed in their proper light. Only a policy of extreme urgency would be justified if its feasibility depended on national product figures that lay in the upper reaches of the range. The feasibility of deferrable or discretionary programs should be based on less optimistic productivity assumptions.

In the tax field similar perplexities arise. I assume the trend of taxation in the future will continue to be in the direction of greater progressivity. The relation of progressivity to productivity is very largely unknown. In fact, we do not know how progressive the tax system really is. We do not know, for instance, the extent to which executive remuneration is determined on a before-taxes basis, and the extent to which it is determined on an after-taxes basis.

Decisions on tax policy should be reached with a consciousness that they are made in a large area of uncertainty. Existence of that uncertainty should lead to a relatively conservative attitude toward increased progressivity of the individual income tax. There are no arguments that increased progressivity will increase productivity, and there are persuasive arguments that it will impair economic incentives, although the statistical record of the United States economy over the last generation indicates that they have frequently been exaggerated. The risks of impairing the rate of growth of the economy are so great that they should not be ignored in making policy decisions.

C. THE POSSIBILITY OF CONTRADICTIONS

The third type of projection transcends the traditional boundaries of economics and requires excursions into the unfamiliar fields of politics and sociology. In fact, one of the distressing things about economics seems to be that the answers to many of the important questions that economists raise must be sought outside their own discipline.

The economic life of the modern industrial economy seems to be dominated, on the one hand, by the efforts of individuals and classes to improve their own well-being independently of any-one else and, on the other hand, by redistributive efforts in the direction of equality. In the redistributive struggle, fiscal policy has played and will probably continue to play a major role. In fact, it may turn out that it is the only effective means whereby redistribution can be brought about—apart from the egalitarian tendencies that seem to be inherent in the process of capitalistic development.

I suggest as a possible hypothesis that, for any group or class, redistribution in its favor and an increase in living standards, which depends on increasing productivity, are partial substitutes for each other. The slower the rate of productivity increase, the more intense will be the struggle for redistribution and vice versa. While it is impossible to prove the correctness of this hypothesis, a comparison of the history of the United States with that of Europe suggests that it is plausible.

If my hypothesis is correct, it may give rise to serious contradictions within the capitalistic process, depending on the answers to some of the questions raised above. It is possible that a slowing down of the rate of productivity increase may increase the demand for redistributive fiscal measures that may in turn retard productivity even further. In this way, a vicious circle leading to economic stagnation may set in. On the other hand, rapid increases in productivity may lead to difficulties of an opposite kind. Redistributive measures may not be undertaken rapidly enough to maintain consumers' purchasing power. These possibilities lead to the conclusion that there may be an optimum rate at which redistribution should be undertaken in the general interest.

It should be one of the major tasks of long-run projections to indicate whether such contradictions are likely to occur, and also to bring to public attention the increases in living standards that can occur if economic growth is unimpeded. I believe the redistributive struggle has received a powerful impetus from the pessimistic conclusions of the classical economists and the static assumptions that have dominated so much of economic analysis.

In some countries, at any rate, a shift of emphasis toward increased productivity is needed. Again, as Schumpeter has so forcefully pointed out, long-term projections should make clear the redistribution that is involved in the growth of mass production, which cheapens items of mass consumption but leaves unchanged the prices of many items—notably domestic service and housing—consumed by the higher income groups. The commonly used practice of deflating all incomes by an index of the cost of living of relatively low income families obscures this process entirely. Of course, these remarks may result from myopic preoccupation with present difficulties. We may someday return to the simple faith of the thirties, when redistribution and economic growth were supposed to go hand in hand.

Economic research that throws light on the relation of economic growth to the distribution and the redistribution of income is as important as any of which I can think. But the way is difficult. A dynamic analysis will make redistributive measures appear less feasible than they do under a static analysis; and such conclusions are likely to be considered biased. Furthermore, the limitations on our knowledge of long-run economic processes are so great that attempts to reach definite opinions are likely to be affected by subjective judgments.

I hope this paper will not be construed as an attempt to deprecate long-run projections in the wider sense of the term. But I do deplore the amount of time and effort that is now going into the statistical computations of projections which may have little more validity than attempts to guess the height of the emperor of China. Study of detailed models can be carried so far as to divert attention from the study of their foundations. Attention should be redirected toward qualitative and quantitative studies of what has happened in the past and of what is happening in other countries. As for the future, knowledge of the past provides so much room for constructive exercise of a wide variety of intuitions and insights that it is premature to attempt to imprison the human intellect in a computing machine.

C O M M E N T

MARY W. SMELKER, *Renyx, Field & Company, Inc.*

There are a number of different kinds of arguments in Mr. Smithies' paper, and it is sometimes difficult to tell whether he is objecting to long-range projections, to full-employment policy in general, or to possible misuse of long-range projections as a tool of full-employment policy. It does emerge clearly, however, that in view of the very incomplete knowledge which economists have of the dynamics of economic growth, he distrusts attempts to alter the institutional structure of the economy for the purpose of attempting to maintain continuous full employment. As an alternative, he would deal with the problem of cyclical fluctuations through automatic stabilizers, such as variations in government receipts supplemented by *ad hoc* measures to alleviate specific situations once the need has been made clear.

In attempting to improve the structural relations within the economy, there is always the danger that some of the factors responsible for economic growth may be weakened or impaired. Since quantitative projections cannot deal explicitly with such intangibles as the strength of economic incentives, it is apparently Mr. Smithies' fear that the use of such projections might give rise to policies which fail to preserve and strengthen such incentives. Thus it is quite conceivable that if a quantitative projection seems to demonstrate that consumer purchasing power will be insufficient to maintain full employment, a tax system might be devised which would favor consumption, but which might penalize enterprise and initiative unduly.

A reluctance to tamper with the economy is indeed prudent if there is a sound basis for believing that the present (or, let us say, pre-Korean) institutional structure is conducive to some sort of middle way between inflationary and deflationary longer-term developments. However, the problem of incentives and obtaining desirable rates of economic growth must be faced whether we rely on so-called automatic stabilizers or on attempts to alter institutions so that the chances for serious cyclical deviations are minimized. A good system of automatic stabilizers is precisely one in which the marginal rate of tax on income changes is high, which in turn entails a high degree of progression in tax incidence. The degree of progressiveness in the tax structure would very likely be higher in a system relying primarily on automatic stabilization than in one in which attempts were made to provide a viable set of long-term relationships. In general, devices which sustain income in the event of an economic downturn, such as progressive taxes, adequate unemployment compensation, and farm price supports, may not be the types of institutional arrangement which maximize personal exertion and efficiency, however desirable and necessary they are from other points of view.

The identification which seems to exist in Mr. Smithies' mind between the highly progressive present income tax, long-range projections, and attempts to equalize the income distribution is a little puzzling. The present tax structure, which he thinks may be injurious to incentives, is certainly not the result of projections of any kind, or of egalitarian theories about the income structure, but mainly of the necessity of channeling about a quarter of the national income into government revenues. If we except the tax increases following the Korean outbreak from consideration, the tax structure, as a whole, has surprisingly little progressiveness, as has been shown by Musgrave and his associates.[1]

The emphasis which Mr. Smithies places on securing high rates of growth of income as compared with securing greater income equality is one with which few would quarrel. It is also true that the maintenance of adequate rewards for individual effort is necessary to realize income growth; nevertheless, incentives are only one in a complex of factors determining the rate of increase in productivity. In a more measurable category are government policies with regard to development of mineral and other natural resources, flood control, and other public works. An analysis of the relation between government developmental expenditures, long-range projections, and economic growth rates would have been an interesting addition to this paper.

MORRIS A. COPELAND, *Cornell University*

Professor Smithies has already recognized that he has not really tackled the subject he was expected to. But his acknowledgment does not go far enough. Clearly an essential part of a long-run projection of the gross national product is a long-run projection of government final-product demand. And for this purpose, it will hardly suffice to make a projection on the basis of existing government programs, even if the term "programs" is construed so broadly as to take account of new legislative implementations from time to time. A review of the past development of government gross national product expenditures makes it urgent, for our long-run projections, to attempt an estimate of

[1] R. A. Musgrave, J. J. Carroll, L. D. Cook, and L. Frane, "Distribution of Tax Payments by Income Groups: A Case Study for 1948," *National Tax Journal*, Vol. IV, No. 1, March 1951.

the further growth of government functions. It may be suggested that the problems which this type of estimate present are in part analogous to those in another area of projection, viz., personal consumption expenditures. In the case of this latter component of final demand, it has been customary to allow for a gradual rise in standards of living of persons considered in their individual and household aspects. We must allow, also, for the rise in standards of living of persons in their collective aspect.

Much of Professor Smithies' paper deals with "the relation of government expenditure and taxation to entrepreneurial incentive or the inducement to invest." On this subject, he seems to speak as a thoroughgoing agnostic. But, somehow, he turns out to be an agnostic with rather definite convictions. His comments run mainly in terms of incentive effects of tax system changes that squeeze the share of profits in the national dividend or diminish the inequality of income size distribution. And he tells us that "There are no arguments that increased progressivity will increase productivity, and there are persuasive arguments that it will impair economic incentives. . . ."

His conception of the subject of the incidence of taxation on incentives is too narrow and the conclusion cited is in need of substantial qualification. His conception is too narrow because it is too aggregative. Surely, in exploring the incentive effects of taxation, we need to consider particular forms of taxation. Let me give two illustrations: (1) it is widely conceded that the corporate income tax discourages corporate equity financing, and (2) it has frequently been pointed out that the real property tax has adverse incentive effects on investment. When an enterprise must choose either a larger investment in plant and equipment and lower variable costs or a much smaller investment and higher variable costs, the real property tax tends to favor the latter alternative. Further, when an enterprise holds proven wasting natural resources, this tax tends to encourage their rapid depletion. I suggest these forms of tax incidence are illustrations of incentive effects that need to be reckoned with in long-run projections.

As to Professor Smithies' assertion that there are no arguments that taxes designed to reduce income inequality will increase productivity, I would refer him to my paper on income size distribution (*American Economic Review*, Vol. 37, pp. 56ff.), where several are cited. There are certainly arguments. He may not like them, but he should not attempt to deny their existence. I will mention one here. Many have argued that the right to live by owning fosters an idle, unproductive class; that decreasing income inequality by decreasing the share of personal income from property will tend to increase the national product.

Professor Smithies is skeptical not only about tax incidence but also of projections themselves. He condemns, in the same breath, long-run and short-run projections as equally fallible guides to fiscal policy. This seems an undiscriminating condemnation. I would call his attention to the fact that the use of very short-run projections merges into the use of preliminary actuals as a basis for a steering wheel fiscal policy.

Finally, let me offer, on behalf of Dr. Brill and of myself, one comment that applies not to Professor Smithies' paper alone, but to the aggregate of all the papers. Nearly all of the discussion has emphasized items that appear in the gross national product account itself. I recall only one mention of the financial structure of the economy (apart from my own reference to the possible narrowing of corporate equities, above). Certainly we need to take account of the trends in the financial structure of the various economic sectors in attempting long-run gross national product projections.

CONCEPTUAL PROBLEMS INVOLVED IN PROJECTIONS OF THE INTERNATIONAL SECTOR OF GROSS NATIONAL PRODUCT

JACQUES J. POLAK

INTERNATIONAL MONETARY FUND

A. THE INTERNATIONAL SECTOR IN GNP TABULATIONS

1. The smallness of "net foreign investment"

IN THE typical tabulation of the gross national product of the United States,[1] the international sector is summarized by the heading "net foreign investment." In magnitude, the item is small in most normal years, and in many abnormal years as well. In 1949, it was $422 million against a GNP of $256 billion. In the 21 years from 1929 through 1949, net foreign investment exceeded 1 percent of GNP only five times. Its statistical unimportance, as measured by its presentation in the GNP tables of the Department of Commerce, may further be inferred from the fact that it was smaller than the "statistical discrepancy" in 16 of the same 21 years. In 8 of these years, the statistical discrepancy would have been smaller if net foreign investment had not been added into GNP (Table 1).

It is to this very small item that this paper is addressed. But before proceeding to a discussion of the techniques of projection in the international sector, it will be necessary to clarify the nature of the item. In the process, we shall also make clear that the smallness is in part arbitrary and the result of the stepchild treatment which this particular item appears to have received from national income statisticians.[2]

2. Treatment of the foreign sector on a net basis

The first arbitrary reason why the foreign element in the social

---

Note: The author is an official of the International Monetary Fund. The views expressed in this paper are his own.

[1] See, for instance, *Survey of Current Business*, "National Income Number," July 1950 (Department of Commerce).

[2] In fact, the foreign sector played an even smaller role in the first national income estimates of the Department of Commerce, when only the net of dividends and interest was included as an entry, "International Balance of Property Income," the last line on income paid out by "Miscellaneous Industries." See *National Income in the United States, 1929-35* (Department of Commerce, 1936), p. 232.

TABLE 1

GROSS NATIONAL PRODUCT, NET FOREIGN INVESTMENT,
AND "STATISTICAL DISCREPANCY," 1929-49
(IN BILLIONS OF DOLLARS)

Year	Gross National Product	Net Foreign Investment	"Statistical Discrepancy"
1929	103.8	0.8	−0.1
1930	90.9	0.7	−0.7
1931	75.9	0.2	1.2
1932	58.3	0.2	1.4
1933	55.8	0.2	1.2
1934	64.9	0.4	0.9
1935	72.2	−0.1	−1.3
1936	82.5	−0.1	0.9
1937	90.2	0.1	1.1
1938	84.7	1.1	−0.1
1939	91.3	0.9	1.4
1940	101.4	1.5	1.6
1941	126.4	1.1	1.6
1942	161.6	−0.2	2.3
1943	194.3	−2.2	0.9
1944	213.7	−2.1	4.0
1945	215.2	−1.4	4.9
1946	211.1	4.6	1.7
1947	233.3	8.9	0.3
1948	255.1	1.9	−2.9
1949	255.6	0.4	−1.9

Source: *Survey of Current Business,* "National Income Number," July 1950 (Department of Commerce).

accounts appears relatively so small is that a general tendency to move in the direction of more "gross" concepts in the national income field has (at least in the United States) stopped short of the foreign sector.[3] In Kuznets' article on "National Income" in the *Encyclopaedia of Social Sciences,* one still finds national income defined essentially as what is now called "personal disposable income." Taking this definition of national income as a starting point, we could write according to the now customary formulae:[4]

[3] Many European countries show the foreign sector "gross"; for example, Denmark, France, the Netherlands, Norway, and Sweden. Sweden, among others, shows invisibles "net," but some countries provide gross figures for the entire foreign sector.

[4] Corporate undistributed profits and similar refinements are omitted here.

National income = Consumption + net home investment +
government deficit + net foreign investment

In this equation, which one also finds implicit or explicit in
the early writings of the Keynes school, all three items—home
investment, the government deficit,[5] and foreign investment—are
on a net basis. Gradually, however, the tendency of national
income statisticians seems to have been to "gross up" the two
former items. Home investment was made gross by adding depreciation on both sides of the equation; the government section,
by adding government receipts and taxes on both sides. Taking
these two steps in reverse order, we first add, on the left, taxes
to disposable income and obtain national income; and on the
right, taxes to the government deficit and obtain governmental
expenditure:

National income = Consumption + net home investment +
government expenditure + net foreign investment

Then we add depreciation to both sides:

Gross national product = Consumption + gross home investment
+ government expenditure + net foreign investment

The reader conversant with modern national income details will
observe many omissions in these equations—indirect taxes, transfer payments, etc. These have been omitted purposely so as not
to clutter up the picture and so as to simplify the point which is
to be made: that in "grossing up" the national income concept,
only the foreign sector has been left out.

Services and donations[6] apart, net foreign investment equals
exports minus imports. It often strikes the not quite so sophisti-
cated reader as odd that in order to arrive at national income or
at GNP, one should *deduct* imports. The answer is that imports
are included in the other elements on the right-hand side of the
equation, and that they have to be excluded to arrive at the net
domestic value added of the consumption goods, investment
goods, and export industries.

But the same sort of argument which leads to the inclusion of
depreciation lends support to the idea of not deducting the import component in the output of consumer goods, investment
goods, and exports. At the last stage of the grossing up process,

[5] Which Robertson called "honorary investment." See "Mr. Clark and the
Foreign Trade Multiplier," *Economic Journal*, Vol. xlix, June 1939.
[6] We shall discuss donations below.

379

we come to what might—if a term is needed—be called gross output:[7]

Gross output = GNP + import of goods and services = Gross value of home consumption + gross value of home investment + gross value of exports

Though I do not want to press too strongly for yet another member of the already proliferating family of national income concepts, the preceding paragraphs will have made clear that one reason why the foreign sector looks disproportionately small in total GNP is the net procedure presently followed with respect to that sector.[8]

3. Elimination of donations from the foreign sector

The second reason why, at least in postwar years, the foreign sector appears so small lies in the treatment of international donations in GNP. In the absence of donations, the surplus on account of goods and services in the balance of payments must be equal to net foreign investment—although each can be measured separately and the difference between the two, if any, usually called "errors and omissions," need not necessarily be allocated to the capital sector of the balance of payments as is implied in the present treatment in the GNP calculations in the United States.

It should be noted that, even in that situation, "net foreign investment" enters into GNP, not because investment in foreign countries has anything to do with the GNP of the United States, but simply because of the numerical equality of net foreign investment to the surplus on account of goods and services. It is this surplus which is the real component of GNP.

If the surplus is met in part by donations, such as European Recovery Program aid or emigrants' remittances, instead of by

[7] This concept differs from that of "Gross Available Resources" as used in a number of countries in that the latter is obtained by deducting exports and hence equals GNP + Imports − Exports. See *National Income Statistics, 1938-1947* (United Nations, 1948).

[8] The practice of treating both the government sector and the foreign sector on a net basis has led to the parallel development in both fields of confused and indeed wrong ideas—the ideas that only a government *deficit* or only an export *surplus* could be expansionary—which have only recently been corrected. Cf. Trygve Haavelmo, "Multiplier Effects of a Balanced Budget," *Econometrica*, October 1945, and J. J. Polak, "The Foreign Trade Multiplier," *American Economic Review*, Vol. xxxvii, No. 5, December 1947.

changes in the United States foreign assets and liabilities position, so that net foreign investment is no longer equal to the surplus of goods and services, the proper entry is the surplus and *not* net foreign investment. Obviously, it makes no difference to activity and income in the United States whether exports are financed by a United States loan or paid in gold (both cases of net foreign investment), or whether they are given away as a grant. Nonetheless, it is net foreign investment and not the surplus on goods and services which appears on the United States GNP account. Why?

The explanation for this can be found in the treatment of other sectors of the economy in GNP accounting. It can most readily be explained by reference to the very simplified balance of payments presented below. In this presentation all transactions in goods and services are combined and, also for simplicity, donations *to* the United States are left out of account.

United States Balance of Payments

Debit	Credit
Goods and services (G&S)	Goods and services (G&S)
Commercial imports, G&S M	Commercial exports, G&S E_1
	Gift exports, G&S
	i. Government E_2
	ii. Private E_3
Donations	
Government	
i. G&S E_2	
ii. Cash D_1	
Private	
i. G&S E_3	
ii. Cash D_2	
Capital (net)	Capital (net)
Net foreign investment	NFI

On the basis of these entries, the net surplus on account of goods and services, which may be considered as the element of GNP associated with the foreign sector, equals $E_1 + E_2 + E_3 - M$. The "net foreign investment" which is actually entered into the GNP calculations by the equality of the two sides of the balance of payments[9] equals $E_1 - M - D_1 - D_2$. Hence, it is lower than

[9] Assigning "errors and omissions" somewhat arbitrarily to the capital account.

the surplus on goods and services by the deduction of all donations, both in kind and in cash. This treatment is made possible by the entries under "government expenditure" and "personal consumption expenditure." Gift exports from the United States[10] financed by government grants are entered as government purchases of goods and services, whether technically they are purchased by the government or not. Gift parcels sent by private persons or through such organizations as CARE are lumped together with (or, more accurately, not distinguished from) personal purchases for domestic consumption. Governmental grants abroad in cash, such as Economic Cooperation Administration dollars made available for procurement in Latin America, are fictitiously entered under "government purchases from abroad." Private cash remittances abroad are, again fictitiously, entered as a specified item of personal consumption, in the general group of "foreign travel and remittances." It will be seen that, by this procedure—matching these scattered items against the net foreign investment item—the addition made to GNP is the same as if all four items were omitted from government and private consumption expenditure, and the net surplus on account of goods and services were entered into GNP.[11]

Here, as in the previous section, there is no one particular treatment which can claim to be the most rational. In order that the difference between government expenditure and government receipts equal changes in the government debt (and similar items), it is necessary to enter both E_2 and D_1 under government expenditure. If personal income minus personal expenditure is to equal personal saving, E_3 and D_2 must be listed as personal expenditure. But, similarly, if the balance of payments is to balance, donations must be entered into it. If all this is done, however, and the surplus on account of goods and services is entered as an element of GNP, all donation items are counted twice.

There are various solutions to this problem of double counting. The one followed in the United States GNP computation is to keep the government and private sections of the social accounts in balance, but to rearrange the balance of payments in such a way as to avoid the double counting and, in the process, to make it virtually unrecognizable as a balance of payments. Thus, while

[10] Such gifts in kind purchased abroad by the U.S. Government are entered under purchases from abroad.

[11] $E_1 - M - D_1 - D_2 + (E_2 + D_1 + E_3 + D_2) = E_1 + E_2 + E_3 - M.$

one can perhaps still understand the treatment of governmental grants in cash as "government purchases from abroad" in the government account, it becomes a little hard to recognize the same item when presented as "sales to United States government" in the account "transactions of the rest of the world with the United States." Clearly the more elegant solution would be to have all three accounts—the government account, the personal account, and the balance of payments—in a form in which each can be read and understood by itself, and to take care of the double counting by an adjustment entry in the GNP total.

4. Foreign aspect of net foreign investment

Even including donations, however, the surplus on goods and services is still a relatively minor factor in relation to the total United States GNP. But, in considering the importance of projecting this element of GNP, we must bear in mind that from an entirely different point of view it is considered a crucial magnitude. The same magnitude—or a closely related magnitude—which carries the colorless name of "net U.S. foreign investment" in the GNP context appears with the flashing title of the "world's dollar shortage" in connection with the major payments problems of the world. The "dollar shortage" can be defined in various ways.[12] It may, for instance, be defined as (1) the surplus of the United States balance of payments on goods, services, and *private* donations, which is equal to net United States foreign investment plus net *official* United States foreign grants, or as (2) the amount of "compensatory official financing"[13] in the United States balance of payments, which differs from the definition under (1) primarily in that it deducts the net outflow of capital from the United States on private account and on government account for special purposes. Whatever the precise definition chosen, the dollar shortage, as an *ex post* statistical concept, tends to come close to the net foreign investment item in GNP, especially if foreign grants are included in this item rather than in government expenditure. While, for national income purposes, the projection of the net foreign investment item may be of relatively minor importance, the accurate forecasting of the balance of payments of the United

[12] Fritz Machlup, "Three Concepts of the So-Called 'Dollar Shortage,'" *Economic Journal,* Vol. LX, March 1950, pp. 46-68.
[13] International Monetary Fund, *Balance of Payments Yearbook,* 1938, 1946, 1947.

States is of cardinal importance in connection with the world's payments problems.

It is important in this connection to stress that the benefit which foreign countries derive from their relations with the United States do not arise primarily from the United States export *surplus* of goods and services, but from the gross total of dollars made available through United States imports plus grants.[14] The elasticity of demand for a good part of the imports from the United States, such as essential foodstuffs and many types of machinery, is small. The elasticity of supply of many commodities exported to the United States is also small, at least in the short run. Accordingly, the gains from trade with the United States on the intramarginal units are very considerable and may well be larger than the gains from additional free imports out of grants. In addition, many countries limit their imports from the United States below the level of market demand at the existing rate of exchange for the dollar—or, in other words, maintain their exchange rate (in terms of units of national currency for one dollar) below the equilibrium rate. In these circumstances, there is a gain even on the marginal trade.[15]

5. *"Supply of dollars"*

To indicate this gross concept of the purchasing power over United States goods and services made available to the rest of the world, the term "supply of dollars" has been frequently used in recent years. This supply of dollars was defined originally[16] as the gross purchases of goods and services, plus private donations, plus the gross outflow of long-term capital. It would, in terms of the postwar situation, require to be amended to include governmental grants as well.

This concept of the supply of dollars, whatever its precise definition, had the advantage of bringing into focus two important aspects which, while not novel, need stressing: (a) that the demand for United States goods and services, i.e., the demand for

[14] United States capital is left out of consideration for a moment. It will be brought in presently.

[15] For the underlying concepts see, e.g., Sidney S. Alexander, "The Relative Cost of Devaluation and Import Restriction as Instruments for Improving the Foreign Trade Balance," International Monetary Fund, *Staff Papers*, Vol. I, No. 3.

[16] Hal B. Lary, *The United States in the World Economy* (Government Printing Office, 1943).

U.S. dollars, can never be considered independently of the supply of dollars by the United States; and (b) that in this supply of dollars, the supply through United States lending of capital is of very great importance, next to the supply by the United States purchase of goods and services.

Both points may require some important qualifications which are of particular importance in the context of the recent postwar years, although, strictly speaking, they also applied earlier.[17] In the first place, the supply of dollars, as a factor influencing, though not uniquely determining, the demand for dollars, should not be considered as equal to the current *flow* of dollars to foreign countries, but consideration should also be given to the *stock* of dollars, gold, and various other assets in the hands of foreign countries. The observation is similar to that applicable to the explanation and forecasting of total consumption in the postwar years; we should not only use the variable "income," which, on the whole, gave a satisfactory explanation before, but should take account of the consumers' accumulated stock of money and "near money." A particular feature of the postwar demand for United States exports was that international reserves, which were actually low in real terms by prewar standards, became excessive in view of the greatly impoverished situation and the urgent needs of the war-stricken foreign countries.

Secondly, it should be stressed that while there are important similarities between the supply of dollars through the purchase by the United States of foreign goods and services, on the one hand, and the export of United States capital, on the other hand, there are also very important differences. The most important difference is that no current resources have to be given in return for dollars obtained by a loan. A second difference is the restriction on dollars obtained through certain loans. Thus loans by the Export-Import Bank are "tied"—i.e., usable only for purchases in the United States—by practice or by law. On account of institutional ties, direct investments by United States companies are likely to lead to exports from the United States rather than from other countries.

For this latter reason, a given amount of additional dollar supply provided by increased United States imports will have a

[17] On these points, cf. J. H. Adler, "The Postwar Demand for U.S. Exports," *Review of Economic Statistics*, Vol. xxviii, February 1946, pp. 23-33.

greater effect[18] in reducing the "dollar shortage" than the same additional supply provided by capital exports. The latter will tend to lead to more "new" demand for imports from the United States, caused by the limitations (legal, contractual, or practical) on the use of these dollars by the country receiving them and will hence contribute correspondingly less to the reduction of the dollar shortage which previously existed. For purposes of policy, therefore, foreign lending or capital exports by means of direct investment of x million dollars is not a substitute for increased United States imports of the same amount.

6. Items to be considered

While net foreign investment may be *entered* into a tabulation of GNP estimated for the future on a net basis, this net figure will always have to be *derived* on a gross basis. It is not intended in this paper to discuss every item of the United States balance of payments, but rather to concentrate on those important items on which it may be possible to shed some additional light. The discussion will be limited, therefore, to imports (Section B), exports (Section C), and official loans and grants (Section D). We shall omit both services and private donations and capital movements.[19]

In the treatment to be followed, we shall use without much distinction the expressions "explanation," "forecast," and "projection." Most forecasting consists in the extrapolation of a relationship; and the same relationship, read with reference to the past, must represent a satisfactory explanation of the variable we want to forecast, if we are to use the relationship with confidence in regard to the future.

B. IMPORTS

1. The standard explanation

Ever since Professor Paish[20] coined the term "marginal propensity

[18] Abstracting from the effect of increased income abroad on demand for imports—a point discussed below.

[19] There is no implication, as Mr. Fabricant seems to suggest in his Comment, that these latter flows are less independent, or of denying their importance or their interrelation with imports and exports. They are omitted simply to limit the discussion. The issue of causal or definitional equality is, therefore, not at all at stake here.

[20] F. W. Paish, "Banking Policy and the Balance of International Payments," *Economica*, Vol. III (N.S.), November 1936, pp. 404-22.

to import," the relationship between fluctuations in income and fluctuations in imports has received a good deal of statistical attention from economists. Taking into account, also, the more classical factor of relative prices as a determinant of imports, a number of attempts have been made in the last 10 years to explain, statistically, fluctuations in United States imports by reference to (a) United States national income or a closely related variable and (b) the relative prices of imports and United States commodities. Usually these calculations have been made in "real" terms, i.e., the volume (quantum) of imports has been explained in terms of fluctuations in real income. Table 2 gives the result of a number of these correlations.

TABLE 2

UNITED STATES DEMAND FOR IMPORTS

Author	Source[a]	Period	Income Elasticity	Price Elasticity	Multiple Correlation
deVegh	1	1919-40	0.7[b]	—	0.90
Chang	2	1924-38	1.27	−0.97	0.95
Adler	3	1922-37	1.01	−0.09	0.92
Chang	4	1919-39	0.89	−0.01	0.84

[a] Sources: (1) Imre deVegh, "Imports and Income in the United States and Canada," *Review of Economic Statistics*, 1941, pp. 130-46; (2) T. C. Chang, "International Comparison of Demand for Imports," *Review of Economic Studies*, 1945-46, pp. 53-67; (3) J. H. Adler, "United States Import Demand during the Interwar Period," *American Economic Review*, 1945, pp. 418-30; and (4) T. C. Chang, unpublished study prepared at the International Monetary Fund (1948).

[b] Elasticity with respect to industrial production index.

Taking this collection of correlations (which cover practically the same period and, with the exception of the first, use very similar data) as a whole, the results are not too satisfactory. The correlations, while high, still leave something to be desired; the income elasticity shows some uncertainty, and the price elasticity appears to be altogether uncertain.

Similar calculations were made by Chang,[21] R. Hinshaw,[22] and the United States Department of Commerce[23] for the five main classes of United States imports. Perhaps the most striking

[21] Sources 2 and 4 of Table 2.
[22] Unpublished study of the Federal Reserve Board.
[23] *Survey of Current Business*, July 1946 (Department of Commerce), p. 18.

aspect of these correlations for the various classes is that the fit is generally a good deal *less* satisfactory than for imports as a whole, although the groups themselves are large enough for us to expect cancellation within them of accidental fluctuations.

When postwar national income data were substituted in these correlations for total imports and for the five classes of imports, they were widely used as a yardstick of comparison between actual imports in 1946, 1947, and 1948 and "expected" or "calculated" imports for these years.[24]

The differences between the actual and the calculated data have been differently interpreted. Thus, allowance has been made for decreased rubber and silk imports caused by the production of synthetic rubber and rayon and nylon. But on the whole these calculations were, for a long time, used as forecasts, if not of the *actual*, then at least of the *normal*, imports into the United States at given levels of income. Thus, in February 1949, the *Survey of Current Business* wrote, under a caption "Imports Still Relatively Low":[25]

"Despite their high dollar value and their larger volume as compared with 1947, commodity imports in 1948 were, in real terms, only 5 per cent above previous high levels reached in 1929 and 1937. On the basis of the prewar relationship between domestic economic activity and imports, at least 1.8 billion dollars of additional imports could have been absorbed here in 1948.

". . . Although actual imports were somewhat closer to calculated imports in the first three quarters of 1948 than in 1947, there was still a large deficiency of imports from Europe and a smaller, though substantial, lack of imports from Asia. After omitting from the calculation for Asia imports of raw silk which has been displaced to a large extent by the use of synthetic fibers, and 250,000 short tons of rubber, the legal minimum volume for domestic synthetic rubber production, the apparent deficiency in imports from Asia and Europe was about 2.5 billion dollars. On the other hand, actual imports from other areas, particularly North America, were about 0.7 billion dollars in excess of the value projected on the 1921-38 relationship between gross national product and imports from those continents.

"The large discrepancy between actual and calculated imports

[24] "The Balance of International Payments of the United States, 1946-48," *Survey of Current Business*, July 1946 and February 1949 (Department of Commerce).
[25] Pp. 30-31.

from Europe was mainly in finished and semi-manufactured goods, those economic classes of imports which showed the greatest deficiency. . . . At the same time, the deficiency in imports from Asia was apparently greatest in crude materials and manufactured foodstuffs, although for crude materials as a whole the deficiency (excluding silk and 250,000 tons of rubber) was more than compensated for by increased imports from South America and Africa.

"Such a development indicates that the 1921-38 relationship for certain economic classes or areas has been somewhat modified and that imports from the Western Hemisphere and Africa may well remain higher than the amount calculated on the basis of historical relationships, because of our increased dependence upon foreign sources for commodities such as nonferrous metals and petroleum."

It may be noted that, while it is admitted that the relationship for imports from the Western Hemisphere may have changed permanently, there is no suggestion that the same applies to Europe or Asia.

The recession of 1949, when the decline in industrial activity in the United States produced at once a decline in imports (including imports from Europe), might well have shattered the myth of the "shortage of imports," and should have made it obvious that the prewar relationship had been broken and that a new relationship had been reestablished on a considerably lower level. Nevertheless, the Department of Commerce, while far more careful and stressing in detail the replacement of imports by domestic production, still concludes that "it is difficult to say whether the future American market for foreign goods may be understated or overstated by projections derived from past relationships between imports and gross national product."[26]

2. Inadequacies of the approach

Surveying these results, we can hardly consider them as satisfactory. All we have by way of explanation of this variable, which is of crucial importance, not only for the United States, but also for the rest of the world, is a number of rather simple explanations of either an aggregate or its standard subdivision into five categories. These correlations have been used widely as (quali-

[26] *The Balance of International Payments of the United States, 1946-1948* (Department of Commerce, 1950), p. 60.

fied) forecasts and, while they have failed to yield good forecasts, they have not (like the early postwar unemployment forecasts) been entirely discarded.[27] It seems useful, therefore, to stress some of the weaknesses of these explanations.

3. Weaknesses in the correlation

In the first place, the correlations for the interwar period appear to have been as high as they were in part by accidental circumstances. Adler[28] recently found the high correlation coefficient between real GNP and the volume of imports of 0.99[29] for the years 1923 to 1937 to be to a large extent "the result of two unique events—the repeal of prohibition in 1933 and the serious drought of 1934-37—which caused United States imports to be larger at

[27] Attention may be drawn here to a general theory as to the fate of forecasts which are not confirmed by events. If the event forecast was a *bad* event—such as the postwar unemployment—which does not materialize, the forecaster is blamed and the forecast forgotten. But if the event is a good event—more dollar exports for Europe—the forecast remains alive, though it tends to become a target rather than a forecast; and the blame for nonfulfillment, if any, attaches not to the forecaster, but to the economic group which should have done more to bring about the good event. The following quotation from the source quoted in the previous footnote is instructive in this connection:

"By contrast, projections made on the basis of prewar experience may overstate the demand in this country for traditional imports from Asia and Europe. Our markets for major interwar exports from Asia, such as silk, rubber, and burlap, were particularly affected by the large-scale use of domestically produced substitutes. At the same time, the products of United States factories also competed far more effectively than before the war with imports of manufactured goods from Europe. An additional development, which may continue to cause lower than prewar imports from these areas relative to domestic incomes was the shift during the war and postwar years from European and Far Eastern countries as sources for certain United States import commodities (see above) to Western Hemisphere countries and Africa, and the emigration of many workers with special skills to the United States or other non-European countries.

"It is possible and even probable, however, that Far Eastern and European export industries may be able to surmount many of these handicaps to traditional exports by greater output and reduced prices, and by appealing to quality preferences of American consumers. The revival and modernization of export industries abroad, and the heretofore unequaled efforts to stimulate exports to this country by means such as the assignment of priorities to export industries and market research, may well result in the expansion of other new types of exports to the United States to offset relative declines in sales of other products to this country."

[28] John H. Adler, Eugene Schlesinger, and Evelyn Van Westerborg, "The Pattern of United States Import Trade since 1923, Some New Index Series and Their Application" (Federal Reserve Bank of New York, 1952).

[29] This correlation is apparently a different one from that referred to in Table 2.

the end of the period than they would have otherwise been. If that part of the increase in imports between 1933 and 1937 which was caused by these two random factors is removed from the series, the coefficient of correlation of imports with gross national product falls to +.83. This adjustment obviously influences any projections of the postwar level of imports to gross national product. Total United States imports for 1948, as estimated from the experience of the interwar period, would be $1,630 million smaller when adjustments are made to take account of the effects of the drought and the repeal of prohibition than when no such correction is made, and would to that extent be closer to actual imports in that year." Thus, the very premise that we had a "good" explanation of U.S. imports, which could with confidence be extrapolated, needs questioning.

It would seem, also, that it will be necessary to deepen our insight into the factors which caused fluctuations in imports and thus to arrive at better explanations and more reliable forecasts.

4. Downward trend in U.S. imports

For the relatively short interwar period on which the existing correlations are based, it was possible to explain fluctuations in imports without the use of a trend factor. Nevertheless the existence of such a trend, at least in the long run, would seem to be plausible and to require investigation before interwar relationships are applied to forecast imports for a period some 20 years later. Thus, the expansion of the American market made possible the economic production within the country of goods previously imported. The stream of migration brought to the United States skills whose products had previously to be bought from abroad. Probably most important, the increase in per capita income directed an increasing proportion of consumption toward services which, while some of them can be imported in the form of tourist services, in any case do not enter into the statistics of commodity imports. It is not surprising, therefore, that the ratio of United States imports to GNP has so far shown a pretty persistent tendency to decline (Table 3).

Table 3 (which is in terms of values and therefore not directly comparable with the correlations underlying the forecasts, all of which were in real or quantity terms) shows a number of interesting features. Taking the 80-year period as a whole, there is a striking decline to about one-third in imports, compared with

TABLE 3

RATIO OF IMPORTS TO GNP, 1869-1949
(IN CURRENT DOLLARS)

Annual Averages	Imports as Percent of GNP
1869-78	7.2
1879-88	6.1
1889-98	6.3
1898-1908	4.6
1909-18	5.0[a]
1920-29	4.4[b]
1930-39	2.8[b]
1937	3.4
1946-49	2.5[b]

[a] It would not seem that this figure was high on account of the war years. For the partly overlapping decade 1904-13, the ratio was 4.8 percent.
[b] Average of percentages for individual years.
Source: *Report to the President on Foreign Economic Policies* (Gray Report) (Government Printing Office), p. 124 and sources mentioned there.

GNP.[30] This decline is, however, by no means smooth. Thus, despite the interruption of many commercial ties in World War I and the persistence of the secular tendencies mentioned, the ratio for the twenties was not much lower than it had been in the early part of the century. The sharp break between the twenties and the thirties may in part be because of the increased tariff. Lastly, the postwar figures appear to be not far below the average of the thirties. But this may well be because of the fact that the four postwar years were all boom years (by the standards of the thirties). Compared with the last previous boom year, 1937, the average postwar percentage was about one-fourth off (2.5 percent as against 3.4 percent).

There is, in any case, sufficient statistical evidence of the existence in the past of a downward trend in imports compared with GNP to make it necessary to allow for this trend in forecasting.

5. Inventory cycles and imports

The regression coefficients found by correlating imports and national income over the interwar period have been mostly determined by the major waves of that period: the rise in the twenties, the decline from 1929 to 1932 or 1933, and the recovery thereafter. For these major swings the income elasticity of demand

[30] A forecaster in the seventies who had been told that the 1949 GNP would be over $250 billion might have forecast imports at $18 billion.

for imports (in real terms) appears to have been close to unity. But inspection of the data shows that the elasticity is far greater for shorter cycles. Thus real GNP increased by about 4 percent from 1936 to 1937 and then declined again by about 4 percent from 1937 to 1938. But the volume of imports increased by 11 percent and then fell by 38 percent, indicating an average elasticity over this short cycle of something like 6. Again, in the short recession in 1949, when real GNP declined only a few percent even on a quarterly basis, the volume of imports declined by 7 percent (third quarter of 1948 to third quarter of 1949).

It seems probable that the high income elasticity of imports in short cycles is associated with inventory fluctuations which dominate both these short cycles and the volume of imports during them. Chart 1, which compares changes in the total volume of United States inventories with the volume of imports cor-

CHART 1

Inventory and Import Fluctuations
in the United States, 1946-50

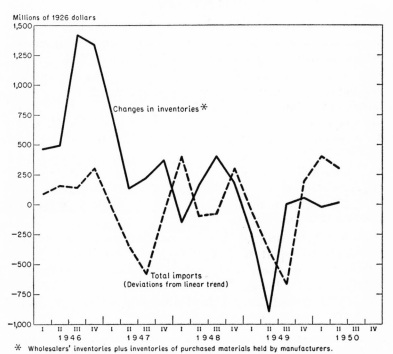

* Wholesalers' inventories plus inventories of purchased materials held by manufacturers.

393

rected for trend, indicates an exceptionally clear relationship between the volume of imports and inventory changes, which warrants more intensive and rigorous investigation. It is not the "goodness of fit," however, which is the most striking attribute of the chart. Even more interesting is the consistency with which imports lag inventory fluctuations—generally by about one-quarter. This consistency of lag tends strongly to support the hypothesis that inventory fluctuations explain the short-run fluctuations in imports.

Our primary concern in this paper is with projections for a relatively long run. In that connection, inventory fluctuations and associated fluctuations in imports, which appear to be characteristic of very short cycles, are not of importance in themselves. But, if undetected, they are important as disturbing elements in the correlation; and, if properly allowed for, they will improve the correlation and lead to more reliable forecasts, even though it is (or has to be) assumed that these short-run fluctuations do not play a role in the period for which the forecast is made.

6. Summary

We have indicated two important respects in which import correlations may be improved. But mere correlation of total imports with a few more explanatory variables than have hitherto been used will not automatically yield a satisfactory basis for forecasting imports. A much more intensive study than has been made so far of the imports of individual commodities or the imports from countries or areas is likely to shed a good deal of additional light on the factors which determine imports. It is not obvious that the detailed analysis of a great many commodities will lead to a more reliable forecast than can be made on the basis of reasonable aggregates; but such an analysis by commodities will probably contribute to finding the most effective way of deriving the best estimate from these aggregates.[31] In making these forecasts it will be realized that we have outgrown the marginal propensity to import as a general-purpose statistical coefficient —though its usefulness as an analytical tool in economic models is by no means exhausted.

Since the United States is the dominant buyer for many world

[31] The importance of changes in inventories, for instance, became quite clear as a result of an unpublished International Monetary Fund study prepared by Mrs. M. Holzman, on the imports into the United States of many individual commodities.

market staples, there is a strong positive correlation between the volume of imports and the prices at which they are purchased. To the extent that one relies only on this (supply) relationship in forecasting United States import prices, one might just as well estimate the value of imports directly on the basis of those internal United States variables which are believed to explain fluctuations in the volume of imports.

The preceding discussion has been concerned mostly with factors which explain changes in the volume of United States imports. Where the objective is to project GNP or the balance of payments in value terms, imports would also have to be projected in such terms. The best procedure for this may be to project the prices of imports separately, in addition to the volume of imports.

C. EXPORTS

In the previous section we have discussed the methods to be employed in explaining (with reference to the past) and in forecasting (with reference to the future) the value of U.S. imports. We have shown the difficulties involved in this operation and pointed toward some unsatisfactory aspects of the work done in this field. But in spite of difficulties and errors, the explanation of fluctuations in U.S. imports is not fundamentally different from the explanation of fluctuations in any other part of GNP. Refinements in technique may be required and, no doubt, in due course be applied; but the entire explanation of U.S. imports runs in terms of variables which themselves are part of the U.S. economy. These include national income or GNP itself. In this respect import forecasting is no different from the forecasting of any other sector in the social accounts, in that the part depends upon the whole, and some knowledge, or provisional estimate, about the whole is necessary before the part can be estimated. This difficulty is faced everywhere, and it can be met by successive approximation, by assumption, or sometimes by policy decisions with respect to the whole. In this respect, therefore, the forecaster of U.S. imports faces no problems different from those that confront, say, the forecaster of the demand for automobiles.

When we pass over to exports, we enter into an entirely new field. The decision to buy U.S. exports lies primarily abroad.[32] In

32 We leave out of account here the donated exports like lend-lease,

order, therefore, to explain U.S. exports, we shall have to explore and bring into our system the decisions and reactions of nonresidents. The amount on which these decisions bear is substantial: $12 billion in commodity exports alone in 1949, nearly 6 percent of the total national income. To make sensible forecasts about these exports, we shall have to know both the underlying situations abroad and the responses of foreigners to these situations with respect to U.S. exports.

It might be thought that the most convenient and most logical way to explain U.S. exports would be to parallel the explanation of U.S. imports. Correlate the income of the world outside of the United States with U.S. exports and you have your relationship, symmetrical to the import equation, which would determine the magnitude of U.S. exports. This procedure was actually followed by Hinshaw and Metzler[33] and by Tinbergen;[34] but it is obviously unsatisfactory, because the "marginal propensities to import from the U.S." of different countries are so widely different that the aggregation of their national incomes for this purpose is not permissible.

But what if we took the national incomes of individual countries and applied to them individually some "marginal propensities to import from the U.S."?[35] It would appear that even this procedure would not work out very satisfactorily for a variety of reasons:

1. In many countries imports are at present subject to quantitative restrictions and the size of imports is, therefore, not only (and as to its short-run fluctuations, not primarily) determined by the demand for imports on the part of its residents, but also (rather) by governmental decisions as to the stringency of the controls.

United Nations Relief and Rehabilitation Administration shipments, or gift parcels.

[33] Randall Hinshaw and Lloyd A. Metzler, "World Prosperity and the British Balance of Payments," *Review of Economic Statistics*, Vol. xxvii, November 1945, pp. 156-70.

[34] J. Tinbergen, "Some Remarks on the Problem of Dollar Scarcity," paper presented to the International Statistical Conference in Washington, September 1947, *Proceedings of the International Statistical Conferences*, Vol. v, pp. 73-97.

[35] An interesting attempt in this direction is made by J. H. Adler in "The Postwar Demand for U.S. Exports," *op.cit.* In an attempt to explain fluctuations in U.S. exports, Adler weights fluctuations in industrial production in foreign countries by their average share in U.S. exports.

2. Even in situations where the government exercises no direct control on imports and where, therefore, the relationship between national income and imports may be presumed to be operative, it may not be particularly fruitful to consider imports as a function of national income. Indeed, in many countries it is probably more reasonable to read this relationship in the opposite direction: the possible value of imports determines the possible level of national income. This level of national income is then brought about by the government's monetary policy, in particular its banking policy and its fiscal policy. Often the equilibrium situation is reached by trial and error; if the monetary policy is too expansionist, reserves dwindle and the policy is then adjusted to the country's possibilities.

3. But even where income is freely determined by market forces rather than by government policy, and where no restrictions are imposed on imports which are demanded on the basis of this level of income, how do we know the level of income to be used in forecasting U.S. exports? Would it be necessary to estimate GNP or national income for all other countries, or to estimate the world's income by a set of simultaneous equations, in order to estimate the exports and the income of the U.S.? To some extent this is indeed the case. But certain short cuts are possible which will enable us to have a reasonable knowledge of U.S. exports without going through the estimation of the national income of all the countries of the world. The reason for this is that, in most foreign countries, factors coming from abroad are the most important factors responsible for fluctuations in national income and, hence, in imports; and quite often these factors outweigh domestic factors in the explanation of changes in imports.

It is, therefore, possible to bring to bear the weight of foreign decisions on U.S. exports without knowledge of the national incomes of foreign countries. There is also much to be said from the purely statistical point of view for an approach which does not hinge on the use of national income data for all countries of the world. In too many countries this sort of statistics is absent or available only in a very rudimentary stage; and, in some countries, national income data, including considerable sections reflecting production outside of the market sphere, are probably a poor indicator in any case of the demand for imports.

We shall indicate below the outlines of a method to estimate

U.S. exports by means of a world system of relationships. The significance of this system lies in its application for long-run forecasting rather than short-run forecasting. For the short run, say, the next year or two, one might well obtain better results by making reasonably informed guesses as to what each country would import from the U.S. But even in making such guesses, it would be helpful to have as a background the knowledge of the relationships in such a general system, although for the short run, information concerning a variety of special factors, such as the inception of a particular development program, the postponement of certain categories of imports, etc., is likely to be more important for accurate forecasting than the ability to make refined allowance for longer-run tendencies.

When we suggest procedures for forecasting or planning the value of U.S. exports, it is obvious that we are dealing with a subject of far greater intrinsic importance than the magnitude of U.S. exports alone. We are dealing with the progress of development abroad; with the balance of payments of whole areas, such as Europe and the Far East; with the conditions for convertibility of currencies or the continuance of discrimination; and, as far as any foreign aid or foreign lending program is concerned, also with U.S. budgetary aspects. We are touching, moreover, in the present world situation on a problem of profound military importance, both in the narrow sense that investment goods exported may have to be produced at the expense of certain military items, and in the much more fundamental sense that an adequate plan for the development of underdeveloped countries may constitute a long-run substitute for military expenditure.

In constructing our model, we must choose the country as our unit. Our intention is to find rules concerning the behavior of countries with regard to their imports. Initially, we shall concentrate on total imports and then separate imports from the United States from these. But can we reasonably speak of the "behavior" of a country in international economic relations as if it has any similarity to the behavior of a consumer, or a firm, or an industry? When we refer to the behavior of a country, we try to reflect in one expression three different sets of behavior:

1. In the first place, there is the behavior of its residents, which we could register for each person individually but which, for reasons of convenience and the availability of statistical data, we

aggregate by countries and sometimes by regions. We could, if we wanted to, study separately the exports from the U.S. to each Canadian province; but it is more convenient to consider all Canadian residents as a group in a study of U.S. exports. If governments followed a neutral monetary policy (whatever that may mean precisely) and did not apply any restrictions to international trade, the behavior of a country would simply be an expression for the aggregate behavior of all its residents.

2. We should take account also, however, of monetary policy measures taken by the government of a country in the light of that country's balance of payments situation. These measures may affect income and thereby imports. Sometimes they may be *direct* measures, such as the institution or retardation of a government's development program; sometimes these measures are more general, the government operating through bank credit, the money supply, taxes, or government expenditure.

3. The government may operate directly on foreign trade rather than through the more general economic variables which determine imports. These latter measures may include such restrictions as import quotas, tariffs, and multiple exchange rates. In our present context, we are little interested in the measures, and more in the effects which they are expected to achieve.

When we speak, therefore, of the behavior of a country as an element in a foreign trade model, we refer to these three aspects of this behavior.

1. *Factors determining other countries' imports*

a. EXPORTS

Among the factors which will primarily determine most countries' (though not the United States') behavior with respect to their imports is the value of their exports. Let us first consider a country whose foreign exchange reserves are at an "equilibrium level." It is not suggested that this implies that the reserves are "adequate" in any absolute sense of the term. For reserves, as for imports, the concept of certain absolute requirements, while useful for programs and plans, is quite unusable to describe the behavior of a country. Therefore, when we refer to an equilibrium level of reserves, we mean this in the sense of what the responsible authorities in the country consider as the amount which the country "can afford" and "must afford."

Let us assume that there is an increase in exports which is not

399

offset by a reduction in domestic demand. This increase will raise incomes by the same amount and it will also affect imports through the three channels of behavior which we have just indicated. The income of exporters will go up and, through the well-known multiplier mechanism, this will lead to an increase in imports. In terms of the simplest multiplier equation, the increase in imports will be less than the increase in exports, provided the marginal propensity to save (or the "marginal propensity to excess-save," or the "marginal propensity to hoard") is greater than zero.

Assuming that this marginal propensity is thus in excess of zero, the country's foreign exchange reserves will go up and the government is likely to stimulate or permit more expansionist developments, thus further increasing the demand for imports.

In those countries where the government relies on restrictive methods at the trade level, it will also attempt to relax these restrictions, increase quotas, lower tariffs, etc.

It is not of great importance for our model in the first instance by which of these three channels the change in exports leads to an increase in imports. In fact, it is most convenient for us if we can combine the reactions through the three channels into a single parameter indicating the behavior of the country. I have indicated this parameter as the "international reflection ratio."[36] It indicates the magnitude in the change in imports which would come about in response to a change in exports. If M stands for the value of imports and X for the value of exports, then the international reflection ratio would be defined as follows:

$$\rho = \Delta M / \Delta X \quad \text{or} \quad \Delta M = \rho \Delta X \qquad (1)$$

If account is taken only of the reactions through the behavior of individuals and the simplest multiplier pattern is followed, it will readily be seen that

$$\rho = \frac{m}{m + s} \qquad (2)$$

where m is the marginal propensity to import and s is the marginal propensity to save. This expression $<$ unity if the marginal propensity to save is positive. Even then, however, ρ will tend to approach unity as reactions through the second and third channels come into play.

[36] J. J. Polak, *An International Economic System* (University of Chicago Press, 1953).

The use of a single parameter to describe the behavior of a country does not imply that the country's response to a particular change will always be the same or will be constant over time. Statistical measurements of ρ have actually been made with some measure of success,[37] but these measurements are of no particular concern to us in this context. For planning purposes, it will be necessary to have a figure for ρ. Possibly it can be obtained from observation of the past; perhaps it can better be estimated in some other manner. In any case, it is probably safe to say that a great many countries have such urgent development needs and are so keenly aware of them that they have a persistent tendency to overimport; in these countries ρ is likely to be very close to unity. Most of them have a very low marginal propensity to save, which would make for a value of ρ of close to unity on account of individual behavior alone; and whatever increases in reserves are left over are likely to be used by the government.

b. LONG-TERM CAPITAL MOVEMENTS

With reference to the past, long-term capital movements may be taken into account in a manner quite similar to that for exports, so that only the total supply of foreign exchange needs would be considered. This procedure is justified because, in the past, it was normal for the total financing of any capital project to come from abroad. Thus a foreign loan of $1 million would tend to lead to investment of the same amount, and hence income of the same amount (less the import component of the investment). Foreign investment of $1 million would then presumably have roughly the same effect on national income and on imports as exports of $1 million.

This simple equivalence of long-term capital imports and exports cannot be assumed to hold with respect to the future. The International Bank for Reconstruction and Development, for instance, does not normally lend to a country the total cost of an investment project, but only the import cost.[38] Until recently, it

---

[37] ibid.

[38] Article IV, Section 3(c) of the Articles of Agreement of the IBRD reads as follows on this subject: "The Bank, if the project gives rise indirectly to an increased need for foreign exchange by the member in whose territories the project is located, may in exceptional circumstances provide the borrower as part of the loan with an appropriate amount of gold or foreign exchange not in excess of the borrower's local expenditure in connection with the purposes of the loan."

was the Bank's policy never to lend for any local currency expenditure in connection with a project. While this policy has now been relaxed, it will continue to be true—and indeed it is desirable—that the value of the projects sponsored by the IBRD will exceed the amount lent by that agency.[39] National legislation in many countries limiting the extent of foreign participation in new industries may also tend in the same direction. It will, therefore, be necessary to make allowance for the fact that, in the future, a capital import of amount L should not, in its effects on imports, be considered as equivalent to an export of the same amount L, but rather to eL, where e stands for the "expansion ratio," that is to say, the ratio of additional investment to additional foreign capital.[40] This expansion ratio is not constant, either between countries or over time. It will, in each case, depend on the whole nature of the country's borrowing plan. We may, therefore, write[41]

$$M = \rho(X + eL) \qquad (3)$$

C. USE OF RESERVES

For purposes of forecasting U.S. exports in the early postwar years, it seemed reasonable to assume that foreign countries would use up virtually all their available resources: the proceeds of their dollar exports, loans, grants, and whatever dollar reserves they felt they could spare. The events of these years seem

[39] Allowance should also be made for the fact that the financing of a particular project with foreign capital does not necessarily indicate a *net* increase of investment over what it would otherwise have been.

[40] See J. J. Polak, "Balance of Payments Problems of Countries Reconstructing with the Help of Foreign Loans," *Quarterly Journal of Economics*, April 1943.

[41] We pass from the somewhat clumsy equation in terms of ΔM, etc., used in (1), to this form in terms of M, etc. It should be understood that all equations are assumed to be linear only in the neighborhood of present values for the variables and that these variables should, accordingly, be considered as differences from present values.

A theoretical point needs to be made here, to which Mr. C. D. Finch of the staff of the Fund has drawn my attention. With respect to exports, we express all the resultant expansion of imports through the coefficient ρ, whether the expansion is brought about directly through the behavior of individuals or indirectly through governmental responses (Section C-1-a). For foreign investment, however, governmental responses are indicated by the expansion ratio e, so that, with reference to the term eL, the reflection ratio should be limited to the first item, i.e., $m/(m+s)$. It may be noted that the *maximum* expansion ratio is $(m+s)/m$, so that the maximum for ρeL equals L. It seemed more convenient to deal with this point in a footnote than to complicate the formulae to allow for it more explicitly.

to lend particular credit to Kindleberger's account of the chronic dollar shortage as a world-wide problem, an account which may perhaps, with slight oversimplification, be phrased: "All other countries will always have a dollar shortage because they will want to spend more dollars than they earn or have."

The experience of 1950, when almost all foreign countries increased their holdings of gold and dollars (by a total of $2.8 billion), must have come as a shock to those who believed in this relatively facile explanation of U.S. exports. There had, however, been numerous indications that this explanation was quite inadequate, at least as far as the European countries were concerned, and reflected only the very peculiar conditions of the early postwar period. Thus, Italy, which had ended the war with virtually no reserves, had acquired $200 million in dollars in 1946, nearly $300 million in gold and all foreign exchange in 1948, and $350 million in gold and all foreign exchange in the course of 1949. While countries had shown themselves prepared to run payment agreement debts up to the limits provided by these agreements in 1946, 1947, and 1948, many of the credit and even grant facilities provided under the Intra-European Payments Scheme of 1949-50 failed to be taken up. There was quite a bit of evidence, therefore, before 1950, that international trade could not be explained in terms of an insatiable hunger for imports limited only by the availability of funds. The desires to acquire reserves, to curb inflation, and sometimes to provide protection to domestic industries all played roles in determining the magnitude of imports.

It may be that the accumulation of dollars and gold abroad in 1950 represents, in part, a lag. Foreign individuals and foreign countries simply have not yet had the time to adjust their spending plans to the increase in income and reserves. In fact, this may be the most important explanation for the accumulation of reserves as far as the underdeveloped countries are concerned; for these countries, I believe, the "Kindleberger effect" is probably the rule rather than the exception. As far as the developed countries are concerned, however, the increase in reserves should be considered primarily as reflecting a deliberate policy. The period 1946-49 was abnormal in the sense that during that period many European countries held "excess reserves," which they gradually used up to finance imports. It may appear odd to speak of "excess reserves" in a time when reserves were low by all standards of adequacy. They were high, though, by one standard: the urgency of the import needs which they could meet. It seems reasonable to consider countries, or perhaps rather governments, as having an indifference curve linking the level of available resources (from both imports and domestic production) to the level of their reserves. This curve would presumably cut the reserve axis at some point where available resources fall far below normal. At that point countries would be prepared to go into short-term debt to keep up the current flow of supplies. On the other hand, the curve would probably rise pretty steeply after some more or less normal reserve had been obtained. Not much more can be said about this curve, but it is important to realize its existence. The adjustment from actual reserves to the "desired reserves" at any particular stage is not immediate. The "excess" is not likely to be spent in a few months. It is budgeted over the future, taking into account not only the present, but also the future, level of desired reserves.

We can consider the period of 1946-49 as one of generally, although not continuously, increasing income and hence gradually increasing "minimum reserves." At the same time, actual reserves for most countries continued to be in excess of minimum reserves and reserves continued, therefore, to be drawn down.

It would not be fruitful to pursue this point further in general terms. Enough has been said to make it clear that we should add to our import equation an allowance for the amount of excess reserves used during the period under consideration. We shall indicate this amount by R_E. It is clear that this symbol will stand for a positive amount when reserves are being run down, i.e., when actual reserves are in excess of "desired reserves," and for a negative amount when the reverse situation prevails.[42] We then obtain the following equation for imports:

$$M = \rho(X + eL) + R_E \qquad (4)$$

It will now be necessary to pass from total imports to the imports from one particular country, the U.S., in the problem which concerns us. For this purpose, let us indicate by a_{ij} the fraction of country i's imports which it buys from country j. The sum of these

[42] Logically, R_E might be derived as an endogenous variable of the system. But there is a pretty narrow limit beyond which it does not pay to allow in the system for more and more relationships and hence to be burdened with more and more residuals, as these relationships do not hold exactly.

fractions over j will obviously equal unity. We then have the the following equation for M_{ij}, the imports of country i from country j:

$$M_{ij} = a_{ij} M_i = a_{ij} [\rho_i (X_i + e_i L_i) + R_{E\,i}] \qquad (5)$$
$$(i = 1, \ldots, n; \; j = 1, \ldots, n; \; i \neq j)$$

When we introduce the coefficient a_{ij}, we do not intend to indicate a purely statistical fraction. Rather it is implied that this coefficient has a certain degree of constancy. This assumption appears justified on the basis of the considerable stability which appears to exist in the pattern of international trade. To be sure, there are long-run shifts reflecting the emergence of new import-trading countries, new consumer demands, and new techniques; and also short-run disruptions, in part on account of the overvaluation or undervaluation of individual currencies. For reasons such as these, it would not be wise to lift the a_{ij}'s for our forecasting purposes from, say, the interwar period. In order to do a reasonable job with reference to forecasting for a rather long period, it will be necessary to take account, as best one can, of knowledge of the shifts. It might be relatively less important to make allowances for the effects of improperly valued currencies. The reason for this is that one ought to assume that, in the longer run, improperly valued currencies will not persist: overvalued currencies will tend to come in for devaluation, and undervalued currencies will tend to lose their special advantage both by increases in prices and by the devaluation of other currencies.

The set of equations shown by (5) indicates all trade flows considered from the import side. Thus it contains some $n(n-1)$ equations explaining the same number of trade flows. In the light of what we have said earlier, it does not seem reasonable to use the same explanation for the United States imports, since these are to only a very minor extent determined by the factors listed.

It is readily seen that this set of equations also provides the exports from each country to each other country and, by summation over the second subscript, the total exports of any country. Thus the exports of country k would equal $\Sigma k M_{ik}$, and if we take k to stand for the U.S., this would provide the answer to the question that concerns us: the estimation of U.S. exports.

While the determination of the magnitude of a country's exports from the importing country's side appears a reasonable procedure as far as the industrial countries, including the U.S., are concerned, it may, in some instances, yield unsatisfactory results for countries whose exports consist of a few raw materials. Within moderate limits our equations may satisfactorily explain the exports of this sort of country also. But if the equations indicate great changes—in particular, great increases—it may be doubtful whether the productive facilities of these countries in their particular export industries will be able to meet such demands. If they are not, the export forecast may be relatively far off, but it cannot be said in advance in which direction it will be off. An attempt to satisfy increases in demand will tend to lead to sharp price increases if the demand is highly inelastic. The export value of the raw material countries will increase much more than if productive facilities have been expanded to meet the increased demand. If, on the other hand, the demand is very elastic—for instance, because there are good substitutes for the particular commodities—the export value may be very much less than if capacity has been expanded in anticipation of the increase in demand.

These objectives point to the necessity of checking the total export figures forecast for particular countries against the likely production possibilities of these countries, and possibly of modifying to some extent our figures in the light of these checks. This type of correction is again not different from that necessary in the forecasting of certain segments of the domestic part of GNP.[43]

There are $n(n-1)$ equations of type 5 to determine $n(n-1)$ trade flows. These equations are adequate to express the relationship of trade flows in terms of each other, but not to determine the absolute amount of any one of them.

We may assume, however, that we know the value of U.S. imports and its distribution. On the basis of the internal variables of the U.S. economy, we can then (with L and R_E as autonomous variables) solve the system and obtain the value of any M_{ij} as well as that of the exports of any one country. In other words, we have, at least ideally:

$$M_{ij} = F_{ij}\,(M_k;\ e_iL_i;\ R_{E_i})\qquad(6)$$
$$(i = 1, \ldots, n;\ j = 1, \ldots, n;\ i \neq j)$$

---

[43] The reader will notice that these corrections are necessary because prices have not been brought into the system explicitly. They could have been introduced, but there is some risk in introducing additional parameters about whose magnitude we do not—and, perhaps for a long time to come, cannot—have any reasonable knowledge.

in which each trade flow is expressed as a function (F_{ij}) of U.S. imports, the capital import and expansion ratios of each country, and the excess reserves of each country. In this expression F_{ij} depends on all the a_{ij}'s in the system as well as on the ρ_i's; and the partial derivative $\partial M_{ij}/\partial M_k$ is constant if equations 6 are linear. In other words, increases in U.S. imports will pull up the entire system of trade flows, and, assuming a constant proportional distribution of these imports, the increases in all trade flows will be proportional to the increase in U.S. imports. If, to give an example, the increase in U.S. imports from $8 billion to $9 billion raises exports from Belgium to Chile in the situation by $1 million, then a further $1 billion increase in U.S. imports (from $9 billion to $10 billion) will raise Belgian exports to Chile by another $1 million.[44]

d. PRACTICAL USE OF THE MODEL

It is believed that the model, in the form in which it has here been presented, cannot be used for immediate practical application; that is, to arrive at precise forecasts. A considerable amount of work would be required to attain estimates for the a_{ij}'s even when countries are grouped into areas; and it may be difficult indeed to obtain reliable estimates of these coefficients, which are marginal, not average, propensities.[45] But even before the information necessary to use the model for forecasting is available, the model itself can be used to obtain qualitative conclusions which may be of great importance for balance of payments forecasting and, perhaps, of even greater importance for balance of payments planning. Some of these conclusions have already been touched upon, but they may be restated here in a somewhat systematic form. Individual conclusions refer to partial effects; that is, they are valid only on the assumption that all of the other factors remain unchanged. Thus, when speaking of changes in the magnitude of U.S. imports, we assume their distribution to be constant; and when we speak of changes in the distribution of U.S. imports, we assume total imports to be constant.

An increase in U.S. imports will lead to a smaller increase in U.S. exports.[46] This is so because (or if one prefers, on the as-

---

[44] In this statement, no account is taken of the effect through R_E, which, in some instances, may be important. For this reason, the fraction $\partial M_{ij}/\partial M_k$ is written as a partial derivative.

[45] If i stands for a country then a_{ii} is zero; but if i stands for an area, a_{ii} is positive, reflecting the marginal intratrade of the area.

[46] This is a *ceteris paribus* statement. If U.S. foreign investment increases

sumption that) the average of the ρ's in the system is less than unity. A further factor tending in this direction is that a general increase in U.S. imports will increase the general level of well-being in other countries and thus raise the level of "desired reserves." This in turn will render R_E negative.

Subject to one important qualification, an increase in U.S. lending will increase U.S. exports more than an equally large increase in U.S. imports. This is so for a variety of reasons: (a) U.S. lending tends to be, to some extent, tied by either legal or institutional arrangements; (b) some U.S. lending, especially that through the IBRD, will have an expansion ratio greater than unity; (c) U.S. lending tends to be concentrated more than U.S. imports in countries which have a relatively high marginal propensity to import from the U.S.

The important qualification to this general statement is that it applies only to such lending as leads to additional investment which otherwise would not have been undertaken. It is limited, therefore, to what might be called project loans in the narrow sense of the word, in that the project would not have been undertaken had it not been for the lending.

The effect of increased U.S. imports on the increase in U.S. exports will be greater the larger the reflection ratio of the country from which the imports are obtained and the larger the marginal share of imports from the U.S. in imports of this country. It will readily be seen that if the U.S. increases its imports from a country i where ρ_i equals unity and a_{ik} equals unity (the subscript k standing for the U.S.), the entire increase in the foreign supply of dollars would come back at once as an increase in U.S. exports. In a long-run equilibrium analysis, account should be taken not only of the immediate return flow, but also of the indirect effects through third and fourth countries. If all ρ's were unity, or if the appropriate average of them were unity, it would be immaterial where the initial expenditure by means of U.S. imports was made, because, ultimately, all of the dollars would tend to flow back to the U.S. But it may even be that the difference from unity of the ρ's in the system is so small all over the world that it will make little difference in the equilibrium situa-

---

at the same time, the statement should be amended to read: An increase in U.S. dollar availabilities from increased U.S. commodity imports and capital exports will lead to a smaller increase in U.S. exports (*vide* point 4 in Mr. Fabricant's Comment).

tion where the U.S. spends its money for imports, so far as the ultimate effect on the total value of U.S. exports is concerned.

The distribution of U.S. imports and lending is of much greater importance for the total flow of world payments than for the value of U.S. exports. It might be inferred from the preceding paragraph that it would be desirable for the U.S., all other things being equal, to concentrate its imports in the countries for which $p_i a_{ik}$ is the highest. This conclusion would be justified if the objective of U.S. imports and lending were to maximize U.S. exports—and even then, the justification for the conclusion might not be strong if the p's all over the world were close to unity. But it does not seem reasonable to assume that the objective of U.S. imports and lending is to maximize U.S. exports.

Apart from the direct objective of individual U.S. imports and individual acts of U.S. lending abroad—to obtain particular commodities or particular investments, or to stimulate particular development possibilities in foreign countries—the general objective of the U.S. supply of dollars may reasonably be described by reference to one of the purposes of the International Monetary Fund: "to facilitate the expansion and balanced growth of international trade and to contribute thereby to the promotion and maintenance of high levels of employment and real income and to the development of the productive resources of all members as primary objectives of economic policy."[47]

In many areas of the world, trade is restricted below the optimum on account of inadequacies of reserves. In a sense, the supplying of dollars by the United States may be considered as a method to oil the mechanism of international payments. Obviously this purpose is not well served if the lubricant flows back as quickly as possible to the place from which it came. It is best served if the lubricant stays in the mechanism for a long time, finding its way through all the channels of trade all over the world. From this point of view, it would be desirable if payments on account of U.S. imports and U.S. lending were directed to countries that (marginally) obtained a *minimum* of their imports from the U.S. and a *maximum* from other countries. In other words, U.S. payments should, from this point of view, be directed to countries with a minimum a_{ik} as well as to countries with a maximum p_i.[48]

---

[47] Articles of Agreement of the International Monetary Fund, Article I (ii).
[48] A comparison—somewhat limping, as are all comparisons—might be

The balance of payments of the U.S. cannot be explained or forecast by reference to U.S. factors alone. In order to build up our model, variables and parameters relating to foreign countries have to be taken into account. The plural *foreign countries* (or *foreign regions*) is essential. No useful purpose is served by opposing to the U.S. a magical "rest of the world" whose balance of payments can be obtained by the easy trick of changing the debit and credit headings in the U.S. balance of payments. This "rest of the world" represents nothing at all in terms useful for economic analysis. It is an amorphous aggregate about the behavior of which no useful statement can be made.

This is perhaps most strikingly indicated with regard to reserves. The observation that the reserves of one particular country, say, France, have increased has a very definite economic meaning and may lead to certain definite consequences. It does not matter for this purpose whether the reserves of all French banks or all French business concerns have come up. Certain action by the French government may be expected in response to the change in *the country's* reserve position. On the other hand, the statement that the reserves of the "rest of the world" have gone up has very little meaning in terms of forecasting events which will follow from this fact. For: (a) the increase in reserves may have occurred in countries which heretofore have had small reserves, and it may then stimulate additional imports; (b) it may have occurred in countries which have had abundant reserves, in which case it is likely to have very little effect on imports; (c) the over-all increase may be compounded of a decrease in countries with adequate reserves and a greater increase in countries with highly inadequate reserves, in which case it may lead to a more than proportional increase in imports; (d) the over-all increase in reserves may be compounded of a decrease in the reserves of countries short of reserves and an increase in the reserves of countries with adequate reserves, in which case it may lead to a reduction in the imports of the rest of the world.

In order to be able to pass beyond meaningless statements of alternative possibilities like the preceding, it will be necessary

---

made with deficit financing policies. It is often argued that deficit financing does not "really" cost the government as much as it appears to cost because part of the additional expenditure will return to the government as additional tax receipts. But it would obviously be absurd to plan deficit financing by so directing the government's payments as to maximize the return from taxes in the first round, or even in all rounds.

to have data on the balances of payments and the reserves of individual countries. The balance of payments of the U.S. taken by itself, read forward or backward, does not contain adequate information for our problem.

Similarly, the solution to the imbalance of world payments cannot be found by looking at the U.S. balance of payments alone. It is merely a truism to say that, if the balance of payments of the U.S. were brought into equilibrium, the "dollar shortage" would be over. While a situation of balance in the payments of the U.S. would *ipso facto* mean balance in the aggregate payments of the "rest of the world," this latter over-all balance could well be compounded of large deficits in some countries and equally large surpluses in others, and if there were no longer a dollar problem, the same balance of payments difficulties might crop up in the form of a sterling problem or a cruzeiro problem, or, simply and more generally, as problems of deficits and surpluses.

Useful balance of payments forecasting must be in terms of the behavior of countries, not simply in terms of definitional relations which can be derived from the social accounts. It is clear from the few equations shown earlier that they contain certain parameters which are intended to describe the behavior of countries. We are not presently concerned with the question as to how much we actually know about this behavior, how regular it is, and with what confidence it can be predicted. The important thing to bear in mind is that these coefficients reflect behavior. The risk of interpreting as causal relationships concurrent changes occurring in the various items in the social accounts is a general risk, and economists and statisticians alike have to be constantly aware lest they fall into the traps which they themselves set when they started out in the social accounting business. In the field of international payments, these risks are no smaller than in other fields of social accounting. With regard to problems such as the dollar shortage or discrimination, this sort of mistake is frequently made.[49] In practice, the need for caution often does not go beyond avoiding the identification of average propensities with marginal propensities; but the problem is, in a sense, more funda-

[49] In this connection I may mention, as an example, Ragnar Frisch, "On the Need for Forecasting a Multilateral Balance of Payments," *American Economic Review*, September 1947. Cf. my comment: "Balancing International Trade: A Comment on Professor Frisch's Paper," *American Economic Review*, March 1948.

mental in that it is necessary to distinguish behavior from observed social accounting relationships.

D. OFFICIAL LOANS AND GRANTS

1. *Introduction*

We now come to the third important element in the balance of payments which we intend to discuss from the forecasting point of view: official loans and grants. These are entered as an "autonomous variable," L, in our system of equations above. We must now find an explanation for this variable.

Although the variable L referred to loans and grants by all countries, this section will deal only with loans and grants by the United States. This is not to minimize grants and loans by other countries, in particular, capital exports by the United Kingdom in the form of releases of sterling balances. But we concentrate here on the loan and grant component of the U.S. balance of payments, not on L as it affects U.S. exports.

2. *No forecast possible*

With regard to such balance of payments items as imports, exports, and tourist expenditures, it is often reasonably safe to rely on "persistence forecasting," i.e., to assume that *natura non facit saltum*, and that what happened recently is likely to continue to happen in the near future. This procedure is, however, particularly inappropriate in the field of foreign grants and loans, because they represent governmental decisions, which change abruptly from one year to the next. Perhaps the most striking example in recent history is the Marshall Plan. It is probably not unreasonable to say that in May 1947, United States aid to Europe for the year 1948 would have been forecast at a few hundred million dollars at most (outside Germany and Austria, and perhaps Italy and Greece). Yet, a few months later, after the Harvard speech of June 5, 1947 and after the Western European countries had presented a four-year plan for $17 to 22 billion, it suddenly became reasonable to estimate this aid for 1948 at a number of billions of dollars. The difference between the two figures reflects a decision, and items which are determined by governmental decisions to such a large extent are obviously not suitable for pure forecasting by economists who are on the outside.

The sections which follow, therefore, do not deal with the forecasting of these decisions, or with methods of forecasting them. Rather they constitute an analysis of the possibility of basing the decisions on rational factors, failing which, one would have to consider them as a matter entirely outside the realm of economics. In these discussions we shall limit ourselves to the *development* aspect of foreign loans and grants. The period of *reconstruction* aid is largely over, except for Korea. Many of the same considerations apply, however, to aid for the two purposes, as the economic problems of reconstruction and development are comparable in many respects.

3. *Magnitude of the need*

It is tempting to seek "objective" figures on the amount of foreign aid required by reference to some standard of need, and it is easy to point to the disparity in per capita income between the underdeveloped countries, on the one hand, and Western Europe and the United States, on the other hand, to show the existence of a vast objective need for more capital. But how much? The underdeveloped countries of the Far East (outside China), Africa, the Near East, and Latin America, with a population of about 1,075 million, have a national income of about $80 billion, or an average of $75 per capita. For the United States, the figure is about 20 times as high. To raise these areas to the U.S. level would require additional income of roughly $1.5 trillion. In the advanced industrial countries, the ratio of capital to income is about four to one. Thus, to produce this much more income, at least $5 trillion might be needed,[50] or $100 billion a year for 50 years, assuming *a stationary population* and the increase of productivity in the underdeveloped countries to the U.S. level with an adequate supply of capital. Even on these assumptions, these countries would reach the 1950 level of the United States only in the year 2000, when the United States would be far ahead of this level.

These figures are presented partly to show the magnitude of the problem, but primarily to make clear by reference to the factors that it cannot usefully be considered from the point of view of absolute needs. This indeed is just as well. While economic planning must be based on statements of objectives which

[50] Using a somewhat lower ratio of capital to income than in the U.S. or U.K.

it is desired to achieve, these objectives themselves do not have the absolute character of "needs" or "requirements" which can somehow be objectively determined.[51] Calculations of "requirements" often deceive by their apparent objectivity those who use the figures as well as those who compute them. It should always be clear that they are nothing but derivations based on arbitrary assumptions, often of some *average* per capita level of consumption. Since *import requirements* are the difference between the computed consumption requirements and estimated domestic supplies and often have to be met at prices much higher than the domestic supply price, they are particularly subject to minor fluctuations in the postulated consumption levels.[52]

4. *What the United States can afford*

Just as the criterion of need does not give us a clue to the proper magnitude of a foreign aid program, so the criterion of what the United States can afford is equally an irrelevant and useless yardstick to apply. In connection with the Marshall Plan, the question of "the limits within which the United States could safely and wisely extend aid to Western Europe"[53] was the subject of wide political discussion and of extensive study by a Presidential committee. But the report of the committee was devoted almost exclusively to the question of the availability of particular commodities, not to the ability of the United States to bear any particular amount of aid in general; and with the disappearance of the world wheat shortage shortly afterward, the entire problem of the ability of the United States to provide foreign aid of any given dollar amount seems to have vanished from public attention.

This is quite reasonable for two reasons. In the first place, the optimum practicable amount of foreign loans and grants for development purposes in the near future to all countries outside the U.S.S.R. sphere is likely to constitute only a small proportion of the United States gross national product. Whether the amount

[51] Except in emergency situations and with reference to the most primary foodstuffs.

[52] A striking example: The computation of minimum meat requirements for the countries of Eastern and Southern Europe which received UNRRA supplies showed a difference in import requirements of a billion dollars a year, according to whether one or another recognized standard of minimum intake was used.

[53] *European Recovery and American Aid* (President's Committee on Foreign Aid, November 7, 1947), p. 3.

is about $1.2 billion as suggested in the Gray Report, or even, say, $5 billion (which would be 6 percent of the national income of the countries concerned), it would, in any case, be within the range of 1 or 2 percent of the $300 billion gross national product.[54] Only if one were to consider large aid to Eastern Europe, the U.S.S.R., and China[55] might the total figure for developmental loans and grants reach a high percentage of GNP—and such aid would then, most obviously, be in substitution of very much larger other demands on the national economy and on the budget. But secondly, and more generally, it should be realized that one cannot in any absolute sense (or in any sense whatever) speak of a country's "ability" to render foreign aid—any more than one can speak of a country's ability to spend money on education or on military preparedness. As put most explicitly in the Act for International Development, development is an objective of United States policy.[56] This objective must be valued on the national scale of values.[57] It must be weighed against alternative uses of United States resources. This process of weighing may yield a particular figure of the amount the United States *is prepared* to spend on foreign aid. But this should not be regarded as the amount which the United States *can afford*. Foreign aid figures of a number of billions a year would have been considered unthinkable 15 years ago. They are not unthinkable now, not because the United States is so much richer—although, of course, it is—but because of a change in the schedule of values.

5. An optimum rate of capital inflow

Does it follow, then, that there is no objective criterion to guide

[54] For a more extensive discussion of the concept of "capacity" for foreign financing, see Horst Mendershausen, "Future Foreign Financing," *Review of Economics and Statistics*, Vol. xxxi, November 1949, pp. 272-74.

[55] Something in the order of the $50 billion, five-year plan proposed by Senator McMahon in February 1950.

[56] Public Law 535, Section 403(a) reads as follows: "It is declared to be the policy of the United States to aid the efforts of the peoples of economically underdeveloped areas to develop their resources and improve their working and living conditions by encouraging the exchange of technical knowledge and skills and the flow of investment capital to countries which provide conditions under which such technical assistance and capital can effectively and constructively contribute to raising standards of living, creating new sources of wealth, increasing productivity, and expanding purchasing power."

[57] Horst Mendershausen, "Foreign Aid with and without Dollar Shortage," *Review of Economics and Statistics*, Vol. xxxiii, February 1951, p. 43.

the decision of policy makers—a decision which forecasters may try to forecast, or perhaps to influence? Or should one fall back on determination by such short-run bottlenecks as were often stressed by the International Bank for Reconstruction and Development in explaining the moderate rate of its lending in the face of enormous need: the lack of detailed plans acceptable to the Bank, or the lack of people who can make such plans? It would seem that considerations of this sort, however pertinent they may be to explaining developments in the short run, would have little place in the making of plans for the longer period—except that the plans themselves should provide for means to break the bottlenecks. No one would base the scope of a long-run program of disease control on the number of physicians presently available.

It would appear that there is such an objective criterion—although it is not precise and not subject to immediate statistical application; that, in fact, there is an *optimum* rate of foreign investment from the point of view of the countries receiving the capital.

It might seem at first sight that as far as capital-importing countries are concerned, forgetting for a moment about the service of the debt, there is no limit to the amount of capital they could absorb, or at least, that this limit would be so far removed that it would have no practical significance. Assuming investment to proceed at a rate no higher than the rate of foreign capital inflow,[58] why should not each country seek to obtain the largest amount of investment and capital inflow that it can?

The answer to this question is primarily in terms of the mobility of goods, both within the country and internationally: it is the lack of mobility, or, in other words, the inelasticity of supply of goods within the country or within certain regions of the country, which sets important limits on the amount of capital a country can absorb.

Let us take the case of perfect mobility of goods, both internally and through imports from abroad, and further assume perfect elasticity of supply in the world as a whole—a reasonable assumption if the country whose problem we study is relatively small.[59] An investment program of magnitude I per annum is

[58] Or, indeed, no higher than the rate of foreign capital inflow times the maximum expansion ratio.

[59] The assumption may not be quite so reasonable as far as the world

416

undertaken, of which I_m is imported capital goods and I_d is demand for domestic labor and supplies. The entire value of I is made available in terms of foreign exchange by, say, a foreign grant. It is clear that I_m raises no problem at all. The goods are imported against payment from the available foreign exchange and, until they begin to be unloaded and thus start to be combined with domestic resources, no call on those resources is made. As far as I_d is concerned, this will lead to a secondary demand for consumer goods, both domestic and imported, and successive rounds of income spending. To the extent that the derived demand is for imports, there is again no problem: they can be financed from the balance of I available. Indeed, assuming $\rho < 1$ (or, more generally, $e\rho < 1$), some of the foreign exchange made available will remain unused. To the extent that the demand is for domestic goods, and their local supply is not infinitely elastic, these will flow in, with perfect mobility, from other parts of the country or from abroad. The price level of all commodities in all parts of the country will remain constant, as any infinitely small increase in prices would call forward additional supplies, either from other regions or from abroad. There is no limit to the investment, assuming the requisite foreign exchange accompanies it.

But this ideal situation is a quite inaccurate description of reality, particularly in underdeveloped countries. In such countries the cost of transport is high. Price differentials between regions are enormous. The cost to the consumer of imports is very considerably above their landed cost—if not because of tariffs, then because of high markups, monopoly-type profits of importers, expensive marketing. These factors make for a rather inelastic supply of consumer goods when, on account of increased demand, local supplies have to be supplemented by imports. Not until the local price rises substantially will imports—from other regions or from abroad—begin to flow in.[60] Thus,

---

supply of food is concerned in connection with large-scale development in all underdeveloped countries simultaneously.

[60] The rise in price occasioned by an increase in demand will be very much greater if the increase shifts the country (or region) from being a net exporter of, say, rice to being a net importer. The same high cost of transportation and trade make for a wide spread between the prices of export goods on the farms and in the villages, on the one hand, and at the export level (f.o.b.), on the other. Hence, for the consumer, the difference between the prices of rice at the rice "export point" and the rice "import point" (to borrow gold standard terms) should be very large indeed. Or,

investment will be accompanied by a rise in local prices even though adequate foreign exchange is available. Some inflation will occur.

Owing to the inflation, real income will be shifted from the population at large to the relatively small wealthier classes. If the money income rates of large sections of the population are relatively inflexible, the shift in income to the higher income groups might even exceed the increase in real income due to the additional investment. In that case, the purpose of the development program—to raise the real income of the low income groups —will be defeated. Hence the existence of an optimum point of foreign investment: the point at which the current loss in real income of the low income groups in the population because of inflation exceeds the discounted[61] prospective increase in real income which may be expected from the new investment.

It is not suggested that a precise, or even a rough, figure can be set for each country or for the underdeveloped world as a whole on the basis of these theoretical principles. Their main justification at this stage is to point out that there is an optimum of this sort. The existence of an optimum can also be observed from the postwar experience of a country which has built a very high rate of investment on the basis of (or at least supported by) large foreign grants. The Philippines, from 1946 to 1949, devoted about 25 percent of its national income to investment.[62] Assistance from the United States in various forms enabled the country for a number of years to proceed in this manner without balance of payments limitations. But it is doubtful whether this rate of investment, with the attending high level of prices, was to the benefit of the population at large. Indeed, it seems quite reasonable to maintain that the Philippines would have been better off with a lower rate of investment.

The fact that one country (or a few)[63] can be shown to have received more than the optimum rate of investment would tend to support the existence of such an optimum. But the optimum obviously does not exist in absolute terms—as x percent of the

in other words, the elasticity of supply beyond the export point may be very small.

[61] Note that a rate of interest is implied—the (very high) subjective rate applicable to the low income groups in the underdeveloped countries.

[62] Economic Survey Mission to the Philippines, October 9, 1950.

[63] Greece also seems to be a case in point of a country receiving more aid than was good for its economy.

national income. A great deal will always depend on the particular nature of the investment program. Above all, the limit will depend on the measures taken by the government to increase the elasticity of supply in the whole economy as well as on measures to increase savings. To give one example: A large public works program in which workers are paid money wages with which they bid up food prices until imports flow in may be seriously inflationary; while the same program may be perfectly tolerable if the government, with the foreign exchange available to it, purchases foodstuffs abroad and distributes them as wages in kind.

It is clear from this that an optimum rate of investment can be determined for each country only on the basis of a plan—not only of the cost and the nature of the program, but also of the manner in which it is to be carried out.

As these plans come gradually into being, and the experience of tolerable and intolerable rates and conditions of investment is gathered in various countries, it will become possible to obtain an impression of the magnitude of the optimum rate of investment.

It might be found that the distance between this optimum and the amount the United States and other capital-exporting countries are prepared to make available is not too great.[64] In our present state of knowledge, however, we cannot give any confident answer to this question.

COMMENT

SOLOMON FABRICANT, *New York University*

1. From among the many interesting things in Mr. Polak's stimulating paper, I can select only a few for examination. There is, first, his proposal for projecting U.S. imports. The ratio of imports to gross national product has followed a downward trend in the past. Given a projection of GNP, he suggests, we may use an extrapolation of the trend in the ratio to project the trend in imports.

My first comment is on the historical trend in the ratio of imports to GNP. Mr. Polak notes the irregularities in the movement of the ratio, but concludes that "in any case," there is sufficient evidence for a downward trend. Yet the irregularities cannot be ignored when we are projecting one or two decades into the future. According to Polak's Table 3, the ratio changed between

[64] After making allowance for domestic saving and private capital imports.

419

adjacent averages by the following number of percentage points: −1.1, +0.2, −1.7, +0.4, −0.6, −1.6, −0.3. The differences among these figures may seem small, but they must be referred to an average percentage of only 4 or 5.

There is, next, the question whether the trend in the above ratio is a simple function of time. Would the ratio continue to fall whatever happened to GNP? Polak himself explains the downward trend by the rise in per capita income. If national income stopped rising more rapidly than population, the ratio of imports to GNP might stop falling. This suggests a revision of the formula for projecting imports.

But we can hardly stop here. Nor would Polak, for he appeals for a "more intensive study . . . of individual commodities" (Section B-6). This might take the form of an investigation of changes in the ratio of imports to output in each of our industries and changes in the relative importance of industries with high and low average import-output ratios. (This, too, is implied by Polak when he speaks of the declining ratio of imports to GNP as the result of increased self-sufficiency and of the rise of the service industries.) Then we would have to explain these changes, before we could use them as a basis for projecting total imports. And this explanation could not avoid bringing in certain developments abroad, so that the explanation of U.S. imports would not run in the simple terms of "variables which themselves are part of the U.S. economy" (Section C). It is safe to say that we would find the historical trend reflecting the net result of a number of forces acting in opposite directions, and that the weights of these forces have been shifting. Were such an analysis available, I am not sure that we would project a trend in the ratio of imports to GNP that continued to decline at the historical average rate, or even declined at all.

2. When it comes to projecting U.S. exports, Polak avoids the major task of dealing with the national products and other domestic variables of countries in the rest of the world by assuming that, unlike the United States, their national products are determined by their exports, and ultimately by the rest of the world's exports to the United States. To construct the projection formula for U.S. exports, it is necessary to derive a few parameters from data for other countries, but these "have a certain degree of constancy" (Section C-1-c). Fundamentally, the only explicit independent variable is U.S. imports.

The justification for this is essentially the claim that "in most foreign countries, factors coming from abroad are the most important factors responsible for fluctuations in national income and, hence, in imports; and quite often these factors outweigh domestic factors in the explanation of changes in imports" (Section C). Here we have the rather widely accepted theory that the U.S. exports depressions (or business cycles). But even if we could have confidence in this explanation of fluctuations, it is difficult to see the justification for applying the argument to *trends*.

Polak is a little vague as to how the parameters are to be derived. Historical data are not satisfactory, for in contrast with the continuity of the U.S. situation, a great "structural" change has occurred in the outside world. The behavior patterns summarized by the parameters can be put only in terms of a new post-World War II set of habits: "a great many countries have such urgent development needs . . . that they have a persistent tendency to overimport" (Section C-1-a); unlike the past, the effect of capital imports must be multiplied by an "expansion ratio" (Section C-1-b); and so on. We may appreciate the need to recognize that the economic world has changed. Nevertheless, two questions require some discussion: first, why no allowance needs to be made also for important changes in the United States; and second, why the changes abroad must be viewed as revolutionary.

Having argued that the "coefficients have a certain degree of constancy," Polak goes on to admit that, "to be sure, there are long-run shifts reflecting the emergence of new import trading countries, new consumer demands, and new techniques; . . ." (Section C-1-c); and to indicate his unwillingness to "imply that the country's response to a particular change will always be the same or will be constant over time" (Section C-1-a). This, it seems to me, takes the heart out of the argument that projections of U.S. exports can be determined primarily by reference to U.S. imports. Once changes in the parameters are admitted, Polak must also admit, as he in fact does (but only with reference to "rather long" periods), that "to do a reasonable job with reference to forecasting . . . it will be necessary to take account, as best one can, of knowledge of the shifts" (Section C-1-c). Polak does not define a "rather long" period; but, if it is one in which such changes may become too important to be ignored, my guess is that it is as short as two decades and possibly even one.

3. Polak assumes that (private) foreign investment is determined by trade. There can, of course, be no question that imports and exports influence foreign investment. A country exporting railroad equipment and financing the export by loans raised within it provides an obvious example, and so does a country exporting oil and hoarding the royalty proceeds abroad. It is also true, however, that foreign investment influences imports and exports, and economists have been studying the mechanism for generations. But Mr. Polak assigns only "official loans and grants" to the role of independent variable. A major difficulty in projecting foreign investment stems out of the complex interaction between investment and trade, and Polak's assumption is an effort to skirt it. I wish it were that easy.

4. One of the conclusions drawn by Polak from his analysis is that "an increase in U.S. imports will lead to a smaller increase in U.S. exports" (Section C-1-d), other things remaining the same. This is mainly because ("or if one prefers," Polak is frank to say, "on the assumption that") foreign countries tend, on the average, to increase their imports less than their exports increase. As change in world imports equals change in world exports, it follows that increase in U.S. imports must be greater than increase in U.S. exports. Is the reasoning (or "assumption") acceptable? Consider the implications: the difference between changes in exports and in imports is (roughly) equal to the change in foreign investment; U.S. imports have an upward trend; therefore, on Polak's theory, there is a secular tendency for U.S. foreign investment to decline. This curious conclusion, it seems to me, can only raise doubts about the theory on which it is based.

5. In his discussion of the optimum rate of capital inflow, Mr. Polak reminds us that the simple aggregate of a nation's income is an incomplete criterion of its economic welfare. His own criterion is in terms of the "low income groups," the "bulk of the population," but I imagine he would not object to taking account of the whole income distribution. This would avoid arbitrary definition of "low income," would allow for inequalities at the lower end of the distribution (which some feel to be more injurious than the disparity between the very rich and the "bulk" of the population), and would give some weight (as most of us would wish) to the impact of development on the "high income" groups. Just what measure of inequality of income distribution

422

is appropriate, where to secure the necessary data for its calculation, and how it should be weighted relative to the average level of income, when judging how far to push an investment program, are questions which reinforce Polak's own conclusion that his criterion is still in the "theoretical" stage.

If we are going to broaden our criterion, perhaps we should allow, also, for the enormous noneconomic costs of change in habits and places of working and living encountered by developmental programs. These costs might go as negative items into the calculation of average real income (with a weight base shifting as adjustments are made and new habits learned), or they might constitute a third element in the criterion. Their inclusion would not make application of the criterion any easier.

6. Mr. Polak's comment on the bottleneck criterion of optimum rate of capital inflow raises again the question of how long the short run is. To increase appreciably the number of physicians in a backward country, to use Polak's example, might well take a generation or more. But bottlenecks never disappear: they only change their form. Economic development is a process in which bottlenecks are constantly being discovered and broken. Education, trade connections, habits of work, commercial (and political) ethics, to speak only of "intangible" capital, must be improved. It is a slow process. This means that the rate of economic development must be planned and benefits of capital inflow must be calculated with an eye to these requirements. Development plans must have a time dimension; and every "optimum rate of capital inflow" also must be "dated."

PART IV

REGIONAL AND NATIONAL PRODUCT PROJECTIONS AND THEIR INTERRELATIONS

WALTER ISARD

MASSACHUSETTS INSTITUTE OF TECHNOLOGY

AND

GUY FREUTEL

WASHINGTON UNIVERSITY

A. INTRODUCTION

WE view the national economy as a space-economy. Resources flow from place to place and thus traverse distance as they pass through the transformation process. In contrast, general equilibrium analysis in the Walrasian tradition essentially treats a single-point, or nonspatial, economy.[1] The same comment applies to general equilibrium analysis in the Keynesian aggregative tradition. For an insight into the operation of the economic system, nonspatial analysis at certain levels of abstraction may be useful. However, when nonspatial models (in particular, the highly aggregative models) are used as a means for understanding or projecting actual quantities, the error due solely to omission of spatial differentiation within the system may be considerable. As will be apparent later, this error is of the same type as that which may arise when aggregates, such as gross national product, national employment, and national energy requirements, are projected without attention to the interrelationships of their components.[2]

The preceding statement poses the problem of choice which faces the analyst making projections of a global quantity, such as gross national product (GNP). On the one hand, he can project

Note: Many of the ideas in this paper are necessarily of an exploratory nature. The kind of regional projection discussed has been largely ignored by economists; much more analysis and subsequent modification of these ideas will be required.

[1] For elaboration, see W. Isard, "The General Theory of Location and Space-Economy," the *Quarterly Journal of Economics*, Vol. LXIII, November 1949, pp. 476-79.

[2] This type of error is clearly revealed and avoided in the excellent study by Harold J. Barnett, "Energy Uses and Supplies, 1939, 1947, 1965," U.S. Bureau of Mines, *Information Circular 7582*, October 1950.

the individual components of the system and their interrelations and then combine these values into a GNP. On the other hand, he can develop statistical short cuts which lean heavily on historical relationships among major aggregates, e.g., time rate of increase of average labor productivity, rate of population growth, percent of population in labor force. The GNP derived in either case is perhaps of limited interest. The difference in method is clearly brought to light by the differences in the problems faced. The analyst attempting directly to project the components must determine the *degree* and *principle* of aggregation that will reduce the number of variables and simplify his problem to the extent consistent with the degree of accuracy required.[3] The analyst who directly projects GNP must select the proper historical trends and relationships. Having determined GNP, he must choose the technique of *disaggregation* which will yield accurate projections for the components. Whether the two methods will yield the same projections, for both GNP and its components, can be tested only by application. If they differ (and this would seem likely), the selection of procedure becomes an important issue.

A similar but somewhat more complex argument applies when we consider the space-economy. From the standpoint of the first method, a system of equations describing an economy subdivided into minute industrial categories is still not completely valid unless it recognizes spatial distinctions. A shoe factory in Tennessee is not the economic equivalent of a shoe factory in Massachusetts, even though similar in all respects except location. Hence, the interrelationships of components in an economic system should be described and constrained by a system of spatially differentiated coefficients, structurally relating the parts of the whole, and not simply by interindustry technological coefficients alone. Both the conceptual complexity and the limitations of data lead to modifications in empirical work and to a search for additional principles of aggregation.

From the standpoint of the second method (direct projection of GNP and subsequent disaggregation), consideration of the space-economy introduces a major problem. Should GNP be derived from separate regional product projections? Or should

---

[3] Accuracy in this context does not imply realized accuracy of the projections, but accuracy given the validity of the data and assumptions entering into the projection.

regional projections be derived from GNP as simply an additional problem in disaggregation, essentially similar to disaggregation into other components of GNP? These questions will be studied in detail in later sections of the paper. The point is that, regardless of one's approach, explicit consideration of the space-economy involves the aggregation or disaggregation problem.

Briefly, some spatial aggregation of economic activity is justified because it is impracticable to study the effect of distance on every individual component of the economic system. In addition, if distance acts on the distribution of economic activity to create a tendency for spatial agglomeration, we can develop principles of aggregation that will aid our analysis. Since we have viewed the economic system as a complex of production processes involving the flow of resources from place to place in the economy, we look to these flows for indications of aggregation principles.

After this introduction, it may seem inconsistent to begin with a discussion of techniques for regional projections in a one-point economy. By doing so, however, we hope to point out the limitations of such analysis, while emphasizing the need for the study of flow phenomena.

B. REGIONAL PROJECTIONS DERIVED FROM GNP PROJECTION: NONINTERREGIONAL TECHNIQUES

To derive a regional projection from a GNP projection, one might first allocate the total among regions on some proportionality basis. For example, if state X produced 12 percent of the GNP in 1950, then 12 percent of the projected GNP for the year T is state X's share for that date. The most immediate objection to such a procedure is the arbitrary selection of the proportionality factor. That the relative shares of the various states, or groups of states, in the GNP will remain constant over time is an unwarranted assumption. Of the many reasons to doubt the validity of such a premise, one is immediately apparent. If examination of historical ratios of gross state product (GSP) to GNP reveal changing relationships, some improvement is obtained with the use of trends. If over the past California shows an increasing proportion of GNP, extrapolation of this trend to some future date yields a better estimate of the share at that time. Since GSP and GNP are highly aggregated quantities affected by many factors (perhaps approaching randomness), they are, in general, fairly stable statistically. The derived relationships change fairly slowly. In general, the shorter the period of projection, the more appropriate is the use of a trend extrapolation.

There is, however, not much to justify confidence in such a procedure other than a statement about the relevance of the past to the future. It is pertinent to ask: What are the variables and relationships on which the projections of GNP are based? Would direct examination of the data for the several regions yield a different result? Examination of the technique used by the Council of Economic Advisers (CEA) to project GNP shows that they have made (1) an estimate of a rate of increase in average productivity, and (2) an estimate of the rate of population increase and labor force participation.[4]

On the basis of these estimates, projections of GNP are derived. Thus, with the simplifying assumption that labor force participation and number of hours worked remain constant,[5] the CEA's technique becomes:

$$\text{GNP}_{t+\theta} = \text{GNP}_t (1 + p)^\theta (1 + z)^\theta \qquad (1)$$

where $t + \theta$ refers to the projected year, t refers to the current or base year, $p = $ rate of population increase, and $z = $ rate of increase in average productivity.

In the first case discussed in this section, the assumption of a constant GSP/GNP ratio meant for purposes of projection that the state parameters p and z were the same as those for the nation as a whole. In the second case, where a monotonically changing GSP/GNP ratio was extrapolated, an implicit assumption was made that these parameters, while different from those appropriate for the nation,[6] continued to be related in a predictable fashion. We cannot ascertain by trend extrapolation whether the changing share is due to a differential in population growth, or productivity change, or both. Without this information we cannot make any statements about the reliability of trend extrapolation.

Now, if a state, say, California, has a different p and z from

---

[4] See the five-year projection by the Council in the *Annual Economic Review*, January 1950, and "Background Material," hectographed, March 1950.

[5] This assumption is maintained throughout the following discussion. It does not affect the logic of the argument.

[6] A difference might be in p, z, or both.

those of the nation as a whole, then the growth of California's gross product is explained by these factors and not by the growth in GNP alone. Moreover, in reality the change in GNP is in part explained by the change in California's gross product. (This is not a complete statement, since obviously the question of the interdependence is here overlooked. But it does serve to emphasize the limitations inherent in a GNP based on extrapolated national parameters. Such a GNP becomes a quantity which can only be viewed as a statistical resultant.)

The weakness of the procedure whereby regional estimates are derived from national parameters is brought to light by the following experiment.

Equation 1

$$\text{GNP}_{t+\theta} = \text{GNP}_t (1+p)^\theta (1+z)^\theta$$

can be rewritten. Let

$$\text{GNP} = \Gamma \cdot L \tag{2}$$

where $\Gamma =$ average labor productivity per hour, and $L =$ number of labor hours, annually.

Then

$$\text{GNP}_{t+\theta} = \Gamma_{t+\theta} \cdot L_{t+\theta} \tag{3}$$

where

$$\Gamma_{t+\theta} = \Gamma_t (1+z)^\theta \tag{4}$$

and

$$L_{t+\theta} = L_t (1+p)^\theta \tag{5}$$

We take California as our region, the year 1930 as t, and the year 1940 as $t + \theta$.

Imagine ourselves in 1930 applying CEA techniques. Since we are not at this point discussing the CEA method per se, we assume that it is entirely valid and accurate for national projections. Thus we may use the actual 1930 to 1940 national population and productivity changes as the basis for a regional projection. If projected GCP_{1940} (gross California product in 1940) does not turn out to be approximately equal to actual GCP_{1940}, then the national rates, p and z, are inapplicable.

Using equations 3, 4, and 5, we set up the following equation for projecting gross California product:

$$\text{GCP}_{t+\theta} = {}_cL_t (1+p)^\theta \cdot {}_c\Gamma_t (1+z)^\theta \tag{6}$$

where $\text{GCP}_{t+\theta} =$ gross California product in year $t + \theta$, ${}_cL_t =$

431

number of labor hours of work performed in California in year t, and $_c\Gamma_t =$ average labor productivity per hour in California in year t.

However, since equation 6 assumes constant labor force participation, and since, because of unemployment, labor force participation was not the same in 1940 as in 1930, it would be wrong to use an unadjusted rate of national population growth as the value for p. It seems best, under these circumstances, to let p represent either the rate of growth of national labor force (including unemployed) or the rate of growth of employed workers in the nation.

When we adopt the former procedure, $p = 1.15$ percent per annum, and $z = 0.0$ percent per annum for the period 1930-40.[7] In 1930 the labor force in California consisted of 2.5 million workers. Since in the same year gross California product (GCP_{1930}) may be estimated at $6.05 billion,[8] average labor productivity per worker in California in 1930 may be set at $2,421.

Substituting these values in equation 6, and changing the units in which $_cL_t$ and $_c\Gamma_t$ are expressed so that these terms represent annual labor force and average productivity per worker per year, respectively, we have:

[7] The average productivity estimate for any given year is derived by the simple and crude technique of dividing GNP in that year by the number in the national labor force for that year.

The zero rate of change in average productivity is primarily due to the fact that the labor force projection for 1940 includes more unemployed than the labor force in 1930. Thus, $GNP_{1940} > GNP_{1930}$, labor force $_{1940} >$ labor force $_{1930}$, unemployment $_{1940} >$ unemployment $_{1930}$, average product per employed worker $_{1940} >$ average product per employed worker $_{1930}$, and average product per worker in the labor force $_{1940}$ is *approximately equal* to the average product per worker in the labor force $_{1930}$.

[8] Since data on gross product for individual states are not available, an approximation had to be made. Data on income payments to individuals are published on both a national and a state basis. Accordingly, we made the assumption that the ratio of income payments to individuals to gross product for California is the same as a similar ratio for the nation. Separate ratios for 1930 and 1940 were computed and on this basis GCP estimates were derived and presumed to approximate the actual GCP's for 1930 and 1940.

The sources for our computations in this experiment were: "Unemployment," Vol. 1, *15th Census of the U.S., 1930* (Bureau of the Census, 1931), pp. 18, 19; Solomon Fabricant, "The Changing Industrial Distribution of Gainful Workers," *Studies in Income and Wealth, Volume Eleven* (NBER, 1949), and quoted in *Historical Statistics of the United States, 1789-1945* (Bureau of the Census, 1949), p. 64; *Survey of Current Business* (Department of Commerce), July 1949, table 2, p. 10.

$$\text{GCP}_{1940} = 2,500,000(1 + 0.0115)^{10} \ (\$2,421)(1 + 0.0000)^{10}$$
$$= \$6.8 \text{ billion}$$

This projected GCP_{1940} contrasts with the actual GCP_{1940}, which may be estimated at approximately \$7.5 billion. The projected increment from 1930 to 1940 of \$0.75 billion contrasts with the approximate actual increment of \$1.45 billion.[9]

In this experiment, the application of national rates p and z to California data for 1930 understates the actual 1930-40 increment in gross product by roughly 50 percent. Presumably this is partly the result of more rapid rates of growth in labor force or employment for California than for the nation as a whole. (The actual rates for California were 1.7 percent and 0.95 percent, respectively.) In part, the understatement can also be attributed to a more rapid rate of increase in average productivity in California. This latter can be partially explained by the increased proportion of the labor force used in high-productivity industries.

Thus on the basis of such a simple projection model, the regional implications of any projected GNP cannot be ascertained without reference to considerations internal to regions. Information about rates of growth of relevant variables pertinent to regions is required. This poses a logical problem in the selection of the proper procedure. If regional implications of national projections cannot be derived without reference to regional rates of change, and if regional rates of change can be discovered only by study of the region under consideration, is it not a superior procedure to begin operations with regional analysis and later reconcile regional projections with national projections? Indeed, this would point to a complete reversal of technique and result in the derivation of national projections from a set of mutually consistent regional projections.

We now focus attention on the possibility of projecting gross regional product (GRP) by using regional rates of change for extrapolating regional aggregates. Using the CEA methodology, we would have the following for region i:

$$_i\text{GRP}_{t+\theta} = {_i\Gamma_{t+\theta}} \cdot {_iL_{t+\theta}} \tag{7}$$

where

$$_i\Gamma_{t+\theta} = {_i\Gamma_t}(1 + _iz)^\theta \tag{8}$$

[9] If we adopt the alternative procedure of allowing p to represent the rate of growth of employed workers in the nation, the value of p is then 0.45 percent per annum and that of z is 0.65 percent per annum. As can be expected, the same result is obtained for projected GCP_{1940}.

and

$$_iL_{t+\theta} = {}_iL_t(1 + {}_ip)^\theta \tag{9}$$

and where $_iz$ = rate of increase in average productivity in region i, and $_ip$ = rate of population increase in region i.[10] From this point of view,

$$GNP_{t+\theta} = \sum_{i=1}^{i=m} {}_iGRP_{t+\theta} \tag{10}$$

There is little reason to suppose that GNP derived in this way will be the same as GNP derived directly from projection of nationally estimated rates of change. But a difference in results does not mean that proceeding from separate regional projections and then summing to obtain the national is preferable to directly obtaining GNP, since we have at this stage taken no account of the interaction of differential regional rates of change. The GNP directly derived may be more valid than that derived by combining separately estimated GRP's. On the other hand, each of the separately derived GRP's is likely to be more valid than a GRP derived from a GNP using national coefficients of change.

C. REGIONAL PROJECTIONS: INTERREGIONAL REACTIONS

It is clear that growth (or decline) of the GRP of a region i is not independent of the direction and rate of change of the GRP of some other region j. Projections of GNP based on extrapolation of past national trends implicitly take account of interregional relations. The task of regional analysis is to make such relations explicit. The simple extrapolation of a trend in the proportion $_iGRP/GNP$ relates the part to the whole without revealing the substance of the relation. Further insight is gained by directly linking growth in one region with that in another. In

[10] To obtain regional rates of change, we need information about the demographic characteristics and industrial structures of the several regions. For example, in estimating $_ip$, we must consider questions of differential fertility rates, migration, and rural-urban population shifts.

A regional p or z can be presumed to be less satisfactory for trend extrapolation than a national p or z, since a region's population and industrial structure are usually subject to a greater degree of variation than those for the nation as a whole.

a two-region economy, regional projections based on regional changes can be simply stated as:

$$_iGRP_{t+\theta} = {}_iGRP_t + \beta\,({}_jGRP_{t+\theta} - {}_jGRP_t) \qquad (11)$$

and

$$_jGRP_{t+\theta} = {}_jGRP_t + a\,({}_iGRP_{t+\theta} - {}_iGRP_t) \qquad (12)$$

where the parameters β and a are determined by statistical observation. This implies mutual interaction by regions i and j on the rates $_jp$, $_jz$, $_ip$, $_iz$. The p's will be determined by fertility rates and migration. The z's may represent over-all increases in productivity due to (1) greater effort or education, (2) the increasing weight in the average of more highly productive occupations, i.e., a shift in industrial structure, (3) technological progress, or (4) an unknown combination of all three. Whatever the source of the changes in the p's and z's, the mutual impact is transmitted by population movements and flows of goods and services between the regions. Population movements aside, the volume and composition of the commodity flows will be determined by the industrial structures of the respective regions.

Usually, however, more than two regions must be considered, and the simple linking of growth factors is inadequate. The economic interrelations between regions depend not only on their industrial structures, but on the distance separating the regions. Presumably, distance attenuates economic relations and the impact of extraregional change.[11]

The effect of the spatial position of a region with respect to other regions can be introduced explicitly through the concept of *income potential*, which parallels Stewart's concept of population potential.[12]

In Stewart's terms the potential of population at any one point A produced by the population P at point B is:

$$_AV_B = \frac{GP_B}{d} \qquad (13)$$

where d is the distance separating A and B, and G is a constant. At point A, the total potential $(_AV)$ is the sum of the separate

---

[11] Obviously, too, the industrial structure of a region depends in part on its distance from other regions.

[12] J. Q. Stewart, "Empirical Mathematical Rules Concerning the Distribution and Equilibrium of Population," *Geographical Review*, Vol. xxxvii, July 1947; "Demographic Gravitation: Evidence and Applications," *Sociometry*, Vol. xi, February-May 1948; and "Potential of Population and Its Relationship to Marketing," *Theory in Marketing* (Irwin, 1950).

potentials. When a population distribution is confined to a surface and is continuous,

$$_AV = \int \frac{1}{d} D dS \qquad (14)$$

where D is the density of population over the infinitesimal area dS. However, since data are available only for large areal units, such as states, Stewart computes total population potential by using the following modification of equation 14:

$$_iV = \sum_{j=1}^{j=m} \frac{1}{d_{ij}} D_j \qquad (i = 1, 2, \ldots, m) \qquad (15)$$

where $_iV$ is the total population potential of state i, D_j is the population of state j, and d_{ij} is the distance between state i and state j.[13] According to Stewart, $_iV$ is a measure "of the influence of people at a distance."[14]

We define the *potential of income* produced by any region j on another region i as

$$_iV_j = \frac{GY_j}{d_{ij}} \qquad (i = 1, 2, \ldots, m) \qquad (16)$$

and the *income potential* produced by all regions on a given region i as

$$_iV = \sum_{j=1}^{j=m} \frac{k_j}{d_{ij}} Y_j \qquad (i = 1, 2, \ldots, m) \qquad (17)$$

where k_j is a constant,[15] and Y_j is the income of region j, which in our context becomes a state or group of states.

Where $_iV$ is low, the region is presumably far from markets. Setting aside inequality of resource distribution, the region tends

[13] The population of each state must be taken to be concentrated at some chosen point within it, and distances must be computed from these points of concentration. As a result, the smaller the area for which data are available, the more accurate and meaningful the computed total population potentials. To determine a value for d_{ii} for computing the potential produced by a state upon itself, a special procedure must be followed. See Stewart, "Empirical Mathematical Rules . . . ," op.cit.

[14] "Demographic Gravitation: Evidence and Applications," op.cit., p. 35.

[15] The expression k_j may be viewed as a factor for converting actual distance into effective economic distance. It may be taken as a weighted average ratio of transport costs over a standard route to transport costs over the given routes connecting region j and region i.

For purposes of this paper, the potential of income is inversely related to the first power of the distance variable simply to illustrate certain relationships. Empirical studies may well indicate another type of inverse relation.

to have few interregional relations because of the high transport costs to markets. Where $_iV$ is high, many interrelations can be expected.

Adding to equation 1 a term to account for interregional relations and the effect of distances separating regions, we may project regional gross product as follows:

$$_i\mathrm{GRP}_{t+\theta} = {}_i\mathrm{GRP}_t(1+p)^\theta (1+z)^\theta + \beta_i \left[\frac{_iV_{t+\theta}}{(1+\rho)_iV_t} - 1 \right] {}_i\mathrm{GRP}_t$$

$$(i = 1, 2, \ldots, m) \tag{18}$$

where p and z are national rates of change, as before; β_i is a positive constant which for each region should vary with the character of its resources;[16] ρ is the rate of change in national income; and $_iV_t$ and $_iV_{t+\theta}$ are the income potentials of region i in years t and $t+\theta$, respectively. According to set of equations 18, the change in $_i\mathrm{GRP}$ depends on internal and external changes. The effects of external changes are mitigated to the extent that they occur at a distance.

A few remarks to explain the construction of this set of equations are in order. Income potential at region i $(_iV_t)$ may rise simply because all regional incomes are rising. Thus, if we use just the concept of income potential in the equations, we shall be taking account of the income effect twice. For the over-all increase in incomes has already been accounted for in p and z, the national rates of change. To avoid such double counting, we use the concept of relative income potential, $_iV_{t+\theta}/[(1+\rho)_iV_t]$. When all regional incomes rise by the same percent, the relative income potential is equal to unity, the second part of the set of equations 18 is zero, and each region's growth directly parallels national growth. This is what one would expect.

It is interesting to note the effects of certain changes. For example, a shift of population toward i will cause $_iV$ to rise (because of larger markets), and conversely for population shifts away from i. If national income rose, but population shifted away from i, the relative income potential would decrease (though the ratio of the income potentials need not). The second quantity to the right of the equations would become negative, thus offsetting to some extent the growth occasioned by i's share in p and z.

[16] For example, a highly localized, immobile resource might tend to raise the β_i for a given region.

437

The value of β_i to be used for projection purposes may be determined by fitting a trend line to past values for β_i. Past values are obtainable, since we know current and past values of p, z, Y_j, and $_iGRP$. β_i represents the effects of peculiarities of regional resource structures. These modify or qualify the distance implications alone which are present in $_iV$. The state of Washington, for example, has closer relations with the Eastern Seaboard than would be indicated by its income potential. Essentially, this is because of the nature of certain of its major resources such as hydro-power, used to produce aluminum which to a large extent is marketed in the New York City area, despite the distance factor. Projecting β_i would result in a true historical approach, comparable to projecting regional rates of growth (and making allowance for complex, but unknown, interrelations).

Thus far, we have lumped all interregional relations into one rough measure, $_iV$. By so doing, we have an operational model in the sense that the required parameters can be statistically derived from obtainable data. Such a procedure, however, necessarily eliminates consideration of the individual regional interrelations, which are basic. A more adequate model would avoid aggregating into the single measure $_iV$ the interregional relations modified by distance. It would consider the separate potentials produced by each region upon region i. The relation of each region to region i might be handled through separate β coefficients and through appropriately qualified incremental income-distance relations.

Set of equations 18 might be modified to read:

$$_iGRP_{t+\theta} = {_iGRP_t}\,(1+p)^\theta\,(1+z)^\theta + \beta_{ij}\Big(\frac{\Delta Y_j}{1+\rho}\cdot\frac{d}{d_{ij}} - 1\Big)$$
$$+ \ldots + \beta_{ik}\Big(\frac{\Delta Y_k}{1+\rho}\cdot\frac{d}{d_{ik}} - 1\Big) + \ldots$$
$$(i = 1, 2, \ldots, m) \qquad (19)$$

where d may be taken as a standard economic distance.

In this manner, it is possible to allow for the effects upon any given region of regional differences in consumption patterns, input requirements, etc., as well as in resource structure. These differences are allowed for only in the sense that they presumably account for the derived value of the several constants ($\beta_{12}, \ldots,$ β_{ij}). Such a model, however, appears to be nonoperational because of the high degree of intercorrelation among the β coefficients and the associated statistical problems.

D. FLOW PHENOMENA
IN INTERREGIONAL ANALYSIS[17]

The preceding sections have suggested statistical techniques for deriving projections of gross *regional* product. Attention has been focused on interregional relations without probing into the essential components, namely, the flow phenomena produced by the interrelated and varied industrial structures of the several regions. Some individuals may feel that analysis can be meaningful only when it incorporates study of such flows.

The accompanying set of charts illustrates certain aspects of these flows. These charts are taken from Professor Ullman's excellent study of the geographic patterns of commodity flows.[18]

Glancing through Ullman's entire collection of charts, one notes the striking differences among states in the length and intensity of flows as evidenced by the destinations of commodity shipments originating within the several states. Charts 1 and 2 show the destination of all commodities originating in Washington and Connecticut, respectively. Washington clearly serves a national market and has trade relations with many states. The market for the products of Connecticut is apparently much more limited in its spatial extent. Connecticut has direct interrelations with fewer states.

With the data aggregated into "all commodities," it is difficult to ascertain the meaning or explanation of this contrast. If we know the composition of the flows and the transport character-

[17] Much of the ensuing analysis has been independently anticipated in the pioneering work of Rutledge Vining, "The Region as an Economic Entity and Certain Variations to Be Observed in the Study of Systems of Regions," *Papers and Proceedings of the American Economic Association,* Vol. 39, May 1949; in ICC Dockets 29885 and 29886, *Testimony of Rutledge Vining;* and elsewhere. The implications of flow analysis have also been stressed by P. R. Crowe, "On Progress in Geography," *Scottish Geographical Magazine,* Vol. LIV, 1938. Also see R. E. Dickinson, "Landscape and Society," *Scottish Geographical Magazine,* Vol. LV, 1939; and G. K. Zipf, *Human Behavior and the Principle of Least Effort* (Addison-Wesley Press, 1949).

[18] E. L. Ullman et al., *Maps of State-to-State Rail Freight Movement,* for 13 states of the United States in 1948, mimeographed, 1951. These charts are based on the 1 percent sample of Class I railroad shipments reported to the Interstate Commerce Commission.

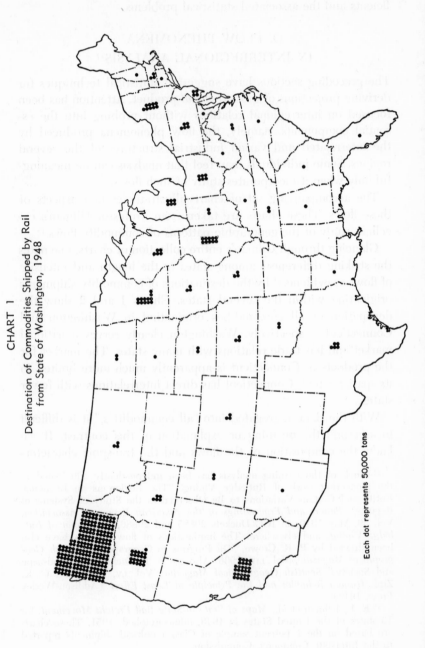

CHART 1

Destination of Commodities Shipped by Rail
from State of Washington, 1948

Each dot represents 50,000 tons

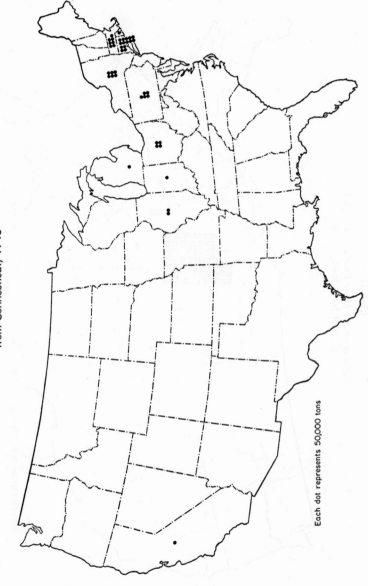

CHART 2

Destination of Commodities Shipped by Rail
from Connecticut, 1948

Each dot represents 50,000 tons

CHART 3

Destination of Mine Products Shipped
by Rail from Iowa, 1948

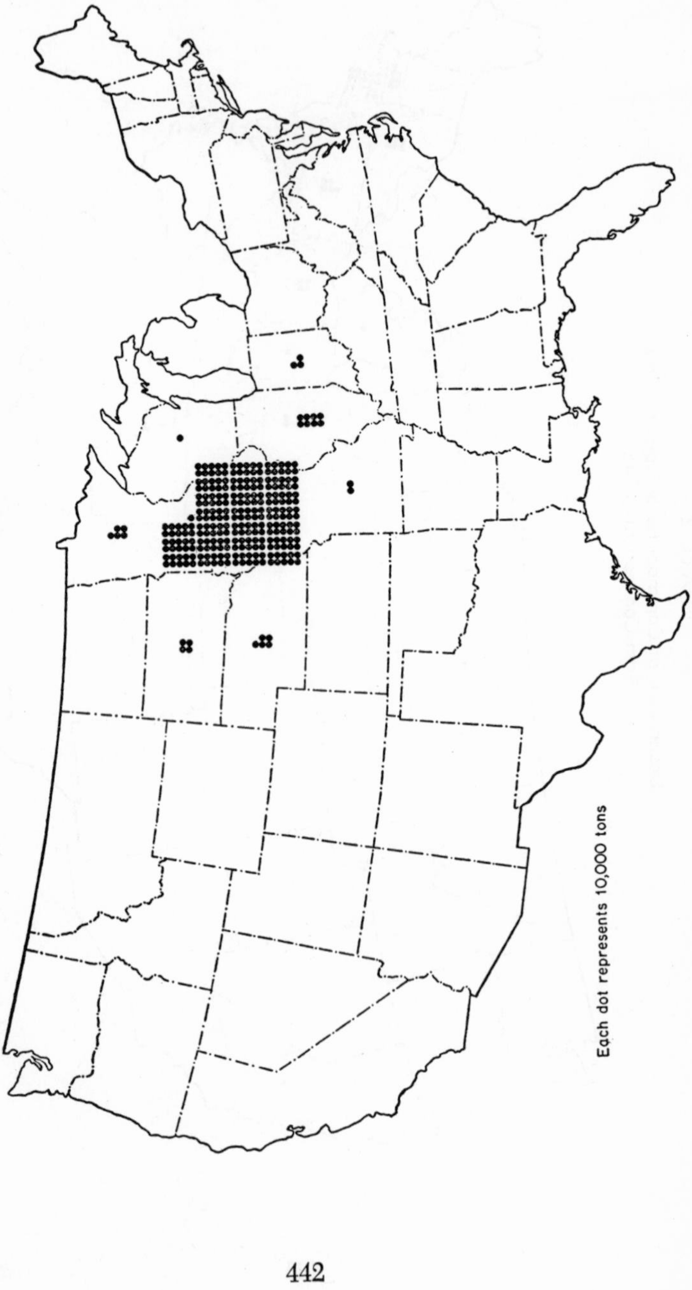

Each dot represents 10,000 tons

CHART 4

Destination of Manufactured and Miscellaneous Products
Shipped by Rail from Iowa, 1948

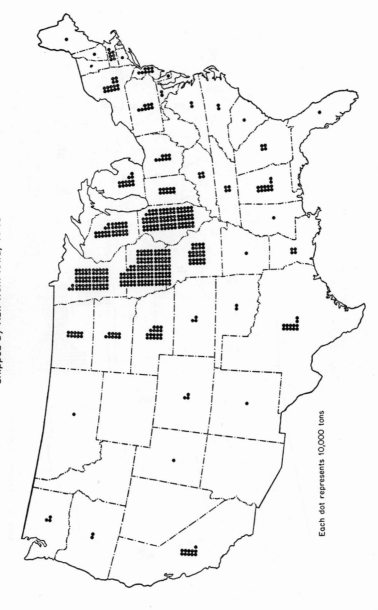

Each dot represents 10,000 tons

CHART 5

Destination of Agricultural Products
Shipped by Rail from Texas, 1948

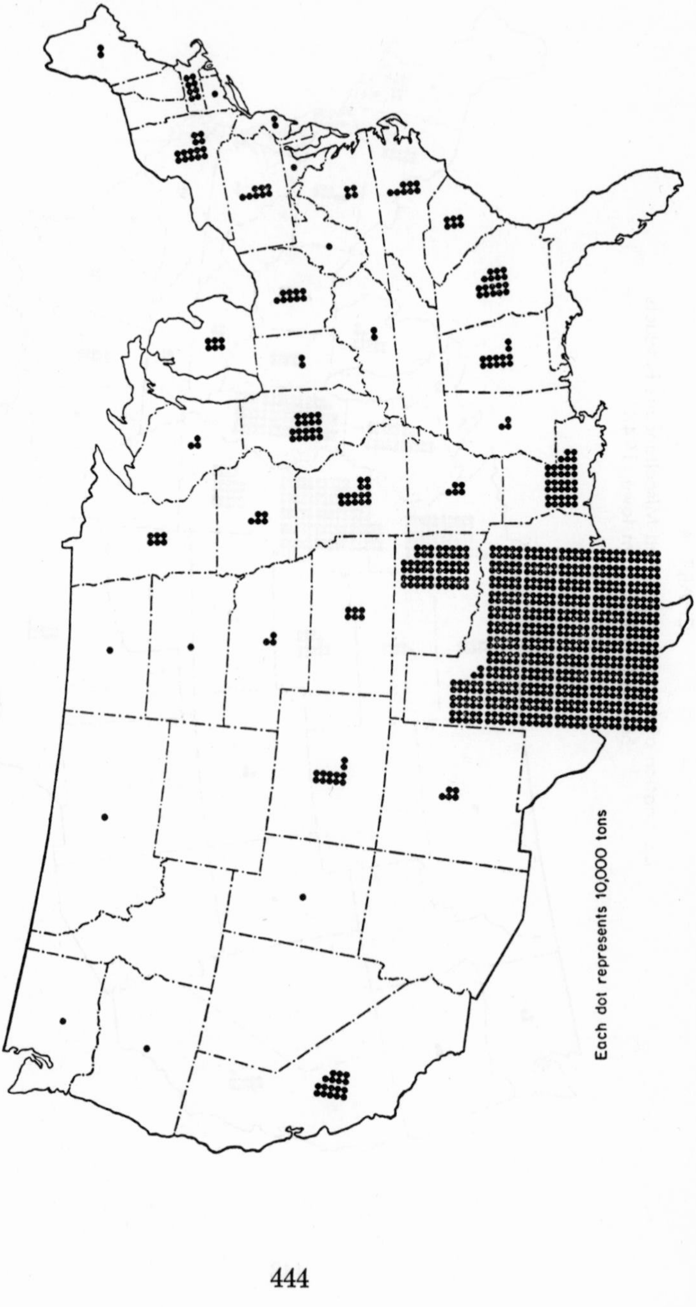

Each dot represents 10,000 tons

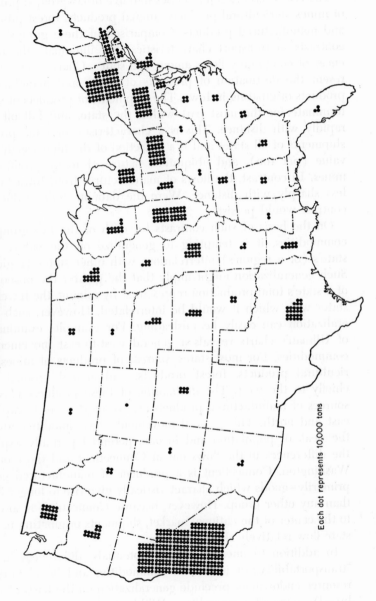

CHART 6

Destination of Agricultural Products Shipped
by Rail from California, 1948

Each dot represents 10,000 tons

445

istics of particular types of commodities, such contrasts have more analytic value.

The ICC classifies commodities into five broad groups: products of mines, agricultural products, animal products, forest products, and manufactured products. Comparison of these groups yields contrasts in transport characteristics that illuminate the differences of commodity flows among the states. Charts 3 and 4 represent the destination of products of mines and manufactured products originating in Iowa. The shipments of products of mines terminate for the most part within the state, and fall off very rapidly with distance. This is a characteristic of mine product shipments of all states and is a reflection of the high weight, low value (per ton), and ubiquitous nature of many products of mines. In contrast, the flows of manufactures from Iowa fall off less sharply with distance. Were the data in dollar value, the contrast would persist.

On the basis of such contrasts for each of the five groups of commodities, it is tempting to generalize on the nature of a state's (or a region's) interrelations with other states (regions). Such generalization might imply that the greater the proportion of a state's total production represented by mining, the fewer the states with which it would be interrelated. However, such generalization can easily be misleading. For example, examination of Ullman's charts reveals a general west-to-east movement of commodities. For most states, *sources* of products of mines, agricultural products, forest products, and animal products are chiefly to the west. The *destination* of these products *plus* the sources of manufactured products are for most states toward the east and north. This general movement of commodities toward the peak of population and income potential partially explains the differences in the flows out of Connecticut and those out of Washington. Connecticut is a producer of manufactured goods primarily—goods which characteristically give rise to longer flows than any other group. However, because Connecticut is so close to the center of the national market, shipments originating in that state flow relatively short distances.

In addition to unequal market potentials, differences in the "transportability" of individual commodities and inequalities of resource endowment preclude generalization on the basis of such broad groups of commodities. Within these groups, there are quite likely to be commodities with transport characteristics so

446

different that the same group when examined for different states or regions shows different flow characteristics. For example, we have selected from Ullman's charts those depicting agricultural product flows out of Texas and California. (See Charts 5 and 6.)[19]

Texas represents the typical pattern of agricultural commodity flows. These flows are usually concentrated within short distances; relatively few cover long distances. In contrast are the much larger national flows of California agricultural products. They are a reflection of California's unique resources for fruit and vegetable production. The nature of Washington's "all commodity" flows can likewise be understood only in the light of its particular resource structure, its distance relations with other regions, and their particular resource structure.

In short, aggregative flow data are helpful in understanding the magnitudes of the major interstate or interregional relationships. But for purposes of analysis, it is essential to study individual commodity flows.

The mutual impact of change in the various regions is channeled through individual commodity flows; hence the most rigorous type of regional projection ought to project each flow. For the present this is not generally a practicable procedure. However, in those instances where a few flows—steel, fuel, etc.—may dominate a region's external relations, there would be great pragmatic value in a general technique for analyzing flows. Such a technique could shed additional light on the problems involved in making projections from econometric, input-output, and other models. For example, the β_i of the simple model presented above will change as the flows change. If an industry (particularly a major industry) shifts from region i to region j, this will be manifest through a change in flows. There will be a change in β_i as the links between the regions change. In addition, there will be the many secondary effects as market and supply area relationships for all the dependent industries are realigned.

An approach in terms of general substitution analysis yields a basis for the explanation and projection of changes in flows. Some of the substitution resulting in alteration of flows can be expressed in standard terms. For example, consider the historical

[19] Since the charts represent tonnage movements and since magnitudes differ in the two states, the reader should be careful to interpret these in a relative sense.

shift of textile plants out of New England, when technological development opened employment to unskilled labor. The movement to the South to take advantage of a cheap labor supply involved, *among other substitutions,* the dominant one of southern unskilled labor (a relatively immobile resource) for skilled New England labor (another geographically conditioned resource).

However, the inclusion of the space factor requires that attention be given to two new basic types of substitutions:[20]

Substitution between transport outlays and other outlays, whether on one or more factors. Two examples are: (a) In glass manufacture, the substitution of natural gas for coal resulted in a shift of the industry to sources of natural gas. Historically, when the direction of the shift was away from the established markets, this amounted to a substitution of transportation outlays for fuel outlays. (b) The problem of the economic justification for an integrated steel mill in New England may be viewed, for the most part, in terms of substitution between transport outlays and all other outlays combined. The mill becomes feasible when the previously high potential outlays on production have fallen sufficiently (due to a growing market, which reduces the diseconomies of scale associated with a limited market) to allow substitution of production outlays for transport outlays involved in satisfying New England steel demand.[21]

There are many other industrial activities which begin development in a region when the increasing regional market has reduced the diseconomies of scale to the point where production outlays can be substituted for transport outlays. Cement production and automobile assembly are two such activities.

Substitution among distance inputs.[22] Analysis in terms of this type of substitution would, for example, help to predict the construction of a Trenton steel mill following the discovery of foreign ore sources. Essentially, the steel industry is transport-oriented, the variation among sites of costs other than transport being

[20] For full elaboration of these types, refer to W. Isard, "Distance Inputs and the Space-Economy," *Quarterly Journal of Economics,* Vol. LXV, May and August 1951.

[21] The reader should bear in mind that in serving the New England market, the transport outlays for a New England mill would be lower than those for a Pittsburgh mill, whereas production outlays would continue to be higher for the former.

[22] A distance input is defined as the movement of a unit of weight over a unit of distance. See Isard, "Distance Inputs and the Space-Economy," *op.cit.,* for full conceptual treatment.

minor for a market of sufficient size. In terms of the New York–Philadelphia market, the Trenton development involves the substitution of distance inputs in the movement of coal and ore for distance inputs in the movement of finished product and scrap.

Thus, whatever the terms of substitution analysis,[23] it does allow prediction of shifts in location of major industrial categories and, as a consequence, the prediction of realignments of flows. For projecting regional development, substitution analysis is a useful supplement to econometric, input-output, and other techniques. And, as in the case of the Pacific Northwest, substitution analysis for a few dominant flows may be a valid technique in itself.

E. REGIONAL PROJECTIONS IN BROAD INDUSTRIAL AGGREGATES

The preceding analysis, developed in terms of flow phenomena, can lead to a model which is, in general, nonoperational (except in a few cases), though substitution analysis seems the most desirable from a theoretical standpoint. On the other hand, the set of equations 18 of Section C, while statistically operational, paid no attention to the industrial structure of the several regions (other than through the derived β coefficients). In this section, we shall examine the possibility of an alternative aggregative approach to regional projections, but one which involves less aggregation than the model represented by the set of equations 18. This permits us to give weight to industrial composition without being forced into nonoperational analysis.

Colin Clark's conceptual classification of all forms of economic activity into primary, secondary, and tertiary has proven extremely useful in regional studies, especially for isolated regional analysis, and for historical comparison of development in different regional economies. However, for purposes of interregional analysis, it conventionally ignores the space element and the influence of distance in shaping flows.

We now inquire how to adapt this framework to regional analysis and projections of regional product (given a national projection). As before, we start with the identity

$$_iGRP_t = {_iL_t} \cdot {_i\Gamma_t}$$

[23] Location studies are essentially comparative cost studies, and these reduce to substitution analysis.

which can be broken down into the identity

$$_iGRP_t = {}_iL_{1_t} \cdot {}_i\Gamma_{1_t} + {}_iL_{2_t} \cdot {}_i\Gamma_{2_t} + {}_iL_{3_t} \cdot {}_i\Gamma_{3_t}$$
$$(i = 1, 2, \ldots, m) \qquad (20)$$

where $_iL_{1_t}$, $_iL_{2_t}$, and $_iL_{3_t}$ represent annual employment in year t in primary, secondary, and tertiary industries, respectively, in region i;[24] and where $_i\Gamma_{1_t}$, $_i\Gamma_{2_t}$, and $_i\Gamma_{3_t}$ represent average productivity in year t in primary, secondary, and tertiary activities, respectively, in the region.

For purposes of projection, it might be assumed in a first model that the existing proportions $_iL_1/_iL$, $_iL_2/_iL$, $_iL_3/_iL$ remain constant. To obtain GRP one year hence, we might multiply current gross product from each of the three categories by (1) unity plus the rate of increase in $_iL$ (total annual regional employment) and (2) unity plus the appropriate rate of increase in productivity derived by historical trends. The trends in each case are regional trends. This procedure, however, has obvious shortcomings.

In a second model, we might allow for a historical shift in the proportion of total employment accounted for by $_iL_1$, $_iL_2$, and $_iL_3$. For the first approximation, we take the given national projection and the shifts in the national categories, L_1, L_2, and L_3, implied there and assume that the same relative shifts apply for the region. Thus, let r_1 be the annual rate of shift into L_1 derived from a trend projection and relevant for year t_1; and let r_2 be the annual rate of shift into L_2 derived from a trend projection and relevant for year t_1. Both r_1 and r_2 can take either a positive or a negative sign depending upon the direction of the shift. A rate r_3 is not necessary since the shift within L to or away from tertiary industries is determined once r_1, r_2, and L are given. Our projection equations become:

$$_iGRP_{t_1} = {}_iL_{1_{t_1}} (1 + r_1)(1 + z_1) \Gamma_{1_{t_0}} +$$
$$_iL_{2_{t_1}} (1 + r_2)(1 + z_2) \Gamma_{2_{t_0}} + ({}_iL_{3_{t_1}} - r_1 \cdot {}_iL_{1_{t_1}}$$
$$- r_2 \cdot {}_iL_{2_{t_1}})(1 + z_3)\Gamma_{3_{t_0}} \qquad (21)$$
$$(i = 1, 2, \ldots, m)$$

where

$$_iL_{1_{t_1}} = {}_iL_{1_{t_0}} (1 + p) \qquad (22)$$
$$_iL_{2_{t_1}} = {}_iL_{2_{t_0}} (1 + p) \qquad (23)$$

---

[24] Any system of classifying industries into a few relatively homogeneous groups would be satisfactory.

and

$$_iL_{3_{t_1}} = {_iL_{3_{t_0}}} \left(1 + p \right) \qquad (24)$$

As before, p is the projected national rate of population increase for the year t_1;[25] and z_1, z_2, and z_3 are nationally projected rates of change in average productivity in primary, secondary, and tertiary activities, respectively. $\Gamma_{1_{t_0}}$, $\Gamma_{2_{t_0}}$, and $\Gamma_{3_{t_0}}$ are average regional productivities for the year t_0 in primary, secondary, and tertiary activities, respectively.

In order to account for regional rather than national rates of change in productivity, s_1, s_2, and s_3 may be substituted for z_1, z_2, and z_3 in equation 21. The former rates refer to change in Γ_1, Γ_2, and Γ_3, respectively, and relate to region i alone. They can be determined from historical trend extrapolation, or from more specific knowledge about changes in industrial productivities, and changes in the relative importance of the components of a particular industrial classification for the region.

Equation 21 can be further revised by substituting regional rates of employment shifts ($_ir_1$ and $_ir_2$) for the national rates (r_1 and r_2). Historical information on regional employment shifts ought to be obtainable in certain cases. When not available, it is still possible to predict, to a limited degree, shifts among primary, secondary, and tertiary activities for a region.

Thus far, interrelations among regions have been omitted. A convenient way of introducing these and other considerations of distance is to use a cross classification, local and interregional. We denote activities as primary local, primary interregional, secondary local, secondary interregional, tertiary local, and tertiary interregional. The classification "local" in each case implies no flows outside the region. Thus, by definition, regional interrelations are manifest only through primary, secondary, and tertiary interregional activities. The influence of the distance factor can enter through reintroduction of the concept of income potential to yield equation 25. Each equation in this set has two main parts. The first reflects intraregional development; the second, interregional.

[25] Use of a national rate of population growth prevents us from directly taking account of differences in fertility among regions, interregional migration, etc. To some extent, however, these other factors which influence regional rates of population growth are reflected indirectly in shifts among types of activity and, later, in different regional productivity rates.

$$_iGRP_{t_1} = {}_{hi}L_{1_{t_1}} (1 + r_1) (1 + s_1) \Gamma_{1_{t_0}} + {}_{hi}L_{2_{t_1}} (1 + r_2)$$
$$(1 + s_2) \Gamma_{2_{t_0}} + ({}_{hi}L_{3_{t_1}} - r_1 \cdot {}_{hi}L_{1_{t_1}} - r_2 \cdot {}_{hi}L_{2_{t_1}})$$
$$(1 + s_3) \Gamma_{3_{t_0}} + {}_{gi}L_{1_{t_1}} (1 + \delta_1) (1 + s_1) \Gamma_{1_{t_0}}$$
$$+ {}_{gi}L_{2_{t_1}} (1 + \delta_2) (1 + s_2) \Gamma_{2_{t_0}} + {}_{gi}L_{3_{t_1}} (1 + \delta_3)$$
$$(1 + s_3) \Gamma_{3_{t_0}} \tag{25}$$

where the subscripts h and g denote local and interregional activity, respectively. In equation 25,

$$\delta_1 = \frac{b_1 \left(\dfrac{_iV_{t_1}}{_iV_{t_0}} - 1 \right)}{_{gi}L_1} \tag{26}$$

where b_1 may be taken as the slope of a simple line of regression measuring the historical relationship between changes in primary interregional employment and $[(_iV_{t_1}/_iV_{t_0}) - 1]$.[26] δ_2 and δ_3 are defined similarly, except for subscripts. In this formulation, r_1 and r_2 can be taken as either national or regional shift rates among local activities only, preferably regional. The term $_{gi}L_{1_{t_1}}$ $(1 + \delta_1) (1 + s_1) \Gamma_{1_{t_0}}$ stands for "gross product of primary interregional industries in region i." Explicitly, the term stands for: (1) the employment in primary interregional activities in region i in time 1, plus or minus the shift in employment as a result of relative changes in the income potential of the region, multiplied by (2) the average productivity in primary activities.

The model, thus far, relies simply on historical observations. Primarily, rates of growth and shifts are determined, and these are modified in ways additional knowledge may suggest. The introduction of income potentials necessarily entails simultaneous determination of GRP for each region. The GRP's are the only unknowns. (An n-region economy will have n equations in the set.) The summation of GRP's obtained through solution of equation 25 may yield a GNP

$$\left(GNP = \sum_{i=1}^{i=m} {}_iGRP \right)$$

considerably different from that which a simple one-point model may yield. As previously, it may be desirable here to introduce a

[26] Since $_{gi}L_{1_1}$ is given in terms of population, δ_1 must be expressed as a pure number. Hence, the term in the numerator of equation 26, which expresses an increment in terms of population, should be divided through by $_{gi}L_1$.

β factor to modify the interregional effects traceable through income potential. This may be required in the light of detailed information from study of flow analysis and projected substitutions involving location shifts and changes in resource utilization. Also, it may be required for purposes of consistency.

The foregoing model encompasses the distance factor in two ways: (1) It recognizes that markets and the spatial extent of economic activities vary. Production and consumption of different commodities balance within areas of varying size. Thus the amount of activity classified as local within a region will depend upon the selection of regional boundaries. In general, the smaller the area the more important it is to consider external relations. (2) It recognizes that, in general, these external relations will be affected by changes in income in all other regions inversely as the distances of these regions from the given region.

As in equations 19, changes in GRP in region i might be linked directly to changes in GRP in every other region by means of β coefficients and separate incremental income-distance relations. This would avoid the undesirable aggregation of linkages in a single measure of income potential. However, as with equations 19, the model becomes nonoperational with such modification. Elaborate and questionable statistical techniques are required to eke out a set of β's from the limited data.

We can push the analysis still further by setting forth the industrial structure of region i in greater detail and by relating each industry in region i to industries in other regions via interregional flows. Such a procedure appears nonoperational except where, as mentioned above, a few major flows dominate the interregional trade of an area. However, with suitable modifications and restrictions, it leads toward an operational input-output model.

Before developing regional input-output analysis, we should try to ascertain to what extent certain manifestations of differential regional rates of growth appear explicitly in equation 25, and to what extent they appear only implicitly, if at all. Among the most readily apparent ones are those associated with population increase, interregional population migration, and rural-to-urban population shifts. Consider, first, population increase and migration, for these are not independent.

In our model, a change in $_{hi}L_1$, $_{hi}L_2$, and $_{hi}L_3$ (employment in local activities) is associated with an average national rate of

453

population increase. On the other hand, the δ_1, δ_2, and δ_3 which relate $_{gi}L_1$, $_{gi}L_2$, and $_{gi}L_3$ (employment in interregional activities) to income potential are regionally differentiated. This means differential rates of change in total employment opportunities in the several regions. If net reproduction in each region exceeds (or is less than) the increase in that region's employment opportunities, we can partially account for emigration (or immigration). Thus, also, we indirectly arrive at over-all regional population projections.[27]

Existing factor immobilities, occupational as well as geographic, are also reflected in the model, especially if no marked changes in immobilities take place. Immobilities dull the response to changes in new employment opportunities and are thus reflected in the historical data from which r_1, r_2, δ_1, δ_2, and δ_3 have been derived.

It is clear that employment in local industries should be differently affected in each region, if employment in interregional activities experiences different rates of change. To some extent, this can be recorded in the model through use of regional rates of shift, $_ir_1$ and $_ir_2$. These rates are based on regional experience and can (for any given year) be viewed as reflecting, in part, previous differential rates of change among regions in the growth of interregional activities.

Closely associated with population growth and migration are changes in spatial population patterns, in particular the rural-to-urban shift. This shift differs in intensity from region to region, and though it does not enter explicitly into the model, it is partially reflected in changes in $_ir_1$ and $_ir_2$ (the rates of shift out of primary and secondary industries).

Consumption patterns also differ from region to region owing partly to differences in income and degree of urbanization, and partly to differences in tastes (though the importance of this latter factor in an era of rapid transportation and mass communication media is uncertain). On the one hand, these differences in consumption patterns are of importance in determining which commodities flow into the region from others and thus affect the pattern of interregional primary, secondary, and tertiary

[27] Note that this technique for deriving regional population projections does not imply that differential rates of population growth among regions will be gradually eliminated. This is assumed, for example, in M. J. Hagood, *Prospects for Regional Distribution of the Population of the United States* (Bureau of Agricultural Economics, November 1949).

activities in other regions. On the other hand, they markedly condition intraregional response to changes in income. Thus, in an agricultural region like the South, the rate of shift out of primary production has tended to be more intense than in an industrial area. These contrasting effects are traceable in our model through the different values of the r's which would be determined from historical data.

One of the significant factors excluded, even implicitly, is the possibility of major, abrupt geographic shifts of industry and changes in resource use caused by technological progress. To some extent, these can be allowed for by the exercise of judgment. The direct influence upon a region of the construction and maintenance of a major atomic energy installation can be roughly gauged. Likewise, the direct influence of continuous casting of steel can be estimated, if this revolutionary process should prove feasible for a large fraction of steel production. In contrast, the model does allow for gradually changing resource use and shifts of location. For example, the gradual shift of industry and population to California is in part explained by the gradual decrease in material orientation, particularly coal and ore orientation. This decrease implies a relative increase in the strength of California's climatic attraction. The β, r, and s coefficients of the model should reflect this and similar developments.

F. THE REGION AS AN ANALYTIC CONCEPT

Thus far we have discussed regional analysis without indicating the implications involved in the use of the concept of a region. As mentioned earlier, a complete analytic description of economic reality would distinguish each component by location, as well as by function or other criteria. Just as the term "industry" is used to sum components sharing similar characteristics, so apparently is the term "region" used to sum components contiguous in space. The empirical content of the "industry" will vary as the criteria selected to distinguish industries. The same holds true for the content of the "region." There appears to be no unique definition of an industry; the criteria for industrial aggregation depend upon the purposes for which the concept is used. Even a cursory examination of the great variety of definitions of a region suggest that it, too, has no unique meaning.

When a group of activities are spatially aggregated into a

region, there are implied certain observable "facts" concerning the internal structure of the region, as well as its external relations, those with other regions. It is implied that each region can be distinguished from other regions according to some workable criteria. The regional boundaries are not randomly drawn. Further, the criteria for regional demarcation should be derived from the framework of analysis to be used. Regional definition or sets of boundaries in use by other disciplines and for other purposes cannot be taken as valid for the economist's use without an examination of their economic meaning. For the economist, a definition is in general derivable only to the extent that his analysis can reveal the role of distance in the functioning of the economic system. Thus, an inquiry into the meaning of a region for economic analysis might begin with an inquiry into the role of space in shaping the economy. This is not the place for an extensive development of such an inquiry, but certain considerations are relevant.

The existence of a spatial dimension in an economic system imposes limitations on economic interaction. Transforming scarce resources into goods and services[28] requires the use of other scarce resources for transport when different phases of the transformation process are separated by distance. At any one point in time, given the existing distribution of resources and the existing techniques of transportation and communication, specialization and division of labor take place with regard not only to function, but to location as well. The relations between phases of the transformation process, and hence their economic interdependence, are reflected through flows of commodities from point to point. Since space acts as a barrier to economic intercourse, primarily through transport costs, the magnitude of these flows will be attenuated by distance. If these flows are regarded as bonds which link components of the system to one another, it can be seen that the greater the magnitude of the flows in any area, the more highly interrelated are the components in that area. Further, if there is a tendency for economic activity to agglomerate around certain focal points, an examination of flows over a wide geographic area will reveal this. As the distance from a focal point becomes greater, the magnitudes of the flows will diminish, some more rapidly than others. Conversely, as a focal point is ap-

[28] Transformation includes transportation of each unit of output to the point of final consumption.

proached, the flows will increase in magnitude. If around such a focal point, a boundary be struck as a locus of points where flows fall to a minimum, it could be said of the components within the boundary that they exhibit a relative maximum (and generally a high degree) of interdependence. (The total magnitude of all the flows within the area is necessarily greater than those linking the area to others.) Such demarcation could be said to embrace a "natural" aggregation over space of economic activities, an aggregation due, in large part, to the impact of distance. Regions of this type might be the regions we seek. Our criterion for regional demarcation would then be internal interdependence of income, as revealed through flow phenomena. Furthermore, if there are such natural aggregations, and if the aggregations display a hierarchical tendency, then we might expect to find regions of varying order.

The preceding remarks serve to focus attention on the necessity of studying flow phenomena in general. Certain considerations help us to systematize the study of these flows in such a way as to shed light more directly on the problem of regional demarcation.

Lösch[29] has developed theoretical grounds for anticipating that economic activities will cluster around foci. Under assumptions of equal distribution of resources, population, technical knowledge, etc., the market area for the product of any producer tends toward a hexagonal shape. The size of this area will be determined by the transport characteristics of the product, on the one hand, and economies of scale, on the other. *Ceteris paribus*, the lower the cost of transporting a unit, the greater the market area; and the greater the economies of scale, the greater the market area. Consequently, goods with different characteristics in these respects will have different market areas. Lösch's system can be envisaged as a plane overlaid with systems of nets of market areas, each net corresponding to a particular product. To minimize transport costs in each plane, these systems should be ordered around a common central point (a first-order center). From this point all commodity flows are outward (given Lösch's highly unrealistic assumptions). Cutting these flows at successively in-

[29] A. Lösch, *Die räumliche Ordnung der Wirtschaft* (2nd edn.; Jena: G. Fisher, 1944). See also N. S. B. Gras, *An Introduction to Economic History* (Harper, 1922); A. Hawley, *Human Ecology: A Theory of Community Structure* (Ronald, 1950); R. D. McKenzie, *The Metropolitan Community* (McGraw-Hill, 1933).

creasing distances from this center reveals irregularly diminishing outward flows as the limits of successively increasing market areas are passed. At the same time, flows in the reverse direction progressively increase in magnitude, though irregularly, as the distance to the closest center of a second order diminishes.

In empirical terms, Lösch's scheme implies that major cities service a large hinterland and that the service function of the major city reduces to fewer and fewer services as the distance from the city increases. Bonds with the major city are attenuated by distance. It further implies an organic relationship between a major city and its hinterland (interdependence of incomes). Bogue has given strong support to this observation in his study of metropolitan dominance. "The metropolitan community appears to be an organization of many mutually interdependent and inter-functioning subcommunities oriented about the hinterland cities which in turn are subdominant to and interdependent with the dominant metropolis, and inter-function with it."[30] Bogue's investigation reveals that the hinterland cities specialize in some functions at a level above that of the small towns, and the metropolitan center at a level above that of the hinterland cities, with no one center dominating all activities.

In terms of flows, this means that the great bulk of flows will traverse relatively short distances; that longer flows will connect foci; and that the greater the distance separating these foci, the smaller the magnitude of the flows and the fewer goods and services represented. Further, this means that intercepting flows equidistant from and on either side of a subdominant center will not yield flows of the same magnitude. The magnitude of flows will be at a relative minimum when the boundary is drawn between two foci oriented toward different foci of a lower order.

If we now recognize that goods and services have market areas of varying size which can be ranked from largest to smallest, we may have a basis for demarcating regions of any order.[31]

[30] D. J. Bogue, *The Structure of the Metropolitan Community* (University of Michigan, 1949), p. 59.

[31] In geographic terminology such regions are "nodal" regions. "They are units possessing an internal structure, comprising a focus (or foci) and surrounding areas tied to the focus. They are bounded by the disappearance or the differential weakening of the tie in favor of a tie to some other focus." Committee on Regional Geography, "Regional Geography," 4th revised outline, February 1950, *American Geography: Inventory and Forecast*. Note also that such criteria eliminate the confusion between the so-called heterogeneous and homogeneous regions. In terms of flows, both "types" of regions

Regions of the ith order can be said to be those in which there is balance between production and consumption of goods of the ith order (corresponding to the ith net of market areas), and relatively little imbalance of higher-order goods, which are those having smaller market areas.

However, Lösch's model and Bogue's averaging techniques fail to catch major flows attributable to inequalities in resource endowment. These flows greatly complicate the orderly Lösch model.[32] However, they may very well be the major substance of interregional relations. This is particularly the case when few, but large, regions (low-order regions) are the subject of analysis. There are relatively few goods of a central function which cross such regional boundaries, these being the goods of first order. Here the flows of resource-oriented goods, where resources are localized, tend to dominate the picture, and to a different extent for the several regions.[33]

---

reduce to the same thing. An area which is heavily specialized in production will have heterogeneous inflows and relatively few outflows. For a region with more diversified production, there may or may not be diversified inflows. Each type will be clearly distinguishable as a region with reference to these criteria, whereas identification in terms of the nature of production obscures the essential role played by space in regional differentiation.

[32] This was observed and stressed by A. Lösch in his empirical work "The Nature of Economic Regions," *Southern Economic Journal*, July 1938; and in part II of his *Die räumliche Ordnung der Wirtschaft*, as cited.

[33] In recent years geographers have shown an intense interest in the development of the regional concept. The Committee on Regional Geography has set forth an outline of its views in some detail. The essence of its approach is the view that the term "region" is an analytic tool, a conceptual device having great value when related explicitly to a particular frame of reference. Thus the concrete determination of any set of regional boundaries will vary among disciplines, but the meaning of the concept should be common to all. In this respect, it is interesting to paraphrase portions of the outline on "Regional Geography," *op.cit.*, to illustrate the relevance of this point of view: Areal differentiation, because of difference from place to place, is necessary in some cases and convenient in most. While permitting the recognition of causes, it does not impose a genetic presentation. It groups data into homogeneous segments of any size whatever, homogeneity being confined to the criteria whereby the units are differentiated. The units thus set apart are regions, each with an internal integrity, defined by its criteria. The region is fixed in a hierarchy of subdivisions. Commonly there is a core area, beyond which lies a marginal area. Distance alone tends to weaken the ties to the focus as the perimeter of the region is approached. All regions are impermanent and, in that sense, fluid. This change may be confined to internal rearrangements of a major region leaving the over-all pattern of regions unaltered: or it may require the reconstitution of one or more areal units. Such change is most likely to affect the boundaries

G. REGIONAL INPUT-OUTPUT ANALYSIS

In the preceding sections, we have discussed techniques for deriving projections of gross regional product using very broad aggregates. In this section, we shall examine the possibility of adapting input-output techniques to regional and interregional analysis as a means of tracing out, in greater detail, industrial interrelations which lie behind regional change.

Input-output analysis, as developed by Professor Leontief, is essentially a Walrasian system of general equilibrium made operational through suitable modifications.[34] As such, it focuses attention on interindustry relations in a spaceless economy. These relations are reflected in structural coefficients, which are derived from technical production functions and household income-consumption patterns. The industrial aggregates are composed of units with similar input-output structures. Given such a system, it is possible (within the limits set by the assumptions) to describe the differential industrial impact of hypothetical changes in the bill of goods. Implicit in such a description is the assumption that differences in location of the units of any aggregate do not have any effect upon the system. However, in fact they do, and the effect of these differences should be considered.

In general, two types of approach are conceivable. The first we shall designate as the "balanced regional" model, and the second, as the "interregional" model. Both can be viewed as at-

---

of regions, since, in any case, these are the most troublesome, being both transitional and critical.

The paraphrase could be extended at length, but the foregoing is enough to show that the conceptual content of the term "region" can be made identical among disciplines without implying any similarities in the empirical content of the term. Our concept of a region is completely compatible with that of the geographer, but our selection of criteria for the demarcation of actual regions may be entirely different from that of the political scientist, the sociologist, etc. In this connection, it is pertinent to suggest that use of existing regional classifications in economic analysis be examined critically for consistency between the criteria that were used to set up the classification and criteria of use to the analyst.

[34] There is a growing body of literature concerned with input-output analysis. The reader unfamiliar with the techniques and the terminology should refer to W. W. Leontief, *The Structure of the American Economy, 1919-1929* (Harvard University Press, 1941), and the following articles by Professor Leontief: "Output, Employment, Consumption, and Investment," *Quarterly Journal of Economics*, Vol. LVIII, February 1944; "Exports, Imports, Domestic Output, and Employment," *Quarterly Journal of Economics*, Vol. LX, February 1946; "Wages, Profit, and Prices," *Quarterly Journal of Economics*, Vol. LXI, November 1946.

tempts to describe the differential industrial and regional impact of a hypothetical change in the bill of goods.

1. *The balanced regional model*

Professor Leontief recently developed a balanced regional model which ties in with our previous discussion of flows.[35] It was pointed out that regions of varying order according to the type of commodity flows crossing regional boundaries could be conceived of. Thus, in the case of a region of order m there will be $1, 2, 3, \ldots, m - 1$ classes of goods flowing across the boundary and a relatively high degree of balance between production and consumption within the region for the remaining $n - m$ goods. For simplicity, the following discussion will consider only one order of regions and classify all goods as either "national" or "local." National goods are those which flow across regional boundaries; local goods are those which balance within the region. However, the analysis can be generalized to cover all orders of regions.

The data for the balanced regional model consist of all the elements usually present in input-output studies. In addition, Leontief's model assumes that the spatial production pattern of all national commodities is known and constant. This constancy of the geographic production pattern is inserted as a useful approximation in lieu of more detailed information. For short-run analysis, it implies that the regional share of total output of a specified national commodity remains the same at all levels of output of that commodity. For longer-run analysis, it implies no locational shifts. This approximation is represented by a set of constants showing the share of each region in the total output of every national commodity.

A second modification of the conventional input-output model concerns the bill of goods. Not only must there be specified a bill of goods for the nation, but also a bill of goods for each region in terms of local goods only.

Further, household demand is not entered into the bill of goods as in the usual procedure. Rather, households are included in the set of structural equations as a local industry. This is desirable in order to retain the local income multiplier effect and to show the impact of derived changes in intraregional employment upon the output of local industries. This is obviously an important

[35] *Studies in the Structure of the American Economy* (Oxford University Press, 1953), part II.

461

source of differential reaction among regions having different industrial structures.

Thus, given the additional information on the geographic production pattern of all national goods and the local bill of goods for each region, the demand for products of local industries of each region can be determined.

The general outlines of Professor Leontief's model are as follows: The outputs of all national commodities are found by multiplying the national bill of goods by the inverse of the matrix of input coefficients. This is straight input-output procedure. Symbolically, this is given by $_NA^{-1}Y$, where Y is the national bill of goods, A^{-1} is the inverse of the matrix of input coefficients, and $_NA^{-1}$ is a section of the inverted matrix which when multiplied by the bill of goods yields required national outputs of national industries.

With knowledge of the outputs of all national industries, the next step is to allocate these outputs geographically. This is done by multiplying each of these outputs by the previously determined set of constants—in this case, simple proportionality factors. Thus, $_jR\,_NA^{-1}Y$ represents the output of national goods required of region j, where the diagonal matrix $_jR$ consists of a set of constants which state the portion of the output of each national commodity produced in region j.

Among the various inputs required in each region to produce the national goods will be those which are of a local character, e.g., local transportation, utilities, construction, etc. We can let the matrix A_{LN} represent the set of input coefficients which state the requirements of local commodities per unit of output of national commodities. Multiplying $_jR\,_NA^{-1}Y$ by A_{LN} we have $A_{LN}\,_jR\,_NA^{-1}Y$, which yields the outputs of local industries required in region j to produce the national goods for which region j is responsible.

However, these outputs of local industries cannot be produced in region j without in turn requiring inputs from local industries and hence requiring additional outputs from them. Thus, we have both direct and indirect requirements. Let A_{LL} represent the set of input coefficients relating inputs of local industries to outputs of local industries. When we invert this matrix and multiply the inverted matrix A_{LL}^{-1} by the term immediately above, we obtain $A_{LL}^{-1}\,_jR\,_NA^{-1}Y$. This last term yields the sum of the direct and indirect requirements, and thus that part of the outputs of local industries in region j attributable to the required production of national goods.

But, in addition to this roundabout source of demand for the output of local industries in region j, there is the demand stemming directly and indirectly from the final demand for local goods within the region itself. This final demand represents that part of the local industry section of the national bill of goods for which a region is responsible, or, in short, what Leontief calls the "local bill of goods," $_jY_L$. Multiplying the local bill of goods by A_{LL}^{-1}, the inverse of the matrix A_{LL} which relates inputs of local industries to outputs of local industries, we obtain A_{LL}^{-1} $_jY_L$. This yields the outputs of local industries required by the local bill of goods in region j. Hence, given the national final demand for all goods and the local bill of goods for region j, the outputs of local industries in region j, represented by the matrix $_jX_L$, can be determined by the equation

$$_jX_L = A_{LL}^{-1}\, _jY_L + A_{LL}^{-1}\, A_{LN}\, _jR_N A^{-1}Y \qquad (27)$$

Through this model, the differential regional impact of a change in the national bill of goods, Y, is traceable.

The limitations and assumptions of the model should be kept clearly in mind. Some stem from the lack of data while others are of a more restrictive nature. For longer-run analysis, the assumption of constant regional proportions of the output of national industries can be adjusted partially to take account of such locational shifts as comparative cost studies and substitution analysis may suggest. For short-run analysis, we need more detailed information on the variation in proportions that takes place with change in the level of national output of a particular commodity.

The input coefficients which enter into all the matrices are not regionally differentiated (as they are in practice). For example, the set of coefficients describing the inputs of various commodities per dollar's worth of a national commodity like steel are the same whether the steel is produced in Fontana, California, or Pittsburgh, Pennsylvania. Also, the input coefficients relating the outputs of local industries to the outputs of other local industries are likewise not regionally differentiated, though, where the information is available, such regional differences in production practice could be incorporated.

The difficulties of bringing households into the system of

structural equations have been discussed elsewhere.[36] In addition, the model assumes that regional consumption patterns are alike when in fact they may differ significantly.

The outflows of national goods from each region are not, in this model, related directly to inflows of the same goods to other regions. Neither inflows nor outflows for a given region are distinguished in terms of region of origin or destination. Hence, while differential regional reactions to hypothesized changes in the national bill of goods are obtained, the interregional relations are not made explicit.

2. The interregional model

The foregoing model was essentially concerned with the derivation of the regional implications of a given national projection. The alternative model discussed below[37] poses a different basic question. It asks, What are the national implications of regional projections?

National aggregates of particular quantities can be viewed as the end result of the operations and interactions of the many components. These components are not directly affected by aggregates. They receive their stimuli through particularized channels (though, to be sure, these stimuli are reflected in the aggregates). National input-output systems are specifically designed to shed light on these channels. The preceding model does so to a still greater extent when it distinguishes between particular types of industries: local, regional of various orders, and national.

Ideally we should trace the connecting links between every producer and consumer in the system. Operational considerations, however, require spatial aggregation as well as industrial aggregation. The interregional model discussed here is advanced as a technique for using only a partial spatial aggregation in an effort to make explicit certain major spatial interrelations. The national economy is divided into meaningful regions, but no distinction is made between classes of commodities. Instead, each component in the system is grouped with others according to

[36] Leontief, "Exports, Imports, Domestic Output, and Employment," op.cit.

[37] The full presentation of this model is contained in W. Isard, "Interregional and Regional Input-Output Analysis: A Model of a Space-Economy," *Review of Economics and Statistics*, Vol. xxxiii, November 1951, pp. 318-28.

similarity of input-output characteristics and location (region, in this case).

Distinguishing productive processes on a basis of location as well as of technology is realistic. In national input-output analysis, industrial processes are classified according to similarity of relationship with other sectors of the economy. But industries having different supply areas and market areas do not have similar relationships with other sectors of the economy regardless of their technical similarity. Inputs of brick to the California construction industry are not "bricks," but "California bricks"; and an expansion of output on the part of the construction industry in New York will not cause the same output reaction in the brick industry in California as in the brick industry in Pennsylvania. On the basis of this and similar considerations, it is inadequate to group components of an economy simply by reference to technical requirements alone. They must also be grouped on a geographical basis.

These considerations lead to the construction of an input-output system in which a given activity in one region and the same activity in another region are considered different industries. The number of industries in the national economy then increases many times, being equal to the number of economic activities in each region summed over all regions. Given n regions and m economic activities, the set of structural equations becomes

$$_k X_i - \sum_{l=1}^{l=n} \sum_{j=1}^{j=m} {}_{kl}a_{ij} \, _l X_j = \, _k Y_i \qquad (28)$$
$$(i = 1, 2, \ldots, m; \; k = 1, 2, \ldots, n)$$

where $_k X_i$ is the output of industry i in region k; $_l X_j$ is the output of industry j in region l; $_{kl}a_{ij}$ is the input coefficient representing the amount of input of industry i in region k per unit of output of industry j in region l; and $_k Y_i$ is the final (bill of goods) demand for the output of industry i in region k.

Such a model focuses attention on commodity flows among regions. To be operational, it requires information on the source and destination of each commodity moving in interregional trade. The model does not imply any distinction between "national" and "local" industries. However, where regions are demarcated according to the criteria developed earlier, the larger the regions, the fewer the interregional flows and the less the information required on the origin and destination of specific commodities.

Hence difficulties in determining the necessary information on interregional commodity flows are a significant factor in limiting the extent to which spatial detail can be retained in this model, and the degree to which spatial interrelations can be made explicit.

Once the degree of aggregation has been determined, the appropriate regions demarcated, and the bill of goods specified, the operation of the model is similar to that of a national input-output model. Since the bill of goods is specified by regions as well as by industries, national totals are only a summation of the interareal and interindustrial adjustments to projections of regional data. Theoretically, within the limitations of the assumptions, the model reveals ". . . how a given autonomous impulse in one region is transmitted to other regions. It can show implicitly how the distance separating regions modifies the impact of this impulse and how the direct and indirect effects play back and forth (instantaneously) from region to region, constantly damped by spatial resistance."[38]

The limitations of the assumption of constant production coefficients have been discussed elsewhere.[39] The additional implications of the assumption of constant coefficients for an interregional model require mention here.

Where constant coefficients refer both to an industry and to the location of that industry, constant geographic patterns of supply are required. Thus regional boundaries must be properly selected to reveal meaningful interregional flows. The requirement of constant geographic patterns of supply also implies comparative stability of relative prices, since major changes in relative prices will in many instances induce changes in the pattern of flows. In a territory in which regions are closely linked by modern methods of communication and transportation and the price system is relatively free to operate, the price relations among regions are likely to be comparatively stable. However, when major political boundaries intervene, as on an international level of analysis, institutional obstructions to the operation of a price system may arbitrarily alter market areas and supply channels.

The assumption of constant coefficients (constant supply channels, in this context) involves an additional restriction even where

[38] *ibid.*, p. 328.
[39] Leontief, *The Structure of American Economy, 1919-1929*, as cited, pp. 38-41.

relative prices are comparatively stable. "Any change in an item of the bill of goods directly calls for a proportional change in each of the inputs required in the production of that item."[40] In terms of changes in a given input requirement, if the input is obtained from more than one region, this implies no change in the relative ability to compete of each of the several regions in supplying that input.

These limitations should not be exaggerated, however. If small changes in the bill of goods are postulated, and if there is excess capacity in the system, the error will be small. In addition, goods which have high transport costs or are otherwise regionally differentiated do have fairly stable market areas. Lastly, if locational studies suggest shifts in supply channels of the inputs for certain goods, these shifts can be approximated by directly entering the inputs by industry and region into the bill of goods.

An important aspect of the interregional model lies in its ability to make allowance for regional differences in production techniques and consumption patterns. (When information on such differences is not available, national coefficients may be used as approximations.) When such regional differences are registered in the model, they are useful in revealing the impact of changes in the bill of goods upon national and regional outputs. The interregional model can be regarded in one sense as yielding a finer industrial breakdown of a national input-output model. Input coefficients are necessarily index numbers in any system of aggregates, and the introduction of regional differentiation in these coefficients presumably reduces the deviation of actual coefficients around the separate indexes. At the same time, the increased number of coefficients permits the expression of a greater number of functional relations. Both factors tend to increase the accuracy of the analysis.

In the pursuit of regional and interregional analysis, the whole range of input-output techniques plays an integral part. It is not simply a matter of selection of one input-output model rather than another. They are all supplementary. Working with the data from a national input-output table is the most direct way to derive input coefficients. The use of these coefficients to obtain rough estimates of state consumption data from state production data yields invaluable information on the types of commodity

[40] Isard, "Interregional and Regional Input-Output Analysis: A Model of a Space-Economy," *op.cit.*

467

flows to be expected and on the subsequent demarcation of meaningful regions. The balanced regional model yields concrete evidence for testing the adequacy of regional boundaries and for devising a hierarchy of regions. Information yielded by this model, used in conjunction with available information on commodity flows, is very helpful in allocating these flows by industry and region of origin and destination.

In another sense, the balanced regional model and the interregional model discussed here are not mutually exclusive. Both are an attack on the same problem from different points of view and, as such, exert a mutual check. The balanced model yields estimates of the regional implications from national projection; the interregional model yields estimates of national implication from regional projections. A priori there is no basis of preference. Both are operational. Both have limitations at different points. Perhaps they should be considered not as alternatives, but as part of the same analytic set of tools for the problem of regional projections.

H. SUMMARY

1. We have pointed out some of the problems in deriving the regional implications of national product projections. These problems include all those involved in the projection of any of the other components of GNP. In addition, they include those which result from the fact that shifts in interindustrial relations and consequent alterations in the interindustrial flow of resources are not independent of similar shifts in interregional relations and the geographic flow of resources.

2. Regional projections using techniques like those used by the Council of Economic Advisers for GNP projections are inadequate without substantial modification. Extrapolation of past relationships between regional gross product and national gross product is extremely weak. The application of national rates of change to regional data for the projection of regional quantities is inadmissible except in the unusual case where these parameters are the same or nearly the same for all regions. Regional projections based on historically derived regional parameters may have a higher degree of validity for any given region. There is little likelihood, however, that the summation of a set of regional projections so derived will be consistent with a national projection directly obtained from national data. Such regional

projections do not take into account the interregional reactions implicit in national projections.

3. Section C, on "Regional Projections: Interregional Reactions," represents an attempt to meet this problem within the framework of CEA methodology by associating growth in one region with growth in another. The simple linking of growth factors is inadequate when more than two regions enter the projection, since economic relations among regions depend not only on their industrial structures, but also on the distances separating them. The concept of income potential is suggested as a possible tool for incorporating the various effects of distance into one rough measure. The resulting model displays the change in any GRP as a function of internal plus external changes, the effect of any external change being modified by the distance at which it occurs. The interregional relations embraced by income potentials may be modified by β coefficients to allow for the effects of particular regional resource structures.

4. The admission of the distance element into the analysis leads to consideration of commodity flows. Examination of these flows into and out of various states reveals a number of regularities and certain striking contrasts. Detailed analysis of these flows can shed considerable light on the nature of interregional relationships, and a rigorous technique for the derivation of regional projections would make full use of such analysis. Shifts in the composition of interregional commodity flows (and, correspondingly, interregional relationships) can be handled in terms of orthodox substitution analysis, or as substitution between transport outlays and other outlays, or as substitution among distance inputs, depending upon the actual circumstances. While it is difficult to envisage a regional projection based upon the projection of every type of commodity flow, substitution analysis can provide a basis for the explanation and projection of shifts in "strategic" flows. Thus it can serve as a useful supplement to other techniques.

5. As an alternative technique for regional projection, it is possible to devise a model in which some aspects of CEA methodology are preserved but with a lesser degree of aggregation. This method pays attention to the industrial composition of the regions. Regional gross product is disaggregated into the product of three major categories of economic activity. These are primary, secondary, and tertiary industries, which are also cross-classified

as local or interregional. Coupling income potential, shift coefficients (representing employment shifts among these types of industry), and productivity change and population growth parameters with this system of aggregates yields a fairly comprehensive interregional projection model. This model is capable of incorporating and yielding information on such long-run interdependent phenomena as population growth, interregional population migration, rural-to-urban population shifts, gradually changing patterns of resource use, and consequent geographic shifts of industry.

6. Central to the problem of regional projections is the proper definition of a region. In our view, the concept of a region is an analytical tool. It is a set of criteria to guide the aggregation of economic activities situated at different points in space. From this point of view, there can be no absolute definition of a region. The criteria selected for demarcation of regional boundaries will vary with the needs of the analyst. As a concept, the region can be defined in perfectly general terms compatible with the needs of all disciplines. For the economist, the concrete definition of a region is tied to an understanding of the role of space in the economic system. Theoretical and empirical considerations suggest that distance acts to create a natural spatial agglomeration of economic activities around foci of varying order of magnitude. This implies a hierarchical order of regions, distinguishable by the nature of the commodity flows across the boundaries selected for demarcation. This orderliness is, however, considerably complicated by major commodity flows resulting from inequalities in resource endowment. Again, this serves to emphasize the necessity of detailed examination of interareal commodity flows in attempting to deal with any problem where economic activities are geographically differentiated.

7. The regional concept and flow analysis can be explicitly introduced into conventional input-output analysis. This can be accomplished with two general types of model. For convenience, we label that developed by Professor Leontief the "balanced regional model" and that developed by Isard the "interregional model." The former may be viewed as an attempt to yield in detail the regional implications of hypothesized shifts in the composition of the national bill of goods. The latter, by contrast, may be considered as an effort to determine the over-all national implication of economic growth and development in the several

regions. Both approaches utilize information on commodity flows and can incorporate information on geographic differences in production practice and consumption pattern.

8. Empirical analysis of the effects of the space factor in an interdependent economy is still in its infancy. An adequate approach to the problem of regional projections really implies the prior solution of a great many theoretical and empirical problems. The approaches touched upon in this paper are, therefore, to be considered primarily as suggested areas for further research.

Adler, J. H., 385n, 387, 390, 396n
Agriculture:
  acreage in use, 160-161, 176
  actual projections in, 108, 110-130, 150-153, 155, 159-174
  assumptions underlying projections, 112-115, 117-119, 121-124, 135-137, 141-142
  exports and imports of farm products, 153-155, 185-187
  feed concentrate balance, 188-189
  income elasticity of demand for farm products, 145-148
  price elasticity of demand for farm products, 144-145
  productivity in, 161, 176
  projections of agricultural prices, 111-117, 121-124, 127-129, 162-167, 171-174
  projections of demand for farm products, 111-125, 127-129, 141-155, 173-175, 185-189
  projections of farm income, 111-112, 169-171
  projections of farm output, 111-125, 155-162, 165-167, 171-178, 185-189
  projections of prices paid by farmers, 111-112, 168-169
  share of farm output in total output, 165-167
  techniques of long-term projection in, 112-125, 129-130
  techniques of short-term projection in, 108-110
  uses for projections, 125-126
Alexander, Sidney S., 384n

Barnett, Harold J., 427n
Barton, Glen T., 84n, 156n, 181, 183
Bean, L. H., 183, 234
Berlinguette, V. R., 71n
Bogue, D. J., 458-459
Boulding, K. E., 133n
Brady, Dorothy S., 337n, 340n, 346n
Brodell, A. P., 156n
Burk, Marguerite C., 127n, 144n, 146n, 148n

Capital formation:
  acceleration principle, 287-298
  actual projections of, 313-318, 323-324

Capital formation (cont.)
  assumptions underlying projections of, 298-304
  comparison of projection with that of CEA, 323-331
  induced and autonomous investment, 288-291, 296-298
  influence of cyclical instability on long-term projections, 318-321
  influence of depreciation allowances on marginal capital-output ratios, 318, 328-331
  methods of projection of, 278-287, 325-327
  natural, warranted, and actual rates of growth in output, 293-295
  projection of, from profits, 281-282
  projection of, from projected increase in output, 283-287, 299-304, 313-323, 326-328
  projection of, by questionnaire methods, 279-280, 326-327
  relation to output or consumption, 283-323, 326-328
Carroll, J. J., 373n
Cavin, J. P., 108n
Chang, T. C., 387
Clark, Colin, 181
Cochrane, W. W., 144n, 156n
Consumption (see Agriculture, Real national product, and Savings)
Cook, L. D., 373n
Cooper, M. R., 156n
Cornfield, J., 191n, 193n, 195, 216, 226
Crowe, P. R., 439n

Davis, Joseph S., 46n
De Vegh, Imre, 387
Dewhurst, J. Frederick, 10n, 101
Dickinson, R. E., 439n
Domar, E. D., 292-295
Dorn, Harold F., 20n, 45n, 46n
Douglas, Paul H., 103
Duesenberry, James S., 236n, 337n, 338n
Durand, John D., 54, 56, 58, 60n

Employment:
  actual projections of, 112, 116, 122, 141-142
  estimates of, 82-84, 180-183

Evans, G. C., 233
Evans, W. D., 191n, 193n, 195, 216, 226
Exports (*see* International sector)

Fabricant, Solomon, 432n
Fellner, William, 292n
Fox, Karl A., 144n, 146n
Frane, L., 373n
Frickey, E. R., 181
Friedman, Rose D., 337n, 340n
Frisch, Ragnar, 411n

Girshick, M. A., 144n
Goldsmith, Raymond W., 75n, 103, 310
Goodwin, Dorothy C., 159n
Gould, J. M., 224
Gras, N. S. B., 457n
Gross national product (*see* Real national product)

Haavelmo, Trygve, 144n, 380n
Hagen, E. E., 139n
Hagood, M. J., 454n
Hansen, A. H., 139n
Harrod, Roy F., 291-295
Hart, A. G., 179, 181, 241
Hawley, A., 457n
Hecht, Reuben W., 84n, 181, 183
Hicks, J. R., 295-298, 347
Hinshaw, Randall, 387, 396
Hoffenberg, M., 191n, 193n, 195, 216, 217, 226

Imports (*see* International sector)
Industrial production capacity (*see* Productive capacity)
Input-output method (*see* Specific industry projections)
International sector:
    explanations of volume of U.S. exports, 395-412, 420-422
    explanations of volume of U.S. imports, 387-395, 419
    foreign countries' exports and level of their imports, 399-401, 407-409, 420-421
    income elasticity of U.S. imports, 386-389, 382-393
    inventory cycles and U.S. imports, 392-394
    long-term capital movements and level of foreign countries' imports, 401-402, 422

International sector (cont.)
    model describing foreign demand for U.S. exports, 404-412, 419-422
    need for, and limits to, foreign aid, 413-419, 422-423
    official loans and grants, 412-419
    optimum rate of capital inflow, 415-419, 422-423
    price elasticity of U.S. imports, 387, 394-395
    relationship between U.S. income and imports, 386-395, 419-420
    supply of dollars, 383-386
    treatment of, in national income accounts, 377-383
    use of reserves and level of foreign countries' imports, 402-404
Isard, Walter, 427n, 448n, 464n, 467n

Jaffe, A. J., 57n
Jaszi, George, 69n
Johnson, D. G., 156n
Johnson, S. E., 159n
Jones, Carl E., 84n

Katona, George, 349n
Kendrick, John W., 69n, 84n
Keynes, J. M., 139n
Kimball, Bradford F., 258
Kiser, Clyde V., 47n
Klein, Lawrence R., 281n, 357n
Koffsky, N. M., 170n
Kuznets, Simon, 30n, 102, 103, 181, 223, 258n, 304, 306-308, 310-312, 337-339, 378

Labor force:
    actual projections of, 59-66, 111-112, 116, 118, 122, 141-142
    assumptions underlying projections of, 43-45, 59-65
    estimates of, 51-59
    measurement of, 51-55
    participation rate, 55-62
    trends in, 55-59
    (*see also* Employment)
Lary, Hal B., 384n
Leontief, W. W., 460-464, 466n
Lewis, H. G., 234n
Lösch, A., 457-459

Machlup, Fritz, 383n
Mack, Ruth P., 348-349, 363n

McKenzie, R. D., 457n
Mendershausen, Horst, 415n
Metzler, Lloyd A., 396
Modigliani, Franco, 236-237, 338n, 349-350
Moulton, H. G., 133n
Musgrave, R. A., 373n

National income (*see* Real national product)
Nourse, E. G., 133n

Paish, F. W., 386
Paradiso, L. J., 234
Polak, J. J., 380n, 400n, 402n, 411n
Population:
  actual projections of, 48-51, 117-118, 120, 122, 142
  assumptions underlying projections of, 45-50
  and fertility, 45-47, 49-51
  and immigration, 47-51
  and mortality, 47-51
Prices:
  influence of price levels on projections, 28, 40-41
  projections of general price level, 111-112, 116, 121-123, 127-129, 137-142, 172-173
Productive capacity:
  estimates of, 241-242, 257-265
  production of mining and manufacturing equipment and, 259-265
  and steel requirements, 241-254
Productivity:
  actual projections of, 111-112, 137
  assumptions underlying projections of, 96-98
  capital, 73-75, 80-81
  concepts, 68-81
  and economic efficiency, 76-79
  effect of interindustry shifts on, 76-79, 93-96
  farm, 82-83, 88-90, 93-95
  man-hour, 73-74, 78-79
  measurement of factor input, 72-75
  nonfarm, 82-83, 91-96
  and technical efficiency, 79-81
  techniques for projection, 96-100
  trends in, 81-96
Projections:
  assumptions underlying, 10-12, 17-23, 38-40
  concepts, 9-10, 275-278

Projections (cont.)
  length of period, 32-35
  margins of error, 25-29
  problems, 12-17, 366-368
  relation to government policy, 365-375
  sustaining of levels, 29-32
  uses of, 35-38, 39-40, 125-126, 365
  (*see also* Agriculture, Capital formation, Employment, International sector, Labor force, Population, Prices, Real national product, Regional product, Savings, Specific industry projections, Steel requirements)

Real national product:
  actual projections of, 111-113, 116, 118, 141-142, 323
  concepts, 68-72
  estimates of, 81-84, 101-104
  projection of components, 23-29
Regional product:
  concept of region, 455-460, 470
  influence of distance on regional interrelations, 434-439, 451-452, 469
  input-output analysis of, 460-468, 470-471
  and interregional commodity flows, 439-449, 469
  projection in broad industrial aggregates, 449-455, 469-470
  projection of, via GNP projections, 429-434, 461-464, 468-471
  use of projections of, to project GNP, 433-434, 464-468, 470-471
Robertson, D. H., 379n
Roos, C. F., 233
Rosa, Robert V., 355n

Samuelson, Paul A., 288-291
Savings:
  and changes in income distribution, 343-346, 364
  and changes in income level, 337-343, 347-350
  and changes in price level, 353-354
  composition of, 354-355, 357
  concepts and attitudes, 334-335, 359-361
  cyclical influences on, 341-343

Savings (cont.)
  and occupational distribution of the population, 350-353
  relative income position and rate of, 336-340, 343-345
  secular constancy of rate of, 337-340
  sources and uses of funds, 354-355, 361-363
  and stocks of consumer durables, 355-359
  and stocks of financial assets, 354-355
  urbanization and rate of, 350-353
Schlesinger, Eugene, 390n
Schultz, Henry, 144
Schumpeter, J. A., 133n
Shavell, Henry, 258n
Shaw, William H., 101, 102, 258n
Siegel, Jacob S., 48n
Smelker, Mary W., 346n
Specific industry projections:
  comparison of importance of derived demand and final demand, 212-214
  comparison of investment and consumption models, 194-214, 225-226
  comparison of results of several types with actual, 193-212, 227-230
  by final-demand blowup method, 192-210, 217
  final-demand projections and, 214-215
  by GNP blowup method, 192, 194-210
  by input-output method, 191-216, 225-232, 321
  measurement of error in, 193-212, 225-231
  by multiple regression method, 192-210, 216-219, 227-232
  types of, 191-193

Steel production capacity:
  estimates of, 266-267
  as a limit to industrial production, 249, 254-255
Steel requirements:
  actual projections of, 246, 252-253
  cyclical sensitivity of, 236-240
  and level of industrial production, 234-251, 253-257, 272
  long-run vs. short-run changes in, 233, 235-236, 242-251
  at maximum levels of industrial production, 253-254, 272
  and rate of change in industrial production, 251-252
  tests of projections of, 245-246, 252-253
  and total productive capacity, 241-251
Stewart, J. O., 435-436
Stigler, G. J., 134n
Strauss, F., 183

Tinbergen, J., 396
Tintner, G., 144n
Tobin, J., 144n

Ullman, E. L., 439-447

Van Westerborg, Evelyn, 390n
Vining, Rutledge, 439n

Warburton, Clark, 139n
Wells, O. V., 138n, 160n, 161n
Whelpton, P. K., 45, 47n
White, Helen L., 48n
Whitman, R. W., 233
Wolfbein, S. L., 57n
Working, E. J., 139n

Yntema, T. O., 234n

Zipf, G. K., 439n

476

RECENT AND FORTHCOMING

PUBLICATIONS OF THE

NATIONAL BUREAU OF ECONOMIC RESEARCH

NATIONAL BUREAU BOOKS *available from bookstores or Princeton University Press, Princeton, New Jersey, except that contributors and subscribers to the National Bureau should order directly from the Bureau.* OCCASIONAL PAPERS, TECHNICAL PAPERS, *and* ANNUAL REPORTS *available from National Bureau of Economic Research, 261 Madison Avenue, New York 16, New York.*

BOOKS

Minimum Price Fixing in the Bituminous Coal Industry	(in press)
Waldo E. Fisher and Charles M. James	
Business Concentration and Price Policy	(in press)
Personal Income during Business Cycles	(in press)
Daniel Creamer	
Mortgage Lending Experience in Agriculture (1954)	255 pp. $5.00
Lawrence A. Jones and David Durand	
Regularization of Business Investment (1954)	539 pp. 8.00
The Frontiers of Economic Knowledge (1954)	376 pp. 5.00
Arthur F. Burns	
The Volume of Corporate Bond Financing since 1900 (1953)	464 pp. 7.50
W. Braddock Hickman	
Shares of Upper Income Groups in Income and Savings (1953)	768 pp. 9.00
Simon Kuznets	
A Study of Moneyflows in the United States (1952)	620 pp. 7.50
Morris A. Copeland	
The Trend of Government Activity in the United States since 1900 (1952)	288 pp. 4.00
Solomon Fabricant	

CONFERENCE ON RESEARCH IN INCOME AND WEALTH

Studies in Income and Wealth

1. *Studies in Income and Wealth, Volume One.* Eight papers on concepts and measurement of national income (1937)	370 pp. 2.50
6. *Studies in Income and Wealth, Volume Six.* Seven papers examining income measurement in relation to government product, income parity for agriculture, international transactions, forecasting national income, and income differences among communities, and dealing with the adequacy of income estimates for computing net capital formation (1943)	302 pp. 3.00
9. *Analysis of Wisconsin Income* (1948)	284 pp. 3.50
Frank A. Hanna, Joseph A. Pechman, Sidney M. Lerner	
10. *Studies in Income and Wealth, Volume Ten.* Eight papers on standardizing basic concepts of national bookkeeping by American, British, and Canadian statisticians; problems of international comparisons of income and wealth; the nation's economic budget and forecasting gross national product and employment; savings and income distribution, and resource distribution patterns (1947)	352 pp. 4.50
11. *Studies in Income and Wealth, Volume Eleven.* Six papers on the industrial distribution of manpower, real incomes in dissimilar geographic areas, national income forecasting, and the saving-income ratio (1949)	464 pp. 6.00
12. *Studies in Income and Wealth, Volume Twelve.* Thirteen papers on national wealth (1950)	608 pp. 6.00

13. *Studies in Income and Wealth, Volume Thirteen.* Ten
papers on size distribution of income (1951)   608 pp. $6.00
14. *Studies in Income and Wealth, Volume Fourteen.* Seven
papers on wealth (1951)   286 pp. 3.50
15. *Studies in Income and Wealth, Volume Fifteen.* Eight
papers on size distribution of income (1952)   240 pp. 3:50
16. *Long-Range Economic Projection* (1954)   490 pp. 9.00
17. *Short-Term Economic Forecasting* (in press)   496 pp. 8.00
18. *Input-Output Analysis: An Appraisal*   (in press)

OCCASIONAL PAPERS

36. *The Labor Force in War and Transition: Four Countries* (1952)   1.00
Clarence D. Long
37. *Trends and Cycles in Corporate Bond Financing* (1952)   .75
W. Braddock Hickman
38. *Productivity and Economic Progress* (1952)   .75
Frederick C. Mills
39. *The Role of Federal Credit Aids in Residential Construction* (1953)   1.00
Leo Grebler
40. *Transport and the State of Trade in Britain* (1953)   1.50
Thor Hultgren
41. *Capital and Output Trends in Manufacturing Industries, 1880-1948*
(1954)   1.50
Daniel Creamer
42. *The Share of Financial Intermediaries in National Wealth and
National Assets, 1900-1949* (1954)   1.50
Raymond W. Goldsmith
43. *Trends and Cycles in Capital Formation by United States
Railroads, 1870-1950* (1954)   1.50
Melville J. Ulmer
44. *The Growth of Physical Capital in Agriculture, 1870-1950*   (in press)
Alvin S. Tostlebe
45. *Capital and Output Trends in Mining Industries, 1870-1948*   (in press)
Israel Borenstein
46. *Immigration and the Foreign Born*   (in press)
Simon Kuznets and Ernest Rubin
47. *The Ownership of Tax-Exempt Securities, 1913-1952*   (in press)
George E. Lent

TECHNICAL PAPERS

7. *Factors Affecting the Demand for Consumer Instalment Sales Credit*
(1952)   1.50
Avram Kisselgoff
8. *A Study of Aggregate Consumption Function* (1953)   1.50
Robert Ferber
9. *The Volume of Residential Construction, 1889-1950* (1954)   1.50
10. *Factors Influencing Consumption: An Experimental Analysis
of Shoe Buying*   (in press)
Ruth P. Mack

ANNUAL REPORTS (GRATIS)

By Arthur F. Burns
30th. *New Facts on Business Cycles* (May 1950)
31st. *Looking Forward* (May 1951)
32nd. *The Instability of Consumer Spending* (May 1952)
33rd. *Business Cycle Research and the Needs of Our Times* (May 1953)
By Solomon Fabricant
34th. *Economic Progress and Economic Change* (May 1954)